The S.O. Combat Manual

Volume II

Fourth Edition

By

James P. Coghill

© Copyright 2018

"Every mother of a son in America should be scared to death
that something like this can be done so easily."
(Mother of a Duke Lacrosse player. CBS 60 Minutes)

4

Dedication

I rejoice in the awakening of the Buddha's and also in the spiritual levels of their sons.

With folded hands I beseech the Buddha's of all directions to shine the lamp of Dharma for all bewildered in the gloom of misery.

With folded hands I beseech all the Buddha's who wish to pass away, to please remain for countless eons and not to leave the world in darkness.

My foes will become nothing. My friends will become nothing. I too will become nothing. Likewise, ALL, will become nothing.

Just like a dream experience, whatever things I enjoy will become a memory. Whatever is passed will not be seen again.

I alone will liberate those not liberated. I alone will release those not released. I alone will relieve those unrelieved. And set living beings in Nirvana!

The Buddha's neither wash away ill deeds with water, nor remove beings sufferings with their hands, nor transfers their realizations to others. Beings are released through the teachings of the truth. The final reality.

Thus by the virtue that has collected through all that I have done, may the pain of every living creature be completely cleared away.

Preface

What you are about to read is the culmination of 10 years of experience and research in the American Injustice System. It comes from direct experience of being branded a sex offender or S.O. and beating the charge. Beating it is the hardest thing I have ever had to do. It is my intention to share this experience with you so you may be better prepared if and when it happens to you. The thing to remember is that every day in this country it is happening to somebody somewhere and you are not immune. No one is.

This author does not care if you're guilty or innocent. This author does not care what you did or didn't do. The only thing this author cares about is that you are insured a fair trial and I don't see how without this manual you're going to get one. That's why this manual is written. What you need to recognize immediately if you're already headed for trial is that the trial is not about making a judgment based on the facts. It's about putting you through an ordeal of such drama and far-reaching repercussions that your confession is obtained and you take a plea bargain. It's a game and your life is the ball, nothing more. That's justice in America.

It may be treated as a game, but the game is still governed by rules. These rules are the criminal statutes, rules of evidence, rules of court, rules of criminal procedure, ethics rules and case law that you must learn till you can quote them without this book and quote them when they apply. If you can do this you stand a better chance of keeping everyone honest and getting a fair trial.

There is no doubt advice in this book is going to piss off a lot of people for various reasons and it doesn't take a genius to figure out in advance who they are and what they represent. That's just tough. If you are an American, you stand by a fair and just legal system. Therefore, if you oppose this book you need to re-evaluate your political philosophy and affiliations accordingly.

Table of Contents

Exhaustion of Remedies

<u>Bijeol v. Benson</u>, 404 F.Supp 595 (S.D. Indiana 1975)
Prisoners must demonstrate attempt at exhausting administrative remedies.

<u>Deltona Corp. v. Alexander</u>, 682 F.2d 888 (11Ith Cir. 1982)
Courts will not require exhaustion when administrative remedy is inadequate, does not exist, would not provide relief commensurate with claim, be so unreasonably delayed as to create serious risk of irreparable injury, when the claim would be denied because it would be clearly denied, or when the administrative action will not resolve the merits.

<u>Fuentes v. Roher</u>, 519 F.2d 379, 387 (2nd Cir. 1975)
These two cases are applicable when you allege that the administrative remedy process itself is unconstitutional. Both cases came from <u>Miller v. Stanmore</u>, 636 F2d 986 (5th Cir. 1981) page 991 note #8.

<u>Lyons v. US Marshals</u>, 840 F.2d 202 (3rd Cir. 1988)
1. Lists the criteria for the non-exhaustion of administrative remedies.
2. If seeking only monetary damages under BIVENS exhaustion is not required.

<u>Maguire v. Wilkinson</u>, 405 F.Supp 637 (D. Conn. 1975)
If no response is elicited, appeal will be deemed denied.

<u>McCarthy v. Madigan</u>, 503 US 117 L.Ed.2d 291, 112 S.Ct. (1992)
<u>Muhammad v. Carlson</u>, 739 F2d 122 (3rd Cir. 1984)
Federal prisoners are not required to exhaust The Federal Bureau of Prisons internal grievance procedure before initiating a Biven's action solely for money damages.

Note: If you're a federal prisoner who is suing the B.O.P. for solely monetary damages you do not have to exhaust your administrative remedies. See: <u>Bivens v. Six Unknown Agents</u>, 403 US 388; <u>McCarthy v. Madigan</u>, 112 S.Ct. 1081

Patsey v. Board of Regents, 457 US 496, 73 L.Ed.2d 172, 102 S.Ct. 2557 (1982)
An individual is not required to exhaust administrative remedies prior to instituting an action under § 1983.

Raines v. Us Parole Commission, 829 F.2d 840 (9th Cir. 1987)
When government failed to raise the exhaustion of administrative remedies in the lower court it made a tactical decision and could not raise the issue for the first time on appeal.

Swoops v. Sublett, 196 F.3d 1008 (9th Cir. 1999)
We consider this appeal on remand from the Supreme Court for further consideration in light of O'Sullivan v. Boerckel, 119 S. Ct. 1728 (1999), decided after issuance of our prior decision in this case. After reconsideration, we conclude that Arizona state prisoners need not appeal an Arizona Court of Appeals' denial of post-conviction relief to the Arizona Supreme Court in order to exhaust their state remedies for federal habeas corpus purposes, except in capital cases or cases involving the imposition of a life sentence.

Tarlton v. US, 429 F.2d 1297 (5th Cir. 1970)
After exhaustion of administrative remedy court will look at same.

Fines/Restitution

Austin v. US, 509 US, 125 L.Ed.2d 488, 113 S.Ct. (1993)
Eighth Amendment excess fines clause held to apply to drug related forfeitures of property to United States under 21 USCS §§881(a)(4) and 881(a)(7).

Bearden v. Georgia, 461 US 660, 76 L.Ed.2d 221, 103 S.Ct. 2064 (1983)
An individual's probation cannot be revoked for the non-payment of a fine.

Montana Dept. Of Revenue v. Kurth Ranch, 114 S.Ct. 1937 (1994)
A punitive civil penalty imposed after a related conviction was barred even though a civil case was litigated contemporaneously with the criminal prosecution.   5. Note: Restitution obligations imposed by either a civil or criminal court may be discharged under bankruptcy. See Pa. Welfare Dept. v. . Davenport, 495 US 552

PA. Welfare Dept. v. Davenport, 495 US 552, 109 L.Ed.2d 588, 110 S.Ct. 2126 (1990)
Restitution obligations in criminal case held to constitute "debts" within meaning of 11 USCS § 101 (11) and are therefore dischargeable under Chapter 13 of the Bankruptcy Code.

State v. Whitney, 151 Ariz. 113, 726 P.2d 210
Defendant was convicted before the Superior Court, Maricopa County, Cause No. CR-137394, Howard F. Thompson, J., for theft of a vehicle, and defendant appealed. The Court of Appeals, Meyerson, J., held that trial judge lacked authority to order payment of restitution to owner of other vehicle damaged in collision with stolen vehicle more than one-half hour after theft. Order of restitution modified.

US v. Arnoldt, 947 F.2d 1120 (4th Cir. 1991)
Fine could not be imposed without sentencing court making specific findings on statutory factors.

US v. Castner, 50 F.3d 1267 (4th Cir. 1995)

Government of Virgin Islands v. Davis, 43 F.3d 41 (3rd Cir. 1994)

In determining imposition and amount of fine, federal district court must consider, among other things, the income, financial resources, and earning capacity of defendant, as well as burden that fine will impose upon defendant and his dependents.

US v. Edmonson, 962 F.2d 1535 (10th Cir. 1992)

US v. Eves, 932 F.2d 856 (10th Cir. 1991)

Fine for costs of incarceration is inappropriate in absence of punitive fine.

US v. Fair, 979 F.2d 1037 (5th Cir. 1992)

Defendant may rely on pre-sentence report to satisfy burden of showing his inability to pay fine or cost of incarceration.

US v. Francisco, 35 F.3d 116 (4th Cir. 1994)

District court is required to make specific factual findings regarding factors for imposition of fine because those findings are essential to effective appellate review of fines imposed and failure to make any findings is grounds for vacation of fine.

US v. Graham, 946 F.2d 19 (4th Cir. 1991)

Defendant's affluence is not appropriate basis for upward departure from fines specified in sentencing guidelines.

US v. Granados, 962 F.2d 767 (8th Cir. 1992)

1. It is incorrect application of sentencing guidelines to impose a fine that the defendant has little chance of paying. 2. Determination that defendant has sufficient assets to pay fine must be based on more than a statement to that effect in the pre-sentence report.

US v. Hannon, US v. Welborn,

There is no statute of limitations applicable to a federal fine. (Authors note: this is not 100% correct: the government has 20 years to collect on fine before it is time barred).

US v. Lindo, 52 F.3d 106 (6th Cir. 1995)

US v. Kassar, 47 F.3d 562 (2nd Cir. 1995)

Written agreement dictating monthly installments of $20,000 towards payment of $600,000 fine imposed by sentencing court to be paid during defendant's probation was ineffective where it was drafted by probation officer; only sentencing court had authority to impose installment schedule to pay fine.

US v. Mack, 655 F.2d 843 (8th Cir. 1981)

Sentence cannot be extended for non-payment of fine.

US v. Rosa, 11 F3d 315 (2nd Cir. 1993)

District court must afford defendant at least minimal opportunity to show that he lacks ability to pay fine proposed by the court.

US v. Walker, 39 F.3d 489 (4th Cir. 1994)

Remand was required for specific findings with regard to defendant's ability to pay fine where pre-sentence report indicated negative net worth and lack of any ability to immediately satisfy fine.

US v. VQDA, 994 F.2d 149 (5th Cir. 1993)

Courts are constitutionally limited in penalty they can impose for nonpayment of criminal fines because of inability to pay.

Fundamental Error

State v. Bunting, 246 P.3d 352
The trial court was obligated to follow case law, which required that six warnings be provided to a submitting defendant prior to a determination of his or her guilt or innocence; the trial court's failure to conduct a colloquy with appellant to ascertain whether her submission on the record was voluntarily made constituted fundamental error.

State v. Cox, 201 Ariz. 467, 468, 37 P.3d 437 (Ariz. App. Div. 1 2002)
Any illegal sentence constitutes fundamental error, that will be reversed on appeal despite a lack of objection in the trial court, and whether the legal sentence is discovered immediately or 100 years later and legal sentence cannot be allowed to stand.

State v. Hardwick, 1 CA-CR 94-0303, COURT OF APPEALS OF ARIZONA, DIVISION ONE, DEPARTMENT E, 183 Ariz. 649; 905 P.2d 1384; 1995 Ariz. App. LEXIS 250; 203 Ariz. Adv. . Rep. 5, November 7, 1995, Filed. REVERSED AND REMANDED
The state's repeated references to an inadmissible document during cross-examination of the defendant constituted fundamental error. Thus, defendant was entitled to reversal of his convictions for child molestation and other related crimes.

State v. Kinney, 241 P.3d 914
Police exceeded the permissible scope of an investigatory detention under the Fourth Amendment by questioning defendant after learning his name did not match the suspect's name. Defendant was not prejudiced by the denial of his motion to suppress his statement, because independent evidence proved that he was prohibited from possessing firearms.

State v. Nettz, (App. Div. .2 1997) 114 Ariz. 296, 560 P.2d 814
A conviction may be set aside despite a lack of objection at trial if fundamental error was committed; fundamental error is such error as goes to the foundation of

the case or which takes from any defendant a right essential to his defense; denial of a fair trial would be such error.

State v. Valenzuela,194 Ariz. 404, 984 P.2d 12; 1999 and Ariz. LEXIS 86; 298 Ariz. Adv. Rep. 26

Fundamental error occurs when the defendant loses a right essential to his defense, was unable to receive a fair trial, or where the error goes to the very foundation of the defendants theory of the case.

Grand Jury

A.R.S. 21-411 Appointment of reporter; transcript.
A. Such transcripts shall be made available to the prosecuting officer and the defendant.

A.R.S. 21-422 Evidence on behalf of a person under investigation.
The person under investigation shall have the right to advice of counsel during the giving of any testimony by him before the grand jury, provided that such counsel may not communicate with anyone other than his client.

A.R.S. 21-422 State grand juries powers of duties.
A. The law applicable to county grand juries, including their powers, duties and functions, applies to the state grand jury except in so far as it is in conflict with this article.

B. The state grand jury shall investigate and return indictments for only those offenses or violations of law arising out of or in connection with:

> 1. Bribery, obstruction of justice, hindering prosecution' or any form of intentional knowing or corrupt misconduct involving any person compensated by public funds.
> 2. Any fraud…
> 3. Perjury, false swearing, unsworn falsification, or violation of Title 13, Chapter 28 in connection with any grand jury proceeding committed by any person testifying before it or any trial or other proceeding involving any indictment returned by a state grand jury.

In Re Grand Jury Matter (Doe), 798 F.2d 91 (3rd Cir. 1986)
Witness had just cause not to answer questions before grand jury if questions are derived from surveillance conducted in violation of Omnibus Crime Control and Safe Streets Act.

In Re Grand Jury Subpoena, 739 F.2d 1354 (8th Cir. 1984)
1. While witness is not entitled to have counsel present in room where grand jury hearing is taking place, witnesses are entitled to have their counsel outside the room and to consult with their counsel whenever necessary.
2. Witness summoned before grand jury is bound legally to testify, for public has right to every individuals evidence.
3. Fifth Amendment privilege against self-incrimination cannot be asserted by grand jury witness in order to protect others from possible criminal prosecution
4. Grand jury witness may not claim Fifth Amendment privilege against self-incrimination as blanket defense; rather, witness must make specific objection in response to specific questions.

In Re Grand Jury Testimony, 832 F.2d 60 (5th Cir. 1987)
District court may order release of grand jury materials if party demonstrates compelling necessity for materials with particularity.

In Re Grand Jury Witness, 835 F.2d 437 (2nd Cir. 1987)
Contemnor must be released when grand jury is discharged: possibility of compliance has ended.

Matter Of Dickinson, 763 F.2d 84 (2nd Cir. 1985)
Simkim v. US, 715 F.2d 34 (2nd Cir. 1983)
Once contemnor establishes that there is no substantial likelihood that continued confinement would accomplish its coercive purpose, the confinement becomes punitive in nature at which point due process requires its termination.

US v. Bissell, 866 F.2d 1343 (11th Cir. 1989)
When indictment is so altered as to charge different offense from that found by grand jury it violates the Fifth Amendment.

US v. Bethety, 32 F.3d 503 (11th Cir. 1994)
Convictions based on modification of essential element not charged by grand jury present reversible error.

US v. Curry, 993 F.2d 43 (4th Cir. 1993)
Defendant had unqualified right to inspect, reproduce, and copy grand jury master list to determine if there was factual basis for motion challenging jury selection procedures.

US v. Dibernardo, 775 F.2d 1470 (11th Cir. 1985)
Federal courts may exercise their supervisory powers over grand juries to remedy violations of recognized rights, protect integrity of federal courts, and deter illegal conduct by government officials.

US v. Eisen, 974 F.2d 246 (2nd Cir. 1992)
Defendant seeking reversal or hearing on alleged grand jury abuse must show prejudice or bias.

US v. Hope, 861 F.2d 1574 (11th Cir. 1988)
Indictment must be dismissed on ground of "duplicity" when two or more separate crimes are joined in single count of indictment.

US v. Koen, 31 F.3d 711 (8th Cir. 1994)
Amendment of indictment is reversible error per se, since amendment usurps constitutionally guaranteed role of grand jury.

US v. Martino, 825 F.2d 754 (3rd Cir. 1987)
Once court determines that there has been prosecutorial misconduct in form of some abuse of grand jury process, it must then determine whether any sanction, such as dismissal of indictment and suppression of evidence, is appropriate.

US v. Mills, 29 F.3d 545 (10th Cir. 1994)
Constructive amendment that broadens an indictment is reversible error per se, because only grand jury can amend indictment.

US v. Powell, 823 F.2d 996 (6th Cir. 1987)
Principal duties of grand jurors are to determine whether probable cause exists to believe that crime has been committed and to protect accused from unfounded prosecutions.

<u>US v. Williams</u>, 899 F.2d 898 (10th Cir. 1990)
Prosecutor has duty to present substantial exculpatory evidence to grand jury.

<u>Woodward v. Tynan</u>, 776 F.2d 250 (10th Cir. 1985)
Normally, grand jury is required to return records to owner upon completion of grand jury's task.

Habeas Corpus

Article 2 § 14 AZ Constitution
"The privilege of the writ of habeas corpus shall not be suspended by the authorities of the state."

Article 2, § 30 AZ Constitution and 5th Amendment of US Constitution.
"The state is required to obtain a new indictment or information to begin a new proceedings."

USCA 6
28 USCA § 2254
McCrae v. Blackburn, 107 S. Ct. 466, 479 US 965, 93 L.ED.2d 411 C. A. 5 (L.A.) 1986
Habeas petitioner who alleged ineffective assistance of counsel on appeal had burden of proving that counsels errors were so serious that counsel was not functioning as counsel guaranteed to petitioner by sixth amendment, or counsel did not entirely failed to challenge prosecution's case.

USCA 6
Walberg v. Israel, 766 F.2d 1071, cert denied 106 S. Ct. 546, 474 U. S. 1013, 88 L.Ed.2d 475 C. A. 7 (Wis.) 1985
If state is not a passive spectator of inept defense, but a cause of the inept defense, burden of showing prejudice resulting from ineffective assistance of counsel is lifted.

A.R.Cr.P. Rule 31.17(b) The appellate courts authority:
[I]ncludes affirming reversing, or modifying the judgment, correcting or reducing the sentence and affirming, modifying or vacating any order made by the lower court, including but not limited to those concerning new trial, arrest of judgment, or dismissal of the indictment or information. The appellate court may in addition remand a case for a new trial, and take any other action that appears just and proper under the circumstances.

A.R.Cr.P. Rule 32.3 (1992)
The Supreme Court in enacting Rule 32 does not intend to restrict by this rule the constitutional scope of habeas corpus.

A.R.S. 13-4124(B)
The court has authority to release a habeas petitioner, but not a rule 32 petitioner – on conditions pending decision on the merits.

Habeas Corpus Ad Prosequendum. Latin: that you have the body to prosecute. Historically a writ in criminal cases to bring before a court a prisoner to be tried on charges other than those for which the prisoner is currently being confined.

Habeas Corpus Ad Subjiciendum Latin: that you have the body to subject to. Historically a writ directed to someone detained another person and commanding that the detainee be brought to court.

Arizona v. Washington, 434 US 497, 501 (1978)
State prisoners double jeopardy claim review on the merits in federal habeas corpus actions prior to re-trial.

Bae v. Peters, 950 F.2d 469 (7th Cir. 1991)
Federal government may grant habeas relief to state prisoner only for violations of federal law.

Beasley v. Holland, 649 F. Supp. 561, appeal dismissed 841 F.2d 1122, cert denied 109 S.Ct. 156, 102 L.Ed.2d 127, S.D. W. VA. 1986
Petitioners claim that witness testimony was false and that such false statements were knowingly used by state officials to obtain his conviction for murder were not supported by any factual basis, at best petitioner failed to raise ground for relief on writ of habeas corpus.

Barry v. Bergen County Probation Dept., 128 F.3d 152, 159-160 (3rd Cir. 1997),cert. denied, 118 S.Ct. 1097 (1998)

Community service obligation imposed upon the defendant satisfied the in custody requirement of § 2254 (a) despite lack of continuous supervision and state's contention that petitioner's failure to complete community service would result in a fine, not imprisonment, because defendant was nevertheless subject to restrictions of his liberty not shared by the general public.

Bell v. US, 48 F.3d 1042 (8th Cir. 1995)

If prisoner chooses to file habeas petition to attack execution of his sentence, prisoner must do so in court with jurisdiction over his present custodian.

Biller v. Lopes, 655 F.Supp. 292 affirmed 834 F.2d 41 D. Conn. 1987

Once petitioner established his infringement of constitutional right, burden shifts to state to establish that error was harmless.

Bribiesa v. Galaza, 215 F.3d 1015, to 18 (9th Cir. 2000)

Dismissal based on state procedural default presents issues of law reviewed de novo.

Burden v. Zant, 510 US 126 L.Ed2.d 611, 114 S.Ct. (1994)

Federal Court of Appeals held to have mistakenly upheld denial of habeas relief, where (1) denial was based on finding not made by federal district court, and (2) evidence supported accused's claim of ineffective assistance of counsel.

California v. Roy, 117 S.Ct. 337 (1996) (per curiam)

The court reversed and remanded for decision of the en banc 9th circuit which had granted habeas relief on the ground that the trial court's erroneous instruction, which fails to include the essential element of intent in a first degree murder charge was not harmless. The court found that the 9th circuit's harmless error analysis which drew primarily from concurrence in Carella v. California, 491 US 263 (1989) and allowed a finding of harmlessness, "only if review of the facts found by the jury establishes that the jury necessarily found the automated element." 81 F.3d 863, 867 (1996), was not sufficiently differential in light of the court's decision in Brecht and O'Neal. Because the error at issue was clearly trial error on the state courts... Applied harmless error analysis of the strict [Chapman] variety, the court determined that the standard set forth in Brecht and O'Neal, rather than analysis suggested in Carella was to be employed in assessing harmless Vel Non. Justice Scalia, concurring in their man, cited Sullivan v. Louisiana, 508 US 275 (1993) and suggested that, because a defendant is entitled to a verdict that he is guilty of each necessary element of the crime, the error at issue here can be harmless only if the jury verdict on the other points effectively embraces one or if it is impossible, upon the evidence, to have found, what the verdict did find without finding this point as well. This analysis, however must still be conducted within the framework of Brecht and O'Neal.

Capps v. Sullivan, 13 F.3d 350 (10th Cir. 1993)
Effect of writ of habeas corpus is to vacate conviction and release petitioner from custody.

Caswell v. Ryan, 953 F.2d 853 (3rd Cir. 1992)
Coleman v. Thompson, 501 US , 115 L.Ed.2d 640, 111 S.Ct. 2546 (1991)
Under "exhaustion" principle, absent valid excuse, a prisoner must first present all federal claims to state court before the district court may entertain a federal habeas petition.

Ceja v. Stewart, 97 F.3d 1246 (9th Cir 1996)
Multiple errors, even if harmless individually, may entitle petitioner to habeas relief if their cumulative effect prejudiced defendant.

Chacon v. Wood, 36 F.3d 1459 (9th Cir. 1994)
Habeas petition challenging underlying conviction is never moot simply because, subsequent to its filing, petitioner has been released from custody.

Clark v. Warden Md. Penitentiary, CA.4 (Md.) 1961, 293 F.2d 479, 82 S.Ct. 1149, 369 US 877, 8 L.Ed.2d 279,cert. denied
Allegations of habeas corpus petition must be accepted as true, for purpose of appeal from denial without hearing, where neither state nor federal courts given hearing on factual issues.

DeAngelo v. Wainwright, 781 F.2d 1516, cert. denied, 107 S.Ct. 444, 479 US 953, 93 L.Ed.2d 392 C.A.11 (Fla.) 1986.
Rule that state prisoner is entitled to federal habeas corpus relief if fourth amendment claim is fully and fairly litigated in state court does not extend to fifth and sixth amendment's as well.

Del Raine v. Carlson, 826 F.2d 698 (7th Cir. 1987)
Relief sought by federal inmate in form of expungement of disciplinary sanction from his record was within habeas corpus jurisdiction; as inmate's objective in seeking relief was to enhance his prospects for parole, in effect he was seeking to accelerate his release from prison.

English v. Cody, 146 F.3d 1257, 1259 (10th Cir. 1998)
Evitts v. Lucy, 469 US 387, 394-96 (1985)
Gideon v. Wainwright, 372 US 335, 344 (1963)
Because this right lies at the very foundation of the adversary system of criminal justice, habeas courts must be particularly vigilant in scrutinizing the adequacy of state rules of procedural default which have the effect of barring federal habeas review of claim of ineffective assistance.

Faye v. Noia, 372 US 391, 401-401 (1963)
"That in a civilized society, government must be accountable to the judiciary for a man's imprisonment; if the imprisonment cannot be shown to conform with the fundamental requirements of law, the individual is entitled to immediate release."

Field v. Calderon, 125 F.3d 757, 7 59-60 (9th Cir. 1997)
The right to the effective assistance of counsel is fundamental and essential to fair trial.

Foster v. Lockhart, 9 F.3d 7 22,727 (8th Cir. 1993)
Writ granted unless state retries petitioner within 120 days to correct constitutional defects that make petitioner's current custody unlawful.

Franklin v. White, 803 F.2d 416, cert. denied, 107 S.Ct. 1904,481 US 1020, 95 L.Ed.2d 510
Due process claims relating to defendant's receipt of fair notice of charge against him are cognizable in habeas corpus. See: USC.A. 5, 14.

Gilliam v. Foster, 75 F.3d 881, 889 (4th Cir. 1996)
Pre-trial habeas review of double jeopardy claim proper because state remedies exhausted.

Glenn v. Dallman, 686 F.2d 418, 4 22-23 (6th Cir. 1982)
Conviction reclassified when petitioner convicted of aggravated burglary but facts and jury instructions only supported conviction for burglary and adverse collateral consequences might result if conviction and not reclassified or grant the petitioner a re-trial on specific issues.

Green v. Abrams, 984 F.2d 41 (2nd Cir. 1993)
Escobar v. O'Leary, 943 F.2d 711 (7th Cit. 1991)
1. Writ of "habeas corpus" functions to grant relief from unlawful custody or imprisonment. 2. A writ of habeas corpus may be granted to person being held in custody in violation of the Constitution or the laws of the United States.

Green v. Arn, 809 F.2d 1257, cert. granted and vacated, 108 S.Ct. 52, 98 L.Ed.2d 17 on remand 839 F.2d 300, cert. denied, 109 S. Ct. 847,102 L.Ed.2d 979 C.A.6 (Ohio) 1987
Absence of counsel during the taking of evidence of defendant's guilt is prejudicial per se and justifies automatic grant of habeas corpus writ without any opportunity for harmless error inquiry.

Gwin v. Snow, 870 F.2d 616 (11th Cir. 1989)
Prisoner seeking injunctive relief which lessens period of confinement must bring claim in a habeas corpus petition.

Harbel Oil Company v. Superior Court, 86 Ariz. 303, 307, 345, P.2d (1959)
The court recognized that it may simply affirm or reverse or it may also issue specific directions.

Harding v. Lewis, 641 F.Supp. 979, Affirmed 834 F.2d 853, Cert. 109 S.Ct. 182, 102 L.Ed.2d 72, 82 S.Ct. 23

Evidentiary hearing on petition for habeas corpus is required in District Court if petitioner has alleged facts which if proven late entitled to relief; no such hearing is required if merits of petitioners claim were resolved in state court.

Harding v. Lewis, 641 F.Supp. 979, affirmed 834 F.2d 853, cert. denied 109 S.Ct. 182, 102 L.Ed.2d 151 D. Ariz. 1986.

Counsels advice to proceed pros se would constitute grounds for habeas corpus relief, due to ineffective assistance of counsel, where there is factual or legal defense, or defendant does not understand attorneys advice. See also: USCA amendment 6.

Harris v. Champion, 15 F.3d 1538 (10th Cir. 1994) Givens v. Green, 12 F.3d 1041 (11th Cir. 1994)
Hollis v. Davis, 941 F.2d 1471 (11th Cir. 1991)

Inexcusable or inordinate delay by state in processing claims for relief may make state process ineffective to protect habeas petitioner's rights and may excuse exhaustion of state remedies.

Hayes v. Morgan, 58 F.Supp. 2d 817, 831 (N.D. Ohio, 1999)

The court granted relief on petitioner's claim that he was denied ineffective assistance of appellate counsel as a result of counsel's erroneous filing of notice of appeal having the wrong case number and failure to take timely corrective action, which resulted in dismissal of petitioner's direct appeal. The conditional grant of relief required the state of Ohio to reinstate petitioner's appeal, with the appointment of new counsel, and provide a full transcript of all proceedings from the lower court to the newly appointed counsel.

Hill v. Lockhart, 28 F.3d 832, 847- 48 (8th Cir. 1994)

Sentence vacated and state ordered to retry penalty for charges on which petitioner convicted. Reclassifying petitioner's conviction.

Holman v. State, 5 Ariz. App. 311, 313, 426 P.2d 411 (1967)
"[A] proceedings commenced by the filing of a petition for a writ of habeas corpus primarily concerns jurisdiction and required that the petitioner be found to be held illegally." See also: State v. Superior Court, 25 Ariz. 226, 231, 215 P.538 (1923).

Hunt v. Warden Md. Penitentiary, CA.4 (Md.) 1964, 325 F.2d 936
Factual allegations in petition for writ of habeas corpus or excepted as true for purpose of appeal from denial of petition without a hearing.

Joyner v. King, 786 F.2d 1317, reh. denied, 795 F.2d 84, cert. denied, 107 S.Ct. 653, 479 US 1010, 93 L.Ed.2d 708 C.A. 5 (LA.) 1986.
Federal evidentiary hearing is mandated where alleged facts, if true, would entitle habeas petitioner to relief or where petitioner did not receive full and fair evidentiary hearing in state court.

Kaufman v. US, 394 US 217, 22 L.Ed.2d 227, 89 S.Ct. 1068 (1969)
Federal Habeas Corpus relief is not to be denied to prisoners alleging constitutional deprivations solely on the ground that relief should have been sought by appeal.

Kirkpatrick v. Blackburn, 777 F.2d 272, certiorari denied 106 S.Ct 2907, 476 US 1178, 9 0 L.Ed. 2d 993, appeal after remand 870 F.2d 276
Petitioner for habeas corpus must establish the trial and error was not merely abuse of discretion, but was so grave as to amount to denial of his constitutional right to substantive due process, that is, that error made trial fundamentally unfair.

Kirkpatrick v. Blackburn, 777 F.2d 272, cert denied 106 S. Ct. 2907, 476 US 1178, 90 L.Ed.2.d 993, appeal after remand 870 F.2d 276, rehearing denied C.A. 5 (L.A.) 1985
If state court is found to have abridged petitioner's constitutional rights, burden shifts to prosecution to show that error was harmless beyond reasonable doubt.

Kontakis v. Beyer, 19 F.3d 110 (3rd Cir. 1994)
Constitutional error in state court is not harmless if it had substantial and injurious effect or influence in determining jury's verdict giving rise to habeas case.

Kotteakos v. US, 328 US 750, 756 (1946) Federal courts apply the Brecht standard of harmless error in harmless error proceedings. Brecht v. Abrahamson, 507 US 619, 623, 629-30 (1993) under this standard habeas relief is automatically granted for structural defects while habeas relief for constitutionally significant trial error is granted only when the error had substantial and injurious effect or influence in determining the jury verdict.

Lajoie v. Thompson, No. 98-35919, UNITED STATES COURT OF APPEALS FOR THE NINTH CIRCUIT, 217 F.3d 663; 2000 US App. LEXIS 14460; 53 Fed. R. Evid. Serv. (Callaghan) 1622; 2000 Cal. Daily Op. Service 5023; 2000 Daily Journal DAR 6731, July 13, 1999, Argued and Submitted, Portland, Oregon , June 23, 2000, Filed. REVERSED and REMANDED.
District court erred in denying inmate's petition for writ of habeas corpus because exclusion of evidence of victim's past sexual abuse by others was unreasonable application of clearly established federal law.

Lawrence v. Lensing, 42 F.3d 255 (5th Cir. 1994)
State prisoner seeking federal habeas review of conviction must assert volition of federal constitutional right.

Leonard v. Nix, 55 F.3d 370 (8th Cir. 1995)
Heffernan v. NORRIS, 48 F.3d 331 (8th Cir. 1995)
Habeas petitioner may excuse procedural bar and abuse of writ by showing cause and prejudice, or actual innocence.

Leonard v. Nix, 55 F.3d 370 (8th Cir. 1995)
Successful habeas petition is prerequisite to §1983 claim that hinges on finding that claimant's Habeas petition is not mooted by petitioner's release from custody, if petitioner faces sufficient repercussions from his allegedly unlawful punishment.

Levine v. Commissioner of Correctional Services, 44 F.3d 121 (2nd Cir. 1995)
Exhaustion requirement is satisfied if petitioner fairly presented the federal constitutional claim to the highest state court.

Long v. AZ. Board of Pardons and Parole, 180 Ariz. 490, 492, 885 P.2d 178, 180 (APP. 1994) "Both legislative and judicial branches of Arizona Government have recognized that a habeas petitioner is entitled to a speedy decision. US Supreme Court has always recognized that the writ must provide quick relief: "Under our constitutional framework the 'great constitutional privilege' of habeas corpus, Exparte Bollman, 4 Cranch 75, 95 (1807) (Marshall, C. J.) has historically provided a prompt and efficacious remedy for whatever society deems to be intolerable restraints." See also: ARS 13-4124(A)

Mabry v. Johnson, 467 US 504, 104 S.Ct. 2543
Petitioner filed petition for writ of habeas corpus. The United States District Court for the Eastern District of Arkansas, William Ray Overton, J., dismissed petition, and petitioner appealed. The United States Court of Appeals for the Eighth Circuit, 707 F.2d 323, reversed, and certiorari was granted. The Supreme Court, Justice Stevens, held that petitioner's acceptance of prosecutor's proposed plea bargain did not create constitutional right to have bargain specifically enforced, and petitioner could not successfully attack subsequent guilty plea. Reversed.

Mayfield v. Ford, 664 F. Supp. 1285 Neb. 1987
Petitioner who has been illegally confined under statute that is unconstitutional is entitled to attack commitment by petition for writ of habeas corpus. See: 28 USC. § 2254.

McClesky v. Zant, 499 US 467, 113 L.Ed.2d 517, 111 S.Ct. 1454 (1991)
Federal habeas petitioner was held to have abused the writ because he did not raise the issue in a prior federal petition.

McFarland v. Scott, 512 US 1 129 L.Ed.2d 666, 114 S.Ct. (1994)
Federal District Court held to have authority, prior to filing of habeas corpus petition, to appoint counsel for indigent capital defendant and to stay execution.

Middleton v. Evatt, 855 F.Supp. 837, 84 (D.S.C. 1994) Aff'd, 77 F.3d 467 (4th Cir. 1996) cert. denied, 117 S.Ct. 199 (1996)

While federal court is bound by state court determination that counsel's alleged deficiencies were a result of trial tactics, it still must undertake its own review to determine whether tactics were reasonable.

Miller v. Fenton, 106 S. Ct. 445, 474 US 104, 88 L.Ed.2d 405, on remand, 796 F.2d 598, cert denied, 107 S. Ct. 585, 479 US 989, 93 L.Ed.2d 587 US NJ. 1985

Voluntariness of a confession is not an issue of fact presumed correct in a federal habeas corpus preceding under 28 USCA S. S. 2254 (d), but it is a legal question meriting independent consideration.

Moon v. Head, 285 F.3d 1301, 1308 (11th Cir. 2002)

Habeas corpus used to challenge suppression of evidence.

Norman v. Ducharme, 871 F.2d 1483 C.A.9 (Wash) 1989.

While his snorkel, factual findings of a state court are presumed correct in the habeas corpus proceeding and will not be set aside unless lacking fair support in record, Court of Appeals may give different legal weight to those facts. See: 28 USC. § 2254 (d).

Note: When a state court rejects the double jeopardy claim, the defendant, after exhausting state remedies, may pursue the claim in a federal habeas corpus actions prior to trial in state court.

Note: Applicants currently in custody shall file a petition for a writ of habeas corpus naming the state officer having custody as respondent. See section 2254 Rules, supra note 1, R.2 (a) 28 USC. Fol. § 2254. Applicant not currently in custody pursuant to the judgment being attacked but subject to future custody shall file a petition for writ of habeas corpus with an added prayer for appropriate relief against the judgment they wish to attack, naming the state officer having custody and the Attorney General for the state where the judgment was injured as respondent. See Id. R. 2 (b). Petition must be typed or legibly handwritten and should follow or closely approximates the form of the model application, the model form for use in application for habeas corpus is located at 28 USC. § 2254, annexed to the rules governing § 2254.

Note: Compare ARS § 13-2010(L)(1) with ARS § 13-4239(G)
A habeas petitioner – unlike a Rule 32 petitioner – has the right to appeal if the writ is denied.

Note: A prisoner seeking to challenge the conditions of his or her confinement should pursue relief through a civil rights claim under 42 USC. § 1983.

Note: In granting habeas relief, a federal court may order the state to resentence a petitioner.

O'Neal v. McAninch, 513 US 130 L.Ed.2d 947, 115 S.Ct. (1995)
Error violating Federal Constitution in state criminal trial held not harmless and federal habeas corpus petitioner held required to win where habeas judge has grave doubt as to harmlessness.

Oaradus v. Arave, 130 F.3d 385 (9th Cir 1997)
Federal habeas corpus relief is limited to claims that alleged constitutional violation in state criminal proceedings.

Osborn v. Shillinger, 997 F.2d 1324 (10th Cir. 1993)
Habeas petitioner's claims must be construed liberally when he appears pro se.

Paxton v. Walters, 120 Ariz. 120, 124, 231 P.2d 458 (1951)
"If the information states no offense it follows that it is a nullity, conferred no jurisdiction upon the court, and necessarily formed no basis for a plea of guilty and for the pronouncement of judgment and sentence thereon by the court. The judgment and sentence rendered are therefore wholly null and void." Id. The court concluded, "That habeas corpus will lie in a case where a person is incarcerated under a void judgment by this court, even if the question were properly raised." See also: State v. Hathcock, 9 Ariz. App. 178, 181, 450 P.2d 419 (1969)

Pearson v. Norris, 52 F.3d 740 (8th Cir 1995)

To prevail on a claim of bias by a state judge in any habeas corpus action, petitioner must actually establish bias or prejudice or prejudice on part of the judge or if, who realistically considering the psychological tendencies and human weakness, judge would be unable to hold the proper balance between the state and the accused, prejudice may be presumed; factors warranting a presumption of prejudice include whether the judge has a pecuniary interest in outcome of the trial or whether judge has been target of personal abuse or criticism from one of the partners. See also: Richmond v. Ricketts, 640 F.Supp. 767 (Ariz. 1986)

Pemberton v. Collins, 991 F.2d 1218 (5th Cir. 1993)

Federal habeas courts asks only whether constitutional violation infected state trial.

Pierre v. Rivkind, 825 F.2d 1501 (11th Cir. 1987)

Writ of habeas corpus extends only to custody and detention; it cannot address collateral or ancillary forms of administrative relief.

Preiser v. Rodriguez, 411 US 475, 494, 499 (1973) At 485-86.

Habeas corpus can be used to challenge incarceration under unconstitutional statute, pre-trial imprisonment based on the defective indictment, confinement in improper institution, denial of constitutional right at trial, invalid guilty plea, unlawful detention by executive or military, or parole violation.

Richardson v. Gramley, 998 F.2d 463 (7th Cir. 1993)

Issue not preserved within state court system is deemed waived on federal habeas corpus review.

Roe v. Flores-Ortega, 120 S.Ct. 1029 (2000)

Reversing the 9th circuit's grant of relief in the California habeas case, the court held that counsel's failure to file notice of appeal where a defendant has not indicated whether he wishes to pursue an appeal is not per se ineffective assistance of counsel. Rather, under the circumstances the reviewing court should first determine whether counsel actually consulted with the defendant concerning available appellate remedies; if so, counsel's performance is deficient only if she fails to follow the defendants instruction; if not, counsel's performance is deficient if a rational defendant would want to appeal, or if the particular defendant has reasonably demonstrated an interest in pursuing an appeal. Prejudice in these circumstances is established upon a showing of reasonable probability that, but for counsel's deficient performance, the defendant would have perfected a timely appeal.

Russell v. Jones, 679 F. Supp. 949 W. D. Mo. 1988
Even if it is assumed that trial defense counsel's performance was deficient in failing to object to testimony, habeas corpus petitioner has burden of showing that admission of evidence deprived him of a fair trial and that he suffered prejudice in that if the evidence had been excluded, results of the trial would have been different.

Sanders v. Sullivan, 701 F. Supp. 996 appeal after remand 701 F.2d 218 S.D. N.Y. (1987)
Habeas petitioner was entitled to evidentiary hearing on issue whether prosecutor knowingly used to perjure testimony at trial upon providing signed an affidavit of key witness from trial and his testimony was perjured, even though there was no support for the contention, that the prosecutor knowingly used testimony.

Scaniq v. US, 37 F.3d 858 (2nd Cir. 1994)
A person under supervised release may be deemed "in custody" for purposes of entitlement to bring habeas corpus proceeding.

Schlup v. Delo, 513 US 130 L.Ed.2d 808, 115 S.Ct. (1995)
Federal habeas corpus petitioner under death sentence held required, to avoid procedural bar, to show only that constitutional violation probably resulted in conviction of one who was actually innocent.

Schwendeman v. Wallenstein, 971 F.2d 313 (9th Cir. 1992)
State habeas claim is considered exhausted when it's been fairly presented to the highest state court.

<u>Seiler v. Thalacker</u>, 101 F.3d 536, 539 (8th Cir. 1996),cert. denied, 117 S.Ct. 1447 (1997)

Court of Appeals explicitly held that Brecht prejudice analysis is not appropriate unless the state courts have conducted <u>Chapman v. California</u> harmless error analysis.

<u>Simon v. US</u>, C.A.8 (Mo) 1958, 253 F.2d 909

Our trial court has held no hearing on petition for habeas corpus it must be assumed upon appeal that factual allegations of petition are true.

<u>Spencer v. Zant</u>, 729 F.2d 1293, reversed 753 F.2d 877, cert granted in part 106 S. Ct. 3331, 478 US 1019, 92 L.Ed.2d 737, affirmed 107 S. Ct. 1756, 481 US 279, 95 L.Ed.2d 262 rehearing denied 107 S. Ct. 3199, 482 US 920 96 L.Ed.2d 686 D. Ariz. 1986

<u>Richmond v. Ricketts</u>, 640 F. Supp. 767 D.C. GA. 1984

<u>McCloskey v. Zant</u>, 580 F.Supp. 338, hearing ordered.

To prevail on a claim of bias by a state judge in a habeas corpus action, petitioner must actually establish bias or prejudice on part of the judge or if, realistically considering the psychological tendencies and human weaknesses, judge would be unable to hold the proper balance between the state and the accused, prejudice may be presumed; factors warranting a presumption of prejudice include whether judge has a pecuniary interest in the outcome of the trial or whether judge has been target of personal abuse or criticism from one of the parties.

<u>State v. Buckley</u>, 153 Ariz. 91, 93, 734 P.2d 1047, 1049 (APP. 1987)

<u>State v. Vargas-Burges,</u> 162 Ariz. 325, 327, 783 P.2d 264, 266 (APP. 1984)

This error is so fundamental that it is not capable of waiver.

<u>State v. Curtis</u>, 185 Ariz. 112

Defendants are precluded from seeking post-conviction relief on grounds that were adjudicated, or could have been raised and adjudicated, in a prior appeal or prior petition for post-conviction relief ("PCR"). See Ariz. R. Crim. P. 32.2, 17 Ariz. Rev. Stat. Ann. ("A.R.S."). But the State can waive preclusion if, when responding to a PCR, the State fails to "plead [***2] and prove . . . preclusion by a preponderance of the evidence." Id.; <u>State v. Hursey</u>, 176 Ariz. 330, 332, 861 P.2d

615, 617 (1993). This petition for review presents the question whether, when preclusion is evident from the petition and from the court's own files, a trial court may screen and summarily dismiss a PCR on grounds of preclusion without putting the State to the burden of a response. That question is one of first impression. Our answer is yes. A claim is precluded that could have [***9] been, but was not, raised in a prior appeal or PCR, unless the "asserted claim is of sufficient constitutional magnitude."

State v. Fuentes, 12 Ariz. APP. 48, 49, 467 P.2d 760 (1970)
Bowman v. State, 103 Ariz. 482, 483, 445 P.2d 841 (1968)
State v. Dunivan, 77 Ariz. 42, 266 P.2d 1077 (1954)
State v. Cowsey, 71 Ariz. 227, 225 P.2d 713 (1950)
Pray v. State, 56 Ariz. 171, 106 P.2d 500 (1940)
When circumstances are substantively identical to one in which the indictment or information was quashed the Supreme Court ruled: "The fact that new information would substantially be the same as the first does not excuse its filing. We have held when a motion to quash information is granted there is no case pending in the superior Court until new information is filed."

State v. Hawkins, 140 Ariz. 88, 90, 680 P.2d 522, 524 (1984)
This being a matter of substance, not procedure, the legislature has the primary authority to grant or deny release.

State v. Poli, 161 Ariz. 151, 153, 776 P.2d 1077, 1079 (APP. 1989)
In Hathcock "courts have a sua sponte duty to examine their jurisdiction."

State v. Rockefeller, 117 Ariz. 151, 153, 571 P.2d 297, 299 (1977)
Twining v. New Jersey, 211 US 78, 29 S. CT. 14, 53 L. Ed. 97 (1908)
Permitting the trial of an accused without a valid information or indictment violates fundamental notions of due process.

State v. Rose, 121 Ariz. 131, 142, 589 P.2d 5, 16 (1978)
When Arizona appellate courts intend further proceedings to take place in the trial court, they specifically so state. See also: A.R.Cr.P. Rule 201(b)

Stringer v. Black, 503 US, 117 L.Ed.2d 367, 112 S.Ct. (1992)
Aggravating circumstances unconstitutionally vague on capital sentencing proceeding held retroactively available to support federal habeas corpus.

Swazo v. Wyoming Department of Corrections, 23 F.3d 332 (10th Cir. 1994)
There is right to counsel in habeas corpus case when district court determines that evidentiary hearing is required.

Taylor v. Wallace, 931 F.2d 698 (10th Cir. 1991)
Inmates action seeking restoration of good time credits is properly pursued via petition for writ of habeas corpus.

Todd v. Schomig, 283 F.3d 842, 849 (7th Cir. 2002)
Habeas corpus used to challenge indictment using perjured testimony, inadmissible evidence of other crimes, impartial tribunal, and delay in execution.

Tucker v. Day, 969 F.2d 155 (5th Cir. 1992)
Failure of appointed defense counsel to provide any assistance at re-sentencing hearing was constructive denial of right to assistance of counsel and warranted habeas relief.

US v. Garcia, 42 F.3d 573 (10th Cir. 1994)
If defendant successfully attacks state conviction through petition of writ of habeas corpus, he may apply for reopening of any federal sentence enhanced by state conviction.

US v. Harris, 12 F.3d 735 (7th Cir. 1994)
Jackson v. Carlson, 707 F.2d 943 (7th Cir. 1983)
Prisoner objecting to incremental level of incarceration, such as segregation, has administrative remedies and if these fail he can apply for habeas corpus, arguing that he is being deprived of liberty without due process of law, providing that he has been given by statute or regulation an entitlement to less restrictive confinement.

Walker v. Lockhart, 763 F.2d 942,cert. denied, 106 S.Ct. 3332, 478 US 1020, 92 L.Ed 738 C.A.8 (Ark) 1985.
Federal habeas corpus power goes only to constitutionality of detention, not to question of guilt or innocence.

Waletzki v. Keohane, 13 F.3d 1079 (7th Cir. 1994)
Habeas corpus is available to challenge duration as well as fact of custody.

Washington v. Delo, 51 F.3d 756 (8th Cir. 1995)
Dismissal of successive or potentially abusive habeas claims is not automatic; if petitioner can show cause for failure to raise or fully develop claims, and prejudice arising therefrom, district court may consider merits of such claims.

Weidner v. Thieret, 866 F.2d 958, reh. Denied C.A. 7 (Ill.) 1989.
Habeas petitioner was entitled to hearing on issue of whether His confession had been coerced; state judge, who ruled that confession was admissible, did not indicate whether he believed or disbelieved any part of either party's evidence, and there were wide discrepancies between police version and defendant's version of interrogation, and it was necessary to know facts underlying confession before federal court could make independent judgment on whether facts crossed threshold of impermissible coercion.

Whitney v. Horn, 280 F.3d 240, 249 (3rd Cir. 2002)
Habeas corpus used to challenge effectiveness of trial counsel.

Wilkerson v. Wyrick, 806 F.2d 161, cert. denied, 107 S.Ct. 2466, 481 US 1071, 95 L.Ed.2d 875 C.A.8 (Mo.) 1986.
Due process is denied when person is convicted without having received fair and reasonable notice of charge against him and such denials of due process are cognizable in federal habeas corpus. See: USC.A. 5, 14.

Willard v. Pearson, 823 F.2d 1141 C.A.7 (Ind) 1987.
Not entitled to habeas corpus relief for alleged violation of state law with respect to joinder of crimes. See: 28 USC. § 2254.

Wilson v. Phend, C.A.7 (Ind) 1969, 417 F.2d 1197
Where petitioner for habeas corpus was dismissed without requiring respondent to answer, petitioner's allegations must be deemed true for purpose of review.

Withrow v. Williams, 507 US 1 123 L.Ed.2d 407, 113 S.Ct. (1993)
Restriction on federal habeas corpus review of Fourth Amendment issues held not to apply to Michigan prisoner's claim that conviction rested on statements obtained without Miranda warnings.

Wray v. Johnson, 202 F.3d 515, 530 (2nd Cir. 2002)
Erroneous admission of evidence was not harmless.

Ya v. Maugans, 24 F.3d 500 (3rd Cir 1994)
Warden of prison or facility where detainee is held is considered "custodian" for purposes of habeas corpus action, as warden has day to day control over prisoner and can produce actual body.

Harmless Error

A.R.S. 13-3987 Harmless Error
Neither a departure from the form or mode prescribed in respect to any pleadings or proceedings, nor in error or mistake therein, shall render the pleadings or proceeding in valid unless it actually it has prejudiced, or tended to prejudice the defendant in respect to a substantial right.

Chapman, 386 US at 23
In Chapman the court held that this formulation is entirely consistent with the standard adopted in Fahy v. Connecticut, 375 US 85 (1963) that the question is whether there is reasonable possibility that the error complained of might have contributed to the conviction.

Lawson v. Borg, 60 F.3d 608, 612-613 (9th Cir 1995)
State court conclusion that in error was harmless is not a finding of fact entitled to the presumption of correctness.

Note: In the case of constitutional error the Supreme Court as stated that it may label the error harmless only upon determination beyond a reasonable doubt that the error did not contribute to the verdict.

Satterwhite v. Texas, 486 US 249, 256 (1988)
If the sixth amendment violation pervades the entire proceeding, harmless error analysis is inapplicable and the violation is enough to overturn a conviction regardless of the severity of the results.

State v. Bass, 198 Ariz. 571, 580-81, ¶ 39, 12 P.3d 596, 805-06 (2000)
State v. Vigil, 195 Ariz. 189, 192, ¶ 13, 986 P.2d 222, 225 (App. 1999)
To define harmless error, a court must be able to conclude beyond a reasonable doubt that the erroneously admitted evidence had no effect on the jury, i.e. that the jury would have convicted the defendant even if the evidence had been excluded...

<u>State v. Tucker</u>, No. 1 CA-CR 12234, Court of Appeals of Arizona, Division One, Department B, 165 Ariz. 340; 798 P.2d 1349; 1990 Ariz. App. LEXIS 106; 57 Ariz. Adv. Rep. 42, March 27, 1990 , As Corrected March 28, 1990. Reconsideration Denied May 25, 1990. Review Denied November 6, 1990.
Defendant's conviction for sexual indecency with a child was improper where the trial court erred in admitting hearsay statements made by the child to police and a social worker and in admitting expert testimony that was common knowledge. Where case comes down to the victim's word against the defendant and there is no physical evidence, improper hearsay evidence and expert testimony require reversal.

<u>State v. Williams</u>, 133 Ariz. 220, 225, 650 P.2d 1202, 1207 P.2d 9, 12 (1980)
The test for determining harmless error is whether there was reasonability... that a verdict might have been different had the error not been committed.

<u>US v. Matco</u>, 950 F.2d 44, 48 n.8 (1st Cir. 1991)
Harmless error analysis inapplicable when counsel absent from sentencing hearing because critical stage of proceedings.

<u>US v. Merino-Balderrama</u>, No. 97-30303, UNITED STATES COURT OF APPEALS FOR THE NINTH CIRCUIT, 146 F.3d 758; 1998 US App. LEXIS 16448; 49 Fed. R. Evid. Serv. (Callaghan) 827; 98 Cal. Daily Op. Service 5680; 98 Daily Journal DAR 7887, June 3, 1998, * Submitted, Seattle, Washington* The panel unanimously found this case suitable for decision without oral argument. Fed. R. App. P. 34(a) and Ninth Circuit Rule 34-4., July 21, 1998, Filed
Defendant's conviction for possession of child pornography was reversed and remanded because it was not harmless error for district court to allow jury to view films where government failed to present evidence that defendant knew films' content.

<u>US v. Morley</u>, 199 F.3d 129, 140 (3rd Cir. 1999)
Erroneous admission of evidence of defendant's prior bad act is not harmless and error because remaining evidence presented by prosecution was not compelling.

<u>US v. Scroger</u>, 98 F.3d 1256 (10th Cir. 1996)
Government has burden of proving that non constitutional error was harmless.

<u>US v. Toles</u>, 297 F.3d 959, 9 67-68 (10th Cir. 2002)
Even if limitation on cross-examination violated defendant's confrontation clause rights, error harmless beyond a reasonable doubt due to overwhelming evidence of defendant's guilt.

<u>US v. Varoudakis</u>, 233 F.3d 113, 126 (1st Cir. 2000) Admission of prior bad act evidence could sway juror's judgment and DOS was not harmless.

<u>US v. Vasquez</u>, 7 F.3d 81, 83 (5th Cir. 1993)
Harmless error analysis inapplicable when court denied defendant statutory right to a point of counsel at evidentiary hearing to determine merits of motion to vacate sentence because not permitted by statute.

<u>Wilson v. Anderson</u>,CA9 (Cal) 1967, 379 F.2d 330, reversed on other grounds, 88 S.Ct. 1133, 390 US 523, 20 L.Ed.2d 81, rehearing denied, 88 S.Ct. 1812, 391 US 929, 20 L.Ed.2d 670
Any harmless error rule applied to violation, by state court, all of provision of federal standard.

Hearsay

F.R.E. Rule 801 (c)

Hearsay, is a statement, other than one made by the defendant while testifying at trial or hearing, offered in evidence to prove the truth of the matter asserted.

A.R.E. Rule 801

Purpose. These rules, and particularly those concerning hearsay, are designed to protect the confrontation clause of federal and state Constitution. See: State v. Allen, 157 Ariz. 755 P.2d 1153 (1988).

State v. Allen, No. CR-87-0087-PR, Supreme Court of Arizona, 157 Ariz. 165; 755 P.2d 1153; 1988 Ariz. LEXIS 78; 9 Ariz. Adv. Rep. 8, June 2, 1988. REVERSED AND REMANDED.

Admission of hearsay statements of unavailable child molestation victim was fundamental error; statements did not fit recognized or residual exceptions and her knowledge of sexual matters could not be ascribed to defendant in light of past abuse.

State v. Damper, 223 Ariz. 572

Murder victim's text message to a friend indicating that she and defendant were fighting was properly admitted into evidence because, while the Sixth Amendment barred testimonial hearsay, the text message was not testimonial because there was no showing that the victim intended or believed that the message might be later used in a legal proceeding.

State v. Tucker, No. 1 CA-CR 12234, Court of Appeals of Arizona, Division One, Department B, 165 Ariz. 340; 798 P.2d 1349; 1990 Ariz. App. LEXIS 106; 57 Ariz. Adv. Rep. 42, March 27, 1990 , As Corrected March 28, 1990. Reconsideration Denied May 25, 1990. Review Denied November 6, 1990.

Defendant's conviction for sexual indecency with a child was improper where the trial court erred in admitting hearsay statements made by the child to police and a social worker and in admitting expert testimony that was common knowledge.

Webb v. Lewis, No. 93-16167, UNITED STATES COURT OF APPEALS FOR THE NINTH CIRCUIT, 44 F.3d 1387; 1994 US App. LEXIS 34997, May 12, 1994, * Submitted, San Francisco, California * The panel unanimously finds this case suitable for submission without oral argument. Fed. R. App. P. 34(a); 9th Cir. R. 34-4. , August 24, 1994, Filed , Further Amended December 8, 1994. Certiorari Denied May 22, 1995, Reported at: 1995 US LEXIS 3515.

The admission of a child declarant's hearsay, which recounted her sexual molestation, violated the accused's confrontation right, because the statements were not made during a medical exam and lacked guarantees of trustworthiness.

Immunity

<u>Allen v. City & County of Honolulu</u>, 39 F.3d 936 (9th Cir. 1994)
Prison official was not entitled to qualified immunity as to claim that he forced inmate to choose between right to outdoor exercise and right to law library access, both of which rights were clearly established.

<u>Armendariz v. Penman</u>, 31 F.3d 860 (9th Cir. 1994)
Supervisor may be liable based on either (1) personal involvement in constitutional deprivation or (2) sufficient casual connection between superior's wrongful conduct and the constitutional violation.

<u>Bagola v. Kindt</u>, 39 F.3d 779 (7th Cir. 1994)
After a prison worker had his hand cut off by the machine he was working on he brought a Bivens action. The court held that the federal worker's compensation statute was not a bar in a Bivens action and appointed him counsel in the lower court.

<u>Benitez v. WLFF</u>, 985 F2d 662 (2nd Cir. 1993)
<u>Jones v. Counce</u>, 7 F3d 1359 (8th Cir. 1993)
Qualified immunity defense fails if public officer violates clearly established right because a reasonably competent official should know the law governing this conduct.

<u>Bivens v. Six Unknown Agents</u>, 403 US 388, 29 L.Ed.2d 619, 91 S.Ct. 1999 (1970)
Supreme Court held that government agents may be held liable for violating constitutional rights.

<u>B.K. Instrument, Inc. v. US</u>, 715 F.2d 713 (2nd Cir. 1983)
<u>Dugan v. Rank</u>, 372 US 609, 10 L.Ed.2d 15, 83 S.Ct. 999 (1963)
There are two instances when the plaintiff can sue the United States directly: 1) Action by an officer beyond his statutorily defined powers; 2) where the powers or the manner of their execution are unconstitutional. B. K. @ 723 724.

Buckley v. Fitzsimmons, 509 US 125 L.Ed.2d 209, 113 S.Ct. (1993)
Prosecutors hold no absolute immunity from 42 USCS §1983 damages claims alleging; 1) fabrication of evidence during preliminary investigation, and 2) making of false statements at a press conference.

Edgar v. City Of Livingston, 40 F.3d 312 (9th Cir. 1994)
State judge does not enjoy judicial immunity from unconstitutional behavior when facts are sufficient to grant party declaratory or injunctive relief against judge.

Gardiner v. Incorporated Village of Endicott, 50 F.3d 151 (2nd Cir. 1995)
For qualified immunity to attach, it is not enough that officer believes his conduct comports with clearly established rights; that belief must also be reasonable.

Guzman - Rivera v. Rivera - Cruz, 55 F.3d 26 (1st Cir. 1995)
1. Absolute immunity protects the prosecutor's role as advocate for the state, not his or her role as an administrator or investigative officer. 2. Prosecutorial conduct is given absolute immunity only if it is intimately associated with the judicial phase of the criminal process.

Hill v. Marshall, 962 F.2d 1209 (6th Cir. 1992)
Smith v. Wade, 461 US 30, 75 L.Ed.2d 632, 103 S.Ct. 1625 (1983)
Prison official could be personally liable in civil rights action for actions taken in the course of his office. SMITH grants punitive damages.

Hunt v. Bennett, 17 F.3d 1263 (10th Cir. 1994)
Hays County Guardian v. Supple, 969 F2d III (5th Cir. 1992)
Eleventh Amendment does not bar state law actions against state officials in their individual capacities.

Mandonado - Denis v. Castillo - Rodriguez, 23 F.3d 576 (1st Cir. 1994) Inadequate training of subordinates may be basis for §1983 claim.

Mendenhall v. Goldsmith, 59 F.3d 685 (7th Cir. 1995)
For purposes of immunity analysis, federal officials are indistinguishable from state officials and receive no greater degree of protection from constitutional claims.

McKinney v. Dekalb County, Ga., 997 F.2d 1440 (11th Cir. 1993)
Canton v. Harris, 489 US 378,103 L.Ed.2d 412, 109 S.Ct. 1197 (1989)
Monell v. Dept. Social Services, 426 US 658, 56 L.Ed.2d 611, 98 S.Ct. 2018 (1978)
Sovereign immunity does not shield governmental entities from suit in § 1983 action alleging inadequacy of official policy or custom.

Mitchell v. Forsyth. 472 US 511, 86 L.Ed.2d 411, 105 S.Ct. 2806 (1985)
Cameron v. I.R.S., 773 F.2d 126 (1985)
The Attorney General and I.R.S. agents do not have absolute immunity.

Morales v. Portuondo, 165 F. Supp.2d 601 (S.D.N.Y. 2001)
Granting relief to codefendant in Kings following prosecutor's confession on air; ordering "unconditional discharge", barring re-trial, and requiring expungement of the record of petitioner's convictions and all references to them in the public record."

Neely v. Feinstein, 50 F.3d 1502 (9th Cir. 1995)
Standard for denying qualified immunity in civil rights action involves two part analysis: whether law governing official's conduct was clearly established, and whether reasonable officer could have believed that conduct was lawful under that law.

Pierson v. Ray, 386 US 547, 19 LEd2d 288, 87 S.Ct. 1213 (1967)
Judges are totally immune from liability for damages for acts committed within their judicial jurisdiction. It is also applicable to prosecutors and legislators (Authors note: this was true in 1967 but today there are a number of other legal avenues available).

Procunier v. Navarette, 434 US 555, 55 L.Ed.2d 24, 98 S.Ct. 855 (1978)
Prison officials not immune from liabilities for official acts when motivated by malicious intent to deprive prisoners of constitutional rights.

Schroeder v. McDonald, 41 F.3d 1272 (9th Cir. 1994)
Prison officials were not entitled to qualified immunity for transferring inmate from minimum security facility to medium security facility without following mandatory prison regulations.

Scott v. Glumac, 3 F.3d 163 (7th Cir. 1993)
Because doctrine of qualified immunity entitles officers to immunize from both civil liability and burdens of litigation, it is important to resolve immunity question at earliest possible stage.

State v. Holsinger, (1977) 115 Ariz. 271, 564 P.2d 1238
Prosecutors failure to disclose to defense counsel that immunity had been granted to the only state witness who tended to corroborate testimony of accomplice in murder prosecution constituted prejudicial error requiring reversal of defendant's conviction, since fact of immunity was irrelevant, not only to test witnesses credibility, but also to determine if witness was herself and accomplice.

Tower v. Glover, 467 US 914, 81 L.Ed.2d 758, 104 S.Ct. 2820 (1984)
Public defenders held NOT IMMUNE from liability in a §1983 action alleging conspiracy with state officials to deprive clients of federal rights.

Wahl v. McIver, 773 F.2d 1169, 1172 (11th Cir. 1985)
Pulliam v. Allen, 466 US 522 , 80 L.Ed2.d 565, 104 S.Ct. 1970 (1984)
Judicial immunity however, concerns only monetary liability and does not bar injunctive relief against judicial officers acting in their judicial capacity (1104 S.Ct. @ 1981). Furthermore, judicial immunity does not bar an award of attorney's fees under 42 USC §1983. Id. at 104 S.Ct. 1982.

<u>Weg v. Macchia</u>, 995 F.2d 15 (2nd Cir. 1993)

Public officials receive protection of qualified immunity if they establish that it was objectively reasonable to believe that their acts did not violate clearly established rights.

<u>White v. Farrier</u>, 849 F.2d 322 (8th Cir. 1988) Cole v. Bone, 993 F.2d 1328 (8th Cir. 1993) Government officials may be held liable for constitutional wrongs caused by their failure to adequately train or supervise subordinates.

Indictment

F.R.Cr.P. Rule 7.0 (b)
Waiver of Indictment An offense punishable by imprisonment for more than one year may be prosecuted by information if the defendant in open court and after being advised of the nature of the charge and of the defendant's right-waves prosecution by indictment.

Alexander v. L.A., 405 US 625,633 (1972)
Fourteenth amendment due process clause requires fair trial but does not require state indictment by grand jury.

Ball v. US, 470 US 856, 864 - 65 (1985)
Proper way to remedy multiplictious convictions is to vacate all but one conviction.

Beverly v. Walker, (N.D. N.Y. 1995) 899 F.Supp. 900
U.S.C.A. Fifth Amendment.
Indictment met constitutional standards, where in each count specified time and place at which alleged crime occurred and set forth the essential elements of crimes and indictment sufficiently informed defendant of charges against him.

Boothe v. Wyrick, W.D. Mo. 1978, 452 F.Supp. 1304
Errors turning on the sufficiency of, or Proper way to remedy multiplictious convictions is to vacate all but one conviction. Amendments to an indictment are not reviewable in federal habeas corpus unless the indictment is constitutionally defective.

Buttrum v. Black, (N.D. GA. 1989) 721 F.Supp. 1268 affirmed 908 F.2d 695, rehearing denied 916 F.2d 719
An amendment of indictment occurs when charging terms of indictment are altered, either literally, or in effect by prosecutor or court after grand jury has last passed upon them.

Cole v. State of Arkansas, 68 S.Ct. 514 (1948)
No principal of procedural due process is more clearly established than that notice of specific charge, and a chance to be heard in a trial of that issue raised by the charge, if desired, are among the constitutional rights of every accused in a criminal proceeding in all courts, state or federal. In Re Oliver, 333 US 257, 68 S.Ct. 499 and cases there cited.

Deckard v. Swenson, D.C. Mo. 1971, 335 F. Supp. 992
Scalf v. Bennett, CA8 (Iowa) 1969, 408 F.2d 325,cert. denied, 90 S.Ct. 175, 396 US 887, 24 L.Ed.2d 161
The writ of habeas corpus will not be used to test indictment unless it is constitutionally defective.

Ex Parte, Bain, 121 US 1, 7 S.Ct. 781, 30 L.Ed. 849 (1987)
The instant that the court amends the indictment, the court loses jurisdiction. At that point in time, there is nothing that can cure the defect. It is jurisdictional defect. Upon an indictment so charged the court can proceed no further. There is nothing for which the prisoner can be held to answer. A trial on such indictment is void.

Ex Parte Wilson, 114 US 417, 426 (1885)
Defendant has the right to insist he shall not be put upon trial, except on the accusation of a grand jury.

Feels v. Soloff, 920 F.2d 1114, 1118 (2nd Cir. 1990)
Fifth Amendment right to grand jury does not pertain to state because not incorporated by the fourteenth amendment.

Forgy v. Norris, (1995, CA8 Ark.) 64 F.3d 399, reh. denied, (1995, CA 8 Ark) 1995 US App. LEXIS 27956
Defendant's constitutional right to notice of charges against him was violated by information charging him with burglary with intent to commit crime punishable by "imprisonment" where he was tried for burglary with intent to commit attempted theft, since information lacked specificity by failing to give adequate notice of burglary charge.

Givens v. Housewright, 786 F.2d 1378, 1381 (9th Cir. 1986)

The information in a citation to a statute which merely defined the degree of murder, identifying murder by torture as one type of first-degree murder, did not provide the defendant adequate notice of the specific charge of first-degree murder by torture.

Gray v. Raines, 662 F.2d 569

Gray was convicted in Arizona state court of second degree or "statutory" rape under A.R.S. § 13-611(B). He argues on this appeal that the Arizona statutory rape law (since repealed) under which he was convicted discriminated against males and therefore violated the Equal Protection Clause of the United States Constitution. He also argues that, because he was charged in the information only with first degree or forcible rape, his right to due process was violated when the trial judge included second degree rape in his charge to the jury. Obviously, the State of Arizona may organize its criminal laws in whatever manner it chooses. The state cannot, however, use a classification scheme to circumvent the constitutional notice requirement imposed on the state when charging a defendant with an offense. The ruling of the Court today applies only to the conviction for second degree rape; the [**15] conviction for lewd and lascivious acts is not disturbed. The writ of habeas corpus is granted and this case is remanded to the District Court for action consistent with this opinion. Reversed and remanded.

Groppie v. Leslie, 404 US 496, 30 L.Ed.2d 632, 92 S.Ct. 582 (1972)

Due process clause requires that minimum net deprivation of life, liberty or property by adjudication be preceded by notice and opportunity for hearing appropriate to nature of case.

Hamilton v. McCotter, 772 F.2d 171 (5th Cir. 1985)

The Constitution, statute, or court rule should be checked to determine whether the state may prosecuted by indictment. Some states may allow prosecution to be commenced either by an information, complaint, or indictment.

Inciso v. US, 429 US 1099, 97 S.Ct. 1118, 51 L.Ed.2d 546 (1977)

US v. Phaester, 544 F.2d 353, 361 (9th Cir. 1976) cert. denied

Furthermore, tardy challenges to an indictment must be construed according to common sense.

Jeffries v. Blodgett, 5 F.3d 1180, 1188 (9th Cir. 1992)

States that do not prosecuted by indictment will usually initiate prosecution by filing on an information or complaint. Offenses which can be prosecuted by grand jury indictment can also be prosecuted by information if in open court the accused waves his right to grand jury indictment after the charges have been read. See: US v. Ferguson.

Kaneshiro v. US, 445 F.2d 1266, 1269 (9th Cir.) (internal quotations omitted) cert. denied, 404 US 992, 92 S.Ct. 537, 30 L.Ed.2d 543 (1971)

When the sufficiency of the indictment challenged after trial, it is only required that the necessary facts appear in any form or by fair construction can be found within the terms of the indictment. Where an indictment is questioned post-trial, reference to a statute will cure some defects. But the defendant must have been given adequate knowledge of the missing elements in order to satisfy the due process requirement, otherwise reference to a statute will not cure the defect in the indictment.

Kincaid v. Sparkman, 175 F.3d 444 (6th Cir. 1999)

A criminal defendant is entitled to be tried on charges contained in the indictment and only on those charges.

Lee v. Madigan, 358 US 228, 232 - 35, 241 (1959)

Johnson v. Sayre, 158 US 103, 114 (1895)

The protection of indictment by grand jury extends to all persons except those serving in the armed forces.

Lowery v. McCaughtry, CA7 (Wis.) 1992, 954 F.2d 422, cert. denied, 113 S.Ct. 104, 506 US 834, 121 L.Ed.2d 63

If state would treat habeas petitioner's claims as waived or forfeited, then there is no available state correction process and exhaustion is not essential.

LTS v. Plenty Arrows, 946 F.2d 62 (8th Cir. 1991)

Verdict cannot be based on an act that could have occurred after return of indictment.

McNally v. US, 483 US 350 97 L.Ed.2d) 292, 107 S.Ct. 2875 (1987) US v. Gimbel, 830 F.2d 621 (7th Cir. 1987)

To be valid, an indictment must allege that the defendant performed acts which, if proven, constituted a violation of the law that he or she is charged with violating.

Mechling v. Slayton, ED. Va. 1973, 361 F. Supp. 770

Generally, the scope of review of a challenged state indictment in federal habeas corpus proceeding is confined to questions of whether the alleged defects go to the jurisdiction of the trial court or deprived defendant of the right to be sufficiently informed of the charges against him.

Nethery v. Collins, 993 F.2d 1154 (5th Cir. 1993)

Deficient indictment will provide basis for federal habeas relief if defect is so significant that convicting court lacked jurisdiction under state law.

Normandeau, 800 F.2d at 958 (internal quotations omitted)

A minor or technical deficiency in the indictment will not reverse the conviction if there is no prejudice.

Note: Indictments that charge the defendant with one act or another, the word "or" may not leave the averment uncertain as to which of the two or more things is meant. An allegation that charges the commission of a crime by one act or another is defective if it does not clearly inform the defendant of the charge so that a defense can be prepared to meet it. The same standard is applied to pleadings in civil cases, where both disjunctive allegations and disjunctive denials generally constitute defective pleadings and are therefore inadmissible.

Note: For an information to be valid you need only contain the same information required in a grand jury indictment.

Note: Each offense must be charged in a separate account in an indictment or complaint.

Note: "Superseding indictment" is an indictment filed without the dismissal of a preceding indictment.

Note: Two circuits have held an indictment is not multiplictious if it divides a series of similar offenses into several counts in order to meet the jurisdictional requirement of the charge to statute, as long as the division into counts is logical and based on distinct time periods or distinct locations.

Pavel v. Hollins, 261 F.3d 210

Appeal from a judgment of the United States District Court for the Northern District of New York (Thomas J. McAvoy, then-Chief Judge), denying petitioner Kenneth G. Pavel's application for a writ of habeas corpus on the ground that Pavel was not convicted in state court in violation of his federal right to effective assistance of counsel. On appeal, Pavel emphasizes that his trial attorney (1) did not prepare a defense, on the theory that the charges against Pavel would be dismissed at the close of the prosecution's case; (2) failed to call two important fact witnesses, with the content of whose putative testimony the attorney was familiar; and (3) did not call as a witness a medical expert. In these circumstances, Pavel argues, his right to effective assistance of counsel was violated. We agree. Accordingly, we reverse the judgment of the District Court, vacate the state court judgment of conviction, and remand the cause. On remand, the District Court shall issue a writ of habeas corpus to Mr. Pavel on the thirtieth calendar day after the issuance of our mandate unless New York State has, by that point, taken concrete and substantial steps to expeditiously retry him. Judgment of [**2] District Court reversed; judgment of conviction vacated, cause remanded.

Peterson v. Jacobson, 2 Ariz. App. 593, at 595, 411 P.2d 31 (1966)

In order to render a valid judgment and sentence in a criminal prosecution, the court must have jurisdiction of both of the offense and of the defendant's person... Jurisdiction of a court to try and punish an individual of a crime cannot be acquired by the court's mere assertion of jurisdiction, but must be invoked or acquired in the mode prescribed by law. If not so invoked, any judgment is a nullity.

Romberg v. Nichols, 953 F.2d 1152 (9th Cir. 1992)
When jury compromises its verdict, verdict shall not stand.

Shepherd v. Rees, 909 F.2d 1234 (9th Cir. 1990)
A trial cannot be fair unless nature of charges against a defendant are adequately made known to him in a timely fashion. See: Strickland v. Washington, (1984)

Spencer v. Coconino County Superior Court, Div. 3, No. 16609-SA, Supreme Court of Arizona, 136 Ariz. 608; 667 P.2d 1323; 1983 Ariz. LEXIS 225, August 3, 1983
The indictment charging the accused with one count each of incest and child molestation regarding the numerous occasions he had sexual relations with his 15-year-old daughter was duplicitous and therefore fatally defective.

State v. Anthony Charles Davis, 206 Ariz. 377, 79 P.3d 64, Ariz. Supreme Court, No. CR-01-0423-PR, CR-01-0423-PR, decided October 30, 2003
This case refers to time elements (During February or March) not allowable, must give dates in close proximity, on or about a given date. See also: State v. Verdugo.

State v. Berry, 101 Ariz. 310, 419 P.2d 337 (1966)
The Supreme Court of Ariz. found there was no essential difference between an information and an indictment.

State v. Curry, 1 CA-CR 94-0617, 1 CA-CR 95-0056 (Consolidated), COURT OF APPEALS OF ARIZONA, DIVISION ONE, DEPARTMENT C, 187 Ariz. 623; 931 P.2d 1133; 1996 Ariz. App. LEXIS 196; 225 Ariz. Adv. Rep. 3, September 10, 1996, Filed , Petition for Review DENIED on February 26, 1997 by Arizona Supreme Court No. CR-96-0579-PR. AFFIRMED IN PART; REVERSED IN PART; REMANDED
Amendment of an indictment was proper where it did not prejudice defendant by depriving him of notice of the charges and where an acquittal of the amended charge provided a double jeopardy defense to a prosecution on the original charge.

State v. Davis, 206 Ariz. 377, 399, 79 P.2d 64, 76 (2003)

The Arizona Supreme Court said, "each offense must be charged in a separate count" in an indictment or complaint. Charging more than one act in a single count is forbidden because it does not provide adequate notice of the charged to be defended, it presents a hazard of non-unanimous jury verdict, and period… makes precise pleading of prior jeopardy impossible in the event of later prosecution.

State v. Hill, (App. Div. 1 1976) 26 Ariz. App. 37, 545 P.2d 999

In order for principal of double jeopardy to apply, the two alleged crimes must have identical components; test to be applied is whether facts charged in latter information would if found true, have justified conviction under earlier information.

State v. Johnson, 2 CA-CR 98-0572, COURT OF APPEALS OF ARIZONA, DIVISION TWO, DEPARTMENT A, 2000 Ariz. App. LEXIS 46; 318 Ariz. Adv. Rep. 3, March 30, 2000, Filed , THIS DECISION IS SUBJECT TO FURTHER APPELLATE REVIEW. MOTIONS FOR RECONSIDERATION OR PETITIONS FOR REVIEW TO THE ARIZONA SUPREME COURT MAY BE PENDING. COUNSEL IS CAUTIONED TO MAKE AN INDEPENDENT DETERMINATION OF THE STATUS OF THIS CASE.

Trial court erred by allowing State to amend criminal information after victim testified, since amended charges were of different nature than original charges and appellant was not afforded adequate opportunity to defend.

State v. O'Grady, 312 US 329, 61 S.Ct. 572, 85 L.Ed. 859, 1941 US Lexis 921

Petitioner pled guilty to the simple burglary and was sentenced to burglary with explosives. Rights under fourteenth amendment due process clause requires defendant to be notified of the charge against him and to be supplied with a copy of the charging document.

State v. Smith, 66 Ariz. 376, 378, 189 P.2d 205 (1948)

Where the Arizona Supreme Court said in 1948… Where the challenge to the information is based upon an omission in the averment of the essential elements of the crime, jurisdiction of the subject matter cannot be conferred by consent... And hence objection to the jurisdiction may be made for the first time in Supreme

Court. The Smith court further said:... We said if an information does not allege a public offense, advantage may be taken thereof at any time. [2][3] we must conclude that it is the settled law of this state that in a criminal case the court acquires no jurisdiction of the subject matter of the alleged offense unless the jurisdictional facts constituting the offenses are set forth in the information, and that where the court is without jurisdiction of the subject matter judgment of conviction will be reversed in this court even on plea of guilty, for jurisdiction cannot be conferred by consent. 66 Ariz. at 379.

State v. Verdugo, (1973) 109 Ariz. 391, 510 P.2d 37
Precise time of act is unnecessary to be proven, if it is alleged that it occurred "on or about" a given date.

State v. Whitney, 159 Ariz. 476, 480, 768P.2d 638,642 (1983) (Citing A.R.Cr.P. Rule 13.3 (a)). Charging more than one act in a single count is forbidden because it does not provide adequate notice of the charge to be defended... Presents a hazard of non-unanimous jury verdict and... Makes a precise pleading of prior jeopardy impossible in the event of a later prosecution.

Thomas v. Harrelson, 942 F.2d 1530
Defendant's murder conviction was affirmed by the Court of Criminal Appeals of Alabama, 455 So.2d 278. Defendant's petition for writ of habeas corpus was denied on the merits without evidentiary hearing by the United States District Court for the Northern District of Alabama, No. CV89-A-27-S,Clarence W. Allgood, J. Defendant appealed. The Court of Appeals, Godbold, Senior Circuit Judge, held that: (1) there was no procedural bar; (2) indictment was constructively amended; and (3) defendant's trial counsel was ineffective for failing to raise issue of constructive amendment. Reversed and remanded.

US v. Abreu, 952 F.2d 1458 (1st Cir. 1992)
Function of bill of particulars is to provide defendant with necessary details of charges against him to enable him to prepare defense, avoid surprise against trial, and protect against double jeopardy.

US v. Anderson, 872 F.2d 1508, 1509 - 20 (11th Cir.)
Remedy for sentence resulting from multiplicity is to vacate all sentences and remand for resentencing. Cert. denied, 493 US 1025 (1989).

US v. Blockburger, 52 S.Ct. 180,284 US 299 (1932)
Each of the offenses created required proof of a different element.

US v. Brandon, 17 F.3d 409,422 (1st Cir.)
Multiplictious indictments violate Fifth Amendment double jeopardy clause, because raises danger that defendant will receive more than one sentence for single crime. cert. denied, 115 S.Ct. 80 (1994).

US v. Caldwell, 176 F.3d 898, 903 (6th Cir. 1999)
Indictment must be sufficiently specific to enable defendant to plead double jeopardy in subsequent proceeding, if charged with the same crime based on the same facts.

US v. Caperell, 938 F.2d 975 (C.A. (Nev.) 1991)
LaMere v. Risley, 827 F.2d 622, 624 (9th Cir. 1987)
Hanling v. US, 418 US 87, 117, 94 S.Ct. 2887, 2907, 41 L.Ed.2d 590 (1974)
An indictment must set forth the elements of the offense charged and contain a statement of facts and circumstances sufficient to inform the defendant of the elements of the specific offense.

US v. Carll, 105 US 611 (1882)
The Carll's reasoning is simple and logical, in that, all statutes state and federal are written disjunctively which separate all the various elements are ways to violate a statute, and if the charging instrument (i.e. indictment, information or complaint) merely mimics the states language, then it is insufficient in alleging offense because it is duplictious. Where the elements of the crime have to be ascertained by reference to the common law or two other statutes, it is not sufficient to set forth the offense in the words of the state. The facts necessary to bring the case within the statutory definition must also be alleged.

US v. Carlock, 806 F.2d 535 (5th Cir. 1986)

US v. MacDonald, 456 US 1, 8, 71 L.Ed.2d 696, 102 S.Ct. 1497 (1982)

Protection from delay in indictment must be found in the due process clause of the Fifth Amendment.

US v. Chandler, (1995, CA8 Ark) 66 F.3d 1460

U.S.C.A. 5

The sufficiency of indictment. Although superseding indictment includes language not provided in criminal statute prohibiting acceptance of gratuity, indictment is considered sufficient if it fairly informs the accused of charges against him and allows him to plead double jeopardy as bar to future prosecution.

US v. Chichy, (C.A.6, Ohio, 1993) 1 F.3d 1501 cert. denied 114 S.Ct. 620, 510 US 1019, 126 L.Ed.2d 584

Indictment is presumed sufficient if it tracks statutory language, cites elements of crimes charged and provides approximate dates in times.

US v. Clements, 22 F.3d 73 (8th Cir. 1994)

Under Fifth Amendment, defendant has a right to be tried only on charges contained in indictment returned by grand jury.

1. The Fifth Amendment requires that the defendant be tried only on charges handed down by grand jury and, that's indictment has been returned, its charges may not be broadened through amendment except by grand jury.

2. Variance rises to the level of reversible error where evidence presented trial, together with jury instructions, raises possibility to defendant was convicted on offense other than that charged in the indictment.

US v.Cochran, 17 F.3d 56 (3rd Circuit 1994)

US v. Pupo, 841 F.2d 1235 (4th Cir. 1988)

Indictment that fails to charge all essential elements of crime must be dismissed.

US v. Critzer, 951 F.2d 306,307 - 08 (11th Cir. 1992) (per curiam)

Court should look only at face of indictment, not at facts government expects to prove.

US v. Crowell, 997 F.2d 146 (6th Cir. 1993)
General rule is that indictment cannot be used as evidence against person.

US v. Delano, 55 F3d 720 (2nd Cir. 1995)
Constructive amendments of indictment are per se violations of the Fifth Amendment chat require reversal even without showing of prejudice.

US v. Dischner, 960 F.2d 870 (9th Cir. 1992)
Indictment must be read as a whole and construed according to common sense.

US v. Douglas, 974 F.2d 1046 (9th Cir. 1992)
US v. Werme, 939 F.2d 108 (3rd Cir. 1991)
Defendant cannot be convicted for offense that was not included in the indictment.

US v. Dubo, 186 F.3d 1177 (9th Cir. 1999)
If properly challenged prior to trial, an indictments complete failure to recite an essential element of the charged offense is not a minor or technical flaw subject to harmless error analysis, but a fatal flaw requiring dismissal of the indictment.

US v. Duncan, 850 F.2d 1104, 1108, n.4 (6th Cir. 1988) (dictum)
US v. Marquardt, 786 F.2d 771, 778 (7th Cir. 1986)
Also pushes indictment may result in multiple sentences for one crime and may suggest to jury that defendant committed several crimes.

US v. Edmonson, 962 F.2d 1535 (10th Cir. 1992)
US v. Gayle, 936 F.2d 1234 (11th Cir. 1991)
Indictment must be competent and forthright attempt to notify accused of extent of his alleged culpability.

US v. Felix, 503 US 378 (1992)
Emphasize that a mere overlap in proof between two prosecutions does not establish a double jeopardy violation. Id at 386. When defendant is charged with the conspiracies containing overlapping proof, courts look at the elements of the conspiracies charged, the overt acts charged, geographic location, timing and participants to determine if the conspiracies are the same offense.

<u>US v. Ferguson</u>, 758 F.2d 843, 850 (2nd Cir. 1985)
Just as defendant may waive trial by jury, defendant may waive similar right of indictment by grand jury.

<u>US v. Fitzgerald</u>, 882 F.2d 397, 399 (9th Cir. 1989) Indictment charging assault and specifying date, location, and victim of alleged assault sufficient under 7 (c) (1) even though failed to define "serious bodily injury", because not impermissibly vague.

<u>US v. Flores</u>, (1995, CA5 Tex.) 63 F.3d 1342
Indictment stating that defendant conducted financial transaction with certain amount of money by attempting to move the money sufficiently alleged violation of money-laundering statute, since it fairly informs the defendant of charge against him and was sufficient to bar future prosecution for same offense.

<u>US v. Fogel</u>, 901 F.2d 23 (4th Cir. 1990)
<u>US v. Long</u>, 900 F.2d 1270 (8th Cir, 1990)
<u>US v. Field</u>, 875 F.2d 130 (7th Cir. 1989)
Purpose of presentation clause of the Fifth Amendment is twofold; It entities defendant to be in jeopardy only for offenses charged by a group of his fellow citizens acting independent of either prosecutor or the judge; and it entitles defendant to be apprised of charges against him so that he knows what he must.

<u>US v. Forbes</u>, 16 F.3d 1294, 1297 (1st Cir. 1994)
Objection that indictment failed to state essential elements of offense can be raised for the first time on appeal under Rule 12 (b) (2). Therefore we hold that Harrod did not waive his objection by failing to object before trial.

<u>US v. Garza - Juarez</u>, 992 F.2d 896 (9th Cir. 1993)
Trial court may dismiss indictment in exercise of its general supervisory powers.

US v. Gatto, (D.N.J. 1990) 746 F.Supp. 432 reversed 924 F.2d 491 rehearing denied

To extent the government is able to do so precise date and place of each event alleged in indictment should be provided to defendant.

US v. Gimbel, (ED. Wis. 1985) 632 F.Supp. 748 reversed, 830 F.2d 621

District Court in considering sufficiency of charges before trial, must regard fax alleged as true and cannot weigh against them contrary aversions by defendant. In weighing sufficiency of charges before trial, District Court must except in limited circumstances, consider only facts, acts and allegations contained within indictment itself.

US v. Gordon, 844 F.2d 1397, 1401 - 02 (9th Cir. 1988)

Failure to dismiss or cure duplictious indictment with special interrogatories and additional instruction requested by defendant inappropriate because risked conviction by non-unanimous jury verdict.

US v. Haddock, 956 F.2d 1534 (10th Cir. 1992)

Duplicity" is the joining of two or more separate offenses in same count; vice of duplicity is that jury may convict the defendant without unanimously agreeing on the defendant's guilt on the same offense.

US v. Harper, 901 F.2d 471 (5th Cir. 1990)

A guilty plea does not bar a prisoner from challenging his indictment on jurisdictional grounds.

US v. Henry, 29 F3d 112 (3rd Cir. 1994)

Bank and wire fraud theories not advanced in indictment could not save indictment on appeal when theories that were advanced in indictment were found to be invalid.

US v. Molinaro, 11 F3d 853 (9th Cir. 1993)

US v. Homick, 964 F2d 899 (9th Cir. 1992)

1. The Fifth Amendment requires that defendant be tried only on charges handed down by grand jury and, thus, after indictment has been returned, its charges may not be broadened through amendment except by grand jury.

2. Variance rises to the level of reversible error where evidence presented at trial, together with jury instructions, raises possibility that defendant was convicted on offense other than that charged in indictment.

US v. Hope, 861 F.2d 1574 (11th Cir. 1988)

Indictment must be dismissed on ground of duplicity when two or more separate crimes are joined in a single count of indictment.

US v. Hord, 6 F.3d 276 (5th Cir. 1993)

US v. Harris, 959 F.2d 246 (D.C. Cir. 1992)

Indictment is multiplicious, and thereby defective, if single offense is alleged in a number of counts, unfairly increasing defendant's exposure to criminal sanctions.

US v. Horodner, 993 F.2d 191, 193 (9th Cir. 1993)

Convictions on two counts of possession of firearm by convicted felon based on possession of same firearm on different dates separated by period when firearm being repaired, barred because it was one uninterrupted course of conduct.

US v. Keith, 605 F.2d 462,464 (9th Cir. 1979)

A claim of defect in indictment can be raised at any time, but challenges should be made at the earliest possible moment... Indictments which are tardily challenged are liberally construed in favor of validity.

US v. Lang, (D.MD. 1991) 766 F. Supp. 389

It is generally sufficient to allege offense in words of statute and state time and place of alleged offense, so long as words of statute fully, directly, set forth all elements necessary to constitute offense.

US v. Littlefield, 105 F.3d 527,528 (9th Cir. 1977) (Per Curiam)
Defendant waves right to indictment because he agreed to proceed by information and reaffirmed choice at plea hearing.

US v. Lopez, 2 F.3d 1342 (5th Cir. 1993)
US v. James, 980 F.2d 1314 (9th Cir. 1992)
Each count of indictment must stand on its own and cannot base its validity on allegations of any other count not specifically incorporated. Generally, failure of indictment to detail each element of charged offense is fatal defect.

US v. Lopez - Alvares, 970 F.2d 583 (9th Cir. 1992)
Indictment must state elements of offense charged in sufficient detail to allow defendant to prepare his or her defense and to avoid double jeopardy.

US v. Marquardt, 786 F.2d 771, 778 (7th Cir. 1986) (dictum)
Multiplictious indictment may prejudice jury against defendant by creating impression of more criminal activity than in fact occurred.

US v. Musacchino, 968 F.2d 782 (9th Cir. 1991)
Court of appeals reviews sufficiency of indictment de novo.

US v. Musacchio, 940 F.2d 486 (9th Cir. 1991)
In indictment, Government must allege essential facts necessary to apprise defendant of crime charged, but is not required to allege its theory of case or list supporting evidence to prove crime alleged.

US v. Normandeau, 800 F.2d 953, 958 (9th Cir. 1986)
An essential purpose of an indictment is to give a defendant notice of a charge so that he may defend or plead his case adequately. Generally the failure of an indictment to detail each element of the charged offense constitutes a fatal defect.

US v. O'Bryant, 998 F.2d 21 (1st Cir. 1993)
Bringing indictment tolls statute of limitations on charges set forth in that indictment.

US v. Podell, 869 F.2d 328, 332 (7th Cir. 1989)
Separate convictions for unlawfully removing and tampering with motor vehicles identification number and unlawfully altering vehicles identification number barred when series of acts directed at one automobile.

US v. Randall, 171 F.3d 195,203 (4th Cir. 1999)
Constructive amendment is per se "reversible error" and must be corrected on appeal even when defendant did not preserve issue by objection.

US v. Robinson, 953 F.2d 433 (8th Cir. 1992)
US v. Arpan, 861 F.2d 1073 (8th Cir. 1988)
Allen v. US, 164 US 482, 41 L.Ed. 528, 17 S.Ct. 1156 (1896)
Supplemental jury instruction of the "dynamite" variety are grounds for "reversible error" due to their strong coercive effect on the jury. When the judge told the jury they had to bring in a decision he effectively denied the defendant the right to a hung jury.

US v. Rosario - Diaz, 202 F.3d 54 (1st Cir. 2000)
If the court permits the jury to convicted defendant on evidence of the crime not included in the indictment, a constitutional right to a grand jury is violated.

US v. Rosnow, 9 F3d 728 (8th Cir. 1993)
Defendant at any time may raise claim that indictment fails to state offense.

US v. Santistevan, (1994, CA10 Utah) 39 F.3d 250
Failure of prosecution to prove essential elements of distribution of cocaine beyond a reasonable doubt violated most fundamental sense of due process and allowed court to raise issue of sufficiency of evidence sua sponte.

US v. Santos - Rivera, 183 F.3d 367, 369 (5th Cir. 1999)
One of the elements required by indictment is that it provide defendant with double jeopardy defense against future prosecutions.

US v. Sharpe, 995 F.2d 49 (5th Cir. 1993)

Challenged, government must explain and support legitimacy of its reasons for sealing indictment.

US v. Spinner, 180 F.3d 514,516 (3rd Cir. 1999)

Failure of indictment to sufficiently state offense is fundamental defect that can be raised at any time. Must also address double jeopardy. The indictment need only allege the essential facts [charges] you need not explain the government theory of the case.

US v. Stevens, 462 F.3d 1169

Robert Stevens appeals a 30-year sentence imposed by the district court after Stevens plead guilty to one count of Receipt of Child Pornography and one count of Possession of Child Pornography, both in violation of 18 U.S.C. § 2252A(a). For the reasons set forth below, we vacate the sentence and remand for resentencing. At the time Stevens committed the crimes, application note 1 to U.S.S.G. § 2G2.2 defined "minor" as "an individual who has not attained the age of 18 years." In 2005, at the time the district court imposed Stevens's sentence, the Sentencing Commission had amended the application note, so that it defined "minor" as "(A) an individual who had not attained the age of 18 years; (B) an individual, whether fictitious or not, who a law enforcement officer represented to a participant (i) had not attained the [**5] age of 18 years, and (ii) could be provided for the purposes of engaging in sexually explicit conduct; or (C) an undercover law enforcement officer who represented to a participant that the officer had not attained the age of 18 years." Stevens argues that this modification is a substantive change rather than a clarification, and that there-fore the district court erred by retroactively applying the amended definition. We agree.

US v. Talbot, C.A.9 (Cal) 1995, 51 F.3d 183

Rule providing that court may permit information to be amended at any time before verdict only if no additional or different offense is charged did not apply to situation in which government replaced citation with an information, which does serve as superseding instrument. F.R.Cr.P. Rule 17 (e) and 18 USC.A.

US v. Telemaque, 244 F.3d 1247, 1249 (11th Cir. 2001)
Conviction vacated because court failed to inform defendant of nature of offense; no determination of whether error was appropriate for harmless error review.

US v. Van Dyke, 14 F3d 415 (8th Cir. 1994)
There is ordinarily no error in giving jury copy of indictment.

US v. Wicks, 187 F.3d 426, 427 (4th Cir. 1999)
To meet constitutional guarantees an indictment must enable defendant to plead an acquittal or conviction in bar of future prosecutions for the same offense.

US v. Woodruff, (1995, CA9 Cal) 50 F.3d 673, 95 Daily Journal DAR 4916
Indictment charging violation of Hobbs Act was sufficient, although it contains no factual allegations as to how interstate commerce was interfered with and did not state any theory of interstate impact, since it set forth all elements of offense charged and insured defendant's right not to be placed in double jeopardy.

US v. Zavala, 839 F.2d 523,526 (9th Cir. 1988) (en Banc)
Indictment charging various drug violations sufficient when tracking statutory language and listed dates of violations. Cert. denied, 488 US 831 (1988)

Wilkinson v. Haynes, W.D. Mo. 1971, 327F. Supp. 967
Sufficiency of state information was not reviewable in federal habeas corpus proceeding unless information was so defective as to deprive state court of jurisdiction.

Wright v. Lockhart, 854 F.2d 309,1988 US App. LEXIS 11221
Amendments to an information are permissible so long as the amendment does not alter degree of the charge crime or unfairly surprise defendant. See also: Lincoln v. State, 287 Ark. 16, 696 S.W.2d 316 (1985)

Ineffective Assistance of Counsel

<u>Blackburn v. Foltz</u>, 828 F.2d 1177

Defendant brought habeas corpus petition subsequent to state conviction for armed robbery, alleging that he was denied the effective assistance of counsel. The United States District Court for the Eastern District of Michigan, Barbara K. Hackett, J., denied petition and defendant appealed. The Court of Appeals, John W. Peck, Senior Circuit Judge, held that defendant was denied the effective assistance of counsel based on combination of counsel's erroneous legal advice concerning possible use of prior convictions if defendant testified, failure to obtain transcript of earlier trial to impeach key eyewitness and failure to investigate lead concerning potential alibi defense. Reversed and remanded with instructions.

<u>Bloom v. Calderon</u>, 132 F.3d 1267 (9th Cir. 1997)

Attorney failed to get expert witness.

<u>Brown v. Myers</u>, 137 F.3d 1154 (9th Cir. 1998)

Attorney was ineffective by failing to investigate defendants alibi defense.

<u>Endicott v. Henry</u>, No. 98-17336, UNITED STATES COURT OF APPEALS FOR THE NINTH CIRCUIT, 2000 US App. LEXIS 1635, December 7, 1999, Argued and Submitted, San Francisco, California , February 3, 2000, Filed , RULES OF THE NINTH CIRCUIT COURT OF APPEALS MAY LIMIT CITATION TO UNPUBLISHED OPINIONS. PLEASE REFER TO THE RULES OF THE UNITED STATES COURT OF APPEALS FOR THIS CIRCUIT. , Reported in Table Case Format at: 2000 US App. LEXIS 13259. ... of habeas corpus REVERSED, case REMANDED

Evidence of an alibi was significant. Counsel's failure to investigate the evidence amounted to a deficient performance, depriving petitioner of the right to effective assistance of counsel.

<u>Foster v. Lockhart</u>, 9 F.3d 722 (8th Cir. 1993)

Attorney's failure to investigate defense is "never" a tactical decision.

Gray v.Lynn, 6 F.3d 265

After affirmance of conviction for attempted first-degree murder, 391 So.2d 1184, petition was filed for writ of habeas corpus. The United States District Court for the Western District of Louisiana, Edwin F. Hunter, Jr., J., dismissed, and petitioner appealed. The Court of Appeals, Garwood, Circuit Judge, 724 F.2d 1199, affirmed. Petitioner filed instant habeas action and district court, upon magistrate's recommendation, dismissed. Petitioner appealed. The Court of Appeals, 917 F.2d 562, affirmed in part, reversed in part, and remanded. On remand, the District Court, Donald E. Walter, J., adopted recommendation of magistrate judge and dismissed petition. Petitioner appealed. On grant of certificate of probable cause, the Court of Appeals, Barksdale, Circuit Judge, held that: (1) trial counsel's failure to object to erroneous jury instruction fell beneath objective standard of reasonable professional assistance, and (2) trial counsel's failure to object to erroneous jury instruction resulted in prejudice to defendant sufficient to undermine confidence in outcome of his trial. Reversed and remanded.

Greene v. Henry, No. 01-15938, UNITED STATES COURT OF APPEALS FOR THE NINTH CIRCUIT, 302 F.3d 1067; 2002 US App. LEXIS 18645; 2002 Cal. Daily Op. Service 9353; 2002 Daily Journal DAR 10492, March 11, 2002, Argued and Submitted, San Francisco, California , September 11, 2002, Filed. REVERSED.

Case remanded with ... Where defendant, convicted of rape, sought a writ of habeas corpus for ineffective assistance of counsel for failure to discredit the victim, the court of appeals denied the writ; victim's contradictory statements to police and court impeached her.

Harris v. Housewright, 697 F.2d 202

Petitioner appealed from the United States District Court for the Eastern District of Arkansas, Garnett Thomas Eisele, Chief Judge, which denied his petition for writ of habeas corpus. The Court of Appeals, Heaney, Circuit Judge, held that petitioner was denied effective assistance of counsel, in that he proved that his attorneys failed to perform with degree of skill with which reasonably competent counsel would perform under similar circumstances and he was prejudiced by his counsels' ineffectiveness. Reversed and remanded.

Holsclaw v. Smith, 822 F.2d 1041

Petitioner, who had been convicted of theft of automobile, sought writ of habeas corpus. The United States District Court for the Northern District of Alabama, No. CV86-A-5225-NE, Clarence W. Allgood, J., denied petition, and petitioner appealed. The Court of Appeals, Tuttle, Senior Circuit Judge, held that failure of trial counsel to raise question of sufficiency of evidence of theft at trial was not strategic decision, but, rather, was outside wide range of professional and competent assistance, resulting in reasonable probability that, but for error, result would have been different, and thus was ineffective assistance. Reversed and remanded with directions.

Holosombach v. White, 133 F.3d 1382

After his conviction for first-degree sodomy was upheld on direct appeal and he was denied state post-conviction relief, state prisoner petitioned pro se for federal writ of habeas corpus. The United States District Court for the Northern District of Alabama, No. CV-94-PT-3137-S,Robert B. Propst, J., dismissed petition. Petitioner appealed. The Court of Appeals, Barkett, Circuit Judge, held that: (1) trial counsel's decision not to conduct any investigation into conceded lack of medical evidence of sexual abuse was not reasonable, and (2) counsel's failure to conduct adequate pretrial investigation into lack of medical evidence prejudiced defendant.

In re Hegstrom, 153 Ariz. 286

The attorney was charged with three counts of unethical conduct after he failed to provide a client with a copy of the reply to the counter-claim, failed to further litigate a matter when he promised to do so, failed to communicate with clients, failed to inform a client of the amount of attorney's fees, and failed to appear at a criminal defendant's rule to show cause hearing. The commission recommended that the attorney be disbarred. On review, the court disbarred the attorney because once the attorney took on the representation of a client; the ethical rules of conduct became a part of the lawyer's contract with his client. In addition, the court reasoned that a breach of the lawyer's contract with his client could be a violation of the lawyer's ethical responsibilities. Finally, the court reasoned that the attorney neglected legal matters entrusted to him pursuant to Ariz. Code Prof. Resp. DR 6-

101(A) and abandoned his clients without notice and to their prejudice. The court disbarred the attorney.

Johnson v. Baldwin, No. 96-35049, UNITED STATES COURT OF APPEALS FOR THE NINTH CIRCUIT, 114 F.3d 835; 1997 US App. LEXIS 11968; 97 Cal. Daily Op. Service 3871; 97 Daily Journal DAR 6573, November 5, 1996, Argued, Submitted, Portland, Oregon , May 23, 1997, Filed. REVERSED and REMANDED

A petition for writ of habeas corpus was dismissed improperly as there was a reasonable probability that, but for defense counsel's errors at petitioner's rape trial, the proceeding's result would have been different.

Mak v. Blogett, 970 F.2d 614 (9th Cir. 1992)
US v. Tucker, 716 F.2d 576, 595 (9th Cir. 1983)
A court may find unfairness and thus prejudice-from the totality of counsel's errors and omissions.

State v. Boozer, 80 Ariz. 8, 291P.2d 786 (1955)
It is the universal rule that if improper statements are made by counsel during the trial it is the duty of opposing counsel to register an objection thereto so that the court may make a correction by proper instruction and if the offense be sufficiently hurtful, declare a mistrial.

State v. Carriger, 132 Ariz. 301, 303, 645 P.2d 816, 818 (1982) When counsel's acts and omissions reduce his role to one approaching that of a neutral observer, a defendant is denied the effective assistance of counsel.

State v. Dambrosio, 156 Ariz. 71, 750 P.2d 14
The petitioner's complaint before the State Bar was specific and in depth, describing numerous instances of ineffectiveness which may be related to counsel's alleged state of intoxication during trial. Additionally, petitioner submitted an affidavit of his trial counsel's former secretary which attested to, among other things, counsel's "severe drinking problem" during petitioner's extensive trial. Taking these contentions as true in the context of whether a "colorable claim" has been presented, I firmly conclude that a colorable claim has been established

entitling petitioner to an evidentiary hearing on his heretofore undetermined claims.

State v. Kerr, 142 Ariz. 426, 640 P.2d 145 (Ct. App. 1994)
State v. Jessen, 130 Ariz. 1, 633 P.2d 410 (1981)
It is the responsibility of defense counsel to ensure that any document necessary to defendant's argument is in the record on appeal.

State v. Krum, 182 Ariz. 108 (February 14th, 1995)
Defendant first sought post-conviction relief when the victim, who was his step-granddaughter, recanted her story to her grandmother. Court appointed counsel advised him that he must supply an affidavit from the victim. When he failed to do so, the trial court dismissed his petition. He brought another petition alleging both the victim's recantation and his counsel's failure to effectively assist him with his first petition. On appeal, the court granted review and reversed the trial court's dismissal because defendant had a right to effective assistance of counsel in a post-conviction proceeding. While the federal constitution did not include a right to counsel in post-conviction proceedings, state law did, at Ariz. Rev. Stat. § 13-4235(B) (1989). The court found that the state law right to counsel was meaningless if it was not a right to effective assistance of counsel. Defendant stated a colorable claim because his allegations that his counsel failed to secure third-party affidavits that the victim had recanted her story indicated a performance below the standard defined by prevailing professional norms. Having stated a colorable claim, he was entitled to an evidentiary hearing. The court granted review of the trial court's summary denial of defendant's petition for post-conviction relief and granted relief. The court remanded the matter to the trial court for proceedings in accordance with the court's opinion. An accused is entitled to be assisted by an attorney who plays the role necessary to ensure that the trial is fair. For that reason, the right to counsel is the right to the effective assistance of counsel.

State v. Krum, 182 Ariz. 108 (May 12th, 1995)
Defendant first sought post-conviction relief when the victim, who was his step-granddaughter, recanted her story to her grandmother. Court appointed counsel advised him that he must supply an affidavit from the victim. When he failed to do

so, the trial court dismissed his petition. He brought another petition alleging both the victim's recantation and his counsel's failure to effectively assist him with his first petition. On appeal, the court granted review and reversed the trial court's dismissal because defendant had a right to effective assistance of counsel in a post-conviction proceeding. While the federal constitution did not include a right to counsel in post-conviction proceedings, state law did, at Ariz. Rev. Stat. § 13-4235(B)(1989). The court found that the state law right to counsel was meaningless if it was not a right to effective assistance of counsel. Defendant stated a colorable claim because his allegations that his counsel failed to secure third-party affidavits that the victim had recanted her story indicated a performance below the standard defined by prevailing professional norms. Having stated a colorable claim, he was entitled to an evidentiary hearing. The court granted review of the trial court's summary denial of defendant's petition for post-conviction relief and granted relief. The court remanded the matter to the trial court for proceedings in accordance with the court's opinion.

State v. Krum, 183 Ariz. 288 (September 21st, 1995)
The state sought review of a decision from the Arizona Court of Appeals holding that defendant was entitled to an evidentiary hearing in a post-conviction relief proceeding under A.R.Cr.P. 32.1(e) whereby defendant contended, through third-party affidavits from his wife and natural grandson, that the victim had recanted her accusations of sexual abuse against defendant. Defendant pled no contest to the attempted sexual abuse of his thirteen-year-old step granddaughter. After the court of appeals affirmed his conviction on direct appeal, defendant filed a petition under A.R.Cr.P. 32.1(e) for post-conviction relief, claiming that the victim had recanted her allegations. The court vacated the decision of the court of appeals holding that defendant was entitled to an evidentiary hearing and affirmed the trial court's judgment denying defendant's petition for post-conviction relief. The court held that defendant's affidavits from his wife and natural grandson did not establish a colorable claim that the victim had recanted her accusation of sexual abuse. The court found that the third-party affidavits showed no personal knowledge and were at most, hearsay evidence of recantation. Neither defendant's wife nor his grandson directly claimed to have heard the victim recant and their affidavits were found to be conclusory and completely lacking in detail, and they did not say when or where or to whom the victim supposedly recanted. The court concluded that such

affidavits would seldom entitle a defendant to relief under A.R.Cr.P. 32. The court vacated the decision of the court of appeals and affirmed the trial court's judgment denying defendant's petition for an evidentiary hearing in a post-conviction relief proceeding. The court concluded that defendant's affidavits from his wife and natural grandson did not establish a colorable claim that the victim recanted her accusation of sexual abuse against defendant.

State v. Lee, 142 Ariz. 210, 220, 689 P.2d 153, 163 (1994)
Quoting Strickland, "the right to counsel is the right to effective assistance of counsel."

State v. Miller, 120 Ariz. to 24, 585 P.2d 244 (1978)
It is also the duty of defendant to see that the record contains the material to which he takes exception.

State v. Radjenovich, No. 1 CA-CR 6438, Court of Appeals of Arizona, Division One, Department A, 138 Ariz. 270; 674 P.2d 333; 1983 Ariz. App. LEXIS 608, December 1, 1983. REVERSED
A defendant received ineffective assistance of counsel in a sexual assault case because counsel failed to interview a single prosecution witness, and was surprised when a defense expert, after learning the prosecution's theory, refused to testify.

Turner v. Duncan, 158 F.3d 449 (9th Cir. 1998)
Trial counsel's failure to investigate and to adequately conduct a pretrial preparation was not a strategic decision and required remand for an evidentiary hearing to determine whether a pretrial investigation would have produced a lesser degree of homicide.

US v. Blaylock, 20 F.3d 1458 (9th Cir. 1994)
Jefferies v. Blodgett, 988 F.2d 923, 940 (9th Cir. 1993)
The ABA standards are regularly used by courts as guidelines in determining whether an attorney's performance falls below reasonable professional standards.

<u>US v. Burton</u>, 575 F. Supp. 1320 (E.D. Tex. 1983)
Defense counsel must be familiar with the laws and facts of the case in order to provide effective assistance of counsel.

In Forma Pauperis

A.R.C. 26.11 Duty of the court after pronouncing sentence after trial, the court shall, in pronouncing judgment of sentence:

(b) If he or she is entitled thereto, advise the defendant that: 2. If the defendant is unable to pay for a certified copy of the record on appeal and the reports transcript, they will be provided by the county.

Baragan v. Eyman, 93 Ariz. 227

Even though an inmate's appeal in forma pauperis was mishandled by the trial court clerk, the required papers were filed with the superior court, the inmate would have the appeal to which he was entitled, and a habeas corpus discharge was denied.

Douglas v. California, 372 US 353, 361 (1963)

Entitlements to free transcripts of all court proceedings under federal law; (indictments, grand jury minutes, discovery, pre-sentence reports, psychologist reports, witness and victim affidavits, police reports, any medical reports, evidentiary hearings, minutes, sentencing and closing arguments, etc.). Whereas if these transcripts are not made available to the appellant, who is striving to litigate his case in court it would constitute a violation of State and Federal regulations that govern the rights of an individual under Article 2 § 4 of the Arizona Constitution and the 14th Amendment to the US Constitution denying "meaningful access to the courts."

Hardy v. US, 375 US 277, 84 S.Ct. 424, 11 L. Ed. 2d 331 (1964)

On direct appeal, if you are determined to be indigent, you will be entitled to transcripts of the entire trial proceedings. See also: Griffin v. Illinois, 351 US 12, 34, 35 (1956)

In re Lopez, 97 Ariz. 328

Once inmate perfected appeal by filing notice of appeal, trial court lost jurisdiction and was without discretion to dismiss appeal or set aside order granting leave to proceed in forma pauperis. Only proper course was to transfer record on appeal.

Jurisdiction

5.22 C.J.S. § 167, p. 202
Jurisdiction to try and punished for a crime cannot be acquired by the major assertion of it, or invoked otherwise than in the mode prescribed by law, and if it is not so acquired or invoked any judgment is a nullity.

Ariz. Const. Art. 6 § 1
No court may acquire complete jurisdiction to hear and determine any cause until it has obtained through due process, prescribed by law, jurisdiction over both subject matter and the parties, and the power to render the particular judgment that was rendered.

Acker v. CSO Chavira, 188 Ariz. 252, 254, 934 P.2d 816, 818 (App. 1997)
Quoting State v. Superior Court, 39 Ariz. 242, 2 47-48, 5 P.2d 192, 194 (1931) a court's inherent authority may be defined as such powers as are necessary to the ordinary and efficient exercise of jurisdiction.

Branch v. Estelle, 631 F.3d 1229, 1233 (5th Cir. 1980)
Absence of jurisdiction in convicting court is, a basis for federal habeas relief cognizable under the due process clause.

Dassinger v. Oden, (App. Div1 1979) 124 Ariz. 551, 606 P.2d 41
Generally, lack of jurisdiction over subject matter can be raised at any time and parties cannot waive the requirement that court have subject matter jurisdiction or by consent confer subject matter jurisdiction upon the court.

Dupnick v. McDougall, 136 Ariz. 39 (1983) 664 P.2d 189
The essential facts are not in dispute. When a defendant is sentenced by the Superior Court to imprisonment and committed to the custody of the Department of Corrections, the Superior Court usually orders the sheriff to take custody of the sentenced to defendant until he can be received by the Department of Corrections. In Maricopa County v. State, supra, the several petitioners sought special action, in the nature of mandamus to compel the director of DOC to accept prisoners. We

held pursuant to A.R.S. 31-201.01 the director had unqualified duty to receive and hold all prisoners sentenced to state prison.

Ex Parte Cannon, 546 S.W.2d 266, 267 (Tex. Cr. App. 1976)
A defect cannot be waived, but can be raised at any point in direct or post-conviction proceedings.

Ex Parte Carlson, 186 N.W. 722, 725, 176 Wis. 538 (1922)
A formal accusation is essential for every trial of a crime. Without it the court acquires no jurisdiction to proceed, even with the consent of the parties, and where the indictment or information is invalid the court is without jurisdiction.

Ex Parte Kirby, 626 S.W.2d 533, 534 (Tex. Cr. App. 1976)
The predicate conclusion of no jurisdiction derives wholly from state laws governing or controlling the validity of a charging document.

First Nat. Bank of Ariz. v. Carruth, (App. Div2 1977) 116 Ariz. 42, 569 P.2d 1380
State courts are bound by decision of federal courts in their interpretation of federal statutes.

Greane v. Haws, (N.D. N.Y. 1996) 913 F.Supp. 136 NO 95-CV-1033
Establishment of jurisdiction should be the first thing a court looks for before it can proceed with the claims. It may be impossible in a 42 USC § 1983 action, however, to determine the jurisdictional issue without essentially determining whether plaintiff has stated a cause of the action. Jurisdiction to adjudicate a section 1983 action arises when a plaintiff demonstrates a violation of his right under constitutional law.

Harding v. Logan, E.D. N.C. 1966, 251 F.Supp. 710
Indictment or information is not to be reviewed by federal habeas corpus unless it is so fatally defective as to deprive court of jurisdiction.

Hilderbrand v. United States, No. 15623, UNITED STATES COURT OF APPEALS NINTH CIRCUIT, 261 F.2d 354; 1958 US App. LEXIS 3266, November 5, 1958

Federal courts had no jurisdiction over a crime committed on a Washington Indian Reservation unless it involved an Indian, and as defendant was not an Indian, the district court had no jurisdiction over him in a murder trial.

Honomichl v. State, 333 N.W.2d 797, 798 (S.D. 1983)

The complaint is the foundation of the jurisdiction of the magistrate or court. If these charging instruments are invalid, there is a lack of subject matter jurisdiction. Without a formal and sufficient indictment or information, a court does not acquire subject matter jurisdiction and thus the accused may not be punished for a crime.

Hooker v. Boles, 346 F.2d 2 85,286 (1965)

No authority need be cited for the proposition that when a court lacks jurisdiction, any judgment rendered by it is void and unenforceable.

Hughes Aircraft Co. v. Industrial Commission, (App. Div1 1979) 124 Ariz. 551, 602 P.2d 41

Normally, jurisdiction of subject matter may be raised at any time, including four first time on appeal.

In re Matter of Green, 313 S.E.2d 1993 (N.C. App. 1984)

The jurisdiction of the court over subject matter has been said to be essential, necessary, indispensable, and an elementary prerequisite to the exercise of judicial power. 21 C.J.S., "Courts" § 18, p. 25. A court cannot proceed with a trial without such jurisdiction existing. It is elementary that the jurisdiction of the court over the subject matter of the action is the most critical aspect of the court's authority to act. Without it the court lacks any power to proceed; therefore, a defense based on this lack of jurisdiction cannot be waived and it may be asserted at any time.

In re Special Grand Jury, No. 81-3527, UNITED STATES COURT OF APPEALS, NINTH CIRCUIT, 674 F.2d 778; 1982 US App. LEXIS 20960; 8 Media L. Rep. 1422, February 8, 1982, Argued , March 17, 1982, Decided, As Amended April 26, 1982.

Denial of motion requesting access to grand jury ministerial records reversed because movants' standing would be based on common law right of access to court records, but would be subject to grand jury secrecy rules.

Jones v. Lopez-Placencia, (App. 1969) 10 Ariz. App. 253, 458 P.2d 120

Jurisdiction is one of three types. Jurisdiction over the person, jurisdiction over the subject matter, and jurisdiction to render particular judgment in question.

Kelly v. Meyers, 263 PAC. 903, 905 (Ore. 1928)

If these sections are unconstitutional, the law is void and offense created by them is not a crime and a conviction under them cannot be a legal cause of imprisonment, for no court can acquired jurisdiction to try a person for acts which are made criminal only by an unconstitutional law.

Leon v. Numkena, (App. Div1 1984) 142 Ariz. 307, 689 P.2d 566

Parties cannot, by consent, give court jurisdiction over subject matter for which court does not otherwise have jurisdiction.

Lopez v. Ariz. Water Co., (App. Div2 1975) 23 Ariz. App. 99, 530 P.2d 1132

The Court of Appeals is bound by prior decisions of the highest court of Arizona.

Nick Luguna Jr. v. State of Arizona, 124 Ariz. 179, 602 P.2d 847, 1979 and Ariz. App. LEXIS 620

Once the defendant has been found guilty of a crime in justice court it may not be held over for prosecution as a felony in Superior Court of a greater offense arising out of the same context.

D.W. Onan & Sons v. Superior Ct. Santa Cruz Co., (1947) 65 Ariz. 255, 179 P.2d 243

The trial court must have jurisdiction of person and jurisdiction of subject matter of action and want of jurisdiction over either person or subject matter is always open to inquiry.

Pazos v. Pima Co. Superior Ct., (App. 1968) 8 Ariz. App. 560, 448 P.2d 130

Court exceeds its jurisdiction where it's act amounts to abuse of discretion.

People v. Hardiman, 347 N.W.2d 460, 462, 132 Mich. App. 382 (1984)

Where an information charges no crime, the court lacks jurisdiction to try the accused.

Petersen v. Jacobson, 2 Ariz. App. 593, 595, 411 P.2d 31, 33 (1966)

In order to render a valid judgment and sentence in a criminal prosecution, the court must have jurisdiction both of the offense and of the defendant's person... Jurisdiction of the court to try and punish an individual accused of a crime cannot be acquired by the court's mere assertion of jurisdiction, but must be invoked or acquired in the mode prescribed by law. If not so invoked, any judgment is a nullity.

Ralph v. Police Court of El Cerrito, 190 P.2d 632, 634, 84 Cal. App.2d 257 (1948)

Without a valid complaint any judgment or sentence rendered is void ab initio.

Rodriguez v. State, 441 S.Ct..2d 1129 (Fla. App. 1983)

Subject matter jurisdiction cannot be conferred by way for our consent, and may be raised at any time.

State v. Chatmon, 671 P.2d 531, 538 (Kan. 1983)

An indictment, information or complaint in a criminal case is the main means by which a court obtains subject matter jurisdiction and is the jurisdictional instrument on which the accused stands trial.

State v. Jones, (App. Div2 1984) 142 Ariz. 302, 689 P.2d 561
When jurisdiction of court has been properly invoked by filing of a criminal charge, disposition of the charge becomes judicial responsibility.

State v. Johnson, 318 Ariz. Adv. Rep. 3
Because the state's motion to amend the information was not based on a technical or formal error in the information, because the amendments changed the nature of the offense charged in count three, and because appellant was not afforded notice of the allegations on both counts one and three and an ample opportunity to defend against them, we conclude that the trial court both erroneously granted the motion to amend the information and denied appellant's motion for a judgment of acquittal. Accordingly, we vacate appellant's convictions and sentences imposed on counts one and three of the information.

State v. Marovich, (1973) 109 Ariz. 45, 504 P.2d 1268
Where the state appellate court reviews case involving federal constitutional error, state must apply federal standard and declare relief that error was harmless beyond a reasonable doubt if it affirms.

State v. Phelps, (1948) 67 Ariz. 215, 193 P.2d 921
The first duty of any court is to determine whether it has jurisdiction in the premises, and in some determining it is acting judiciously.

State v. Poli, 161 Ariz. 151, 153, 776 P.2d 1077, 1079 (App. 1989)
Courts have a sua sponte duty to examine their jurisdiction.

State v. Smith, 66 Ariz. 376, 378, 189 P.2d 206 (Ariz. 1948)
In Arizona, that mode of law to invoke or bestow jurisdiction upon the state trial court is Rule 2.2, 2.3 and 13.2 of the Arizona Rules of Criminal Procedure and, Article 2 § 30 of the Arizona Constitution, for indictment, information or complaint. Where challenge to the information is based upon an omission in the averment of the essential element of crime, jurisdiction of the subject matter cannot be conferred by consent...and hence objections to the jurisdiction may be made for the first time in the Superior Court.

State v. Superior Ct. of Pima Co., (App. 1968), 7 Ariz. App. 170, 436 P.2d 948
Although jurisdiction of both offense and person are required in criminal cases, an objection as to jurisdiction of person may be waived. Jurisdiction over the person is a defect that is waived by failure to raise the defense prior to entering of a plea.

Stillwell v. Markham, 10 P.2d 15, 16, 135 Kan. 206 (1932)
The subject matter jurisdiction of a criminal case is related to the cause of action in general, and more specifically to the alleged crime or offense which creates the action. The subject matter of a criminal offense is the crime itself. Subject matter in its broadest sense means the cause; the object; the thing in dispute.

US v. Apex Distributing Co., Nos. 15701, 15702, UNITED STATES COURT OF APPEALS NINTH CIRCUIT, 270 F.2d 747; 1959 US App. LEXIS 3351, September 21, 1959
Orders dismissing criminal actions, with prejudice, based upon government's failure to comply with discovery order were not appealable under Criminal Appeals Act because orders were not "sustaining motions in bar" or based on defects in indictment.

US v. Cote, No. 93-30441, UNITED STATES COURT OF APPEALS FOR THE NINTH CIRCUIT, 51 F.3d 178; 1995 US App. LEXIS 13508, January 13, 1995, Argued and Submitted, Portland, Oregon , March 16, 1995, Filed ,
As Amended on Denial of Rehearing and Suggestion for Rehearing En Banc June 2, 1995. Once mandates reversing convictions issued, the trial court had authority to retry defendants, as long as the double jeopardy clause was not violated; double jeopardy did not bar a retrial where reversals were based on incorrect jury instructions.

US v. Dahlheim, No. 93-30275, UNITED STATES COURT OF APPEALS FOR THE NINTH CIRCUIT, 1994 US App. LEXIS 18006, July 13, 1994, ** Submitted, Portland, Oregon** The panel finds this case appropriate for submission without argument pursuant to Fed. R. App. P. 34(a) and 9th Cir. R. 34-4., July 19, 1994, Filed , THIS DISPOSITION IS NOT APPROPRIATE FOR PUBLICATION AND MAY NOT BE CITED TO OR BY THE COURTS OF THIS CIRCUIT EXCEPT AS PROVIDED BY THE 9TH CIR. R. 36-3. , Reported in Table Case Format at: 29 F.3d 635, 1994 US App. LEXIS 26258. Certiorari Denied November 28, 1994, Reported at: 1994 US LEXIS 8529.

A conviction was not void even though the issuance of the indictment by a grand jury of fewer than seven members violated the Oregon Constitution.

US v. Mathews, No. 86-3867, UNITED STATES COURT OF APPEALS FOR THE NINTH CIRCUIT, 833 F.2d 161; 1987 US App. LEXIS 15628, September 9, 1987, Submitted * * The panel finds this case appropriate for submission without oral argument pursuant to Ninth Circuit Rule 34-4 and Fed. R. App. P. 34(a).., November 27, 1987, Filed

Federal subject matter jurisdiction was conferred when certain facts alleged in the indictment were proven by defendant's guilty plea and the plea was made knowingly and intelligently.

US v. Montalvo, No. 90-10078, No. 90-10080, No. 90-10081, No. 90-10082, No. 90-10585, No. 90-10586, UNITED STATES COURT OF APPEALS FOR THE NINTH CIRCUIT, 1992 US App. LEXIS 18863, March 13, 1992 *, Submitted, March 13, 1992 **, Argued and Submitted, San Francisco, California * The panel finds US v. Montalvo, Nos. 90-10078, 90-10080 and US v. Matsuzaki, Nos. 90-10081, 90-10082 appropriate for submission without oral argument pursuant to Fed. R. App. P. 34(a) and Ninth Cir. R. 34-4. ** US v. Bueno, No. 90-10585 and US v. Cincola, No. 90-10586., August 4, 1992, Filed , THIS DISPOSITION IS NOT APPROPRIATE FOR PUBLICATION AND MAY NOT BE CITED TO OR BY THE COURTS OF THIS CIRCUIT EXCEPT AS PROVIDED BY THE 9TH CIR. R. 36-3. , Reported as Table Case at 972 F.2d 1346, 1992 US App. LEXIS 28663.

The sentencing judge, who did not preside at the trial, failed to exhibit sufficient familiarity with the case when he entered the sentences.

US v. Price, No. 02-10196 , UNITED STATES COURT OF APPEALS FOR THE NINTH CIRCUIT, 314 F.3d 417; 2002 US App. LEXIS 26745; 56 ERC (BNA) 1028; 2002 Cal. Daily Op. Service 12404; 2002 Daily Journal DAR 14622; 33 ELR 20146, December 6, 2002, Argued and Submitted, San Francisco, California , December 26, 2002, Filed

The Double Jeopardy Clause did not bar a defendant's federal criminal prosecution for violating the Clean Air Act, even though a county agency previously assessed against defendant a civil penalty for the same conduct.

US v. Roberts, Nos. 78-2738, 78-2806, UNITED STATES COURT OF APPEALS, NINTH CIRCUIT, 618 F.2d 530; 1980 US App. LEXIS 17817, March 15, 1979, Argued , May 7, 1980, Decided

A prosecutor's suggestion that a witness testifying under a plea agreement was credible because a detective was monitoring his testimony constituted reversible error because the government could not vouch for the witness's credibility.

US v. Ruiz, No. 00-50048, UNITED STATES COURT OF APPEALS FOR THE NINTH CIRCUIT, 241 F.3d 1157; 2001 US App. LEXIS 3357; 2001 Cal. Daily Op. Service 1793; 2001 Daily Journal DAR 2293, October 12, 2000, Argued and Submitted, Pasadena, California , March 5, 2001, Filed , Certiorari Granted January 7, 2002, Reported at: 2002 US LEXIS 7.

Defendant's right to receive undisclosed Brady material could not be waived through a plea agreement; prosecutor could not withhold recommendation for downward departure based on such a waiver.

US v. Siviglia, 686 Fed.2d 832, 835 (1981) A court lacking jurisdiction cannot render judgment but must dismiss the cause at any stage of the proceedings in which it becomes apparent that jurisdiction is lacking.

US v. Travis, No. 83-1238, UNITED STATES COURT OF APPEALS FOR THE NINTH CIRCUIT, 735 F.2d 1129; 1984 US App. LEXIS 21349, April 11, 1984, Argued and Submitted , June 19, 1984, Decided

Even though defendant implicitly waived prosecution by indictment, providing the district court with jurisdiction to sentence, order was vacated and remanded where government breached its promise under the plea agreement to stand mute at sentencing.

US v. Walker, No. 76-1193, UNITED STATES COURT OF APPEALS FOR THE NINTH CIRCUIT, 575 F.2d 209; 1978 US App. LEXIS 13066, January 13, 1978
Conviction was reversed where district court's supplemental instruction constituted an amendment to the indictment, and was confusing and subject to an interpretation that was prejudicial to defendant.

US v. Wiora, C. A. No. 97-50485, UNITED STATES COURT OF APPEALS FOR THE NINTH CIRCUIT, 1999 US App. LEXIS 4041, November 4, 1998, Argued and Submitted, Pasadena, California , March 9, 1999, Filed , RULES OF THE NINTH CIRCUIT COURT OF APPEALS MAY LIMIT CITATION TO UNPUBLISHED OPINIONS. PLEASE REFER TO THE RULES OF THE UNITED STATES COURT OF APPEALS FOR THIS CIRCUIT. , Reported in Table Case Format at: 1999 US App. LEXIS 11658.
Enhancement of appellant's sentence for failing to release his kidnapping victim was inappropriate where there was no evidentiary hearing to determine the credibility of witnesses and disputed facts regarding access to vehicles.

White v. Davidson, (1935) 46 Ariz. 1, 46 P.2d 1073
Objection to jurisdiction of court can raise only question whether court had jurisdiction of subject matter and of person.

Jury

28 USC. §1865 (b) (2000)
A juror must be US citizen at least 18 years old, resident for at least one year in judicial district in which trial is held, failed to read, write, understand and speak English, mentally and physically capable of performing jury service, and free from criminal conviction or pending charges punishable by more than one year in prison.

A.R.Cr.P. Rule 22.3 Further review of evidence and additional instructions.
After the jurors have retired to consider their verdict, it they desire to have any testimony repeated, or if they or any party request additional instructions, the court may recall them to the courtroom and order the testimony read or give appropriate additional instructions. The court may also order other testimony read or give other instructions, so as not to give undue prominence to the particular testimony or instructions requested. Such testimony may be read or other instructions given only after notice to the parties.

US v. Robinson, 953 F.2d 433 (8th Cir. 1992)
US v. Arpan, 861 F.2d 1073 (8th Cir. 1988)
Allen v. US, 164 US 482, 41 L.Ed 528, 17 S.Ct. 154 (1896)
Supplemental jury instructions of the "Dynamite" variety are grounds for reversible error due to their strong coercive effect on the jury. When the judge told the jury they had to bring in a decision he effectively denied the defendants right to a hung jury.

Bruce v. State, 126 Ariz. 271,614 P.2d 813
The Superior Court, Pima County, Cause No. 181680, Richard N. Roylston, J., granted special action relief after City Court of the city of Tucson denied request for jury trial, and State appealed. The Court of Appeals, 126 Ariz. 313, 614 P.2d 855, affirmed, and State's petition for review was granted. The Supreme Court, Holohan, V C. J., held that: (1) City Court of the city of Tucson did not have subject-matter jurisdiction to try defendant on charge of aggravated assault on police officer even though charge was designated a misdemeanor by its filing in city court, and (2) since aggravated assault on police officer and assault on second

victim were equivalent of simple battery at common law, which was not crime requiring jury trial, and charges did not constitute crimes involving moral turpitude which would require jury trial, defendant had no constitutional right to trial by jury on assault charges, even though potential sentence on all charges could exceed six months if sentences were ordered served consecutively. Opinion of Court of Appeals vacated; remanded with directions.

Burton v. Johnson, 948 F.2d 1150 (10th Cir. 1991)
1. Doubts regarding bias must be resolved against juror.
2. A jury's dishonesty, of itself, was evidence of juror's bias.

Dyers v. Calderon, 151 F.3d 970 (Ninth Circuit 1998)
The presence of a biased juror cannot be harmless, the error requires a new trial without a showing of actual prejudice because it introduces any structural defects not subject to harmless error analysis.

Estelle v. Williams, 425 US 501, 503, 96 S.Ct. 1621, 1692, 48 L.Ed.2d 126 (1976)
Arizona law is clear that for a juror to see the accused in jail garb is inherently prejudicial.

Fields v. Brown, 431 F.3d 1186 (9th Cir. 2005)
The presence of a biased juror introduces a structural defect not subject to harmless error analysis.

Fields v. Woodford, 309 F.3d 1095 (9th Cir. 2002) 10.1.1.1.
Presence of a biased juror cannot be harmless, error requires new trial without showing of actual prejudice. 10.1.1.2. Either actual or implied juror bias may support challenge to cause.

Floyd v. Garrison, 996 F.2d 947 (8th Cir. 1993)
Fifth Amendment guarantee of equal protection requires that procedures used to select jury pools be racially non-discriminatory.

Francis v. Franklin, 471 US 307, 85 L.Ed.2d 344, 105 S.Ct. 1965 (1985)
Sandstrom v. Montana, 442 US 510, 61 L.Ed.2d 39, 99 S.Ct. 2450 (1979)
Trial courts instructions cannot impermissibly shift the burden of proof to the defendant.

Ho v. Carey, 332 F.3d 587 (9th CIR 2003)
When jury instruction omits a necessary element of the crime, constitutional error has occurred.

Holland v. Illinois, 493 US 474, 107 L.Ed.2d 905, 110 S.Ct. 803 (1990)
Prosecutor's exercise of preemptory challenges to exclude all black potential jurors from white defendant's petit jury held not to violate defendants Sixth Amendment right to trial by impartial jury.

Hughes v. US, 258 F.3d 453, 460 (6th Cir. 2001)
The trial granted based on ineffective assistance of counsel claim because counsel failed to strike juror who admitted bias.

Hunter v. Clark, 934 F.2d 856 (7th Cir. 1991)
Fifth Amendment requires that criminal trial judge give "no adverse inference" jury instruction when requested by defendant to do so.

James v. Kentucky, 466 US 341, 80 L.Ed.2d 346, 104 S.Ct. 1830 (1984)
The judge failed/refused to give requested instructions. The Supreme Court reversed and held that state statutes did not take precedent over constitutional law and that the judge had to give the requested instruction.

Jeffries v. Blodgett, 974 F.2d 1179 (9th Cir. 1992)
Fifth Amendment prohibits prosecutor from commenting to jury on defendant's failure to take stand in his own defense.

Lawson v. Borg, 60 F.3d 608 (9th Cir. 1995)
Jury exposure to facts not in evidence deprives defendant of Sixth Amendment rights to confrontation, cross - examination, and assistance of counsel.

Lord v. Wood, No. 97-99025, No. 97-99026 , UNITED STATES COURT OF APPEALS FOR THE NINTH CIRCUIT, 184 F.3d 1083; 1999 US App. LEXIS 15709; 99 Daily Journal DAR 7167, November 19, 1998, Argued and Submitted, San Francisco, California , July 14, 1999, Filed , Certiorari Denied February 28, 2000, Reported at: 2000 US LEXIS 1730. Writ of certiorari denied, Motion granted by Lambert v. Lord, 528 US 1198, 120 S. Ct. 1262, 146 L. Ed. 2d 118, 2000 US LEXIS 1730 (2000)... of his trial REVERSED. State's appeal dismissed... A competent attorney would not have failed to put three witnesses on the stand who, if believed, would have cleared petitioner of murder; counsel's failure to do so constituted deficient performance that was prejudicial to petitioner's defense.

Mach v. Stewart, 137 F.3d 630 (9th Cir. 1997)
During voir dire, statement of one prospective juror who is later dismissed were found to have the potential of tilting entire panel or conduct, further voir dire to ascertain impact of jurors statements was reversible error.

Menendez v. Terhune, 422 F.3d 612 (6th Cir. 2006)
Jury instruction that fails accurately to reflect law is reversible error.

Morgan v. Illinois, 504 US 119 L.Ed.2d 492, 112 S.Ct. (1992)
Illinois trial court held to violate due process by refusing to ask potential jurors on voir dire, in capital case, if they would automatically impose death penalty if the defendant was convicted.

Murphy v. Florida, 421 US 794 (1975)
The court indicated that under the same circumstances in a federal trial it would have overturned the conviction pursuant to its supervisory power Id. at 797 - 98.

Nethery v. Collins, 993 F.2d 1154 (5th Cir. 1993)
Burton v. Johnson, 948 F.2d 1150 (10th Cir. 1991)
1. Doubts regarding bias must be resolved against juror.
2. A juror's dishonesty, of itself, was evidence of juror's bias.
3. Racially based exclusion of even a single juror violates equal protection clause.

Patton v. Yount, 467 US 1025 (1984)

Smith v. Phillips, 455 US 209, 215-18 (1982)

Chandler v. Florida, 4 4 90 US 560, 575, 581 (1981)

Marshall v. US, 360 US 310 (1959)

Essentially the defendant must make a showing of prejudice which the court then may inquire into.

Perkins v. Komarnyckyj, 172 Ariz. 115, 118, 834 P.2d 1260, 1263 (1992)

We were unable to conclude that Benenati suffered any prejudice from it. See also: State v. McDaniel.

Powers v. Ohio, 499 US 400, 113 L.Ed.2d 411, 111 S.Ct. 1364 (1991)

White criminal defendant held to have standing to raise equal protection objection to prosecutor's allegedly race-based exercise of peremptory challenges to exclude black perspective jurors.

Rogers v. State, (1974) Ark. 144, 515 SW2d 79, cert. denied, 421 US 930, 44 L.Ed.2d 87, 95 S.Ct. 1656

14th amendment requires that counsel be permitted to in terra gate prospective jurors about racial bias.

Romberg v. Nichols, 953 F.2d 1152 (9th Cir. 1992) When jury compromises its verdict, verdict shall not stand.

Rushen v. Spain, 464 U. S. 114, 119 (1983)

Contact between judge and jury raises special considerations. A judge has discretion in replying to request or inquiries from the jury, but should consult counsel before responding and should do so only in open court. Failure to follow up this rule is subject to harmless error review.

Sandstrom v. Montana, 442 US 510, 524 (1979)

Jury instruction shifting burden of proof on mental state unconstitutional. Sandstrom v. Montana, Id at 515. The Sandstrom court held that even though some juror might have considered the challenge instruction to be a permissive presumption, the fact that won the reasonable juror could have interpreted as shifting to Burton required the court to treat as a mandatory presumption. Id at 519.

Shaw v. Hahn, 56 F.3d 1128 (9th Cir. 1995)
A person has equal protection right not to be excluded from jury solely on basis of race.

Shephard v. Maxwell, 384 US 333 (1966)
Irwin v. Dowd, 366 US 717 (1961)
Exposure of the jurors to knowledge about the defendant's prior criminal record and activities is not alone sufficient to establish a presumption of reversible prejudice, but on voir dire jurors should be questioned about their ability to judge impartiality.

Smith v. Phillips, 455 US 209 (1982)
During trial one of the jurors had been actively seeking employment in the District Attorney's Office.

Spain v. Rushen, 883 F.2d 712 (9th Cir. 1989)
Defendant has constitutional right to appear before jury free of shackles.

State v. Anderson, No. 1 CA-CR 4537, Court of Appeals of Arizona, Division One, Department B, 128 Ariz. 91; 623 P.2d 1247; 1980 Ariz. App. LEXIS 699, December 30, 1980, Rehearing Denied February 4, 1981. Review Denied February 18, 1981.
Judgment and sentence reversed, and case remanded ... Failure to give a requested instruction on the definition of "private parts" to limit the jury's inquiry to the proper evidence was reversible error where the jury was allowed to speculate as to what constituted private parts.

State v. Benati, 381 Ariz. Adv. Rep. 3 (2002)
Benati contends that trial court erred in responding to jurors question during deliberation, arguing the communication occurred outside his presence and was without his knowledge or consent. The general rule in Arizona is that reversible error occurs when a trial judge communicates with jurors after they have retired to

deliberate, unless defendant and counsel have been notified and given an opportunity to be present.

State v. Bingham, 176 Ariz. 146, 147, 859F.2d 769, 770 (App. 1993)
We have found it necessary to strike jurors who believed police officers to be more credible than others. Reversible error results from failure to strike a juror for bias even when preemptory challenge is later used to strike juror.

State v. Davis, 117 Ariz. 5, 570 P.2d 776 (App.1977)
Trial court's ex-parte communication to jurors not prejudicial because it merely restated jury instructions.

State v. Fletcher, 149 Ariz. 187, 717 P.2d 866 (1986)
The test of whether erroneous jury communications required reversal is whether it can be said beyond a reasonable doubt that the defendant was not prejudiced by the communication.

State v. Holder, 155 Ariz. 83, 745 P.2d 141
In his appeal to the court of appeals, defendant contended that he was entitled to raise Batson for the first time on appeal, that Batson applied to his case, and that the record established a prima facie showing of the discriminatory exercise of preemptories. The court of appeals agreed with the defendant and remanded to the trial court for a hearing to determine whether the prosecution could now meet its burden of providing a racially neutral explanation for the exercise of its peremptory challenges.

State v. Huerta, 170 Ariz. 584, 585, 826 P.2d 1210, 1211 (App. 1991) rev. other grnds.
We have found it necessary to strike jurors who believed that the charge alone showed the defendant's guilt.

State v. Jackson, 144 Ariz. 53, 695 P.2d 742 (1985)
Certain basic instructions including a reasonable doubt instruction, must be given by the court following closing arguments even though the jury had been previously instructed prior to the receipt of evidence.

State v. Koch, 138 Ariz. 99, 673 P.2d 297 (1983)

A trial judge may not communicate with a jury unless the defendant and counsel have been notified and given the opportunity to be present. See also: State v. Shumway, 137 Ariz. 585, 672 P.2d 929 (1983)

State v. Korzep, 165 Ariz. 490, 799 P.2d 831

Defendant was convicted in the Superior Court, Yuma County, No. Cr-14519, Douglas W. Keddie, J., of manslaughter and she appealed. The Court of Appeals affirmed, 164 Ariz. 175, 791 P.2d 1058, and review was granted. The Supreme Court, Gordon, C.J., held that defendant was entitled to instruction that a person is justified in using deadly physical force against another to the extent that the person reasonably believes that the use of deadly physical force is necessary to prevent the other person's commission of aggravated assault, even when the other person is a member of the defendant's household. Vacated in part and remanded.

State v. Mata, 125 Ariz. 233, 240-41, 609 P.2d 48, 55-56 (1980)

However if it may be said beyond reasonable doubt, that there was no prejudice to the defendant, a communication between judge and jury outside the presence of the defendant and counsel is harmless error. Id at 241, 609 P.2d at 56.

State v. McDaniel, 136 Ariz. 188, 665 P.2d 70 (1983)

When no notification was given to defendant prior to responding to the jury's questions, such communications between judge and jury violated this rule and was error.

State v. McDaniel, 136 Ariz. 188, 665 P.2d 70 (1983), cert. denied, 499 U. S. 952, 111 S.Ct. 1426 113 L.Ed.2d 478 (1991)

Where no notification was given the defendant prior to responding to the jury's questions, such communications between judge and jury violated this rule and was error. Where no notification is given to defendant prior to responding to the jury's questions, such communications between judge and jury violated A.R.Cr.P. 22.3 and was error.

State v. Maldonado, 1 CA-CR 02-0519 , COURT OF APPEALS OF ARIZONA, DIVISION ONE, DEPARTMENT B, 206 Ariz. 339; 78 P.3d 1060; 2003 Ariz. App. LEXIS 180; 412 Ariz. Adv. Rep. 6, November 6, 2003, Filed , Motion granted by State v. Maldonado, 2004 Ariz. LEXIS 28 (Ariz., Mar. 16, 2004). Convictions reversed; case remanded for... Defendant was entitled to new trial after she was convicted of being accomplice to sexual conduct with minor and child abuse because court's failure to impanel lawful number of jurors was fundamental error. Defendant was entitled to 12-person jury.

State v. Rich, 184 Ariz. 179, 907 P.2d 1382 (1995)
Counsel is present for four questions but was not for the fifth. In answering the jury's last question as it did, "all the evidence has been presented to you" the court neither explicitly nor implicitly commented on the evidence. See also: State v. Robin, 112 Ariz. 467, 543P.2d 779 (1975)

State v. Rodriguez, 131 Ariz. 400, 644 P.2d 888, 890 (App. 1981)
When jurors remarks indicate misgivings about impartiality, and juror should be struck for cause.

State v. Rojas, 1 CA-CR 91-1800, COURT OF APPEALS OF ARIZONA, DIVISION ONE, DEPARTMENT C, 177 Ariz. 454; 868 P.2d 1037; 1993 Ariz. App. LEXIS 279; 154 Ariz. Adv. Rep. 66, December 23, 1993, Filed REVERSED AND REMANDED
A trial court abused its discretion in denying defendant's motion for mistrial on the ground that, before deliberations began, a juror asked when the trial court would sentence and sent a sympathy note and money to the child molestation victims.

State v. Sanchez, No. 5702-PR, Supreme Court of Arizona, 135 Ariz. 123; 659 P.2d 1268; 1983 Ariz. LEXIS 161, January 28, 1983, Rehearing Denied March 8, 1983. ... of Appeals vacated; reversed and remanded.
Defendant was entitled to a new trial when a trial court failed to submit a form of verdict on insanity and a jury was not told it must return a verdict of not guilty by reason of insanity if it found defendant insane.

State v. Shumway, 137 Ariz. 585, 672 P.2d 929 (1983)
A trial judge may not communicate with a deliberating jury unless the defendant and counsel have been notified.

State v. Strayar, 119 Ariz. 607, 583 P.2d 263 (App. 1978)
The communication essentially consisted of a refusal to answer the jury's question and a restatement of the court's instruction that the jury was charged with determining the facts. Although the trial court's action gave the parties no opportunity to object or voice their concerns regarding the judge's procedure until it [was] too late.

State v. Thompson, 68 Ariz. 368, 389 - 92, 206 P.2d 1037, 1039 - 40 (1949)
Challenging a juror for bias is a substantial right.

State v. Tittle, 147 Ariz. 339
The court found that a self-defense instruction constituted fundamental error and impermissibly shifted the burden of proof by requiring the jury to decide defendant's conduct was justified prior to acquitting him. The court reversed and found that the failure of the trial court to inform the jury of each side's burden of proof was fundamental error, because defendant testified that he acted in self-defense. The court found that an out-of-state robbery conviction could be used to establish an aggravating circumstance under A.R.S. § 13-703(F)(1), because the offense was punishable by life imprisonment or death under Arizona law as it existed at the time of the robbery conviction. Further, the court held that as a matter of law, a robbery conviction constituted an aggravating circumstance within the meaning of § 13-703(F)(2); therefore, the robbery conviction could properly constitute two aggravating circumstances, § 13-703(F)(1), (2), on remand. The court found that the imposition of the death sentence and/or a finding of a new aggravating circumstance on remand would not offend double jeopardy, because he was originally given the death penalty. The court reversed the decision of the trial court and remanded for a new trial not inconsistent with its opinion.

Sullivan v. Louisiana, (1993, US) 124 L.Ed.2d 182, 113 S.Ct. 2078, 93 CDOS 3934, 93 Daily Journal DAR 6962, 7 FLW Fed S. 341
Constitutionally deficient jury instruction reasonable doubt, for purpose of prosecutor's burden of proving guilt beyond reasonable doubt, is not amendable to harmless error analysis and always invalidates conviction.

Sullivan v. Louisiana, 508 US, 124 L.Ed.2d 182, 113 S.Ct. (1993)
US v. Taylor, 997 F.2d 1551 (DC Cir. 1993)
Constitutionally deficient criminal jury instruction as to definition of reasonable doubt. For purposes of proving guilt beyond reasonable doubt, held not amenable to harmless error analysis on appeal and would always invalidate a conviction.

Test v. US, 420 US 29, 42 L.E.2d 786, 95 S.Ct. 749 (1975)
Regarding inspection of the jury "Wheel" and "List."

US v. Adcox, 19 F.3d 290 (7th CIR 1994)
When trial court answers jury questions it has a duty to answer with concrete accuracy.

US v. Ajiboye, 961 F.2d 892 (9th Cir. 1992)
If trial judge inquiries into numerical division of deadlocked jury and then gives ALLEN charge, charge is per se coercive and requires reversal.

US v. Aragon, 983 F.2d 1306 (4th Cir. 1993)
When jury can choose between conflicting evidence that decision should stand.

US v. Barnett, 968 F.2d 1189 (11th Cir. 1992)
Federal juries should not be concerned with the consequences of their verdict on the defendant.

US v. Berroa, 46 F.3d 1195 (D.C. Cir. 1995)
Giving ALLEN charge which contained additional statements not found in ABA approved instruction, and which omitted other required statements, was presumptively coercive and was reversible error.

US v. Blakey, 14 F.3d 1557 (11th Cir. 1994)
Prosecutor may not make suggestions, insinuations, and assertions calculated to mislead jury.

US v. Blood, 435 F.3d 612 (6th Cir. 2006)
Jury instruction that fails accurately to reflect law is reversible error.

US v. Boonphakdee, 40 F.3d 538 (2nd Cir. 1994)
Criminal defendant has right to jury charge which reflects defense theory.

US v. Brooks, 145 F.3d 446
Motion in limine to preclude government from introducing certain evidence in criminal trial was granted by the United States District Court for the District of Massachusetts, Edward F. Harrington, J., and the government appealed. The Court of Appeals, Selya, Circuit Judge, held that: (1) government had right to interlocutory appeal of the order, which extirpated evidence that the government considered to be substantial proof of specified elements of the charged offenses, even though ruling was on motion in limine rather than a suppression order; (2) appeal was timely though jury was sworn before Court of Appeals stayed proceedings; (3) district court abused its discretion in granting motion; (4) appeal divested the district court of its authority to swear a jury and start the trial, and it actions in doing so were nullities; and (5) district judge would be removed from further participation in the case and case would be assigned, on remand, to a different district judge. Vacated and remanded with directions.

US v. Brumel - Alvarez, 991 F.2d 1452 (9th Cir. 1992)
Jury, not prosecutor, has the duty to sift through inconsistencies of testimony to weigh credibility of witnesses and to resolve any ambiguities in evidence.

US v. Carter, 965 F.2d 804 (10th CIR 1992)
1. Questions from jury must be answered in open court and only after providing counsel an opportunity to be heard…
2. Government bears burden of proof to show courts exparte communication with jury was harmless error.

US v. Carter, 973 F.2d 1509 (10th Cir. 1992)
1. Question from jury must be answered in open court and only after providing counsel an opportunity to be heard.
2. Government bears burden to show trial court's ex parte communication with jury was harmless error.

US v. Carter, 910 F.2d 1524 (7th Cir. 1990)
Defendant in criminal trial is entitled to have jury consider any theory of defense that is supported by law and that has some foundation in evidence.

US v. Cartwright, 6 F.3d 294 (5th Cir. 1993)
Jury charge must be both legally accurate and factually supportable; court may not instruct jury on charge that is not supported by evidence.

US v. Cavanaugh, 948 F.2d 405 (8th Cir. 1991)
US v. Sotelo - Rivera, 906 F.2d 1324 (9th Cir. 1990)
If evidence would permit jury to find defendant guilty of a lesser included offense, defendant is entitled to instruction on that offense.

US v. Coppins, 953 F.2d 86 (4th Cir. 1991)
For all offenses for which imprisonment for more than 6 months is authorized, the right of jury trial exists, but there is no flat rule that there is no right to a jury trial when the possible sentence is less than six months.

US v. Dalaney, 732 F.2d 639 (8th Cir. 1984)
If a single juror is improperly influenced verdict is an unfair as if all were.

US v. Davis, 965 F.2d 804 (10th Cir. 1992) Failure to instruct jury as to required element of offense charged would mandate reversal.

US v. Duhart, No. 73-2570, UNITED STATES COURT OF APPEALS FOR THE NINTH CIRCUIT, 496 F.2d 941; 1974 US App. LEXIS 8750, May 8, 1974
Erroneous jury instruction resulted in the reversal of a conviction for assault with intent to commit rape because the jury could have convicted defendant of the offense despite his lack of intent to commit rape.

US v. Eagle Elk, 820 F.2d 959 (8th Cir. 1987)
Criminal defendant in federal court has non - waivable right to unanimous jury verdict.

US v. Frazin, 780 F.2d 1461 (9th Cir. 1986)
When jury deadlocks, defendant should be afforded opportunity to request that jury be reinstructed on burden of proof or on its member's duty to decide according to their own conscience.

US v. Frega, 179 F.3d 793 (9th Cir. 1999)
When a jury makes explicit its difficulties a trial judge should clear them away with concrete accuracy.

US v. Gallerani, 68 F.3d 611 (2nd Cir. 1995)
Due process requires the trial court to charge the jury on all elements of the crimes alleged in the indictment. A court's failure to instruct jury on some of the elements of a charged crime has the effect of relieving the prosecution of part of its burden of proof in obtaining conviction. The allegedly erroneous instruction must be considered in the context of the charge as a whole but the complete omission of an element of offense violates due process. Permitting the jury to find a defendant guilty of multiple crimes it found that any one crime had been committed by his co-conspirators, was erroneous.

US v. Galloway, 316 F.3d 624 (6th Cir. 2003)
A prosecutor cannot express his personal opinion before jury.

US v. Gaudin, 515 US 506, 132 L.Ed.2d 444, 115 S.Ct. 2310 (1995)
The Constitution gives any criminal defendant the right to have a jury determines, beyond a reasonable doubt, is guilty of every element of crime with which he is charged.

US v. Gaudin, 997 F.2d 1267 (9th Cir. 1993)
When trial judge deprives jury of its fact-finding duty, this violates the criminal defendant's due process rights.

US v. Gee, 266 F.3d 8 5 (7th Cir. 2000)
If a jury rationally could find in the defendants favor on some material issue, then the jury must be instructed on that subject.

US v. Gomez, 67 F.3d 1515 (CA 10 Utah 1995)
By answering jury's questions in open court without defendant or his counsel present, district court violated defendant's 5th amendment right to be present at any stage of criminal proceedings, but error was harmless where answers given were not factually inaccurate and no inferences from testimony were required to provide them. A Fifth Amendment violation occurred by answering jury's question in open court without defendant or his counsel present, if district court violated defendants constitutional right to be present at any stage of criminal proceedings, but error was harmless where answer is given that were not factually inaccurate and no inferences from testimony were required to provide them.

US v. Gray, 105 F.3d 956 (5th Cir. 1999)
If District judge so favors prosecution during trial that judge appears to predispose jury toward finding of guilt and appears to take over prosecutorial role, due process violation occurs.

US v. Haddon, 927 F.2d 942, 948 - 49 (7th Cir. 1991)
Trial court prediction of length of trial during voir dire was harmless error because subsequent instruction cured any inference of guilt.

US v. Hall, 116 F.3d 1253 (8th Cir. 1997)
If exposed to extrinsic evidence improperly influenced only one juror, verdict is as unfair as if all jurors were.

US v. Hall, 989 F.2d 711 (4th Cir. 1993)
A defendant is constitutionally entitled to mentally competent jurors and to enforce this right, jury's verdict must be set aside if defendant presents clear evidence of juror's incompetence to understand issues and to deliberate at time of his services.

US v. Hove, 52 F.3d 233 (9th CIR 1992)

Omission of essential element of offense from jury instruction is plain error and cannot be harmless.

US v. Hunt, 794 F.2d 1095 (5th Cir. 1986)

Proof beyond a reasonable doubt is proof that leaves one firmly convinced of defendant's guilt.

US v. Lampkins, 47 F.3d 175 (7th Cir. 1995)

Discrimination in jury selection on basis of gender violates equal protection.

US v. Lorenzo, 995 F.2d 1448 (9th Cir. 1993)

Trevino v. Texas, 503 US 118 L.Ed.2d 193, 112 S.Ct. (1992)

Batson v. Kentucky, 476 US 79. 90 L.Ed.2d 69, 106 S.Ct. 1712 (1986)

Purposeful racial discrimination is selection of the venire violates a defendant's right of equal protection. (see Batson) Accused's objection under equal protection clause to states race based use of peremptory challenges prior to the Supreme Court's decision in Batson v. Kentucky held preserved for review by the Supreme Court. (see Trevino)

US v. Manning, 23 F.3d 570 (1st Cir. 1994)

Arguments urging jury to act in any capacity other than an impartial arbiter of the facts in the case before it are improper.

US v. McFarland, 34 F.3d 233 (9th Cir. 1995)

Omission is an essential element of offense from jury instruction is plain error in cannot be harmless. And 235 - fails to instruct jury that conviction for offense required the defendant knew conduct was unlawful.

US v. McFarland, 34 F.3d 1508 (9th Cir. 1994)

District court may not substitute alternate jurors unless defendant has given express waiver of his rights.

US v. Nelson, 27 F.3d 199 (6th Cir. 1994)

When trial judge omits from jury instructions element of offense necessary to find defendant guilty, omission is plain error.

US v. O'Brien, 14 F.3d 703 (1st Cir. 1994)

Jury can freely choose to credit particular testimony while discounting other testimony that arguably points in a different direction.

US v. Ojebode, 957 f.2d 1218 (5th CIR 1992)

Jury's verdict cannot stand if the instructions provided to the jury do not require it to find each element of the crime under the proper standard of proof.

US v. Pace, 10 F.3d 1106 (5th Cir. 1993)

Any doubt about credibility of witnesses or about inferences that can be drawn from evidence should be resolved in favor of jury verdict.

US v. Perz - Tosta, 36 F.3d 1552 (11th Cir. 1994)

Reasonable inferences from circumstantial evidence, rather than mere speculation, must support jury's verdict.

US v. Peterson, 236 F.3d 848 (7th Cir. 2001)

1. To render a guilty verdict, jury must hear sufficient evidence to avoid resorting to excessively strained inferences or guesswork. 2. When a verdict may have rested on any of several grounds, one of which lies improper, the conviction cannot be upheld.

US v. Porter, 764 F.2d 1 (1st Cir. 1985)

Decision to allow jury to take notes and use them during deliberations is matter within discretion of trial court, and absent abuse of discretion, action of trial court will not be disturbed.

US v. Pruitt, (1985 CA 11 Ala) 763 F.2d 1257, cert. denied, (1986) 474 US 1084, 88 L.ed.2d 896, 106 S.Ct. 856

Jury may be instructed to consider uncharged offenses in order to determine whether charged offenses are related in continuous pattern of criminal activity.

US v. Randazzd, 80 F.3d 623 (1st CIR 1996)
Failure to submit entire element of crime to jury, when request is made, is treated as structural and is reversible error without regard to harm.

US v. Riffe, 28 F.3d 565 (6th Cir. 1994)
Refusal to give accurate jury instruction is reversible if it impairs defendant's theory of the case and is not covered adequately by instructions given.

US v. Rigsby, 45 F.3d 120 (6th Cir. 1995)
Requirement that defendant receive fair trial by panel of impartial, "indifferent" jurors is basic requirement of due process.

US v. Robertson, 45 F.3d 1423 (10th Cir. 1995)
Criminal defendant has Sixth Amendment right to jury pool comprised of fair cross-section of the community.

US v. Sarkisian, 197 F.3d 996 (9th Cir. 1999)
Defendant's sixth amendment rights are violated even if only one juror was unduly biased or improperly influenced.

US v. Shears, 762 F.2d 397 (4th Cir. 1985)
US v. Delvecchio, 707 F.2d 1214 (11th Cir. 1983)
Jeopardy attaches when jury is impaneled and sworn.

US v. Schweihs, 971 F.2d 1302 (7th Cir. 1992)
US v. Washington, 819 F.2d 221 (9th Cir. 1987)
District court must give instruction regarding any legitimate theory of defense that is supported by evidence, and failure to do so is reversible error. Defendant is entitled to instruction on any defense recognized in law and supported by sufficient evidence to allow reasonable jury to find in defendant's favor.

US v. Strauss, 999 F.2d 692 (2nd Cir. 1993)
Jury is exclusively responsible for determining witness credibility.

US v. Thomas, 895 F.2d 1198 (8th Cir. 1990)
Court need not instruct jury that defendant will receive mandatory sentence if he or she is found guilty. Jury was not to consider punishment of defendant or loss of parole under sentencing guidelines.

US v. Trega, 179 F.3d 793 (9th CIR 1995)
When jury makes explicit its difficulties a trial judge should clear them away with concrete accuracy.

US v. Waldon, 206 F.3d 597, 607 (6th Cir. 2000)
No abuse of discretion when defendants inadvertently observed in shackles while being transported by Marshall's because court instructed jury that it was not evidence of guilt.

US v. Winfield, 997 F.2d 1076 (4th Cir. 1993)
Convictions based on theories not submitted to the jury cannot stand.

US v. Vastola, 989 F.2d 1318 (3rd Cir. 1993) Where there has been an inconsistent verdict, criminal defendant is protected against jury irrationality and error by review of sufficiency of evidence.

US v. Vasquez Lopez, 22 F.3d 900 (9th Cir. 1994)
Constitution forbids all parties in either criminal or civil trials from challenging prospective jurors solely on account of their race.

US v. Zuniga, 989 F.2d 1109 (9th Cir. 1993)
Even if alibi evidence is weak, insufficient, inconsistent, or of doubtful credibility, alibi instructions should be given.

Weaver v. Thompson, 197 F.3d 359 (9th Cir. 1999)
In other charge analysis, fundamental question is whether jury was improperly coerced, less infringing defendants, due process rights.

Mail

Bieregu v. Reno, 59 F.3d 1445 (3rd Cir. 1995)

Prisoners do not forfeit their First Amendment rights to use of the mails. In the context of the First Amendment and prison mail, "censorship" means altering or withholding delivery of particular letter. Prison officials not entitled to qualified immunity in suit alleging constitutional violations by opening prisoner's incoming legal mail outside his presence.

Brewer v. Wilkinson, 3 F.3d 816 (5th Cir. 1993)

Lemon v. Dugger, 931 F.2d 1465 (11th Cir. 1991)

"Special Mail" may not be opened by prison officials outside the presence of the inmate. "Special Mail" is mail from federal prisoner directed to attorneys, designated state & federal officials, and representatives of news media, and it is not to be opened by prison officials. Prison official's interference with plaintiff's legal mail violates both plaintiff's constitutional right of access to the courts and his First Amendment rights of free speech.

Foster v. Basham, 932 F.2d 732 (8th Cir. 1991)

Prison mail room policy of preventing inmate's access to telephone directory listings of attorneys sent to inmates through the mail was unconstitutional.

Gramdgna v. Johnson, 846 F.2d 675 (11th Cir. 1987)

Practice of allowing prisoner's mail to accumulate before forwarding it to prisoners unconstitutionally infringed on their right of access to the courts.

Hall v. Curran, 818 F.2d 1040 (2nd Cir. 1987)

A pointed case on censorship and the inextricably meshed rights of both the writer and intended recipient of mail.

Knop v. Johnson, 977 F2d 996 (6th Cir. 1992)

Prisoners could not be required to designate particular attorneys in order to activate privileged treatment of their legal mail.

<u>Loggins v. Delo</u>, 999 F.2d 364 (8th Cir. 1993)

Letter by prison inmate to brother in which some unkind remarks were made about the female mail room officer did not implicate "security concerns," and thus, imposition of disciplinary action on inmate for such letter violated the First Amendment.

<u>Mayer v. State</u>, 184 Ariz. 242

A notice of appeal by a pro se inmate was deemed filed when it was properly addressed and delivered to prison authorities for forwarding to the clerk of the superior court.

<u>O'Donnell v. Thomas</u>, 814 F.2d 524 (8th Cir. 1987)

<u>Wycoff v. Brewer</u>, 572 F.2d 1260 (8th Cir. 1978)

In both cases prison officials opened three (3) court letters and the appellate court either remanded the case for factual findings or declared the action unconstitutional.

<u>Phelps v. US Federal Government</u>, 15 F.3d 735 (8th Cir. 1994)

<u>Griffin v. Lombardi</u>, 946 F.2d 604 (8th Cir. 1991)

Prison inmates have a recognized First Amendment interest in receiving mail. Prisoners constitutional right to send and receive mail may be restricted only for legitimate penological interests.

<u>Procunier v. Martinez</u>, 416 US 396, 40 L.Ed.2d 224, 94 S.Ct. 1800 (1974) 11.

The inmate must be notified of the rejection of a letter written by or addressed to him. The author must be given a reasonable opportunity to protest the decision. Complaints must be referred to a prison official other than the person who originally disapproved the correspondence. Mail censorship regulations violated the First Amendments protections of lawful expression.

<u>Ramos v. Lamm</u>, 639 F.2d 559 (10th Cir. 1980)

<u>Collins v. Schoonfield</u>, 344 F.Supp. 257 (D. Maryland 1972)

Officials could not determine what was, or was not, legal mail.

Turner v. Safley, 482 US 78, 96 L.Ed.2d 64, 107 S.Ct. 2254 (1987)
Mail restrictions on inmate correspondence held not to violate the First Amendment (see case for the particulars).

Van Cleave v. US, 854 F.2d 82 (5th Cir. 1988)
Sizemore v. Williford, 829 F.2d 608 (7th Cir. 1987)
Prisoner's complaint that his daily newspaper were permanently withheld and intentionally never delivered by prison officials implicated his substantive rights as guaranteed by First Amendment.

Mandamus

Allied Chemical Corp. v. Daiflon, Inc., 449 US 33, 66 L.Ed.2d 193, 101 S.Ct. 188 (1980)
Remedy of mandamus is a drastic one, to be invoked only in extraordinary situations.

Doughty v. Underwriters at Lloyd's, London, 6 F.3d 856 (1st Cir. 1993)
It is a prerequisite to mandamus relief that ruling below be palpably improper and that suitor's entitlement to claimed relief be plain as a matter of law.

In Re Glass Workers Local No. 173, 983 F.2d 725 (6th Cir. 1993)
Mallard v. US Dist. Court for S. Dist. of Iowa, 490 US 296. 104 L.Ed.2d 318, 109 S.Ct. 1814 (1989)
Mandamus may be issued when petitioner shows there is no other means available to obtain desired relief and that his right to issuance of the writ is clear and undisputable.

Matter of Continental Illinois Sec. Litigation, 985 F.2d 867 (7th Cir. 1993)
One of less controversial functions of mandamus is to assure that lower court complies with spirit as well as letter of mandate issued to that court by higher court.

Potomac Electric Power Co. v. ICC, 702 F.2d 1026 (D.C. Cir 1983)
Congress has empowered federal courts to issue writ such as Mandamus if necessary to effectuate or prevent frustration of orders previously issued.

US v. Gunderson, 978 F.2d 580 (10th Cir. 1992)
Mandamus cannot be used as a substitute for an appeal.

US v. Horn, 29 F.3d 754 (1st Cir. 1994)
Advisory mandamus is appropriate when issue presented is novel, of great public importance, and likely to recur.

Socer v. Scott, 942 F.2d 597 (9th Cir. 1991)
Prisoner who alleges cause of action under the Mandamus Act need not rely upon implied or private right of action under any other statute.

Marriage and Divorce

42 USC § 667 (b) (2)Federal child support and establishment of paternity act. Requires that state receiving federal funds allow a rebuttal presumption in judicial or administrative proceedings for the award of child support.

Acuna v. Sullivan, 765 F.Supp. 510 (E.D. Arkansas 1991)
1. Validity of marriage is determined by law of place where it was celebrated.
2. Under Texas law, marriage is void if either party was previously married and the prior marriage is not dissolved.

Barnes v. State of Mississippi, 992 F.2d 1335 (5th Cir. 1993)
State may enact abortion law calculated to inform woman's free choice, not hinder it.

Bennett v. Bennett, 595 F.Supp. 366 (D.C. D.C. 1984)
Where mother violated father's child custody rights under decree which was required to be recognized by the court, she could be made to compensate father for the harm done.

Bruce v. Hartford Life & Accid. Ins., 907 F.2d 585 (5th Cir. 1990)
Under Louisiana law, divorce actions abate on death of either party.

Cooper v. State Of Utah, 684 F.Supp. 1060 (D. Utah 1987)
Right to lawful marriage, without fear of criminal prosecution, is part of fundamental right to marry protected by the Fourteenth Amendment.

Depuy v. Dupuy, 686 F.Supp. 568 (E.D. Virginia 1988)
Under Virginia law, wife was entitled to recover attorney fees incurred in enforcing New York divorce judgment which required her former husband to make support payments.

Hassan v. Lubbock Independent School Dist., 55 F.3d 1075 (5th Cir. 1995)
Children do not shed their constitutional rights at the schoolhouse door.

<u>Holbert v. West</u>, 730 F.Supp. 50 (E.D. Kentucky 1990)
Generally, common law rule is that under age marriage of person over age seven is not "void" from onset but is merely "voidable" and valid until declared void by the court.

<u>Hullett v. Towers</u>, Perrin, Forster & Crosby. Inc., 38 F.3d 107 (3rd Cir. 1994)
Under Pennsylvania law, for purposes of interpretation. property settlement agreement is treated same as any other contract.

<u>In Re Marriage of Gilbert</u>, 945 P.2d 238, 88 WA. App. 362 (Wash. App. Div. 1, 1997)
You must show that to impose child support would be unjust or inappropriate in your particular circumstances. You must show that you are indigent. Due to being in prison, and that the amount you are being asked to pay is excessive. Most states mandate a support order of at least $25 for parents with less than $600 a month in combined net income. (Per child, $25). You should consider seeking a reduction in payments in light of this ruling through your respective county. See also: A.R.S. 25-100; 25-1012; 46-402.

<u>In Re Frawley</u>, 112 BR 32 (D. Colorado 1990)
Under Colorado law, two essential requirements must be met to establish a common law marriage; agreement between parties and cohabitation.

<u>In Re Soderling</u>, 998 F.2d 730 (9th Cir. 1993)
Under California law, all community property is liable for debts or either spouse incurred before or during marriage.

<u>In Re Spirtos</u>, 56 F.3d 1007 (9th Cir. 1995)
Under California law, when one party fails to perform his or her obligations under divorce decree, other party may sue him or her under contract principles for failing to perform.

<u>Labram v. Havel</u>, 43 F.3d 918 (4th Cir. 1995)
Generally, spouse may not recover for loss of consortium if he was not married to victim of primary wrong at time victim suffered her injuries.

113

Mullins v. State Of Oregon, 57 F.3d 789 (9th Cir. 1995)

When child is abandoned by his parents and placed with state agency, state's paramount concern must be swift and suitable placement of the child.

P.O.P.S. v. Gardner, 998 F.2d 764 (9th Cir. 1993)

Rights to marry, have children, and maintain relationship with children are fundamental rights protected by the Fourteenth Amendment and thus, strict scrutiny is required of any statutes that directly and substantially impair those rights.

Qutb v. Strauss, 11 F.3d 488 (5th Cir. 1993)

Parent's right to rear children without undue governmental interference is a fundamental component of due process.

State v. Korzep, 165 Ariz. 490, 799 P.2d 831

Defendant was convicted in the Superior Court, Yuma County, No. Cr-14519, Douglas W. Keddie, J., of manslaughter and she appealed. The Court of Appeals affirmed, 164 Ariz. 175, 791 P.2d 1058, and review was granted. The Supreme Court, Gordon, C.J., held that defendant was entitled to instruction that a person is justified in using deadly physical force against another to the extent that the person reasonably believes that the use of deadly physical force is necessary to prevent the other person's commission of aggravated assault, even when the other person is a member of the defendant's household. Vacated in part and remanded.

Steen v. CIR, 923 F.2d 603 (8th Cir. 1991)

Under Iowa law, property inherited both before and during marriage can be considered in determining a property settlement.

Stubbs v. Metropolitan Life Ins. Co., 653 F.Supp. 299 (S.D. Texas 1986)

Under Texas law, granting of wife's petition for annulment of marriage on grounds of fraud made the marriage a nullity and restored the parties to the state which existed before the marriage.

<u>Trammel v. US</u>, 445 US 40, 63 L.Ed.2d 186, 100 S.Ct. 906 (1980)
A spouse can testify against the other party if the marriage is irretrievably broken.

<u>US v. Kapnison</u>, 743 F.2d 1450 (10th Cir. 1984)
Wife testified against her husband and the appellate court upheld her testimony.

<u>US v. White</u>, 974 F.2d 1135 (9th Cir. 1992)
Public policy interests in protecting integrity of marriages and ensuring spouses freely communicate with one another underlie marital communications privilege.

<u>Waters v. Gaston County</u>, N.C., 57 F.3d 422 (4th Cir. 1995)
Federal Constitution embraces a fundamental right to marry.

<u>Willoughby v. Willoughby</u>, 758 F.Supp. 656 (D. Kansas 1990) 26.
Under Kansas law, after petition for divorce is filed, district judge is permitted to issue an order which restrains the parties from disposing of property. A life insurance policy is property subject to division in divorce.

<u>Winston v. Delaware Children & Youth Service</u>, 748 F.Supp. 1128 (E.D. Penn. 1990)
Parent's liberty interest in a relationship with their child continues even when custody has temporarily been granted to the state or another parent.

Medical

Boyd v. Knox, 47 F.3d 966 (8th Cir. 1995)
Prison official's knowledge of deliberate indifference to prisoner's serious medical needs may be established by circumstantial evidence.

Estelle v. Gamble, 429 US 97, 50 L.Ed.2d 251, 97 S.Ct. 285 (1976)
Elementary principles of the cruel and unusual punishment clause of the Eighth Amendment establish the government's obligation to provide medical care for those whom it is punishing by incarceration.

Fields vs, Gander, 734 F.2d 1313 (9th Cir. 1984)
Bee v. Greaves, 744 F.2d 1378 (10th Cir. 1984)
Individual has a constitutionally protected interest in making his own decision whether to accept or reject the administration of potentially dangerous drugs.

Felce v. Fiedler, 974 F.2d 1484 (7th Cir. 1992)
Riggins v. Nevada, 504 US 118 L.Ed.2d 479, 112 S.Ct. 1810 (1992)
There is a liberty interest in not being subjected to involuntary administration of antipsychotic drugs except when there is an overriding justification for their use and a determination of medical appropriateness.

Gill v. Mooney, 824 F.2d 192 (2nd Cir. 1987)
Prison officials are more than merely negligent if they deliberately defy express instructions of prisoner's doctors.

Green v. Carlson, 446 US 14, 64 L.Ed.2d 15, 100 S.Ct. 1468 (1980)
Suit against prison warden for money damages in a wrongful death.

Hampton v. Holmesburg Prison Officials, (1976, CA3 PA) 546 F.2d 1077
Source of pre-trial detainees right to medical treatment is found in due process clause or an equal protection clause, with decisions interpreting cruel and unusual punishment clause of eighth amendment serving as a useful analogies.

Johnson v. Clinton, 763 F.2d 326 (8th Cir. 1985)
Prison inmate stated a claim for cruel and unusual punishment by alleging that prison warden had denied him necessary surgery for a hernia and that he was being forced to work beyond his physical capacity, thus endangering his life.

Miltier v. Beorn, 896 F.2d 848 (4th Cir. 1990)
Failure to respond to inmates known medical needs raises an inference that there was a deliberate indifference to those needs in violation of the Eighth Amendment.

Neely v. Fienstein, 50 F.3d 1502 (9th Cir. 1995)
Mental hospital officials are liable to patient in civil rights action if they exhibit conscious indifference amounting to gross negligence.

Roba v. US, 604 F.2d 215 (2nd Cir. 1979)
Prisoner has right not be forcibly transported when he is in a life threatening situation.

Shannon v. Lester, (1975, CA6 Tenn.) 519 F.2d 76
Persons detained in custody are entitled to medical treatment when necessary on account of illness or injury, and refusal of prison authorities, with knowledge of condition, to provide medical treatment may constitute violation of due process clause of 14th amendment.

Torraco v. Maloney, 923 F.2d 231 (1st Cir. 1991)
Prison officials deliberate indifference to inmate's serious medical needs constitutes Eighth Amendment violation and gives inmate cause of action under §1983.

US v. Charters, 829 F.2d 479 (4th Cir. 1987)
Forcible medication with antipsychotic drugs implicates individual rights to freedom from physical invasion and freedom of thought as well as right to privacy protected by the Constitution and the common law.

Weaver v. Clarke, 45 F.3d 1253 (8th Cir. 1995)

Harris v. Coweta County, 21 F.3d 388 (11th Cir. 1994)

Prison official violates Eighth Amendment by being deliberately indifferent either to prisoner's existing serious medical needs or to conditions posing substantial risk of serious future harm.

Woodall v. Fote, 648 F.2d 272 (5th Cir. 1981)

Ramos v. Lamm, 639 F.2d 559 (10th Cir. 1980)

Inmates must be provided with medically necessary mental health treatment.

Miranda

Alston v. Redman, 34 F.3d 1237 (3rd Cir. 1994)

Edwards v. Arizona, 451 US 477, 68 L.Ed.2d 378, 101 S.Ct. 1880 (1981)
Suspect who has requested presence of counsel cannot be questioned concerning any crime, not just one that got him in custody.

Illinois v. Perkins, 496 US 292, 110 L.Ed.2d 243, 110 S.Ct. 2394 (1990)
Illinois undercover law enforcement officer posing as fellow inmate was held not required to give MIRANDA warnings to suspect.

Jocks v. Tavernier, 316 F.3d 128 (2003)
The appropriate remedy for violations of Miranda rights is exclusion of the evidence at trial.

Miranda v. Arizona, 384 US 436, 16 L.Ed.2d 694, 86 S.Ct. 1602 (1966)
A person being arrested must be told that he/she has the right to remain silent and that if they chose to do so an attorney will be appointed for them.

Miranda v. AZ., No. 759 Argued Feb. 28 – Mar. 1, 1966 decided June 13, 1966 GO> 384 US 436
When the accused is interrogated in a room cut off from the world or placed in a stressful condition the testimony gathered is inadmissible regardless of whether the accused was informed of his rights.

Sanna v. Dipalo, 265 F.3d 1 (1st CIR 2001)
When a person in police custody requests the presence of an attorney the authorities must cease interrogation.

US v. Allee, 299 F.3d 996 (8th CIR 2002)
Inquiry into defendant's silence following Miranda warnings constitutes trial error. (This would also apply to right to counsel.)

US v. Baker, 999 F.2d 412 (9th Cir. 1993)
Due process requires that defendant's be able to exercise their constitutional right to remain silent and not be penalized at trial for doing so.

US v. Bland, 908 F.2d 471 (9th Cir. 1990)
Miranda warning given to defendant was inadequate where defendant was not informed that he had a right to have an attorney during questioning.

US v. Bonner, 302 F.3d 776 (7th CIR 2002)
A defendant's right to silence, coupled with her right not to have any reference to her silence made at trial, exists even before defendant receives Miranda warnings.

US v. Bowman, 907 F.2d 63 (8th Cir. 1990)
Statement given by defendant before MIRANDA warnings could be used for impeachment.

US v. Burson, 952 F.2d 1196 (10th Cir. 1991)
Once defendant invokes his right to remain silent, it is impermissible for the prosecution to refer to any Fifth Amendment rights which the defendant has exercised.

US v. Butler
Because of the inherently coercive nature of custodial interrogations, a person must be advised of his Miranda rights, prior to questioning.

US v. Carpenter, 963 F.2d 736 (5th Cir. 1992)
Fifth Amendment shields suspects from interrogation about any offense, charged or uncharged.

US v. Carter, 953 F.2d 1449 (5th Cir. 1992)
Use of the defendant's post - arrest silence for its substantive value is prohibited, as is its use for impeachment purposes.

US v. Cordova, 990 F.2d 1035 (8th Cir. 1993)
Reading of Miranda rights is required whenever a suspect is interrogated while in custody.

US v. Covington, 783 F.2d 1052
Defendant was charged with carnal knowledge of his 13-year-old daughter within the special maritime and territorial jurisdiction of the United States. The United States District Court for the District of Hawaii, Samuel P. King, J., suppressed the defendant's statements. Government appealed. The Court of Appeals, Circuit Judge, held that the exclusionary rule of Miranda and Edwards does not apply to statements obtained by foreign law enforcement officers in violation of foreign law and, therefore, if an investigator was acting as a law enforcement officer of the Marshall Islands, rather than as a law enforcement officer of the United States, the exclusionary rule would not apply, but a determination was required as to whether the trustworthiness of the confession satisfied due process standards. Reversed and remanded.

US v. Gelzer, 50 F.3d 1133 (2nd Cir. 1995)
Statements made during custodial interrogation are generally inadmissible unless suspect has first been advised of his rights.

US v. Ghent, 279 F.3d 1121
Petitioner sought federal habeas corpus relief following affirmance, on direct appeal, 43 Cal.3d 739, 239 Cal.Rptr. 82, 739 P.2d 1250, of his conviction by original jury for first-degree murder, attempted rape, and assault with intent to commit rape, and of death penalty imposed pursuant to second jury's verdict in special circumstances retrial. The United States District Court for the Northern District of California, William A. Ingram, Chief District Judge, denied petition. Petitioner appealed. The Court of Appeals, Reinhardt, Circuit Judge, held that: (1) admission of testimony in violation of Miranda violated petitioner's due process rights; (2) erroneous admission of psychiatrist's testimony did not have substantial or injurious effect on original jury's verdict; (3) erroneous admission of psychiatrist's testimony during special circumstances retrial warranted habeas relief; (4) jurors' brief glimpses of petitioner in restraints did not rise to level of due process violation; and (5) failure to give lesser-included instruction did not

prejudice petitioner. Affirmed in part, reversed in part, and remanded with directions.

US v. Henley, 984 F.2d 1040 (9th Cir. 1993)
When officer has reason to know that suspect's answer may incriminate him, even routine questioning may amount to interrogation.

US v. Hurst, 228 F.3d 751 (6th CIR 2000)
Interrogation triggers the need to give Miranda warnings.

US v. Johnson, 56 F.3d 947 (8th Cir. 1995)
After giving Miranda warnings to suspect in custody, if suspect indicates in any manner. at any time, prior to or during questioning, that he wishes to remain silent, interrogation must cease.

US v. Johnson, 42 F.3d 1312 (10th Cir. 1994)
US v. Walton, 10 F.3d 1024 (3rd Cir. 1993)
When Miranda violation is alleged to have occurred, burden of proof rests with government to prove validity of waiver by preponderance of evidence.

US v. Little, 18 F.3d 1499 (10th Cir. 1994)
There is no per se rule requiring police to advise detainee of right to refuse to answer questions (Authors Note: under NO circumstances volunteer information or respond to questioning without the presence of counsel).

US v. Menesses, 962 F.2d 420 (5th Cir. 1992)
Confession induced by assurance that there will be no prosecution is not voluntary.

US v. Moreno Flores, 33 F.3d 1164 (9th Cir. 1994)
Garcia v. Singletary, 13 F.3d 1487 (11th Cir. 1994)
Defendant who is in custody must be given MIRANDA warnings before police officers may interrogate him.

US v. Soto, 953 F.2d 263 (6th Cir. 1992)

Defendant did not waive his MIRANDA rights by initiating conversation with police officer regarding how inventory of defendant's belongings following his arrest should be conducted.

US v. Swint, 15 F.3d 286, 290 (3rd CIR 1994)

Confession involuntary because defendant thought statements were off the record "proffer" and officers did not clearly inform defendant's statements were on the record.

US v. Waldemer, 50 F.3d 1379 (7th Cir. 1995)

Defendant may not be convicted solely on his own uncorroborated admissions made after crime has ended.

US v. Whaley, 13 F.3d 963 (6th Cir. 1994)

Minnick v. Mississippi, 498 US 146, 112 L.Ed.2d 489, 111 S.Ct. 486 (1990)

Police cannot re-interrogate suspect who does not initiate discussion of his offense after invoking right to counsel.

Miscellaneous

Article 2 § 26 AZ. Constitution: Bearing Arms.

The right of the individual citizen to bear arms in defense of himself or the state shall not be impaired, but nothing in this section shall be construed as authorizing individuals or corporations to organize, maintain or employ an armed body of men.

A.R.S. 13-103 Abolition of Common Law Offenses and Affirmation Defense; definition. 1. All common law offenses and affirmative defenses are abolished. No conduct or omission constitutes an offense or an affirmative defense under this title or under another statute or ordinance. 2. For the purpose of this section, "affirmative defense" means a defense that is offered and that attempts to excuse the criminal actions of the accused or another person for whose actions the accused may be deemed accountable. Affirmative defense does not include any justification defense pursuant to Chapter 4 of this title or any defense that either denies an element of the offense charged or denies responsibility including alibi, misidentification, or lack of intent.

A.R.S. 11-261 Authority to procure liability and errors and omission is insurance covering officers, agents and employees.

US Bankruptcy became official in 1933.

The road to bankruptcy began with contract between King of France and the 13 United States of North America. See www.yale.edu/lawweb/avalon.

Oct. 28, 1977 US as a corporation declared insolvency. 26 IRC 165 (g)(1); U.C.C. 1-201(23); CRS 39-22-103.5;

Westfall v. Braley, 10 Ohio/88, 75 Am. Dec. 509

Adams v. Richardson, 337 S.W. 2d 911

Ward v. Smith, 7 Wall 447

Since May 9, 1933, the US has been in a state of declared national emergency. Senate Resolution 9, 93rd Congress, 1st session, forward, 1973.

27 CFR vol. 1; 27 CFR 72, 11, page 1122-1123

Any of the following types of crime (federal or state); Offenses against revenue laws; burglary; counterfeiting; forgery; kidnapping; larceny; robbery; illegal sale or possession of a deadly weapon; prostitution (including soliciting, procuring, pandering, white slaving, keeping a house of ill fame and like offenses); extortion; swindling and confidence games; and attempting to commit, conspiring to commit, or compounding any of the foregoing crimes. Addiction to narcotic drugs and use of marijuana will be treated as if such were commercial crime.

ARC 610 Religious beliefs or opinions. Evidence of the beliefs or opinions of a witness on matters of religion is not admissible for the purpose of showing that by reason of their nature the witness's credibility is impaired or enhanced. See: Art. 2 §2 AZ. Constitution

Kelley v. Abdo, 209 (ARIZ. 521, 444 ARIZ. ADv. REP. 9, 105 P.3d 167, 2005 APP.Lex1511 (Ct. APP. 2005)

State v. Towery, 186 ARIZ. 168, 920 P.2d 290 (1996)

State v. Rankovick, 159 ARIZ. 116, 765 P.2d 518 (1988)

New Trial

Antevski v. Volkswagenwerk Aktiengesellschaft, 4 F.3d 537 (7th Cir. 1993)
US v. Douglas, 874 F.2d 1145 (7th Cir. 1989)
If verdict is based on false testimony district judge has discretion to grant injured party a new trial.

Blancha v. Raymark Industries, 972 F.2d 507 (3rd Cir. 1992)
Even in the absence of timely objection, court could grant new trial if error in instructing jury resulted in miscarriage of justice.

Dakota Industries Inc. v. Ever Best Ltd., 28 F3d 910 (8th Cir. 1994)
New trial is required when district court erroneously submits question of law to jury to decide.

Durrough v. State, (1981, Tex. Crim.) 620 SW.2d 134
Defendant may be tried second time for offense when prior conviction for that same offense is set aside on appeal; where reversal grants appellant new trial, he may be tried on original indictment or on new indictment charging same offense.

Jackson v. Virginia, (1979) 443 US 307, 61 L.Ed.2d 560, 99 S.Ct. 2781
If state court reverses and characterizes it as based on weight of evidence or does not characterize it at all, insufficiency of verdict will create double jeopardy bar.

Lama v. Borras, 16 F.3d 473 (1st Cir. 1994)
Winter v. Brenner Tank, Inc., 926 F2d 468 (5th Cir.)
District court may order a new trial even when verdict is supported by substantial evidence.

Newell Puerto Rico, Ltd. v. Rubbermaid Inc., 20 F.3d 15 (1st Cir. 1994)
EEOC v. Clear Lake Dodge, 25 F.3d 265 (5th Cir. 1994)
District court may grant new trial where verdict returned is against great weight of evidence.

Note: Based upon new evidence, a new trial may be had anytime within 2 years. A new trial based on ineffective of assistance of counsel may be had any time if your attorney failed to present evidence, known to him at the time, to the trial or sentencing court.

Overbee v. Van Waters & Rogers, 765 F.2d 578 (6th Cir. 1985)
Morse v. US, 270 US 151, 70 L.Ed 518, 46 S.Ct. 241 (1926)
A motion for a new trial suspends the finality of a judgment.

TS v. Davis, 15 F.3d 1393 (7th Cir. 1994)
Defendant is entitled to new trial if there is a "reasonable possibility" that jury's verdict has been affected by material not properly admitted as evidence.

US v. Davis, 960 F.2d 820 (9th Cir. 1992)
If newly discovered evidence established that defendant in narcotics case had been convicted solely on uncorroborated testimony of crooked cop involved in stealing drug money. Interest of justice would support new trial.

US v. Greer, 223 F.3d 41 (2nd Cir. 2000)
Motion for a new trial must be granted if trial was not fair to the moving party.

US v. Hall, 85 F.3d 367 (8th Cir. 1996)
Trial court may grant new trial based on taint of even a single juror.

US v. Hobson, 825 F.2d 364 (11th Cir. 1987)
US v. Haimowitz, 725 F.2d 1561 (11th Cir. 1984)
To justify new trial, evidence must be discovered following trial, movant must show due diligence to discover evidence, evidence must not be merely cumulative or impeaching, evidence must be material to issues before court and evidence must be of such nature that new trial would probably produce new result.

US v. Honer, 225 F.3d 549 (5th Cir. 2000)
New trial is necessary when there is significant possibility that improperly admitted prejudicial evidence and substantial impact on verdict, viewed in light of entire trial.

US v. Levy - Cordero, 156 F.3d 244 (1st Cir. 1998)
New trial must be ordered whenever substantial rights are affected by error at criminal trial and the government cannot prove harmless beyond a reasonable doubt.

US v. Tory, 52 F.3d 207 (9th Cir. 1995)
Cumulative effect of the errors relating to armed robbery count deprived defendant of fair trial and required new trial on armed robbery court.

US v. Walker, 25 F.3d 540 (7th Cir. 1994)
To win new trial based on recanted testimony, defendant must show that recantation is true, that jury might have reached different result if it were not for false testimony, and that witness' testimony took defendant by surprise.

Parole / Probation

<u>Bearden v. Georgia</u>, 461 US 660, 76 L.Ed.2d 221, 103 SCt 2064 (1983)
An individual's probation cannot be revoked for non – payment of a fine.

<u>Board of Pardons v. Allen</u>, 482 US 369, 96 L.Ed.2d 303, 107 S.Ct. 2415 (1987)
Montana statute, providing that parole board shall release prisoner on parole when certain prerequisites are met, held to create liberty interest protected under Fourteenth Amendment.

<u>Caporale v. Gasele</u>, 940 F.2d 305 (8th Cir. 1991)
Defendant's claim that Parole Commission "double counted" by using same factors to depart from guidelines as it used to establish offense severity level was reviewable: double counting violates Parole Act.

<u>Ceniceros v. US Parole Commission</u>, 837 F.2d 1358 (5th Cir. 1988)
Parole Commission is bound by its own regulations unless it can show good cause for deviating from them.

<u>Cook v. Tx D.O.C. Justice Planning Dept.</u>, 37 F.3d 166 (5th Cir. 1994)
1. Section 1983 action is appropriate remedy for recovering damages resulting from illegal administrative procedures.
2. Section 1983 is appropriate legal vehicle to attack unconstitutional parole procedures.
3. Prior convictions held void by Court of Appeals in prior decision should not be considered by parole board in determining parole eligibility of prisoner.

<u>DeWitt v. Ventetoulo</u>, 6 F.3d 32 (1st Cir. 1993)
State is not obliged by Constitution to parole its prisoners, but having done so, it is obliged to afford them due process when it revokes parole.

<u>Fernandez v. US</u>, 941 F.2d 1488 (11th Cir. 1991)
Actions of parole commission may be challenged only in habeas corpus proceedings initiated pursuant to §2241 in district in which individual is incarcerated.

Green v. ARN, 839 F.2d 300 (6th Cir. 1988)
Petitioners release from parole did not moot her habeas corpus action, considering the collateral consequences which might flow from her criminal conviction.

Maynard v. Havenstrite, 727 F.2d 439 (5th Cir. 1984)
Evans v. Dillahunty, 711 F.2d 828 (8th Cir. 1983)
Probation officers are absolutely immune for erroneous PSI reports. The Commissioner is cloaked with the same immunity.

Minnesota v. Murphy, 465 US 420, 79 L.Ed.2d 409, 104 S.Ct. 1136 (1984)
A probationer confronted with incriminating questions at a meeting with his probation officer ordinarily will have no problem effectively claiming the privilege against self-incrimination at the time disclosures are requested.

Moody v. Daggett, 429 US 78, 50 L.Ed.2d 236, 97 S.Ct. 274 (1976)
A parolees liberty involves significant values protected by the due process clauses of the Fifth and Fourteenth Amendments.

Note: Supervised release is not mandatory in all instances. A judge may depart from the guidelines for of the rational preparing listed in Title 18 USC. 3553B and 3583.
May" is used in the statutory language while the language of the guidelines, is "shall" is mandatory.

O'Bremski v. Maass, 915 F.2d 418 (9th Cir. 1990)
State habeas corpus petitioner was entitled to have his release date considered by a parole board that was free from bias or prejudice.

Patten v. North Dakota Parole Board, 783 F.2d 140 (8th Cir. 1986)
State statutes, rules, and regulations can create a constitutionally protected liberty interest in parole.

Perry v. US Parole Comm'n, 831 F.2d 811 (8th Cir. 1987)

Gagnon v. Scarpelli, 411 US 778, 46 L.Ed.2d 656, 94 S.Ct. 1756 (1973)

Morrissey v. Brewer, 408 US 471, 33 L.Ed.2d 484, 92 S.Ct. 2593 (1972)

At a parole revocation hearing a probationer is entitled to less than the full panoply of due process rights accorded a defendant at a criminal trial. 16. The minimum requirement of due process includes, inter alia, written notice of the claimed violations of parole.

Powell v. Ducharme, 998 F.2d 710 (9th Cir. 1993)

Once inmate serving life sentence serves discretionary minimum term set by Indeterminate Sentence Review Board, inmate must be considered for parole at expiration of that term.

State v. Pima Co. Adult Probation Dept., 147 Ariz. 146, 708 P.2d -1337 (1985)
A.R.S. 12-251

Probation officers are officers, agents and employees of the judicial department of the state.

State v. Wagstaff, 164 Ariz. 485, 794 P.2d 118 Defendant was convicted in the Superior Court, Maricopa County, Daniel E. Nastro, J., No. CR-152707, of child molestation. Defendant appealed and filed petition for review of denial of post-conviction motion. The Court of Appeals, 161 Ariz. 66, 775 P.2d 1130, affirmed conviction, modified sentence and granted petition for review. The Supreme Court, Gordon, C.J., held that: (1) statute providing for mandatory lifetime parole and conviction for dangerous crime against children did not provide penalty for violation of parole which violated separation of powers, and (2) discretionary sentence of lifetime parole for second-degree offenders without clear sanctions violated separation of powers. Judgment of Court of Appeal approved as modified; sentence imposing lifetime parole vacated.

Taylor v. US Parole Commission, 734 F.2d 1152 (6th Cir. 1984)

The parole commission abused its discretion in ruling that single piece of hearsay evidence established by preponderance of evidence that parolee had engaged in new criminal conduct.

US v. Barth, 899 F.2d 199 (2nd Cir. 1990)
Probation officer should commit oral modifications to condition of probation to writing.

US v. Copeland, 20 F.3d 412 (11th Cir. 1994)
Same protections granted those facing revocation of parole are required for those facing revocation of supervised release.

US v. Granderson, 511 US, 127 L.Ed.2d 611, 114 S.Ct. (1994)
Duration of imprisonment following probation revocation for drug possession held to be governed by originally applicable Federal Sentencing Guidelines imprisonment range, rather than by term of probation.

US v. Lamberti, 847 F.2d 1531 (11th Cir. 1988)
Statements made by parolee during interrogation to his parole officer without prior administration of Miranda warnings are admissible at trial.

US v. McCormick, 54 F.3d 214 (5th Cir. 1995)
Court must expressly find that there is "good cause" to deny defendant right to confront and cross-examine adverse witness in parole revocation hearing.

US v. Smith, 953 F.2d 1060 (7th Cir. 1992)
Constitutional power of the President to grant reprieves and pardons for offenses against the United States entails an unreviewable power to reduce a sentence imposed by a court.

US v. Stevens, 986 F.2d 283 (8th Cir. 1993)
Decisions to revoke probation and imprison person who is attempting to make his victims whole should not be taken lightly.

US v. Stites, 56 F3d 1020 (9th Cir. 1995)
Cooperation with probation officer is not required of defendant at peril of increased imprisonment.

US v. Tippens, 39 F.3d 88 (5th Cir. 1994)

Persons on supervised release have procedural due process rights in context of revocation hearings.

White v. White, 925 F.2d 287 (9th Cir. 1991)

Parolee has right to confront and cross-examine adverse witnesses at parole revocation hearing.

Young v. Kann, 926 F.2d 1396 (3rd Cir. 1991)

Supt. Massachusetts Corr. Inst. v. Hill, 472 US 445, 86 L.Ed.2d 356. 105 S.Ct. 2768 (1985)

Prisoner has constitutionally protected liberty interest in good time credit.

Perjured Testimony

ARS 13-2702 Perjury: Classification;
Purpose The function of the perjury statute is to protect the administration of government from the debilitating effects of false testimony. See also: Franzi v. Superior Court ex rel. County of Pima, 139 Ariz. 556, 679 P.2d 1043 (1984)

Blacks Law Dictionary: Crimen Falsi A term derived from common-law where perjured testimony is considered null and void.

Bonin v. Calderon, 59 F.3d 815, 844 (9th Cir 1995)
If the prosecutor knowingly uses perjured testimony or knowingly fails to disclose a testimony is false, the conviction must be set aside if there is any reasonable likelihood that the false testimony could have affected the jury verdict.

Brown v. Wainwright, (1986 CALL FLA) 785 F.2d 1457
Prosecution violated due process clause when it knowingly allowed material testimony to be introduced at trial, failed to step forward and make falsity known, and knowingly exploited false testimony in closing arguments.

State v. Lada Bouche, (1985) 146 VT 279, 502 A.2d 852
Conviction obtained through states knowing use of false evidence, either solicited by state or allowed to go uncorrected, violates fourteenth amendment of US Constitution.

Plain Error

F.R.Cr.P. Rule 52(b)
Plain error or defects affecting substantial rights may be noticed although they were not brought to the attention of the court.

Note: The Supreme Court has characterized plain error as error, deviation from a legal rule is "error" unless the rule has been waived.

<u>Johnson v. US</u>, 520 US 461, 465 (1997)
Failure to assert right usually results in forfeiture, but plain error rule mitigates. The plain error doctrine recognizes that where a defendant's substantial personal rights are at stake, the rule forfeiture should been slightly if necessary to prevent a grave injustice.

<u>State v. Garcia-Contreras</u>, 191 Ariz. 144, 953 P.2d 536
Defendant was convicted by jury upon retrial in the Superior Court, Maricopa County, No. CR 91-02873, Stephen A. Gerst, J., of child molestation charges. Defendant appealed. Following remand, the Court of Appeals affirmed convictions. Granting petition for review, the Supreme Court, Zlaket, C.J., held that: (1) defendant's choice not to be present at jury selection, after trial court denied request for continuance to allow defendant's civilian clothing to arrive, was not voluntary and did not constitute waiver of right to be present; (2) denial of continuance was abuse of discretion; and (3) error in denying continuance was structural error that was not subject to harmless error review. Convictions reversed; case remanded for new trial.

<u>US v. Battle</u>, 289 F.3d 661, 664-65 (10th Cir. 2002)
Plain error review because double jeopardy and other sentencing objections not raised by defendant before trial court.

<u>US v. Clarke</u>, 227 F.3d 874, 884 (7th Cir. 2000)
Must look at records as a whole to determine whether prosecutor's misconduct denied defendant the fair trial.

US v. Fuchs, 218 F.3d 957 (9th Cir. 2000)
A trial court commits plain error when (1) there is error, (2) that is plain, and (3) the error affects substantial rights.

US v. Joyner, 191 F.3d 47, 55 (1st Cir. 1999)
Plain error review of effect of prosecutor's remarks on jury must be reviewed in light of the entire record.

US v. Leo-Maldonado, 302 F.3d 1061, 1064 (9th Cir. 2002)
An appellate court may review for plain error if an objection is on specific. Review of untimely objection to sufficiency of indictment limited to plain error review.

US v. Mendoza-Paz, 286 F.3d 1104, 1113 (9th Cir. 2002)
Plain error review because defendant failed to object to alleged improper lay opinion testimony at trial.

US v. Olano, 507 US 725, 732 (1993)
Deviation from a legal rule is error unless the rule has been waived. Appellate courts plain error review is discretionary, and should be exercised only if it "seriously affects the fairness, integrity or public reputation of judicial proceedings".

US v. Rogers, 126 F.3d 655, 658 (5th Cir. 1997)
Because impermissible in court identification allowed, error will receive increased scrutiny.

US v. Schwayder, 312 F.3d 1109, 1120 (9th Cir. 2002)
When defendant fails to raise objection at trial, courts should take great care in exercising their discretion to reverse for plain error.

US v. Sesay, 313 F.3d 591, 596 (D.C. Cir. 2002)
Plain error review because defendant failed to renew request to pursue line of questioning of witness that had been foreclosed by a pre-trial ruling.

US v. Spinner, 152 F.3d 950, 956 (D.C. Cir. 1998)
Plain error because government failed to present any evidence on an essential element of crime.

US v. Syme, 276 F.3d 131, 154 (3rd Cir. 2002)
Prejudice presumed in cases of constructive amendment to indictment.

US v. Tyler, 281 F.3d 84,100 (3rd Cir. 2002)
Plain error review because defendant failed to raise confrontation clause challenge at trial.

US v. Velarde-Gomez, 224 F.3d 1062, 1069 (9th Cir. 2000)
Although specific objections are required to preserve an issue on appeal, a facially vague objection can be sufficient to preserve a constitutional error.

US v. Wolfe, 245 F.3d 257, 261 (3rd Cir. 2001)
A court's deviation from a legal rule constitutes error. A court's deviation from a legal rule constitutes error.

Plea Agreement

<u>Bonvillain v. Blackburn</u>, 785 F.2d 545 (5tb Cir. 1986)
Unkept plea bargain is basis for grant of habeas relief if petitioner can prove existence of allegedly broken plea.

<u>Gonzalez v. US</u>, 33 FM 1047 (9th Cir. 1994)
<u>Toro v. Fairman</u>, 940 F.2d 1065 (7th Cir. 1991)
Strickland standard for ineffective assistance of counsel claims extends to assistance with guilty pleas.

<u>Grabowski v. Jackson County Public Defender's Office</u>, 47 F.3d 1386 (5th Cir. 1995)
To be valid, guilty plea must be knowingly, intelligently and voluntarily entered; defendant must be shown to understand nature of charges and consequences of plea.

<u>Margalli - Olvera v. I.N.S.</u>, 43 F.3d 345 (8th Cir. 1994)
1. Plea agreements are contractual in nature and are interpreted according to general contract principles. 2. When government promises in plea agreement to remain silent or to refrain from making recommendation, its failure to do so is a breach of plea agreement.

Note: Fully ninety percent of the pleas entered into each year are "blind pleas" (non-binding, open guilty pleas). However, it is possible avoid this death trap by having your attorney get together with the judge and the prosecutor and enter into a BINDING Sentencing Agreement. See Federal Rule of Criminal Procedure 119e (1) (C). (Authors Note: See how dishonest they are? A plea agreement is a contract between you and the state. Who ever heard of a contract containing requirements the state doesn't have to abide by simply because they don't want to? The courts and their officers don't tell people this walking in. Only one word can be used to describe these conditions. FRAUD! <u>Don't get suckered into a trick bag!</u>)

Note: Incarcerated individuals who are citizens of other countries can apply for a transfer to that country. Due to The onerous sentences given out in this country there is an excellent chance they will serve much less of their sentence in that country.

Pardue v. Burton, 26 F.3d 1093 (11th Cir. 1994)
Claim that plea was not knowing and voluntary because defendant did not know of his full pleading alternatives may not be subject to harmless error analysis.

US v. Anderson, 970 F.2d 602 (9th Cir. 1992) If district court finds that government breached plea agreement, defendant will be entitled to appropriate relief, and district court may, in its discretion, grant defendant option of withdrawing his plea and re-pleading or proceeding to trial.

US v. Asset, 990 F.2d 208 (5th Cir. 1993)
Government is not permitted to breach its part of plea agreement in such a way that frustrates defendant*s reasonable expectations under plea agreement.

US v. Baldacchino, 762 F.2d 170 (1st Cir. 1985)
Santobello v. New York, 404 US 257, 30 L.Ed.2d 427, 92 S.Ct. 495 (1971)
The Supreme Court has recognized that plea bargain agreements must be attended by safeguards to insure the defendant what is reasonably due in the circumstances.

US v. Clark, 55 F.3d 9 (1st Cir. 1995)
1. Courts are guided in interpreting plea agreements by general principles of contract law. 2. If specific performance is sufficient remedy for government's breach of plea agreement defendant must be resentenced by different judge.

US v. Corbitt, 996 F.2d 1132 (11th Cir. 1993)
Judicial participation in plea negotiations is plain error, and defendant need not show actual prejudice.

US v. Cornelius, 999 F.2d 1293 (8th Cir. 1993)
Before guilty plea is entered, defendant must explicitly waive privilege against self-incrimination, right to jury trial and right to confront one's accusers.

US v. De La Fuente, 8 F.3d 1333 (9th Cir. 1993)
1. Government's due process violation by breaching plea agreement that required motion for sentence below mandatory minimum because of defendant's substantial assistance could be remedied by sentence below statutory minimum; remedy was not withdrawal of plea. 2. Breach of plea agreement implicates constitutional guarantee of due process.

US v. Field, 39 F.3d 15 (1st Cir. 1994)
Guilty plea cannot be truly voluntary unless defendant possesses understanding of the law in relation to the facts.

US v. Gaev, 24 F.3d 473 (3rd Cir, 1994)
Plea agreement of conspirators cannot be used as evidence of a defendant's guilt.

US v. Harlan, 35 F.3d 176 (5th Cir. 1994)
North Carolina v. Alford, 400 US 25, 27 L.Ed.2d 162, 91 S.Ct. 160 (1970)
Defendant entering "Alford Plea' pleads guilty, but affirmatively protests his factual innocence to charged offense.

US v. Jones, (D.C. Cir. 1995)
When prosecutor secures plea with promise, promise must be fulfilled.

US v. Laliberte, 25 F.3d 10 (1st Cir. 1994)
Generally, the longer defendant waits before bringing motion to withdraw guilty plea, more forceful his or her reasons in support of withdrawal must be.

US v. Maddox, 48 F.3d 555 (D.C. Cir. 1995)
1. Fact that it is left to district court's discretion whether to accept or reject guilty plea does not allow court to reject plea on arbitrary basis. 2. District court's exercise of discretion in deciding whether to accept or reject guilty plea is not unfettered. 3. Trial judge must provide reasoned exercise of discretion in order to justify rejecting guilty plea which has been agreed to by prosecution and defense.

US v. Premachandra, 32 F.3d 346 (8th Cir. 1994)
Incompetent defendant cannot make a valid guilty plea.

US v. Savage, 978 F.2d 1136 (9th Cir. 1992)
Neither defendant nor government is bound by plea agreement until approved by the court.

US v. Skinner, 25 F.3d 1314 (6th Cir. 1994)
In interpreting plea agreement government is to be held to literal terms of agreement and, ordinarily, must bear responsibility for any lack of clarity.

US v. Traynoff, 53 F.3d 168 (7th Cir. 1995)
Government must fulfill agreements that reasonably cause criminal defendants to take damaging actions or to plead guilty.

US v. Vega, 11 F.3d 309 (2nd Cir. 1993)
District court may permit withdrawal of guilty plea prior to sentencing upon showing by defendant of any fair and just reason.

US v. Velasco, 953 F.2d 1467 (7th Cir. 1992)
Agreement between government and defendant are taken very seriously by the court and government must scrupulously perform and keep any agreement it makes.

US v. Velez, 1 F.3d 386 (6th Cir. 1993)
Plea agreement entered into between government and defendant is not binding on district court upon sentencing.

US v. Walsh, 7 F.3d 1064 (1st Cir. 1993)
Court may accept a guilty plea even when defendant denies guilt but thinks plea would be to his advantage.

US v. Wright, 43 F.3d 491 (10th Cir. 1994)

Smith v. US, 876 F.2d 655 (8th Cir. 1989)

In pleading guilty, defendant waives all challenges to prosecution except those related to jurisdiction.

Presence of the Accused

F.R.Cr.P. Rule 43
(a) The defendant's right to be present has been codified in rule 43 of the federal rule of criminal procedure, which provides: the defendant shall be present at the arraignment, at the time of the plea, at every stage of the trial including the impaneling of the jury and the return of the verdict, and at the imposition of sentence.

A.R.Cr.P. Rule 26.6 (d) (2)
Paragraph (d) (2) precluded statements made by defendant during preparation of a pre-sentence report in one case from being admitted at trial in any later unrelated case.

Arnett v. Ricketts, et al., respondent, 665 F.Supp. 1437, 1987 US Dist. Lexis 7103
After he was found guilty of first-degree murder, Arnett was interviewed by a probation officer, Gerald Snell, for the purpose of preparing a pre-sentence report. The probation officer did not inform Arnett of his constitutional right to remain silent and have the assistance of an attorney, or that his answers could be considered by the trial judge in deciding an appropriate sentence.

Cohen v. Senkowski, 290 F.3d 485, 489 (2nd Cir. 2002)
Prescreening of prospective jurors is a material stage of trial at which the defendant has a constitutional right to be present.

Diaz v. US, 223 US 442, 445-55 (1912)
Defendant in felony case has right to attend all stages of trial from impaneling of jury to delivery of verdict.

Estelle v. Smith, 451 US 454 (1981)
The court may not, during the capital sentencing hearing, and when making the sentence determination, rely upon statements obtained through the custodial presentation interview without the aid of counsel.

Hoffman v. Arave, 236 F.3d 523, 540-41 (9th Cir. 2001)

Although defendant was denied right to counsel during pre-sentence interview, a critical stage of proceeding, error is subject to harmless error review. The court concluded that under Estelle, the Fifth Amendment applied to inculpatory statements made during a pre-sentence interview with a probation officer. The state's reliance on US v. Benlian, 63 F.3d 824 (9th Cir. 1995) for the proposition that any pre-sentence interview in a capital case is not a critical stage is equally unavailing. In Benlian we reiterated our adherence to the Bauman v. US, 692 F.2d 565 (9th Cir. 1982) holding in a non-capital case where the defendant waived the right to counsel. See: Benlian, 63 F.3d at 827.

Jones v. Cardwell, 686 F.2d 754,756 (9th Cir. 1982)

The reasoning that underlies the decision in Estelle supports application of the Fifth Amendment privilege to the sentencing procedure in the instant case.

Powell v. Alabama, 287 US 45 (1932)

It is central in the principle of Powell v. Alabama that in addition to counsel's presence at trial, the accused is guaranteed that he need not stand alone against the state at any stage of the prosecution, formal or informal, in court or out, where counsels absence might irrigate from the accused's right to a fair trial.

Rice v. Wood, 44 F.3d 1396 (9th Cir. 1995)

Criminal defendant charged with felony has right to be present at every stage of his trial.

State v. Gray, (1977, Minn.) 256 NW.2d 74

Accused has constitutionally protected right, under fourteenth amendment to be present, after indictment, at every critical stage in criminal proceedings; before criminal proceeding can take place in absence of accused, it must be clear that the defendant himself is intentionally abandoning known right; unless accused has effectively waived right to be present, reversal of conviction is required unless and his absence was not prejudicial beyond reasonable doubt; defendants absence from pre-trial suppression hearing was violation of due process clause of the fourteenth amendment.

US v. Ash, 413 US 300 (1973)

The court redefined in modified its (critical stage) analysis. According to the court, the (core purpose) of the guarantee of counsel is to assure assistance at trial (when the accused was confronted with both the intricacies of the law and the advocacy of the public prosecutor.) but assistance would be less than meaningful in the light of developments in criminal investigation and procedure if it is limited to formal trial itself; therefore counsel is compelled at pre-trial events that might appropriately be considered to be part of the trial itself.

US v. Herrerra-Figuerara, 918 F.2d 1430 (9th Cir. 1991)

We exercised our supervisory power to require that probation officers permit defense attorneys to accompany defendants in all pre-sentence interviews.

US v. Novaton, 274 F.3d 968, 998 (11th Cir. 2001)

Confrontation clause violated when critical stage of trial conducted while defendant involuntarily absent.

Pre-Sentence Report

F.R.Cr.P Rule 18 USC. §3552(d)
Requires that the Pre-sentence Interview (PSI) be disclosed to a defendant at least 10 days prior to the date set for sentencing.

Hoffman v. Arave, 236 F.3d 523, 540-41 (9th CIR 2001)
Although defendant was denied right to counsel during pre-sentence interview, a critical stage of proceedings, error is subject to harmless review.

James Allan Arnett v. James R. Ricketts, 665 F.SUPP. 1437 (1987 US DIST) LEX157103
After he was found guilty of 1st degree murder Arnett was interviewed by a probation officer, Gerald Snell. The probation officer did not inform him of his constitutional right to remain silent and to have an attorney present or that his answers could be considered by the trial judge in deciding an appropriate sentence.

Note: A defendant has an equal right to prepare and present a pre-sentence report to the judge in a criminal case. Defendant's Pre-sentence Report (P.S.R.) may be prepared by various and sundry legal aid groups throughout the country and usually have a very positive effect at a defendant's sentencing.

US Dept. Of Justice v. Julian, 486 US 1, 100 IL.Ed.2d 1, 108 S.Ct. 1606 (1988)
P.S.I. reports are usually available to a criminal defendant under the Freedom of Information Act.

US v. Abanatha, 999 F.2d 1246 (8th Cir. 1993)
Immunized information about defendants prior involvement in drug dealing should not have been included in defendants pre-sentence report.

US v. Arefi, 847 F.2d 1003 (2nd Cir. 1988)
Even if a misstatement in a sentencing report is "harmless" and does not require re-sentencing. It must still be corrected or clarified.

US v. Blythe, 944 F.2d 356 (7th Cir. 1991) 8.1. Sentencing Judge is not bound by pre-sentence reports recommendations concerning sentence. Defendant may waive right to receive pre-sentence report at least ten days prior to date set for sentencing by failing to assert his rights at the appropriate time.

US v. Herrera-Figuerara, 918 F.2d 1430 (9th CIR. 1991)
We exercise our supervisory power to require that probation officers permit defense attorneys to accompany defendants in all pre-sentence interviews.

US v. Huckaby, 43 F.3d 135 (5th Cir. 1995)
There is a general presumption that courts will not grant third parties access to pre-sentence investigation reports.

US v. Kerley, 838 F.2d 932 (7th Cir. 1988)
US v. Benson, 836 F.2d 1133 (8th Cir. 1988)
1. Due process is violated when information on which defendant is sentenced is materially untrue or is misinformation. 2. Government must prove facts in pre-sentencing report by preponderance of evidence.

US v. Manotas - Mejia, 824 F.2d 360 (5th Cir. 1987)
Failure of district court to correct any factual inaccuracy in pre-sentence investigation report may be raised for first time on appeal and requires re-sentencing.

US v. Scam, 716 F.2d 463 (7th Cir. 1983)
Trial court which relies on confidential pre-sentence report in sentencing a defendant should state in record whether it is relying on undisclosed information and should provide on the record a summary of information if it is so relying.

US v. Streeter, 907 F.2d 781 (8th Cir. 1990)
Confrontation clause of Sixth Amendment applies at evidentiary hearing regarding disputed facts in pre-sentence report.

Preservation of Rights for Review

<u>Lawson v. Borg</u>, 60 F.3d 608, 612-613 (9th Cir 1995)
State court conclusion that in error was harmless is not a finding of fact entitled to the presumption of correctness.

Note: If a party fails to preserve in issue raised in a pre-trial motion in limine by contemperance objection at trial, an appellate court may nonetheless hear the issue under certain circumstances.

<u>State v. McCann</u>, 200 Ariz. 27, 21 P.3d 845 (2001)
This state asks us to reconsider the holding , asserting that the US Supreme Court overturned the basis for our , <u>State v. Ragan</u>, 103 Ariz. 287, 440 P.2d 907(1965) and <u>State v. Renaud</u>, 108 Ariz. 417, 418, 499 P.2d 712, decision in <u>Parke v. Raley</u>, 506 US 20, 113 S. Ct. 517, 121 L.Ed.2d 391(1992). We agree and hold that ever bumble presumption of regularity attaches to prior convictions used to enhance a sentence or as an element of crime. After the courts Parke decision, many of our sister jurisdictions adopted the presumption of regularity for prior convictions used to enhance sentences or as balance of a crime. For instance in <u>Massachusetts v. Lopez</u>, 426 Mass. 657, 690 N.E.2d 809, 814(1998), the Massachusetts Supreme Court said : many other states have specifically relied on the Parke decision to reject collateral ** 848 challenges too long closed convictions by plea where sentencing enhancements involved. We conclude that a collateral challenge, like the defendant's, to a prior conviction by guilty plea, if the challenge is to advance and all, it must be accomplished by sufficient credible and reliable evidence to rebut a presumption that the prior conviction was valid. If a defendant meets this burden, then an evidentiary hearing may be warranted at which the burden will be honored by the Commonwealth to show that the defendant's plea proceedings were conducted anyway that protected his constitutional rights.

<u>US v. Joost</u>, 133 F.3d 125, 129 (1st Cir. 1998)
Motion in Limine to have prior convictions excluded not sufficient to preserve issue for appeal in absence of further objection.

US v. McNeil, 184 F.3d 770, 7 76-77 (8th Cir. 1999)

Motion in the limine to exclude evidence is not sufficient to preserve issue for appeal.

US v. Williams, 81 F.3d 1321, 1325 (4th Cir. 1996)

Defendant's motion in limine sufficient to preserve objection when defendant clearly identified ruling sought and trial court ruled upon motion. vacated in part, 110 F.3d 62 (4th Cir. 1997)

Prison Administration

Barfield v. Brierton, 883 F.2d 923 (11th Cir. 1989)

Olim v. Wakinekona, 461 US 238, 75 L.Ed.2d 813, 103 S.Ct. 1741 (1983)

Montayne v. Haymes, 427 US 236, 49 L.Ed.2d 466, 96 S.Ct. 2543 (1976)

Inmates usually possess no constitutional right to be housed at one prison instead of another.

Battle v. Anderson, 447 F.Supp 516 (S.D. New York 1977)

Wolfish v. Levi, 439 F.Supp 114 (S.D. New York 1977)

People are sent to prison AS punishment not FOR punishment.

Beard v. Livesay, 798 F.2d 984 (5th Cir. 1986)

Meachum v. Fano, 427 US 215, 49 L.Ed.2d 451, 96 S.Ct. 2532 (1976)

Where substantive limitations have in fact been placed on discretion of prison officials in classifying inmate's security status, protectable liberty interest has been created.

Bennett v. Arkansas, 485 US 395. 99 L.Ed.2d 455, 108 S.Ct. 1104 (1988)

Seizure of federal Social Security benefits to help defray cost of maintaining state prison system held to conflict with federal law.

Block v. Rutherford, 468 US 576, 82 L.Ed.2d 438, 104 S.Ct. 3227 (1984)

Lack of contact visits does not violate an inmates constitutional rights.

Caldwell v. Miller, 790 F.2d 589 (7th Cir. 1986)

Payne v. Block, 714 F.2d 1510 (11th Cir. 1984)

An inmate has the right to expect prison officials to follow its policies and regulations.

Cochrane v. Quattrocchi, 949 F.2d 11 (1st Cir. 1991)

Prison visitor retains Fourth Amendment right to be free from unreasonable searches and seizures.

Falcon v. Us Bureau Of Prisons, 52 F.3d 137 (7th Cir. 1995)
Prisoner who seeks quantum change in level of confinement must use writ of habeas corpus, while prisoner who seeks anything else must use civil rights action.

Giano v. Senkowski, 54 F.3d 1050 (2nd Cir. 1995)
Prison walls are not a barrier separating inmates from protections of Constitution.

Griffin v. Lombardi, 946 F.2d 604 (8th Cir. 1991)
Turner v. Safley, 482 US 78. 96 L.Ed.2d 64, 107 S.Ct. 2254 (1987)
Prison officials must "put forward" legitimate governmental interest to justify regulation impinging on constitutional right to inmates and must provide evidence that interest proffered is reason why regulation is adopted or enforced.

Hall v. Lombardi, 996 F.2d 954 (8th Cir. 1993)
When prison regulations contain language of mandatory nature (shall, will. must) they are interpreted as creating a protectable liberty interest.

Hazen v. Reagen, 16 F.3d 921 (8th Cir. 1994)
It is impermissible to transfer inmate in retaliation for exercise of constitutional right.

Helling v. McKinney, 509 US 1125 L.Ed.2d 22, 113 S.Ct. (1993)
Health risk allegedly posed by prison personnel's exposure of inmate to environmental tobacco smoke held to form proper basis of claim for relief under federal constitutions Eighth Amendment.

Holloway v. Hornsby, 23 F.3d 944 (5th Cir. 1994)
Complaints about validity of incarceration or treatment accorded inmates are entitled to timely and meaningful consideration.

Howard v. State, 237 Ariz. p. 203, 204 (1925)
When therefore, the superintendent of the prison receives the commitment which is only authorized for detaining any man within that prison, he may only do what that commitment orders him, to wit, receive and safely keep the defendant for the time

specified therein. If, without legal justification, he does more than is necessary to so safely keep him, he is violating the inmate's constitutional rights.

Hudson v. Palmer, 468 US 517, 82I L.Ed.2d 393, 104 S.Ct. 3194 (1984)
The Fourth Amendment has no applicability to the prison cell.

Johnson v. Hay, 931 F.2d 456, 461 (8th Cir. 1991)
Hunter v. Bryant, 502 US 224, 228 (1991) (per curiam)
Government official not required to guess, at peril, future development of constitutional doctrine, and cannot be held liable or violation of extremely abstract rights.

Jones v. Diamond, 636 F.2d 1364 (5th Cir. 1981), cert denied,453 US 950, 102 S.Ct. 27, 69 L.Ed.2d 1033 (1981)
Confinement of pre-trial detainees with convicted persons is unconstitutional, maintaining jail security or unless physical facilities do not permit operation.

LeMaire v. Maass, 2 F.3d 851 (9th Cir. 1993)
1. Ordinarily, lack of outside exercise for extended periods for inmates is sufficiently serious deprivation and thus meets requisite harm necessary to satisfy objective test for Eighth Amendment violation.
2. Injunction requiring prison to install intercom and leave open door of quiet cells in disciplinary segregation unit (DSU) in order to allow inmates to summon guards for assistance could be applied to all inmates, even those with no serious health problems; previously health inmate may have a medical emergency or be injured in a fall or accident.

Long v. Norris, 929 F.2d 1111, 1115 (6th Cir. 1990)
Public officials are presumed to be aware of the law governing their conduct. Public officials cannot rely on ignorance of even most esoteric aspects of law to avoid liability.

Lucero v. Gunter, 52 F.3d 874 (10th Cir. 1995)
Although random urine testing of inmates does not violate Fourth Amendment, procedures for selecting inmates for testing must be truly random; procedures are not random if field officers have discretion to select targets with no limiting guidelines.

Mackey v. Dyke, 29 F.3d 1086 (6th Cir. 1994)
Howard v. Grinage, 6 F.3d 410 (6th Cir. 1993)
Prisoner had clearly established right to be released from segregation after he no longer qualified for confinement in administrative segregation.

McCabe v. Arave, 827 F.2d 634 (9th Cir. 1987)
Prison regulation that restricted inmates to ten books or to ten books and ten magazines violated prisoners' First Amendment rights.

McGuckin v. Smith, 974 F.2d 1050
State prisoner brought pro se civil rights action against several prison medical authorities and private orthopedic specialist doing consulting work for state Department of Corrections. The United States District Court for the District of Arizona, Alfredo C. Marquez, J., dismissed without prejudice claims against certain defendants and granted summary judgment in favor of other defendants. Prisoner appealed. The Court of Appeals, Reinhardt, Circuit Judge, held that: (1) dismissal without prejudice of certain defendants was appealable "final decision"; (2) District Court acted improperly by failing to notify prisoner of asserted deficiencies in complaint before dismissing his claims against one defendant or to permit prisoner to amend complaint to rectify omissions; (3) District Court should not have dismissed "misnamed" defendant who actually existed, especially as prisoner showed good cause for failing to serve that defendant within time prescribed by civil rule; and (4) prison doctor and specialist did not act with deliberate indifference to prisoner's serious medical needs. Affirmed in part, reversed in part, and remanded.

Meachum v. Fano, 427 US 215, 49 L.Ed.2d 451, 96 S.Ct. 2532 (1976)
The court has the right to determine whether an inmate is being deprived of a "State Created Right" or "Liberty Interest" granted him by a rule, statute, or regulation promulgated by the government.

Miller v. Bensen, 51 F.3d 166 (8th Cir. 1995)
Inmate had no right to prison employment under state law, and thus no constitutionally protected property interest in prison employment.

Norman v. Taylor, 9 F.3d 1078 (4th Cir. 1993)
Lack of serious injury is not fatal to Eighth Amendment excessive force claim under §1983 by prison inmate.

Moyo v. Gomez, 40 F.3d 982 (9th Cir. 1994)
Prison inmates can be "employees" for purposes of Title VII in some circumstances.

Note: Federal prisoners who self-surrender at their designated prisons, versus those taken into custody along the judicial process, automatically receive preferential consideration when applying for furloughs and custody level classifications. See B.O.P. Program Statement 5100 and Form BP 15

Pell v. Procunier, 417 US 817, 41 L.Ed.2d 495, 94 S.Ct. 2800 (1974)
Procunier v. Martinez, 416 US 396, 40 L.Ed.2d 224, 94 S.Ct. 1800 (1974)
The general public has the right to associate with a prisoner.

Purvis v. Ponte, 929 F.2d 822 (1st Cir. 1991)
Prison officials have duty under both the Eighth and Fourteenth Amendments to protect prisoners from violence at hands of other prisoners.

Ramos v. Lamm, 639 F.2d 559 (10th Cir. 1980)
Sweet v. South Carolina Dept. of Corrections, 519 F.2d 854 (4th 1975)
Inmates must be furnished materials for personal hygiene and cell cleaning.

Robins v. Doe, 994 F.Supp. 214 (S.D. N.Y. 1998)

Dolphin v. Manson, 626 F.Supp. 229 (D. Conn. 1986)

Holding that the prolonged confinement of pre-trial detainees in a facility statutorily designated for convicted persons raises the specter of a constitutional violation.

Ruiz v. Estelle, 679 F.2d 1115 (5th Cir. 1982)

Although there are no constitutionally mandated minimums for space requirements per inmate, 40 square feet per inmate would be minimum recommended.

Schroeder v. McDonald, 41 F.3d 1272 (9th Cir. 1994)

Inmate has sufficient liberty interest in confinement at minimum security facility to trigger due process protection when he was transferred to medium security facility; prison regulations spoke in mandatory terms about how classification of prisoners would be conducted.

Slone v. Herman, (1993, CA Mo.) 983 F.2d 107, reh. denied, (CA8) 1993 US App. LEXIS 1984

Prison inmate's liberty interest was violated in violation of two processes when prison officials failed to release him after court order suspending inmates sentence had become final, regardless of whether officials agreed with order.

Stone v. City Of San Francisco, 968 F.2d 850 (9th Cir. 1992)

In prison reform litigation courts must be careful to take into account interests of state and local authorities. However, principles of restraint dissolve when federal constitutional rights have been violated.

Weaver v. Graham, 450 US 24, 101 S.Ct. 960

State prisoner sought writ of habeas corpus challenging application to him of change in state law with respect to good time or gain time credits. The Supreme Court of Florida, 376 So.2d 855, denied the application and certiorari was granted. The Supreme Court, Justice Marshall, held that: (1) for a criminal or penal law to be ex post facto, it must be retrospective and it must disadvantage the offender affected by it; (2) the effect, not the form, of the law, determines whether to ex post facto; (3) fact that statute reducing good time credits was enacted in conjunction

155

with other statutes providing additional bases for credits against sentence did not save it from an ex post facto challenge; and (4) as applied to a prisoner whose crime was committed before its effective date, the statute reducing the amount of good time credit violated the ex post facto clause. Reversed and remanded.

Wishon v. Gammon, 978 F.2d 446 (8th Cir. 1992)
Prisoners have a right to nutritionally adequate food.

Young v. Quinlan, 960 F.2d 351 (3rd Cir. 1992) While prison administration may punish it may not do so in a manner that threatens physical and mental health of prisoners.

Wildon v. Seiter, 501 US 294, 111 S.Ct. 2321 Prisoners brought action against prison officials alleging cruel and unusual punishment. The United States District Court for the Southern District of Ohio, James L. Graham, J., granted officials' motion for summary judgment and prisoners appealed. The Court of Appeals for the Sixth Circuit, 893 F.2d 861, affirmed. Certiorari was granted. The Supreme Court, Justice Scalia, held that prisoners claiming that conditions of confinement constituted cruel and unusual punishment were required to show deliberate indifference on part of prison officials. Vacated and remanded.

Pro Se

Anderson v. US, 948 F.2d 704 (11th Cir. 1991)
Defendant who seeks post-conviction relief has statutory right to proceed pro se.

Baker v. Cuomo, 58 F.3d 814 (2nd Cir. 1995)
Curtis v. Bembenek, 48 F.3d 281 (7th Cir. 1995)
In reviewing pro se complaint, Court of Appeals must employ standards less stringent than if complaint was drafted by counsel.

Burt v. Hennessey, 929 F.2d 457 (9th Cir. 1991)
Pro se litigant was entitled to recover actual costs reasonably incurred in prosecuting a civil action (complicated but informative).

Caldwell v. Amend, 30 F.3d 1199 (9th Cir. 1994)
Houston v. Lack, 487 US 266, 101 L.Ed.2d 245, 108 S.Ct. 2379 (1988)
Prisoner's pro se motion for judgement N.O.V. was deemed filed on date motion was placed in prison's "legal Mailbox," as opposed to date of its receipt by court clerk.

Carabal Sandoval v. Honsked, 35 F.3d 521 (11th Cir. 1994)
Pro se party may sign documents such as objections and brief on behalf of spouse, unless to do so would result in manifest injustice.

Church v. Sullivan, 942 F.2d 1501 (10th Cir. 1991)
US v. Treff, 924 F2D 975 (10th Cir. 1991)
While defendant has the right to conduct his own defense, he has no right to some sort of hybrid representation where he acted as co-counsel.

Faile v. Upjohn, 988 F.2d 985, 988 (9th Cir. 1993)
An uncorroborated pro se litigant completes service under F.R.C.P 5(b) upon submission to prison authorities for forwarding it to the party to be served.

Faretta v. State Of California, 422 US 806, 45 L.Ed.2d 562, 95 S.Ct. 2525 (1975)
An individual has a constitutional right to represent himself.

Good v. Allain, 823 F.2d 64 (5th Cir. 1987)
When dismissal of pro se complaint is warranted, it should generally be without prejudice to afford plaintiff opportunity to file an amended complaint.

Munz v. Nix, 908 F.2d 267 (8th Cir. 1990)
Wolff v. McDonnell, 418 US 539, 41 L.Ed.2d 935, 94 S.Ct. 2963 (1974)
Johnson v. Avery, 393 US 483, 21 L.Ed.2d 718, 89 S.Ct. 747 (1969)
Where there is no personal right to a jailhouse lawyer, a prison must allow prisoners to assist one another unless there is available to prisoners a reasonable alternative means of legal assistance.

Noll v. Carlson, 809 F.2d 1446 (9th Cir. 1987)
Pro se litigant bringing civil rights suit in forma pauperis is entitled to five procedural protections: 1. Process issued and served. 2. Notice of any motion thereafter made by defendant or the court to dismiss the complaint and the grounds therefore. 3. On opportunity to at least submit a written memorandum in opposition to such motion. 4. In the event of dismissal, a statement of the grounds therefore. 5. An opportunity to amend the complaint to overcome the deficiency unless it clearly appears from the complaint that the deficiency cannot be overcome by amendment.

Note: Your right to receive assistance from a jailhouse attorney is protected in law. If prison staff interfere with the activities of a jailhouse lawyer they are liable for monetary damages in their official and personal capacities via a 1983 Bivens Action, 403 US 388.

Note: You have the constitutional right to represent yourself in court and that if you have an attorney he is merely your agent and is bestowed only with the authority you voluntarily grant him. See the Sixth Amendment. Also see Title 28 USC. 1654 and Faretta v. California, 422 US 806. 1169.

Puett v. Blandford, 912 172d 270 (9th Cir. 1990)

Party proceeding in forma pauperis (pro se) is entitled to have summons and complaint served by United States Marshal.

Shabazz v. Askins, 14 F.3d 533 (10th Cir. 1994)

Because prison inmate appealing from summary judgment against him in a civil rights suit was appearing pro se, Court of Appeals construed his pleadings liberally.

Sills v. Bureau of Prisons, 761 F.2d 792 (D.C. Cir. 1985)

Adkins v. DuPont De Nemours, 335 US 331, 93 I Ed2d 43, 69 S.Ct. 85 (1948)

To guarantee that no citizen shall be denied an opportunity to commence, prosecute, or defend an action . . . in any court . . . solely because his poverty makes it impossible for him to pay or secure the costs," Congress enacted 28 USC. § 1915, which permits federal courts to authorize the maintenance of an action without prepayment of fees.

Simmons v. Abruzzo, 49 F.3d 83 (2nd Cir. 1995)

Ferran v. Town Of Nassau, 11 F.3d 21 (2nd Cir. 1993)

Boag v. MacDougall, 454 US 364, 70 L.Ed.2d 551, 102 S.Ct. 700 (1982)

Haines v. Kerner, 404 US 519, 30 L.Ed.2d 652, 92 S.Ct. 594 (1972)

Pro se litigants pleadings are to be construed liberally and held to less stringent standard than formal pleadings drafted by lawyers; if court can reasonably read pleadings to state valid claim on which litigant could prevail, it should do so despite failure to cite proper legal authority, confusion of legal theories, poor syntax and sentence construction, or litigant's unfamiliarity with pleading requirements.

Talley v. Lane, 13 F.3d 1031 (7th Cir. 1994)

To insure that pro se complaints are given fair and meaningful consideration, they are liberally construed however in artfully pleaded.

<u>Taylor v. List</u>, 880 F.2d 1040 (9th Cir. 1989)

Sixth Amendment, right to self-representation includes right of access to law books, witnesses and other tools necessary to prepare defense.

<u>US v. Halverson</u>, 973 F.2d 1415 (8th Cir. 1992)

Pro se filings are not considered when appellant is represented by counsel.

<u>Valandingham v. Bojorquez</u>, 866 F.2d 1135 (9th Cir. 1989)

Prisoner litigating pro se has the right to undertake legal investigation and documentation of his claims in the manner that an attorney would, subject to the security and disciplinary requirements of a prison.

Prosecutorial Misconduct

Ariz. Constitution Article 6 § 27

Judges shall not charge juries with respect to matters of fact, nor comment thereon, but shall declare the law. No case shall be reversed for technical error in pleadings or proceedings when upon the whole case it shall appear that substantial justice has been done.

Bell v. Evatt, 72 F.2d 421 (4th Cir. 1995)

Prosecutor's closing argument of prejudicial facts not in evidence, personal knowledge of facts not in evidence, or in inflammatory comments about defendant are grounds for reversing convictions.

Berger v. US, 295 US 78, 88 (1935)

The prosecutor's duty in a criminal prosecution is to seek justice. As such, the prosecutor should prosecute with earnestness and vigor, but may not use improper methods calculated to produce a wrongful conviction. If the use of such methods impact the fairness of trial to make the resulting conviction and a denial of due process, it may justify a mistrial or reversal of conviction.

Blacklege v. Perry, 417 US 21, 28-29 (1974)

Subsequent prosecution for more serious charge after defendant successfully appeals conviction violated due process.

Bragan v. Poindexter, 249 F.3d 476, 481 (6th Cir. 2001)

Prosecutorial discretion is not unfettered and government acts are unconstitutional if intended to penalize defendant for exercise of constitutional right, or carried out in bad faith. Such conduct usually involves either selective prosecution, which denies equal protection of the law, or vindictive prosecution, which violates due process.

Bruno v. Rushen, 721 F.2d 1193 (9th Cir. 1983)

Prosecutors comments, attacking defendants exercise of his constitutional right to counsel and integrity of defense counsel were improper, and since remarks were made at important stage of trial, were extensive and were not accidental, but calculated to wrongfully impute guilt to defendant, error was not harmless.

Darden v. Wainwright, 477 US 168, 181 (1986)

US v. Young, 470 US 1, 11-12 (1985)

Donnelley v. De Christo Foro, 416 US 637,643 (1974)

A criminal conviction is not to be lightly overturned on basis of prosecutor's comments alone; statements must be viewed in context of entire proceedings in order to determine whether conduct affected fairness of trial appellate review of prosecutorial misconduct therefore consists of a two-part test: first, was the prosecutors conduct actually improper; second, did the misconduct taken in the context of the trial as a whole, violate the defendant's due process rights.

Faile v. Upjohn, 988 F.2d 985, 988 (9th Cir. 1993)

An uncorroborated pro se litigant completes service under F.R.C.P 5(b) upon submission to prison authorities for forwarding it to the party to be served.

Floyd v. Meachum, (1990, CA2 Conn) 907 F.2d 347

Cumulative effect of three categories of improper remarks of prosecutor during his summation in-state trial including both inflammatory comments and erroneous statements of law resulting in violation of defendant's due process right since case involved not one of the few isolated episodes but represented an escalating prosecutorial misconduct from initial to closing summation.

G.L.J. A presumption of vindictive prosecution arises only with a defendant is affirmatively exercising constitutional rights.

Freeman v. Lane, 962 F.2d 1252 (1992)

US v. Buege, 578 F.2d 187 (7th Cir.), cert. denied, 436 US 871, 99 S.Ct. 203, 58 L.Ed.2d 183 (1978)

US v. Fearns, 501 F.2d 486 (7th Cir. 1974)

Which established that the prosecutor's comments violated the Constitution. No reasonable strategic explanation has been given or exists for wide counsel would forego this issue on appeal.

James v. Kentucky, 466 US 341, 80 L.Ed.2d 346, 104 S.Ct. 1830 (1984)
The judge refused to give requested instructions, the Supreme Court reversed and held that state statutes did not take precedent over constitutional law.

Jenkins v. Artuz, 294 F.3d 284, 294 (2nd Cir. 2002)
Prosecutor's failure to correct government witnesses false testimony and subsequent attempt to bolster witnesses credibility violated defendants due process rights.

Kincaid v. Sparkman, 175 F.3d 444-46 (6th Cir. 1999)
Due process violated because prosecution made repeated reference to petitioners prior charges.

Mastracchio v. Vose, 274 F.3d 590,602 (1st Cir. 2001)
Prosecutor's failure to correct witnesses false statement was improper because prosecutor had knowledge of statements falsity; however, this error was not violation of due process.

Napue v. Illinois, 360 US 264, 269 (1959)
Muni v. Holohan, 294 US 103, 112 (1935) (per curiam)
The prosecutor may not knowingly present false testimony and has a duty to correct testimony that he or she knows to be false.

Note: Vindictive prosecution is when a prosecutor uses the charging process to violate due process by penalizing the exercise of constitutional or statutory right.

Note: In situations in which it is reasonably likely that a prosecutor has acted vindictively, and a row bobble presumption of vindictiveness may arise. Otherwise, the defendant must show actual vindictiveness in order to prevail.

Nulph v. Cook, 333 F.3d 1052 (9th Cir. 2003)
The presumption of vindictiveness can be over, only if the state proffers "objective information from the record concerning identifiable conduct on the part of the defendant occurring after the time of the original sentencing proceeding."

People of Territory Of Guam v. Aqualo, 948 F.2d 1116 (9th Cir. 1991)
US v. Duncan, 850 F.2d 1104 (6th Cir. 1988)
US v. Coin, 753 F.2d 1510 (9th Cir. 1985)
Failure to give jury instruction on defense when some evidence supported it is reversible error.

Pollard v. Delo, 28 F.3d 887 (8th Cir. 1994)
Direct comments by prosecutor on defendant's failure to testify violate Fifth Amendment's privilege against self-incrimination.

Pool v. Superior Court, 139 Ariz. 98, 677 P.2d 261 (1984)
Following trial court's denial of defendant's motion for dismissal of new indictment on grounds of double jeopardy and prosecutorial vindictiveness, defendant sought relief by special action. The Supreme Court, Feldman, J., accepted jurisdiction and held that: (1) prosecutor's improprieties in cross-examining defendant warranted, if not required, mistrial; (2) prosecutor would not have been entitled to engage in abusive, argumentative and harassing conduct even if defense had been guilty of serious misconduct; and (3) prosecutor's misconduct was so egregiously improper as to compel conclusion that prosecutor intentionally engaged in conduct which he knew to be improper, that he did so with indifference, if not a specific intent, to prejudice defendant for purpose of avoiding significant danger of acquittal which had arisen, and to prejudice jury and obtain conviction no matter what the danger of mistrial or reversal, and thus, jeopardy attached and re-trial was barred.

State v. Bailey, 647 P.2d 170, 132 Ariz. 472 (1982)
An attorney may not refer to evidence which is not in record or "testify" regarding matter not in evidence.

State v. Bowie, 580 P.2d 1190, 119 Ariz. 336 (1978)
Opening statements should not contain any facts which prosecutor cannot prove a trial.

State v. Childs, 553 P.2d 1192, 113 Ariz. 318 (1976)
In arguments to jury, attorneys are allowed wide latitude in discussing evidence and inferences they can legitimately be drawn therefrom; however, arguments

before jury as to evidence which has been excluded by the court, withdrawn after objection, or as to matters which are simply not in evidence may constitute reversible error is sufficiently prejudicial.

State v. Denny, 579 P.2d 1101,119 Ariz. 131 (1978)
Conviction will be overturned for prosecutorial misconduct when prosecutor's behavior has caused accused to have an unfair trial.

State v. Dutton, 478 P.2d 87, 106 Ariz. 463 (1970)
Attorneys have wide latitude in their remarks to jury, provided they are supported by evidence.

State v. Freader, 696 P.2d 1373, 144, 224 (Ariz. App. 1985)
Prosecutor must be held to higher standard of conduct than an ordinary attorney, and has obligation to ensure that justice is done.

State v. Freeman, 559 P.2d 152, 114 Ariz. 32 (1976)
Wide latitude is permitted in prosecution of closing argument to jury, because closing arguments are not evidentiary in nature and those counsel are allowed to comment on the evidence which has been introduced and to argue reasonable inferences therefrom.

State v. Gendron, 168 Ariz. 153, 155, 812 P.2d 626,628 (1991)
Fundamental error is of such dimension that it cannot be said; it is possible for a defendant to have had a fair trial.

State v. Hardwick, 183 Ariz. 649, 905 P.2d 1384 (App. 1995)
Court found reversible and fundamental error which deprives the defendant of a fair trial, when the prosecution repeatedly referred to the damaging contents of an unadmitted document, a document which would not have been admitted, because it was hearsay and improper expert opinion.

State v. Henry, 176 Ariz. 569, 863 F.2d 861 (1993)
Prosecutor was held to have made improper remark in closing argument, asking whether the word "psychopath" came to mind while the defendant was testifying,

Id. 176 Ariz. at 581, 863 P.2d at 873. It the court found that the remark was improper appeal to the passions and fears of the jury. See also State v. Comer, 165 Ariz. 413, 426, 799 P.2d 333, 346 (1990).

State v. Minnitt, 203 Ariz. 431
During defendant's first two trials the prosecutor presented evidence from an officer that the prosecutor knew was false. The trial court found that the prosecutor had been involved in serious misconduct, but denied defendant's motion to dismiss, concluding that the mistrial resulted from the jury's inability to reach a verdict, rather than from the prosecutor's and the officer's misdeeds. The Supreme Court found that the prosecutor's misdeeds were not isolated events but became a consistent pattern of prosecutorial misconduct that began in 1993 and continued through retrial in 1997. The Supreme Court found that the defense counsel's knowledge of the falsehood did not nullify the prosecutor's behavior. Therefore, the Supreme Court concluded that the double jeopardy provision in Ariz. Const. art. 2, § 10, should have barred the third retrial because in both the 1993 and 1997 trials the prosecutor engaged in extreme misconduct that he knew was grossly improper and highly prejudicial, both as to defendant and to the integrity of the system. Even though defendant was convicted in the third trial which was free from falsehoods, the third trial was improper. The Supreme Court vacated defendant's convictions and sentences and instructed the trial court to dismiss the charges against defendant with prejudice.

State v. Noriega, 690 P.2d 775, 142 Ariz. 474 (1984)
A prosecuting attorney is held to a higher standard of conduct than an ordinary attorney.

State v. Prentiss, 163 Ariz. 81, 786 P.2d 932 (1989)
A prosecutor is held to a higher standard of conduct then an ordinary attorney, and then a prosecutor is duty bound to seek justice and not intentionally overlaid providing evidence which might damage his case or aid the eight years, is clear that refusal to allege mitigating circumstances, which the sentencing judge might consider, metals unduly with judicial power.

State v. Rainey, 672 P.2d 188, 137 Ariz. 523 (App. 1983)

In closing arguments excessive and emotional language is the red and other weapon of counsel's forensic arsenal, limited by principle that attorneys are not permitted to introduce our comment upon evidence which has not previously been offered and placed before the jury.

State v. Schneider, 715 P.2d 297,148 Ariz. 441 (App. 1985)

It is improper for prosecutor to thank court for favorable ruling on his objections.

State v. Sullivan, 635 P.2d 501, 130 Ariz. 213 (1981)

Test for determining whether the prosecutors closing remarks are improper is a two-part test: the remarks must not only call to attention of jurors matters which they could not be justified in considering, but must appear to have probably influenced the jury's verdict.

State v. Zappia, 448 P.2d 119, 8 Ariz. App. 549, cert. denied, 90 S.Ct. 132, 396 US 861, 24 L.Ed.2d 113 (1968)

Prosecutor may not ask questions which cast prejudicial or unfavorable insinuations without being prepared and able to prove facts implied by question.

Tart v. State, (1981, Okla Crim) 634 P.2d 750

Prosecution is forbidden from giving his personal opinion of defendant skills and defendant may be denied his right to fair trial where prosecutor's statement of opinion might unduly influence jury. This is especially true when prosecutor makes unconscionable misrepresentations of law in stating his opinion as to defendant's guilt.

Turner v. Marshall, 63 F.3d 807, 818 (9th Cir. 1995)

Reviewing both individual and cumulative impact of alleged instances of prosecutorial misconduct. Although prosecutorial discretion is broad, it is not unlimited, and courts have a responsibility to protect individuals from prosecutorial conduct that is based upon an unconstitutional motive.

US ex rel. Shaw v. De Robertis, (1985, CA7 Ill.) 755 F.2d 1279

In order to constitute direct violation of 14th amendment, prosecutors improper comment must be misconduct so egregious that it deprives defendant of fair trial; whether prosecutor's comments made defendants trial so unfair as to deny due process requires determination as to whether comments changed results of trial; whether misconduct violates fourth amendment is mixed question of fact and wall and reviewing court is to reach de novo resolution of issue.

US v. Alexander, 287 F.3d 811, 818 (9th Cir. 2002)

Upholding requirement that defendant proof selective prosecution or vindictive prosecution defense.

US v. Austin, 786 F.2d 986 (10th Cir. 1986)

Courts and prosecutors generally are forbidden from mentioning that codefendant has either pled guilty or been convicted.

US v. Beckman, 298 F.3d 788, 793 (9th Cir. 2002)

Prosecutors questions regarding defendants prior arrest in conviction was improper.

US v. Blakely, 14 F.3d 1557 (11th Cir. 1994)

Prosecutor may not make suggestions, insinuations, and assertions calculated to mislead jury.

US v. Childress, 58 F3d 693 (D.C. Cir. 1995)

Prosecutor may not use bully pulpit of closing argument to inflame passions or prejudices of jury or to argue facts not in evidence.

US v. Eyster, 948 F.2d 1196 (11th Cir. 1991)

Prosecutors improper vouching for credibility of prosecution witness tainted trial and required reversal of convictions.

US v. Frederick, 78 F.3d 1370

Defendant challenged the judgment of conviction of the United States District Court for the District of Arizona for aggravated sexual assault against his minor stepdaughter. Defendant raised a number of issues on appeal, which included prosecutorial vouching; improper comments by the prosecutor about defendant's counsel, and prejudicial testimony by government witnesses that suggested defendant had committed similar offenses against others. Reversed and remanded.

US v. Garcia-Guizar, 160 F.3d 511, 520 (9th Cir. 1998)

Prosecutor's description of defendant as "a liar" was improper because it constitutes personal opinion regarding defendant's credibility.

US v. Gray, 291 F.3d 30, 35 (D.C. Cir. 2002)

Concerns over vindictiveness centers on whether prosecutor's actions are designed to punish defendant for asserting legal right.

US v. Grissom, 44 F.3d 1507 (10th Cir. 1995)

Defendant is entitled to good faith or theory of defense instruction if it is supported by sufficient evidence for jury to find in defendant's favor.

US v. Hands, 184 F.3d 1322, 1328-29 (11th Cir. 1999)

Prosecutor's misstatement of evidence was reversible error because evidence of defendant's guilt was not overwhelming.

US v. Hermanek, 289 F.3d 1076, 1099 (9th Cir. 2002)

Prosecutors who portray themselves as participants in criminal investigation by using term "we" and "us" to refer to steps taken in investigation impermissibly vouched for the credibility of government's witness.

US v. Hernandez-Herera, 273 F.3d 1213, 1217 (9th Cir. 2001)

Prosecutor violates due process by taking retaliatory action for defendant's exercise of protected right.

US v. Hook, (1986, CA10 Okla) 780 F.2d 1526,cert. denied, (US) 90 L.Ed.2d 199, 106 S.Ct. 1657

Due process prohibits prosecutors closing argument from expressing his personal opinion regarding evidence presented or guilt accused.

US v. Jones, 592 F.2d 1038, cert. denied, 99 S.Ct. 2179, 441 US 951, 60 L.ED.2d 1056 C.A. Ariz. 979.

Government's inability to produce evidence which it promised the jury in opening statement would appear to harm the government's case rather than the defense.

US v. Lanoue, 137 F.3d 656, 664 (1st Cir 2000) Successful assertions of vindictive prosecution are most common where a defendant advances some procedural or constitutional right in his then punished for doing so.

US v. Martinez, 974 F.2d 589 (5th Cir. 1992)

1. Sixth Amendment secures for a criminal defendant right to present closing argument. 2. Failure to allow closing argument constitutes plain error in absence of a waiver.

US v. McPhee, (1984, CA5 Tex.) 731 F.2d 1150

Defendants due process rights or violated by prosecutors closing statements blatantly implying existence of serious extrinsic offenses and statements that "we want you to find him guilty because a bunch of other reasons" or court gave no cautionary instruction to jury and evidence was not overwhelming.

US v. Nickens, 955 F.2d 112 (1st Cir. 1992)
US v. Iglesias, 915 F.2d 1524 (11th Cir. 1990)

It is improper for prosecutor to inject personal beliefs about the evidence into closing argument or to call the defendant a liar.

US v. Nionaguian, 741 F.2d 1434 (D.C. Cir. 1984)

Prosecutor may not urge jurors to convict defendant in order to protect community values, preserve civil order, or deter future lawbreaking.

US v. Reed, 2 F.3d 1441 (7th Cir. 1993)
It is not only permissible but advisable in closing argument to refute meritless accusations.

US v. Rosa, 17 F.3d 1531 (2nd Cir. 1994)
It is improper for prosecutor to mischaracterize evidence or refer in summation to facts not in evidence.

US v. Rosales-Lopez, (1980 CA9 Cal) 617 F.2d 1349, affirmed, (1981) 451 US 182, 68 L.Ed.2d 22, 101 S.Ct. 1629
Defendants right to due process of law is violated where prosecution increases severity of alleged charges in response to exercise of constitutional or statutory right, and vindictiveness is normally found where government has occasioned to re-indict or retry defendant following exercise of procedural right; however action of prosecutor in re-indict in defendant is not vindictive where charges contained in second indictment exposed defendant to no greater risk of punishment than did those contained in the first indictment.

US v. Salameh, 152 F.3d 88 (2nd Cir. 1998)
Prosecutor must scrupulously refrain from injecting his credibility and overall knowledge into any part of the trial.

US v. Sardelli, 813 F.2d 654 (5th Cir. 1987)
US v. LeQuire, 943 F.2d 1554 (11th Cir. 1991)
Both direct and indirect comments on defendant's failure to testify can invalidate a conviction. Prosecutor's elicitation of testimony on five occasions about previous conviction of defendant was reversible error despite curative instructions.

US v. Smith, 982 F.2d 681,684 (1st Cir. 1993)
Prosecutor statements that defendant was guilty, improper because a personal belief rather than simply the position of government.

US v. Smith, 982 F.2d 681 (1st Cir. 1993)
US v. Easley, 994 F.2d 1241 (7th Cir. 1993)
US v. Williams, 989 F.2d 1061 (9th Cir. 1993)
Prosecutor should not inject his personal beliefs into his presentation of argument.

US v. Stokes, 124 F.3d 39, 45 (1st Cir. 1997)
It is hornbook law that a federal court may dismiss an indictment if the accused produces evidence of actual prosecutorial vindictiveness sufficient to establish due process violation, or even if he demonstrates a likelihood of vindictiveness sufficient to justify a presumption.

US v. Suarez, 262 F.3d 468, 479 (6th Cir. 2001)
Vindictive prosecution may arise from pre-trial increase in severity after defendant asserts protected right.

US v. Taren - Palma, 997 F.2d 525 (9th Cir. 1993)
Opening argument, like closing, should not refer to matters that are not to be presented into evidence.

US v. Tocco, 135 F.3d 116, 130 (2nd Cir. 1998)
Prosecutor's improper reference to other evidence during examination of government's witness was not violation of due process because jury was promptly given curative instruction and there was ample evidence to support conviction.

US v. Tomblin, 42 F.3d 263 (5th Cir. 1994)
Statements in closing argument that presuppose defendant's guilt can be the sort of foul blows long held improper.

US v. Vallie, 284 F.3d 917, 921-22 (8th Cir. 2002)
Prosecutors question to defendant concerning prior unrelated offense was improper.

US v. Weinstein, 762 F.2d 1522, 1542 (11th Cir. 1985)

Prosecution's misconduct must be sufficient to justify reversal, must be so pronounced and persistent that it permeates the entire atmosphere of the trial.

US v. Wilson, 262 F.3d 305,314 (4th Cir. 2001)

Vindictive prosecution claim arises when prosecution violates due process by bringing more serious charges after defendant exercises right to appeal. Upholding requirement that defendant provide proof of vindictive prosecution defense.

US v. Yee - Chan, 17 F.3d 21 (2nd Cir. 1994)

Incompetent summation can construe ineffective assistance of counsel.

Viereck v. US, (1943) 318 US 236, 87 L.Ed 734, 63 S.Ct. 561

Federal prosecuting attorney, in his remarks to the jury may not indulge an appeal wholly irrelevant to any facts or issues in case, purpose and effect of which can only be to arouse passion and prejudice.

Washington v. Estelle, 648 F.2d 276, 279 (5th Cir.), cert. denied, 454 US 899, 102, S.Ct. 402, 70 L.Ed.2d 216

Blankenship v. Estelle, 545 F.2d 510 (5th Cir. 1977), cert. denied, 444 US 856,100 S.Ct. 115, 62 L.Ed.2d 75 (1979)

The admission of prejudicial evidence and improper argument justified federal habeas relief only if, in the context of the entire trial, the heirs contributed as "crucial, critical, highly significant factors.

Reasonable Doubt

Fiore v. White, 531 US 225, 2 28-29 (2001)

In Re Winship, 397 US 358, 364 (1970)

The due process clause requires the government to prove beyond reasonable doubt every element of the crime with which the defendant is charged. Due process is violated when defendant convicted for operating without permit despite fact that prosecution failed to show defendant did not possess hazardous waste permit. The reasonable doubt standard applies in both state and federal proceedings.

Patterson v. New York, 432 US 197 (1977) at 210

The court has repeatedly stated that "the due process clause requires the prosecution to prove beyond a reasonable doubt all of the elements including the definition of the offense of which the defendant is charged."

Sullivan v. Louisiana, 508 US 275, 278 (1993)

The Winship reasonable doubt standard protects three interests. First, it protects the defendant's interest in being free from unjustified loss of liberty. See 397 US at 363. Second, it protects the defendant from the stigmatization resulting from conviction. Third, it engenders community confidence in the criminal law by giving "concrete substance" to the presumption of innocence. Id. at 3 63-64. In this regard, the court stated that it is critical that the moral force of the criminal law not be diluted by a standard of proof that leaves people in doubt whether innocent men are being condemned. Id. at 364. In his concurring opinion, Justice Harlan noted that the standard is "bottomed on a fundamental value determination of our society that it is far worse to convict an innocent man than to let a guilty man go free." Id. at 372 (Harlan J. Concurring). The Winship requirement applies to elements that distinguish a more serious crime from a less serious one, as well as to those elements that distinguish criminal from noncriminal conduct. Thus, a state may not distinguish between similar offenses that have different elements, maximum penalties without requiring the prosecution to prove beyond a reasonable doubt the facts upon which the distinction turns, because the same interests are implicated.

Religion

American Life League, Inc. v. Reno, 47 F.3d 642 (4th Cir. 1995)
Free exercise clause forbids government from adopting laws designed to suppress religious belief or practice.

Berger v. Rensselaer Cent. School Corp., 982 F.2d 1160 (7th Cir. 1993)
Under the First Amendment establishment clause, government may not aid a religion, aid all religions or favor one religion over another.

Brown v. Borough Of Mahaffey, Pa., 35 F.3d 846 (3rd Cir. 1994)
At minimum, First Amendment enjoins government from intentionally burdening religious worship.

Church Of Lukumi Babalu Aye. Inc. v. City Of Hialeah, 508 US 124 L.Ed.2d 472. 113 S.Ct. (1993)
City ordinances regulating animal sacrifice, but effectively prohibiting only sacrifice as practiced by Santeria religion, held void under First Amendment's free exercise of religion clause.

Ferguson v. C.I.R., 921 F.2d 588 (5th Cir. 1991)
Protection of free exercise clause extends to all sincere religious beliefs; courts may not evaluate religious truth.

Kreisner v. City Of San Diego, 1 F.3d 775 (9th Cir. 1993)
Government practice or statute violates establishment clause if its purpose is to endorse religious custom or viewpoint.

Kreisner v. City Of San Diego, 988 F.2d 883 (9th Cir. 1993)
Religious speakers have same right to access to public forums as others.

Lawson v. Dugger, 840 F.2d 779 (11th Cir. 1988)
Restrictions imposed by prison officials on inmate's access to religions literature should be scrutinized under strict MARTINEZ standard of review as restrictions impinged on First Amendment right of non-prisoners.

Malik v. Brown, 16 F.3d 350 (9th Cir. 1994)

Adoption of Muslim names by converts to the Islamic faith is an exercise of religious freedom.

State v. West, 168 Ariz. 292

Examination questions at trial regarding religious beliefs designed to enhance witness credibility are improper under both Ariz. Const. art. 2, § 12 and Ariz. R. Evid. 610. It is equally improper to impeach a defendant's credibility by showing the presence or absence of religious beliefs. The prohibition against questioning a defendant on religious beliefs applies when the credibility of the witness is being attacked. If the use of religion constitutes fundamental error, the failure to object does not preclude the appellate court from addressing it.

State v. West, 168 Ariz. 292

Thomas v. Gunter, 32 F.3d 1258 (8th Cir. 1994)

Prison officials are not free to restrict inmates' exercises of their religion arbitrarily and unreasonably.

Thompson v. Comm. Of Kentucky, 712 F.2d 1078 (6th Cir. 1983)

1. While in prison inmates retain their right to exercise their religious beliefs. 2. Although prisoners do not retain same rights as the outside they may not be denied basic rights of conscience.

US v. Boyll, 774 F. Supp. 1333 (D. New Mexico 1991)

Prohibiting non - Indian member of Native American Church from importing peyote through mail and possessing it with intent to distribute would impose substantial burden on free exercise of religion, was not justified by compelling government interest, and would violate free exercise clause.

Walker v. San Francisco Unified School Dist., 46 F.3d 1449 (9th Cir. 1995)

One way in which general governmental program can be "skewed towards religion" for establishment clause purposes is if program creates symbolic union between church and state.

<u>Werner v. McCotter</u>, 49 F.3d 1476 (10th Cir. 1995)
Religious Freedom Restoration Act, encompasses claims of prisoners alleging interference with free exercise of religion and is to be applied retroactively.

<u>Wilkinson v. State</u>, 172 Ariz. 597 Rules enacted by a department of corrections governing religious visitation for inmates was invalid as it was not promulgated in accordance with the Arizona Administrative Procedure Act.

Rule 32

Rule 32.1.

Scope of remedy Subject to the limitations of Rule 32.2, any person who has been convicted of, or sentenced for, a criminal offense may, without payment of any fee, institute a proceeding to secure appropriate relief.

Any person who pled guilty or no contest, admtted a probation violation, or whose probation was automatically violated based upon a plea of guilty or no contest shall have the right to file a post-conviction relief proceeding, and this proceeding shall be known as a Rule 32 of-right proceeding.

Grounds for relief are:

a. The conviction or the sentence was in violation of the Constitution of the United States or of the State of Arizona;

b. The court was without jurisdiction to render judgment or to impose sentence;

c. The sentence imposed exceeded the maximum authorized by law, or is otherwise not in accordance with the sentence authorized by law;

d. The person is being held in custody after the sentence imposed has expired;

e. Newly discovered material facts probably exist and such facts probably would have changed the verdict or sentence. Newly discovered material facts exist if:

> 1) The newly discovered material facts were discovered after the trial.
> 2) The defendant exercised due diligence in securing the newly discovered material facts.
> 3) The newly discovered material facts are not merely cumulative or used solely for impeachment, unless the impeachment evidence substantially undermines testimony which was of critical significance at trial such that the evidence probably would have changed the verdict or sentence.

f. The defendant's failure to file a notice of post-conviction relief of-right or notice of appeal within the prescribed time was without fault on the defendant's part; or

g. There has been a significant change in the law that if determined to apply to defendant's case would probably overturn the defendant's conviction or sentence; or

h. The defendant demonstrates by clear and convincing evidence that the facts underlying the claim would be sufficient to establish that no reasonable fact-finder would have found defendant guilty of the underlying offense beyond a reasonable doubt, or that the court would not have imposed the death penalty.

HISTORY:
Amended May 7, 1975, effective Aug. 1, 1975; amended June 2, 1992, effective Sept. 30, 1992; amended Oct. 31, 2000, effective Dec. 1. 2000.

NOTES:
[2000 AMENDMENT]
Changes in the first and second paragraphs and in subsection (f) are to meet and accommodate the requirements of Montgomery v. Sheldon, 181 Ariz. 256, 889 P.2d 614 (1995) (opinion supplemented, 182 Ariz. 118, 893, P.2d 1281), and its progeny. A petition when authorized under Montgomery is referred to in the above provision as an "of-right" proceeding. Relief pursuant to subsection (f) will continue to be unavailable to all post-conviction relief proceedings not "of-right". See Moreno v. Gonzalez, 192 Ariz. 131, 962 P.2d 205 (1998).

The addition of new subparagraph (h) is warranted by the U.S. Supreme Court's pronouncement that claims of actual innocence are not cognizable under the federal habeas corpus remedy. Herrera v. Collins, 506 U.S. 390, 113 S.Ct. 853 (1993). This claim is independent of a claim under subparagraph (e). A defendant who establishes a claim of newly discovered evidence does not need to comply with the requirements of subparagraph (h).

In approving the 2000 amendments to Rule 32, the Arizona Supreme Court did not have the benefit of the comments of a statewide commission which was empaneled that year by the Attorney General of Arizona to investigate and assess the administration of the death penalty in the State of Arizona. Accordingly, further amendments to Rule 32 may be necessary following the issuance of that commission's recommendations. In particular, the topics of deadlines and time periods and victims' rights may need to be addressed at that time.

[1992 AMENDMENT]

COMMENT TO RULE 32.1 (E). Impeachment evidence will rarely be of a type which would probably have changed the verdict at trial. However, where newly-discovered impeachment evidence substantially undermines testimony which was of critical significance at trial, the court should evaluate whether relief should be granted on the grounds that the evidence probably would have changed the result. Dicta in cases such as State v. Fisher, 141 Ariz. 227, 250-51, cert. denied, 469 U.S. 1066, 105 S.Ct. 548 (1984), suggesting that a defendant will always be barred from relief if newly-discovered evidence is solely for impeachment, have never been incorporated into the Arizona Rules of Criminal Procedure and should not preclude relief deemed necessary in the court's discretion to avoid a miscarriage of justice.

[1975 AMENDMENT]

GENERAL. Under previous Arizona procedure, there were seven avenues for post-conviction relief: appeal, federal habeas corpus, Arizona habeas corpus, writ of coram nobis, motion for new trial or newly discovered evidence, motion to modify or vacate judgment (under Civil Rule 60 (c)), and delayed appeal. Each had different mechanics, requirements and time limits.

THE UNIFIED PROCEDURE OF RULE 32:
    (1) Consolidates the last five avenues into a single comprehensive remedy;
    (2) Requires, subject to a limited exception, the consolidation of all claims in a single petition;
    (3) Permits summary dismissal of frivolous claims;
    (4) Provides for a full-scale evidentiary hearing on the record in order to limit federal habeas corpus review to questions of law, Townsend v. Sain, 372 U.S. 293 (1963); and
    (5) Allows filing of petitions for post-conviction relief in the court in which the judgment and sentence were rendered.

RULE 32.1.

This rule catalogs the possible grounds for relief. It is based upon Rule 35 of the Alaska Rules of Criminal Procedure and incorporates the essence of ABA, Standards Relating to Post-Conviction Remedies (Approved Draft, 1968) [hereinafter cited in comments to Rule 32 as ABA, Standards] within the drafting structure of the second Revised Uniform Post-Conviction Procedure Act (1966) [hereinafter cited in comments to Rule 32 as Uniform Act]. It is intended that this rule encompass all the grounds presently available in Arizona under a writ of habeas corpus, Ariz. Const. Art. 2, § 14; Ariz. Rev. Stat. Ann. §§ 13-2001 to -2027 (1956); a writ of coram nobis, Ariz. Const. Art. 6, § 5 (Cum. Supp. 1972), e.g., State v. Kruchten, 101 Ariz. 186, 417 P.2d 510 (1966), cert. denied, 385 U.S. 1043 (1967); a motion for a new trial on newly-discovered evidence, 1956 Arizona Rules of Criminal Procedure Rule 310 (3); a motion filed under Ariz. R. Civ. P. 60 (c); a motion for delayed appeal, Ariz. Sup. Ct. R. 16 (a); plus those available under federal habeas corpus procedures, 28 U.S.C. § 2241 (c) (1970). The available grounds are detailed in order to notify prisoners, and the federal courts, of the availability of relief, see Case v. Nebraska, 381 U.S. 336 (1965), to encourage the consolidation of all grounds for relief in a single petition and to justify the preclusion of claims not so raised. See Rule 32.2. These same purposes are served by the detailed checklist of grounds contained in the proposed form. See comment to Rule 32.4 (a) and Form 25.

With the exception of paragraph (d), no showing of any form of custody is required as a precondition for relief, thereby eliminating, in large part, one aspect of federal and state habeas corpus law. See, e.g., Peyton v. Rowe, 391 U.S. 54 (1968).

No filing fee is required in accordance with Ariz. Rev. Stat. Ann. § 13-2023 (1956) which prohibits the charging of a fee in habeas corpus proceedings.

RULE 32.1 (A). Most traditional collateral attacks are encompassed within paragraph (a). Claims of denial of counsel, of incompetency of counsel, and of violation of other rights based on the federal or Arizona constitution are included.

RULE 32.1 (B). Paragraph (b) retains the basic attack on jurisdiction universally recognized as a ground for collateral attack. See ABA, Standards, supra, at § 2.1 (a) (iii).

RULE 32.1 (C). This provision follows ABA, Standards, supra, at § 2.1 (a) (iv). See also Uniform Act, supra, at § 1 (a) (3). It is intended to allow an attack on a sentence even though the petitioner does not contest the validity of the underlying conviction.

RULE 32.1 (D). This paragraph is not intended to include attacks on the conditions of imprisonment or on correctional practices or prison rules. Paragraph (d) is intended to include claims of more traditional types -- e.g., miscalculation of sentence, questions of computation of good time -- which result in the defendant's remaining in custody when he should be free. Appeals from the conviction and imposition of probation must be filed within 20 days of the entry of judgment and sentence. See Rules 31.3, 26.1 (b) and 26.16 (a).

RULE 32.1 (E). Paragraph (e) replaces the 1956 Arizona Rules of Criminal Procedure, Rule 310 (3). The rule reduces the requirements of the 1956 Arizona Rules of Criminal Procedure Rule 310 (3) from absolute preconditions for relief to factors for the court to weigh in deciding whether or not a new trial is justified. See Wexler & Silverman, Representing Prison Inmates: A Primer on an Emerging Dimension of Poverty Law Practice, 11 Ariz. L. Rev. 385, 400-04 (1969) [hereinafter cited in comments to Rule 32 as Wexler & Silverman].

Subparagraph (e) (3) substitutes for the 1-year limit of the 1956 Arizona Rules of Criminal Procedure, Rule 308, a requirement that the judge take into consideration the prisoner's promptness in bringing forth new evidence. This provision will prevent abuse of process, e.g., a prisoner's lying-in-wait until an essential prosecution witness dies, but avoids setting a specific time limit.

RULE 32.1 (F). This provision is based on Ariz. Sup. Ct.R. 16 (a). The scope is intended to be the same as that of the present rule. It includes the situation in which the defendant fails to appeal because the trial court, despite the requirements of Rule 26.11, did not advise him of his appeal rights, and the situation in which the defendant intended to appeal and though timely appeal had been filed by his attorney when in reality it had not. See 31.3; see generally Wexler and Silverman, supra, at 397-4000; e.g., In re Acosta, 97 Ariz. 333, 400 P.2d 328 (1965). The delayed appeal procedure is retained to provide a remedy in those cases in which the grounds to be raised on appeal are not appropriate for a collateral attack on the conviction -- e.g., non-constitutional errors in the conduct of the trial. Moreover, the delayed appeal provision preserves the defendant's right to a general review of the record for fundamental error where his failure to file a timely appeal was not his fault. See Arizona Rev. Stat. Ann. § 13-1715 (B) (1956); Anders v. California, 386 U.S. 738 (1967).

RULE 32.1 (G). Paragraph (g) encompasses all claims for retroactive application of new constitutional and nonconstitutional legal principles. The language is based upon ABA, Standards, supra, at § 2.1 (a) (vi).

JUDICIAL DECISIONS
ANALYSIS

CONSTRUCTION
IN GENERAL.
Where defendant pled guilty to aggravated assault, he waived any right to direct appeal in that action and the Supreme Court of Arizona was without jurisdiction to hear that appeal in defendant's death penalty case; if he wished to challenge the validity of his plea, he had to do so through the post-conviction relief procedures provided by Ariz. R. Crim. P. 32. State v. Cropper, 205 Ariz. 181, 399 Ariz. Adv. Rep. 15, 68 P.3d 407, 2003 Ariz. LEXIS 61 (2003).

Ariz. R. Crim. P. 32.1(f) is atypical of the eight possible grounds for post-conviction relief listed in Rule 32.1(a) through (h); it merely provides a procedural mechanism whereby a defendant who has failed to appeal through no fault of his or her own can obtain jurisdiction in an appellate court. In contrast, the remaining seven grounds state substantive rule 32 claims on which a trial court, operating as a reviewing court, can directly vacate or modify a defendant's conviction or sentence or order that the defendant be released from prison. State v. Rosales, 205 Ariz. 86, 398 Ariz. Adv. Rep. 9, 66 P.3d 1263, 2003 Ariz. App. LEXIS 66 (Ct. App. 2003).

To find that a defendant who seeks leave to file a delayed appeal under Ariz. R. Crim. P. 32.1(f) waives all other claims would compel defendants to include all known substantive rule 32 claims in their first petition, along with the motion for leave to file a delayed appeal; such defendants would therefore be forced to litigate all their known rule 32 claims, including their request for a delayed appeal, before appealing to the appellate court. This order of proceedings might make sense in some cases, and nothing in this decision should be understood to prevent it, in many other cases, however, it would not. State v. Rosales, 205 Ariz. 86, 398 Ariz. Adv. Rep. 9, 66 P.3d 1263, 2003 Ariz. App. LEXIS 66 (Ct. App. 2003).

Trial court, in evaluating a delayed appeal request for post-conviction relief, does not review the trial, conviction, or sentence; at most, it may be called on to make limited factual findings about post-trial communication between counsel and defendant regarding an appeal; thus, if a defendant who successfully obtains leave to file a delayed appeal under Ariz. R. Crim. P. 32.1(f) is permitted to bring a substantive post-conviction relief proceeding after the conclusion of the appeal, the trial court will be functioning as a reviewing court for the first time, albeit that technically it will be addressing the second petition. State v. Rosales, 205 Ariz. 86, 398 Ariz. Adv. Rep. 9, 66 P.3d 1263, 2003 Ariz. App. LEXIS 66 (Ct. App. 2003)

By requesting leave to file a delayed appeal pursuant to Ariz. R. Crim. P. 32.1(f), a petitioner does not waive all other potential claims under the other grounds found in rule 32.1, thereby rendering them precluded; the Court of Appeals concludes that, for practical and policy reasons, no waiver occurs under those circumstances. To begin with, finding no such waiver is consistent with the purpose of the preclusion rule, which essentially requires a defendant to raise all known claims for relief in a single petition to the trial court, thereby avoiding piecemeal litigation and fostering judicial efficiency. State v. Rosales, 205 Ariz. 86, 398 Ariz. Adv. Rep. 9, 66 P.3d 1263, 2003 Ariz. App. LEXIS 66 (Ct. App. 2003).

Petitions for post-conviction relief and petitions for review of a lower court's decision on a petition for post-conviction relief are not "appeals" within the meaning of subsection (f). Moreno v. Gonzalez, 192 Ariz. 131, 962 P.2d 205 (1998).

WITH OTHER LAW

Pursuant to Ariz. R. Crim. P. 32.2, habeas petitioners may not be granted relief on any claim which could have been raised in a prior Ariz. R. Crim. P. 32 petition for post-conviction relief. Only if a claim falls within certain exceptions (subsections (d) through (h) of this rule) and the petitioner can justify why the claim has been omitted from a prior petition will the preclusive effect of Ariz. R. Crim. P. 32.2 be avoided. McKinney v. Schriro, -- F. Supp. 2d --, 2006 U.S. Dist. LEXIS 268 (D. Ariz. Jan. 3, 2006).

CHANGE IN THE LAW

Defendant's second post-conviction relief proceeding was precluded under Ariz. R. Crim. P. 32.2(a) because a prior case was not an Ariz. R. Crim. P. 32.1(g) "significant change in the law;" after the case, the law remained precisely the same, and for purposes of Rule 32.1(g), a change in the law could not be established by the subjective opinions of counsel, and therefore, the superior court erred in granting post-conviction relief. State v. Shrum, 220 Ariz. 115, -- Ariz. Adv. Rep. --, 203 P.3d 1175, 2008 Ariz. LEXIS 239 (2008).

New rule requiring that a jury must decide whether aggravating circumstances exist in capital cases did not apply retroactively to petitioners' cases, which were final; thus, the trial court properly denied post-conviction relief for petitioners. State v. Towery, 204 Ariz. 386, 394 Ariz. Adv. Rep. 14, 64 P.3d 828, 2003 Ariz. LEXIS 16 (2003), cert. dismissed, 539 U.S. 986, 124 S. Ct. 44, 156 L. Ed. 2d 702 (2003).

Where counsel, at prior proceedings had failed to raise claim based upon a change in law because he did not believe the law was applicable to petitioner at the time, counsel had sufficient reason for failing to argue the claim, the claim would constitute a significant change in the law, and the trial court's preclusion finding was an abuse of discretion. State v. Jensen, 193 Ariz. 105, 970 P.2d 937 (Ct. App. 1998).

CLAIM PRECLUSION.

Lack of a controlling precedent in the Arizona Supreme Court or in the Arizona Courts of Appeals led to certifying questions of whether habeas corpus petitioner could raise his ineffective assistance of trial counsel and unintelligent plea claims by alleging, pursuant to subsection (f) of this rule, that failure to file a timely petition for review was without fault on his part and whether any mandatory rule of state law barred petitioner from raising these claims at such a late date. Binford v. Rhode, 116 F.3d 396 (9th Cir. 1997).

DEFENDANT'S RIGHTS

Petitioner for post-conviction relief, who had entered a guilty plea to kidnapping and waived his right to a jury trial at the time of the entry of the plea, did not also waive his right to be sentenced by a jury because he did not know he possessed this right when he entered his guilty plea. State v. Ward, 211 Ariz. 158, 118 P.3d 1122, 2005 Ariz. App. LEXIS 114 (Ct. App. 2005).

Even though Rule 32 does not give an indigent defendant the right to appointed counsel in a discretionary proceeding, that does not mean that a court is forbidden from appointing counsel when, in the interest of justice, appointment of counsel seems necessary. State v. Smith, 184 Ariz. 456, 910 P.2d 1 (1996).

DISCOVERY

After filing only his post-conviction relief notice, inmate requested various materials used at his trial or available at that time, alleging, without elaboration, that they were needed to present an effective defense; however, his claim, unsupported by an actual post-conviction relief petition, was insufficient. Canion v. Cole, 210 Ariz. 598, 456 Ariz. Adv. Rep. 15, 115 P.3d 1261, 2005 Ariz. LEXIS 79 (2005).

ENHANCEMENT OF SENTENCE
--CONVICTIONS INADMISSIBLE.

Defendant's motion for post-conviction relief was granted where some of the six counts to be used as historical prior convictions to enhance her sentences under A.R.S. § 13-604 on other counts covered by the plea agreement were contrary to a supreme court ruling; enhancement under the statute was impermissible if the same felonies were tried together. State v. Ofstedahl, 208 Ariz. 406, 431 Ariz. Adv. Rep. 3, 93 P.3d 1122, 2004 Ariz. App. LEXIS 109 (Ct. App. 2004).

ERROR

Trial court erred in ruling that a recent United States Supreme Court opinion regarding a defendant's right to a jury during sentencing, which was decided when petitioner's request for post-conviction relief was pending, was not applicable to the petitioner. Moreover, the petition for post-conviction relief was considered the equivalent of a direct appeal. State v. Ward, 211 Ariz. 158, 118 P.3d 1122, 2005 Ariz. App. LEXIS 114 (Ct. App. 2005).

Defendant challenged enhanced sentence for aggravated robbery; the petition for relief was denied, but while his petition for review was pending, he filed a notice of supplemental authority and supplemental briefing containing information which made it clear the issue should have gone to a jury, which was fundamental, not harmless, error. State v. Resendis-Felix, 209 Ariz. 292, 438 Ariz. Adv. Rep. 3, 100 P.3d 457, 2004 Ariz. App. LEXIS 181 (Ct. App. 2004).

EVIDENCE
--IN GENERAL.

Motion for new trial is properly denied if the testimony of a proffered witness does not appear reliable or credible to the trial court. State v. Dunlap, 187 Ariz. 441, 930 P.2d 518 (Ct. App. 1996), cert. denied, 520 U.S. 1275, 117 S. Ct. 2456, 138 L. Ed. 2d 214 (1997).

--NEWLY DISCOVERED

When DNA evidence was discovered after defendant's first degree murder and sexual abuse trial, the superior court needed to make additional specific findings of fact and conclusions of law to facilitate the Supreme Court's review of defendant's request for post-conviction relief. State v. Tankersley, 211 Ariz. 323, -- Ariz. Adv. Rep. --, 121 P.3d 829, 2005 Ariz. LEXIS 132 (2005).

Newly discovered evidence of drug use and of lying about drug use would have probably changed the verdict. State v. Orantez, 183 Ariz. 218, 902 P.2d 824 (1995).

--NOT NEWLY DISCOVERED

Question whether an asserted claim was of "sufficient constitutional magnitude" to require a knowing, voluntary and intelligent waiver for purposes of Rule 32.2(a)(3), depended not upon the merits of the particular claim, but rather merely upon the particular right alleged to have been violated. Stewart v. Smith, 202 Ariz. 446, 378 Ariz. Adv. Rep. 86, 46 P.3d 1067, 2002 Ariz. LEXIS 89 (2002).

Where it was undisputed that defendant in murder case knew another person had allegedly confessed to the murder well before trial and did nothing to bring the evidence forward but allowed the trial to proceed instead, that the trial court erred in granting defendant a new trial. State v. Saenz, 197 Ariz. 487, 4 P.3d 1030, 2000 Ariz. App. LEXIS 52 (Ct. App. 2000).

Testimony was not "newly-discovered." Federal courts overwhelmingly do not consider evidence newly-discovered when a defendant who voluntarily chose not to testify comes forward later to offer testimony exculpating a co-defendant. The court of appeals agreed with the federal view. State v. Dunlap, 187 Ariz. 441, 930 P.2d 518 (Ct. App. 1996), cert. denied, 520 U.S. 1275, 117 S. Ct. 2456, 138 L. Ed. 2d 214 (1997).

EXHAUSTION OF REMEDIES

Prisoner, who filed habeas petition days before his motion for reconsideration was determined in state superior court, prematurely filed the habeas petition because his conviction had not become final but was still under consideration in a state court post-conviction proceeding, meaning he had not exhausted his remedies. Lopez v. Schriro, -- F. Supp. 2d --, 2005 U.S. Dist. LEXIS 28060 (D. Ariz. November 8, 2005).

FILING

If a pro se prisoner timely gave his notice of petition for post-conviction relief to the Arizona Department of Corrections for mailing, his notice must be considered timely filed. State v. Rosario, 195 Ariz. 264, 987 P.2d 226 (Ct. App. 1999).

Questions regarding whether, in light of amendments to Rule 32.2(b), federal habeas petitioner could raise his claims pursuant to subdivision (f) of this rule, by alleging that his failure to file a timely petition for review or a Rule 32 petition was without fault on his part, were certified to Supreme Court. Moreno v. Gonzales, 116 F.3d 409 (9th Cir. 1997).

While Rule 32.4(a) establishes the time limits within which a petitioner must file a notice of post-conviction relief, it also provides that a petitioner may pursue, at any time, claims for relief based on subsections (d), (e), (f) and (g) of this rule. State v. Pruett, 185 Ariz. 128, 912 P.2d 1357 (Ct. App. 1995).

GUILTY PLEA

The trial court erred in granting defendant's petition for post-conviction relief and ordering a new sentencing hearing where, when the appellate court vacated defendant's prior convictions on appeal, the terms of his plea agreement were altered. State v. Szpyrka, 223 Ariz. 390, 573 Ariz. Adv. Rep. 14, 224 P.3d 206, 2010 Ariz. App. LEXIS 6 (Ct. App. 2010).

Post-conviction relief under Ariz. R. Crim. P. 32.1 was properly denied because the corpus delicti rule did not apply to admissions made by petitioner at an in-court guilty plea where the statements were made under the supervision and protection of the trial court, which ensured that the plea was knowing and voluntary. State v. Rubiano, 214 Ariz. 184, 495 Ariz. Adv. Rep. 9, 150 P.3d 271, 2007 Ariz. App. LEXIS 7 (Ct. App. 2007).

HABEAS CORPUS

Prisoner's habeas petition under 28 U.S.C.S. § 2254 was denied as untimely because he did not file his state post-conviction motion under Ariz. R. Crim. P. 32 until after the limitations period expired under 28 U.S.C.S. § 2244 so that the state motion did not toll, renew, or refresh the limitation period and the prisoner failed to show entitlement to equitable tolling. Norman v. Ryan, -- F. Supp. 2d --, 2009 U.S. Dist. LEXIS 62626 (D. Ariz. July 20, 2009).

Federal habeas petitioner did not have an available state court remedy under this rule. His speculation regarding the content of original and missing images was insufficient to show that defense access to the material would probably have made a difference in his trial or sentencing and petitioner was not diligent in securing the facts regarding the photographic evidence. Henry v. Ryan, -- F. Supp. 2d --, 2009 U.S. Dist. LEXIS 21510 (D. Ariz. Mar. 17, 2009).

Habeas petitioner's claim that she was denied her right to a public trial due to her case being referred to a court commissioner appointed as a judge pro tempore did not fall within the scope of the exceptions enumerated in Ariz. R. Crim. P. 32.1(d), (e), (f), (g), or (h). Kajander v. Schroeder, -- F. Supp. 2d --, 2009 U.S. Dist. LEXIS 7183 (D. Ariz. Jan. 30, 2009).

State prisoner was not entitled to habeas corpus relief because his claims that: (1) His guilty plea was not knowing, intelligent, and voluntary; (2) Appellate counsel was ineffective; (3) His constitutional rights were violated by the cumulative deficiency of trial, appellate, and post-conviction relief counsel; and (4) Arizona's death penalty statute was unconstitutional, were technically exhausted but procedurally defaulted for purposes of Ariz. R. Crim. P. 32.1(d)-(h), Ariz. R. Crim. P. 32.2(a)(3) and (b), and Ariz. R. Crim. P. 32.4(a). Djerf v. Schriro, -- F. Supp. 2d --, 2008 U.S. Dist. LEXIS 89565 (D. Ariz. Sept. 29, 2008).

Because there was neither absent nor inadequate state corrective process in Arizona to adjudicate petitioner's claims, he was subject to the exhaustion requirement in 28 U.S.C.S. § 2254(b); petitioner's allegations concerning the competence of appellate counsel had to be presented in a state post-conviction-relief petition, which would not be initiated until after his direct appeal proceedings were concluded. Velazquez v. Schriro, -- F. Supp. 2d --, 2007 U.S. Dist. LEXIS 55370 (D. Ariz. July 27, 2007).

Rule 32 encompasses the relief available by writ of habeas corpus. Coley v. Gonzales, 55 F.3d 1385 (9th Cir. 1995).

INEFFECTIVE ASSISTANCE OF COUNSEL
Court erred in denying the inmate's successive notice of post-conviction relief filed pursuant to Ariz. R. Crim. P. 32, because the inmate asked for the appointment of different counsel to evaluate whether he might have a claim of ineffective

assistance of his previous counsel that he could raise in the subsequent proceeding, and this was sufficient to avoid a summary dismissal of his notice. State v. Petty, -- Ariz. --, 590 Ariz. Adv. Rep. 29, 238 P.3d 637, 2010 Ariz. App. LEXIS 142 (Ct. App. 2010).

In an assault case, denial of the inmate's petition for post-conviction relief was proper, the inmate who was not denied effective assistance of counsel where counsel did not question the inmate's reasons for rejection of state's plea offers, and counsel was under no obligation to inquire of the inmate what, if any, plea offer she might be willing to accept. State v. Vallejo, 215 Ariz. 193, 505 Ariz. Adv. Rep. 27, 158 P.3d 9161, 2007 Ariz. App. LEXIS 90 (Ct. App. 2007).

Because prejudice is an essential component of any Sixth Amendment ineffective assistance of counsel claim, claim that a defendant has been prejudiced by deficient performance before disposition of the charges at the trial level is purely speculative. A defendant may bring ineffective assistance of counsel claims only in a post-conviction proceeding -- not before trial, at trial, or on direct review. State ex rel. Thomas v. Rayes, 214 Ariz. 411, 501 Ariz. Adv. Rep. 14, 153 P.3d 1040, 2007 Ariz. LEXIS 32 (2007).

Although petitioner's claim of ineffective assistance of counsel on appeal was a cognizable "Rule 32" claim under this rule, petitioner failed to present a colorable claim of ineffective assistance of appellate counsel which would have changed the outcome. Petitioner's aggravated sentences for aggravated assault and first-degree burglary did not exceed the statutory maximum, therefore the Apprendi rule did not apply and the outcome of petitioner's appeal would not have been different if counsel had raised an Apprendi claim on direct appeal. State v. Febles, 210 Ariz. 589, 455 Ariz. Adv. Rep. 3, 115 P.3d 629, 2005 Ariz. App. LEXIS 86 (Ct. App. 2005).

Defendant failed to raise a colorable claim of ineffective assistance of counsel because a concrete plea offer was not made by the state; an extension of constitutional principles did not include counsel's failure to investigate possibilities of a plea offer made by the state. State v. Jackson, 209 Ariz. 13, 435 Ariz. Adv. Rep. 14, 97 P.3d 113, 2004 Ariz. App. LEXIS 135 (Ct. App. 2004).

By raising one claim of ineffective assistance of trial counsel in a direct appeal, all later ineffectiveness of trial counsel claims would be precluded. State v. Spreitz, 202 Ariz. 1, 378 Ariz. Adv. Rep. 5, 39 P.3d 525, 2002 Ariz. LEXIS 16 (2002).

An allegation of ineffective assistance of counsel is encompassed within this rule as a claim that a defendant's conviction or sentence was in violation of the Constitution of the United States or the State of Arizona. State v. Herrera, 183 Ariz. 642, 905 P.2d 1377 (Ct. App. 1995).

INMATE TRANSPORT ORDER

Where an inmate sentenced to death for first-degree murder requested organic and neurological testing, the superior court properly entered an order requiring the Arizona Department of Corrections to transport the prisoner rather than the county sheriff. The superior court's order was a valid exercise of its inherent authority under §§ 12-122, 12-123(B); the transport order did not significantly infringe on the department's executive authority. State Ex Rel. Ariz. Dep't of Corr. v. Kiger, 224 Ariz. 252, 229 P.3d 264, 2010 Ariz. App. LEXIS 62 (Ct. App. 2010).

JURISDICTION

Appellate court determined that it did not have jurisdiction to hear a petitioner's appeal from the denial of post-conviction relief because, even though the state agreed defendant should receive a new jury trial during sentencing, the petitioner waived his right to appeal by entering a plea agreement. State v. Celaya, 213 Ariz. 282, 481 Ariz. Adv. Rep. 3, 141 P.3d 762, 2006 Ariz. App. LEXIS 78 (Ct. App. 2006).

A trial court has jurisdiction under this rule to determine a claim of ineffective assistance of appellate counsel. State v. Herrera, 183 Ariz. 642, 905 P.2d 1377 (Ct. App. 1995).

--PRECLUSION

Petitioner seeking habeas corpus relief under 28 U.S.C.S. § 2254 was precluded by Ariz. R. Crim. P. 32.2(a)(3) and Ariz. R. Crim. P. 32.4 from obtaining relief in state court because the post-conviction relief court decided that issue against the petitioner and the petitioner had not sought review of the determination on his petition for review to the Arizona Supreme Court, and the petitioner did not assert any exception under Rule 32.1(d)-(h); those claims were technically exhausted but procedurally defaulted absent a showing of cause and prejudice or a fundamental miscarriage of justice. Rogovich v. Schriro, -- F. Supp. 2d --, 2006 U.S. Dist. LEXIS 37041 (D. Ariz. June 6, 2006).

JURISDICTION -- PRECLUSION

Inmate's claim alleging that the United States Supreme Court's decision in Atkins prohibited execution of the mentally ill was not colorable under Ariz. R. Crim. P. 32.1(g) where the Supreme Court held that U.S. Const. Amend. VIII prohibited execution of the mentally retarded, not the mentally ill; the inmate could not return to state court to exhaust the claim because it did not allege facts or law exempting it from preclusion and untimeliness under Ariz. R. Crim. P. 32.2(a)(3) and 32.4(a). Doerr v. Ryan, -- F. Supp. 2d --, 2010 U.S. Dist. LEXIS 20225 (D. Ariz. Feb. 10, 2010).

PRESENTENCE CUSTODY CREDIT

Where petitioner was incarcerated pursuant to drug charges, even though also subject to a probation hold in connection with an assault case, trial court's refusal to grant him 227 days of presentence incarceration credit against his sentence for the drug conviction was improper and subject to post-conviction relief. State v. Brooks, 191 Ariz. 155, 953 P.2d 547 (Ct. App. 1998).

PROCEDURAL DEFAULT

Certain habeas corpus claims were barred by procedural default where the inmate could not be granted post-conviction relief under Ariz. R. Crim. P. 32.2 on any claim that could have been raised in a prior post-conviction petition; Arizona's preclusion rule is an adequate and independent bar to federal review. The claims did not fall within certain exceptions set forth in this rule, and the inmate did not justify why the claims were not presented in a timely manner. Jones v. Schriro, 450 F. Supp. 2d 1047, 2006 U.S. Dist. LEXIS 63137 (D. Ariz. 2006).

State prisoner procedurally defaulted his Eighth Amendment challenge to execution by lethal injection where he did not raise it in compliance with this rule;

prisoner failed to exercise due diligence in obtaining evidence to support his claim that lethal injection was administered so as to cause extreme suffering and torture, nor did he explain why he did not seek evidence between the time Arizona introduced execution by lethal injection and the time the supplemental petition for post-conviction relief was filed. Williams v. Stewart, 441 F.3d 1030, 2006 U.S. App. LEXIS 9633 (9th Cir. 2006).

Subsection (c)(2) clearly states that a continuance will only be granted under "extraordinary circumstances." A simple need for more time, after sufficient time has already been permitted, does not constitute extraordinary circumstances, particularly where the petitioner fails to articulate any issue of actual prejudice, or show that a fundamental miscarriage of justice occurred; without actual prejudice the argument for excusing the procedural default is incomplete. Crook v. State of Ariz., -- F. Supp. 2d --, 2005 U.S. Dist. LEXIS 35315 (D. Ariz. 2005).

In habeas corpus proceeding, district court erred in failing to consider procedural default when it held that issue of ineffective assistance of counsel at sentencing was properly before it. Martinez-Villareal v. Lewis, 80 F.3d 1301, cert. denied, 519 U.S. 1030, 117 S. Ct. 588, 136 L. Ed. 2d 517 (1996).

RETROACTIVE CHANGE IN LAW

A defendant may to receive relief from a conviction if he is entitled to benefit from a retroactive change in the law, including retroactive statutory amendments. Because legislative acts occurring after a conviction may entitle a defendant to Rule 32 relief, criminal convictions give the state no vested right immune from modification by the legislature. State v. Rios, -- Ariz. --, 588 Ariz. Adv. Rep. 5, 237 P.3d 1052, 2010 Ariz. App. LEXIS 132 (Ct. App. 2010).

RIGHT TO APPEAL

Application of A.R.S. § 13-4033(C) to preclude defendant from a direct appeal would deny him his right to appeal under Ariz. Const. art. 2, § 24 without personal notice of the potential consequence, because defendant's failure to appear for sentencing did not itself demonstrate a knowing, voluntary, and intelligent waiver of his right to appeal. Since Ariz. Const. art. 2, § 24 entitled a criminal defendant to appellate review in all cases, not merely those that involved potential claims remediable under Ariz. R. Crim. P. 32.1, A.R.S. § 13-4033(C) was unconstitutional to the extent it was applied to deprive such defendants of their right to direct appeal. State v. Soto, 223 Ariz. 407, 575 Ariz. Adv. Rep. 4, 224 P.3d 223, 2010 Ariz. App. LEXIS 18 (Ct. App. 2010).

RIGHT TO COUNSEL

If, after searching the record, appointed counsel in a post-conviction relief (PCR) proceeding can find no tenable issue to submit, counsel may so inform the court and defendant; the defendant will then be entitled to proceed pro se, and may also be entitled to an appropriate extension of time in which to file a PCR petition; until the trial court makes its required review and disposition, however, counsel is obligated to remain on the case. Lammie v. Barker, 185 Ariz. 263, 915 P.2d 662 (1996).

The pleading defendant does not have a right to appointed counsel in post-conviction relief (PCR) proceedings beyond the trial court's mandatory consideration and disposition of the PCR. Lammie v. Barker, 185 Ariz. 263, 915 P.2d 662 (1996).

The purpose of having counsel remain on the case in Rule 32 proceedings after the defendant has elected to proceed pro se is not to file a post-conviction relief (PCR) petition or petition for review, even though counsel believes there is not tenable basis for it, on behalf of the pro se defendant; rather, counsel's only function at that point is to assist the pro se defendant should that defendant or the trial court discover a viable issue that counsel had not previously considered or when, in the interest of justice, appointment of counsel seems necessary. Lammie v. Barker, 185 Ariz. 263, 915 P.2d 662 (1996).

SECOND PETITION

A pleading defendant must be afforded an opportunity to assert a claim regarding the effectiveness of the attorney representing him on the first petition for post-conviction relief; the obvious method is by means of a second petition for post-conviction relief. State v. Pruett, 185 Ariz. 128, 912 P.2d 1357 (Ct. App. 1995).

SEPARATE CONVICTIONS

Trial court did not abuse its discretion in denying defendant's petition for post-conviction relief, as it could properly impose consecutive terms of probation for two unrelated convictions for which defendant had been separately charged. State v. Bowsher, 223 Ariz. 177, 573 Ariz. Adv. Rep. 7, 221 P.3d 368, 2009 Ariz. App. LEXIS 793 (Ct. App. 2009).

SENTENCE
--DEATH SENTENCE

Where defendant was convicted of first degree burglary and felony murder, the jury did not abuse its discretion in rendering a verdict of death. The Supreme Court of Arizona rejected defendant's challenge to the constitutionality of Arizona's death by lethal injection statute, A.R.S. § 13-757(A); a challenge to the protocol to be used during a lethal injection must be made by petition filed pursuant to this rule. State v. Kuhs, 223 Ariz. 376, 576 Ariz. Adv. Rep. 13, 224 P.3d 192, 2010 Ariz. LEXIS 13 (2010).

--NOT UPHELD

A.R.S. § 13-604.01(I) does not include attempted sexual conduct with a victim under the age of twelve; the sentence imposed against defendant was illegal because the court could not supply a punishment the legislature did not enact. State v. Gonzalez, 216 Ariz. 11, 507 Ariz. Adv. Rep. 12, 162 P.3d 650, 2007 Ariz. App. LEXIS 119 (Ct. App. 2007).

-- RESTITUTION

Post-conviction relief was denied defendant who contested a restitution order in favor of the prison after he was convicted of escape; the order was vacated and the case was remanded for a redetermination of the restitution order because the statutes directed an award of restitution only for damages that flowed directly from defendant's criminal conduct. State v. Guilliams, 208 Ariz. 48, 428 Ariz. Adv. Rep. 3, 90 P.3d 785, 2004 Ariz. App. LEXIS 76 (Ct. App. 2004).

TIMELINESS

When defendant filed a state notice of post-conviction post-conviction relief after the one-year statute of limitations set forth in 28 U.S.C.S. 2244(d) had expired, even if a state court had accepted the notice of post-conviction relief as permissible under this rule, the state petition would have had no tolling effect on the limitations period under 28 U.S.C.S. § 2244(d). Section 2244(d) does not permit the re-initiation of a one-year limitations period that ended before a state petition was filed. Burris v. Schriro, -- F. Supp. 2d --, 2006 U.S. Dist. LEXIS 64014 (D. Ariz. Aug. 18, 2006).

Rule 32.2. Preclusion of remedy

a. Preclusion. -- A defendant shall be precluded from relief under this rule based upon any ground:

> 1) Still raisable on direct appeal under Rule 31 or on post-trial motion under Rule 24;
>
> 2) Finally adjudicated on the merits on appeal or in any previous collateral proceeding;
>
> 3) That has been waived at trial, on appeal, or in any previous collateral proceeding.

b. Exceptions. -- Rule 32.2(a) shall not apply to claims for relief based on Rules 32.1(d), (e), (f), (g) and (h). When a claim under Rules 32.1(d), (e), (f), (g) and (h) is to be raised in a successive or untimely post-conviction relief proceeding, the notice of post-conviction relief must set forth the substance of the specific exception and the reasons for not raising the claim in the previous petition or in a timely manner. If the specific exception and meritorious reasons do not appear substantiating the claim and indicating why the claim was not stated in the previous petition or in a timely manner, the notice shall be summarily dismissed.

c. Standard of proof. -- The state shall plead and prove any ground of preclusion by a preponderance of the evidence. Though the state has the burden to plead and prove grounds of preclusion, any court on review of the record may determine and hold that an issue is precluded regardless of whether the state raises preclusion.

HISTORY: Amended June 2, 1992, effective Sept. 30, 1992; amended Oct. 31, 2000, effective Dec. 1, 2000.

NOTES:
EDITOR'S NOTE
Prior comments were consolidated and amended effective December 1, 2002. R-01-0015.

COMMENT
Rule 32.2(a)(1) precludes relief for any claims that still may be considered by a trial or appellate court under Rule 24, which governs post-trial motions, or under Rule 31, which governs appeals.

The pre-1992 version of Rule 32.2(a)(3) indicated that a defendant must "knowingly, voluntarily and intelligently" not raise an issue at trial, on appeal, or in a previous collateral proceeding before the issue was precluded. See Fay v. Noia, 372 U.S. 392 (1963). While that is the correct standard of waiver for some constitutional rights, it is not the correct standard for other trial errors. Accordingly, some issues not raised at trial, on appeal, or in a previous collateral proceeding may be deemed waived without considering the defendant's personal knowledge, unless such knowledge is specifically required to waive the constitutional right involved. If an asserted claim is of sufficient constitutional magnitude, the state must show that the defendant "knowingly, voluntarily and intelligently" waived the claim. For most claims of trial error, the state may simply show that the defendant did not raise the error at trial, on appeal, or in a previous collateral proceeding, and that would be sufficient to show that the defendant has waived the claim. See Stewart v. Smith, 202 Ariz. 446, 46 P.3d 1067 (2002).

Amendments in 2000 to subsection (b) intended to conform to recent statutory changes include a requirement that a defendant set forth the substance of the specific exception and the reasons for not raising the claim in the previous petition or in a timely manner. The failure to identify the specific exceptions will allow for dismissal without prejudice on the notice alone. Additionally, the amendments add a claim of actual innocence as an exception to preclusion.

Subsection (c) was amended in 2000 to conform to recent statutory changes.

JUDICIAL DECISIONS
ANALYSIS

IN GENERAL

Pursuant to this rule, state prisoners may not be granted relief on any claim which could have been raised in a prior Rule 32 proceeding. Only if a claim falls within subsection (d), (e), (f), or (g) of Rule 32.1 and the petitioner can justify why the claim was omitted from a prior petition will the preclusive effect of this rule be avoided. Gerlaugh v. Lewis, 898 F. Supp. 1388 (D. Ariz. 1995), aff'd, 129 F.3d 1027 (9th Cir. 1997), cert. denied, 525 U.S. 903, 119 S. Ct. 237, 142 L. Ed. 2d 195 (1998).

CONSTRUCTION

Prisoner did not set forth a basis for an evidentiary hearing on his claims for federal habeas relief because he did not diligently pursue the facts underlying his claims in the state courts: the prisoner failed to present his sufficiency of the evidence claim, his claim of juror bias, and his claim for prosecutorial misconduct on appeal, as required by Ariz. R. Crim. P. 31 and 32.2; he also failed to raise his claim of juror bias and to request a hearing on the issue through a post-trial motion under Ariz. R. Crim. P. 24.1(d). As a result, the prisoner failed to give the state courts the necessary opportunity to make additional factual findings related to his claims and thus was denied an evidentiary hearing under 28 U.S.C.S. § 2254(e)(2). Ruderman v. Ryan, -- F. Supp. 2d --, 2010 U.S. Dist. LEXIS 70271 (D. Ariz. July 13, 2010).

--IN GENERAL

Under the 1998 version of this rule, a claim found to be "precluded" under paragraph (a)(2) appears to be a classic exhausted claim and may therefore be subject to consideration in federal habeas; in contrast, a claim that has been "waived" under paragraph (a)(3) is procedurally defaulted and therefore barred from federal court consideration, absent a showing of cause and prejudice or fundamental miscarriage of justice. Poland v. Stewart, 169 F.3d 573, 1998 U.S.

App. LEXIS 35750 (9th Cir. 1999), cert. denied, 528 U.S. 845, 120 S. Ct. 117, 145 L. Ed. 2d 99 (1999).

--WITH OTHER LAW
There was no federal constitutional right to the assistance of counsel in connection with state collateral relief proceedings, even where those proceedings constituted the first tier of review for an ineffective assistance of counsel claim; thus, Ariz. R. Crim. P. 32.2 was an adequate and independent basis to support the state court judgment for federal habeas purposes. Mariano Martinez v. Schriro, 623 F.3d 731, 2010 U.S. App. LEXIS 19928 (9th Cir. Sept. 27, 2010).

Pursuant to this rule, habeas petitioners may not be granted relief on any claim which could have been raised in a prior Ariz. R. Crim. P. 32 petition for post-conviction relief. Only if a claim falls within certain exceptions (subsections (d) through (h) of Ariz. R. Crim. P. 32.1) and the petitioner can justify why the claim has been omitted from a prior petition will the preclusive effect of this rule be avoided. McKinney v. Schriro, -- F. Supp. 2d --, 2006 U.S. Dist. LEXIS 268 (D. Ariz. Jan. 3, 2006).

APPLICABILITY
Inmate's claim alleging that the United States Supreme Court's decision in Atkins prohibited execution of the mentally ill was not colorable under Ariz. R. Crim. P. 32.1(g) where the Supreme Court held that U.S. Const. amend. VIII prohibited execution of the mentally retarded, not the mentally ill; the inmate could not return to state court to exhaust the claim because it did not allege facts or law exempting it from preclusion and untimeliness under Ariz. R. Crim. P. 32.2(a)(3) and 32.4(a). Doerr v. Ryan, -- F. Supp. 2d --, 2010 U.S. Dist. LEXIS 20225 (D. Ariz. Feb. 10, 2010).

Certain habeas corpus claims were barred by procedural default where the inmate could not be granted post-conviction relief under this rule on any claim that could have been raised in a prior post-conviction petition; Arizona's preclusion rule is an adequate and independent bar to federal review. Because the inmate alleged neither cause and prejudice nor that a fundamental miscarriage of justice would occur if those claims were not reviewed on the merits, the preclusive effect could not be avoided. Jones v. Schriro, 450 F. Supp. 2d 1047, 2006 U.S. Dist. LEXIS 63137 (D. Ariz. 2006).

Where it was not clear that the Arizona state courts would find his claim procedurally barred, or that the district court erred in dismissing defendant's due process claim under 28 U.S.C. § 2254(b)(2) because it was not clear that his claim was not colorable, district court was encouraged to consider defendant's request that the court stay his habeas petition and hold his exhausted claims in abeyance while allowing him to exhaust his federal due process claim in the state courts. Cassett v. Stewart, 406 F.3d 614, 2005 U.S. App. LEXIS 7596 (9th Cir. 2005), cert. denied, 546 U.S. 1172, 126 S. Ct. 1336, 164 L. Ed. 2d 52 (2006).

In reversing the United States Court of Appeals for the Ninth Circuit, the Supreme Court relied on the response to a certified question from the Arizona Supreme Court that Ariz. R. Crim. P. 32.2 did not require courts to evaluate the merits of a particular claim but only to categorize the claim; therefore, Rule 32.2 determinations were independent of federal law, and the district court had properly rejected respondent's habeas petition as procedurally barred and the circuit court had erred in ruling otherwise. Stewart v. Smith, 536 U.S. 856, 122 S. Ct. 2578, 153 L. Ed. 2d 762, 2002 U.S. LEXIS 5165 (2002).

A petition for post-conviction relief is analogous to a direct appeal for a pleading defendant. Although procedurally different, a post-conviction relief proceeding is similar to a direct appeal in that both ensure that a defendant is afforded due process of law and both ultimately seek the same relief, a new trial. State v. Rosas-Hernandez, 202 Ariz. 212, 370 Ariz. Adv. Rep. 7, 42 P.3d 1177, 2002 Ariz. App. LEXIS 42 (Ct. App. 2002).

EXCEPTIONS

State prisoner's claim that the prosecutor engaged in prejudicial misconduct by eliciting bad character evidence that the prisoner had a biker reputation was dismissed as procedurally barred because the prisoner did not fairly present the claim to the state courts; the claim was technically exhausted but procedurally defaulted because the prisoner no longer had an available state remedy. Wood v. Schriro, -- F. Supp. 2d --, 2006 U.S. Dist. LEXIS 12360 (D. Ariz. Mar. 20, 2006).

State prisoner's objections to a magistrate's recommendation to deny his 28 U.S.C.S. § 2254 petition were overruled because the magistrate properly concluded that the claims were procedurally defaulted and that the prisoner failed to show cause for the default or prejudice attributable to the default. Further, the prisoner did not show actual innocence and did not assert any applicable exceptions to preclusion under this rule. Tacquard v. Schriro, -- F. Supp. 2d --, 2005 U.S. Dist. LEXIS 27393 (D. Ariz. Nov. 4, 2005).

Questions regarding whether, in light of amendments to subdivision (b) of this rule, petitioner could raise his claims pursuant to Rule 32.1(f) by alleging that his failure to file a timely petition for review or a Rule 32 petition was without fault on his part were certified to Supreme Court. Moreno v. Gonzales, 116 F.3d 409 (9th Cir. 1997).

Where counsel, at prior proceedings had failed to raise claim based upon a change in law because he did not believe the law was applicable to petitioner at the time, counsel had sufficient reason for failing to argue the claim, the claim would constitute a significant change in the law, and the trial court's preclusion finding was an abuse of discretion. State v. Jensen, 193 Ariz. 105, 970 P.2d 937 (Ct. App. 1998).

Question whether an asserted claim was of "sufficient constitutional magnitude" to require a knowing, voluntary and intelligent waiver for purposes of Rule 32.2(a)(3), depended not upon the merits of the particular claim, but rather merely upon the particular right alleged to have been violated. Stewart v. Smith, 202 Ariz. 446, 378 Ariz. Adv. Rep. 86, 46 P.3d 1067, 2002 Ariz. LEXIS 89 (2002).

INEFFECTIVE ASSISTANCE OF COUNSEL
Court erred in denying the inmate's successive notice of post-conviction relief filed pursuant to Ariz. R. Crim. P. 32, because the inmate asked for the appointment of different counsel to evaluate whether he might have a claim of ineffective assistance of his previous counsel that he could raise in the subsequent proceeding, and this was sufficient to avoid a summary dismissal of his notice. State v. Petty, --

Ariz. --, 590 Ariz. Adv. Rep. 29, 238 P.3d 637, 2010 Ariz. App. LEXIS 142 (Ct. App. 2010).

Death-sentenced Arizona prisoner was not entitled to Fed. R. Civ. P. 59(e) reconsideration of the district court's order denying his petition for a writ of habeas corpus under 28 U.S.C.S. § 2254 where none of the prisoner's exhibits called into question the authority relied on by the district court in determining the lack of available state remedies for the prisoner's unexhausted ineffective assistance of post-conviction counsel claims. Smith v. Ryan, -- F. Supp. 2d --, 2009 U.S. Dist. LEXIS 123375 (D. Ariz. Dec. 23, 2009).

Because a prisoner never presented a claim of ineffective assistance based on appellate counsel's failure to raise an allegation of cumulative error, he was now precluded under Ariz. R. Crim. P. 32.2(a)(3) and 32.4 from presenting the claim in state court and could not establish the claim as cause for procedural default for purposes of habeas relief. McKinney v. Ryan, -- F. Supp. 2d --, 2009 U.S. Dist. LEXIS 73958 (D. Ariz. 2009).

Inmate's habeas petition was dismissed as untimely because, regarding the inmate's argument that some of the claims were of "sufficient constitutional magnitude" that the state had to show that the inmate knowingly, voluntarily, and intelligently waived the claim of ineffective assistance, the claims were not immune from 28 U.S.C.S. § 2244(d). Finley v. Schriro, -- F. Supp. 2d --, 2009 U.S. Dist. LEXIS 7179 (D. Ariz. Jan. 30, 2009).

Even though a defendant failed to raise the claim of ineffective assistance of counsel in her first petition, the issue was still reviewable because her first post-conviction relief counsel could not have alleged that post-conviction counsel, himself or herself, was ineffective. State v. Bennett, 213 Ariz. 562, 490 Ariz. Adv. Rep. 12, 146 P.3d 63, 2006 Ariz. LEXIS 125 (2006).

Rule 32.2 did not clearly require the defendant to raise a claim of ineffective assistance of counsel on appeal; therefore, the procedural default is inadequate to bar federal review. Lambright v. Stewart, 241 F.3d 1201, 2001 U.S. App. LEXIS 3364 (9th Cir. 2001).

Absent a showing of cause and prejudice, defendant's claim of ineffective assistance of counsel was procedurally defaulted and could not be considered in federal habeas, where issue had been declared precluded by waiver under subsection (a)(3). Poland v. Stewart, 151 F.3d 1014 (1998), reh'g denied, 169 F.3d 573 (9th Cir. 1999).

Defendant precluded from arguing that new evidence concerning defendant's background, which was available at his trial and previous appeals, should be heard in a petition for post-conviction relief due to his original counsel's ineffective presentation of the evidence. State v. Mata, 185 Ariz. 319, 916 P.2d 1035, cert. denied, 518 U.S. 1042, 117 S. Ct. 20, 135 L. Ed. 2d 1110 (1996).

PROCEDURAL DEFAULT
RELIEF DENIED
Prisoner's habeas petition under 28 U.S.C.S. § 2254 was denied because some claims were procedurally barred on state grounds due to the fact that the trial court denied those issues under (a)(3) of this rule, which precludes from post-conviction relief claims that could have been raised on appeal, and no cause or fundamental miscarriage of justice was shown. Gordon v. Schriro, -- F. Supp. 2d --, 2009 U.S. Dist. LEXIS 121138 (D. Ariz. Dec. 30, 2009).

Trial court did not err in failing to consider mitigation evidence under A.R.S. §§ 13-701, 13-702 and in considering the prisoner's drug use as an aggravating factor; the prisoner was precluded from relief under this rule because he failed to fairly present the claims to the post-conviction review court, and a return to state court would be futile because the time for the prisoner to file a direct appeal under Ariz. R. Crim. P. 31.3 had elapsed. Deberry v. Schriro, -- F. Supp. 2d --, 2009 U.S. Dist. LEXIS 99081 (D. Ariz. Oct. 22, 2009).

Defendant's second post-conviction relief proceeding was precluded under Ariz. R. Crim. P. 32.2(a) because a prior case was not an Ariz. R. Crim. P. 32.1(g) "significant change in the law;" after the case, the law remained precisely the same, and for purposes of Rule 32.1(g), a change in the law could not be established by the subjective opinions of counsel. State v. Shrum, 220 Ariz. 115, -- Ariz. Adv. Rep. --, 203 P.3d 1175, 2008 Ariz. LEXIS 239 (2008).

State prisoner was not entitled to habeas corpus relief because his claims that: (1) His guilty plea was not knowing, intelligent, and voluntary; (2) Appellate counsel was ineffective; (3) His constitutional rights were violated by the cumulative deficiency of trial, appellate, and post-conviction relief counsel; and (4) Arizona's death penalty statute was unconstitutional, were technically exhausted but procedurally defaulted for purposes of Ariz. R. Crim. P. 32.1(d)-(h), Ariz. R. Crim. P. 32.2(a)(3) and (b), and Ariz. R. Crim. P. 32.4(a). Djerf v. Schriro, -- F. Supp. 2d --, 2008 U.S. Dist. LEXIS 89565 (D. Ariz. Sept. 29, 2008).

Habeas petitioner's claim of judicial bias on resentencing was precluded pursuant to Ariz. R. Crim. P. 32.2(a)(3) because it was not raised at trial or on appeal. Gallegos v. Schriro, 583 F. Supp. 2d 1041, 2008 U.S. Dist. LEXIS 89567 (D. Ariz. 2008).

Although respondent argued that the trial judge responded improperly and inaccurately to a question from the jury during deliberations, respondent did not establish that the particular right alleged to have been violated was of sufficient constitutional magnitude to require a knowing, voluntary and intelligent waiver for purposes of this rule. Because the issue regarding the judge's answer was not raised on appeal in an earlier post-conviction proceeding, it was precluded. State v. Swoopes, 216 Ariz. 390, 513 Ariz. Adv. Rep. 4, 166 P.3d 945, 2007 Ariz. App. LEXIS 185 (Ct. App. Sept. 19, 2007).

In seeking habeas relief, an inmate challenged counsel's failure to investigate mitigation evidence, which had been addressed already by the PCR court on independent and adequate state grounds. This claim was procedurally barred following a determination by the PCR court that the claim could have been raised on direct appeal to the state supreme court. Van Adams v. Schriro, -- F. Supp. 2d --, 2007 U.S. Dist. LEXIS 38145 (D. Ariz. May 22, 2007).

Court denied an inmate's 28 U.S.C.S. § 2254 petition, which asserted procedurally defaulted claims and meritless claims of ineffective assistance of counsel; a state court's finding that the inmate's claims were barred by this rule was an adequate and independent state ground for rejecting the inmate's claims. Ross v. Goddard, -- F. Supp. 2d --, 2006 U.S. Dist. LEXIS 65903 (D. Ariz. Sept. 14, 2006).

Petitioner seeking habeas corpus relief under 28 U.S.C.S. § 2254 was precluded by paragraph (a)(3) and Ariz. R. Crim. P. 32.4 from obtaining relief in state court because the post-conviction relief court decided that issue against the petitioner and the petitioner had not sought review of the determination on his petition for review to the Arizona Supreme Court, and the petitioner did not assert any exception under Rule 32.1(d)-(h); those claims were technically exhausted but procedurally defaulted absent a showing of cause and prejudice or a fundamental miscarriage of justice. Rogovich v. Schriro, -- F. Supp. 2d --, 2006 U.S. Dist. LEXIS 37041 (D. Ariz. June 6, 2006).

Prisoner failed to comply with the requirements of Ariz. R. Crim. P. 32.9, and failed to fairly present claims of prosecutorial misconduct to the Arizona Supreme Court; although the claims were technically exhausted, they were procedurally defaulted because they did not allege facts or law exempting them from preclusion and untimeliness. Wood v. Schriro, -- F. Supp. 2d --, 2006 U.S. Dist. LEXIS 12360 (D. Ariz. Mar. 20, 2006).

State inmate's motion for reconsideration of the denial of his motion for evidentiary development in support of various habeas corpus claims was denied as, inter alia, his claim that the trial court erred by failing to replace counsel due to irreconcilable differences was procedurally barred by Ariz. R. Crim. P. 32.2(a)(3); where claim was not one for ineffective assistance of counsel as it was directed at the trial court, it should have been raised on direct appeal. Murray v. Schriro, -- F. Supp. 2d --, 2006 U.S. Dist. LEXIS 3446 (D. Ariz. Jan. 26, 2006).

Although several sentencing claims by a death-sentenced Arizona inmate were procedurally defaulted under paragraph (a)(3) of this rule and under Ariz. R. Crim. P. 32.4(a); the inmate was entitled to consideration of his claim that the trial court violated U.S. Const. amends. VIII and XIV by failing to consider and weigh relevant mitigating evidence under A.R.S. § 13-703 because the Arizona Supreme Court's actual review of the trial court's consideration and weighing of mitigating evidence sufficiently exhausted the claim for purposes of 28 U.S.C.S. § 2254(b)(1). Lopez v. Schriro, -- F. Supp. 2d --, 2005 U.S. Dist. LEXIS 26901 (D. Ariz. 2005).

Defendants were precluded from seeking post-conviction relief on grounds that were adjudicated, or could have been raised and adjudicated, in a prior appeal or prior petition for post-conviction relief. State v. Curtis, 185 Ariz. 112, 912 P.2d 1341 (Ct. App. 1995). (Disapproved to the extent that the question of whether an asserted ground is of sufficient constitutional magnitude to require a knowing and intelligent waiver, depends on the merits of the particular grounds, in Stewart v. Smith, 202 Ariz. 446, 46 P.3d 1067 (Ariz. 2002)).

SUMMARY DISMISSAL
Pursuant to 28 U.S.C.S. § 2254, the court dismissed certain aspects of six of the inmate's claims, and nine of the claims, under Ariz. R. Crim. P. 32.4 and this rule, because the issues were not raised in state court and were procedurally barred. Murray v. Schriro, -- F. Supp. 2d --, 2005 U.S. Dist. LEXIS 22296 (D. Ariz. Sept. 29, 2005).

When preclusion is evident from the petition and from the court's own files, a trial court may screen and summarily dismiss a prior appeal or prior petition for post-conviction relief on grounds of preclusion without putting the state to the burden of a response. State v. Curtis, 185 Ariz. 112, 912 P.2d 1341 (Ct. App. 1995). (Disapproved to the extent that the question of whether an asserted ground is of sufficient constitutional magnitude to require a knowing and intelligent waiver, depends on the merits of the particular grounds, in Stewart v. Smith, 202 Ariz. 446, 46 P.3d 1067 (Ariz. 2002)).

WAIVER

Where petitioner state prisoner filed a petition for federal habeas relief, the district court determined petitioner's ineffective assistance of counsel claims were waived under this rule by her failure to bring them in the first petition for post-conviction relief. Celaya v. Stewart, 691 F. Supp. 2d 1046, 2010 U.S. Dist. LEXIS 17091 (D. Ariz. Feb. 25, 2010).

Capital prisoner's constitutional rights were not violated by the denial of his severance motion to require habeas relief because the state court's determination that the claim had been waived under Ariz. R. Crim. P. 32.2 constituted an adequate state procedural bar and the prisoner did not attempt to demonstrate cause and prejudice or a fundamental miscarriage of justice. McKinney v. Ryan, -- F. Supp. 2d --, 2009 U.S. Dist. LEXIS 73958 (D. Ariz. 2009).

State death row inmate was denied habeas relief under 28 U.S.C.S. § 2254; the inmate's ineffective assistance of counsel claims were procedurally barred as waived under (a)(3) of this rule. Lee v. Schriro, -- F. Supp. 2d --, 2009 U.S. Dist. LEXIS 324 (D. Ariz. Jan. 6, 2009).

Rule 32.3. Nature of proceeding and relation to other remedies.

This proceeding is part of the original criminal action and not a separate action. It displaces and incorporates all trial court post-trial remedies except post-trial motions and habeas corpus. If a defendant applies for a writ of habeas corpus in a trial court having jurisdiction of his or her person raising any claim attacking the validity of his or her conviction or sentence, that court shall under this rule transfer the cause to the court where the defendant was convicted or sentenced and the latter court shall treat it as a petition for relief under this rule and the procedures of this rule shall govern.

HISTORY: Amended June 2, 1992, effective Sept. 30, 1992; amended July 28, 1993, effective Dec. 1, 1993; amended Oct. 31, 2000, effective Dec. 1, 2000.

NOTES:
COMMENT

[1992 AMENDMENT]
COMMENT TO RULE 32.3: The court does not intend to restrict by this rule the constitutional scope of the writ of habeas corpus.

[1973 PROMULGATION]
This section provides that all Rule 32 proceedings, regardless of the grounds presented and their past characterizations, are to be treated as criminal actions. The characterization of the proceeding as criminal assures compensation for appointed counsel and the applicability of criminal standards for admissibility of evidence at an evidentiary hearing except as otherwise provided.

Rule 32 is intended to provide a standard procedure for accomplishing the objectives of all constitutional, statutory, or common law post-trial writs and remedies except those specified in this section. As required by Ariz. Const. art. 2, § 14, the writ of habeas corpus is retained. See Ariz. Rev. Stat. Ann. §§ 13-2001 et seq. (1956). However, it is subordinated to the remedy provided by this rule in much the same way as the federal writ of habeas corpus, 28 U.S.C. § 2241 (1970) is subordinated for federal prisoners to the motion to vacate judgment. 28 U.S.C. § 2255 (1970). United States v. Hayman, 342 U.S. 205 (1952).

Rule 32.4. Commencement of proceedings
a. Form, filing and service of petition. -- A proceeding is commenced by timely filing a notice of post-conviction relief with the court in which the conviction occurred. The court shall provide notice forms for commencement of all post-conviction relief proceedings. In a Rule 32 of-right proceeding, the notice must be filed within ninety days after the entry of judgment and sentence or within thirty days after the issuance of the final order or mandate by the appellate court in the petitioner's first petition for post-conviction relief proceeding. In all other non-capital cases, the notice must be filed within ninety days after the entry of judgment and sentence or within thirty days after the issuance of the order and mandate in the direct appeal, whichever is the later. In a capital case, the clerk of the Supreme Court shall expeditiously file a notice for post-conviction relief with

the trial court upon the issuance of a mandate affirming the defendant's conviction and sentence on direct appeal. Any notice not timely filed may only raise claims pursuant to Rule 32.1(d), (e), (f), (g) or (h). The notice shall bear the caption of the original criminal action or actions to which it pertains. On receipt of the notice, the court shall file a copy of the notice in the case file of each such original action promptly send copies to the defendant, the county attorney, the defendant's attorney, if known, and the attorney general or the prosecutor, noting in the record the date and manner of sending the copies. If the conviction occurred in a court other the Superior Court, the copy shall be sent to the office of the prosecuting attorney who represented the state at trial. The state shall notify any victim who has requested notice of post-conviction proceedings.

b. Notification of appellate court. -- If an appeal of the defendant's conviction, sentence, or both is pending, the clerk, or the court, within 5 days after the filing of the notice for post-conviction relief, shall send a copy of the notice to the appropriate appellate court, noting in the record the date and manner of sending the copies.

Appointment of counsel
1)Capital cases. -- After the Supreme Court has affirmed a defendant's conviction and sentence in a capital case, the Supreme Court, or if authorized by the Supreme Court, the presiding judge of the county from which the case originated, shall appoint counsel for the defendant pursuant to A.R.S. § 13-4041 and Rule 6.8 if the defendant is determined to be indigent. If the appointment is made by the presiding judge, a copy of the court's order appointing counsel shall be filed in the Supreme Court.

Upon the filing of a successive notice, the presiding judge shall appoint the previous post-conviction counsel of the capital defendant unless counsel is waived or good cause is shown to appoint another qualified attorney from the list described in A.R.S. § 13-4041.

On the first notice in capital cases, appointed counsel for the defendant shall have one hundred twenty days from the filing of the notice to file a petition raising claims under Rule 32.1. A capital defendant proceeding without counsel shall have one hundred twenty days from the filing of the notice to file a petition. On the filing of a successive notice, appointed counsel, or the defendant if proceeding without counsel, shall file the petition within thirty days from the filing of the notice. On a showing of good cause, a defendant in a capital case may be granted a sixty day extension in which to file the petition. Additional extensions of thirty days may be granted for good cause. If a petition for post-conviction relief is not filed within one hundred and eighty days from the date of appointment of counsel, or one hundred and eighty days from the date the notice is filed, or the date a request for counsel is denied if the defendant is proceeding without counsel, the defendant or counsel for the defendant shall file a notice in the Supreme Court, advising the court of the status of the proceedings. Thereafter, defendant or counsel for the defendant shall file status reports in the Supreme Court every sixty days until the petition for post-conviction relief is filed.

2) Rule 32 of-right and non-capital cases. -- Upon the filing of a timely or first notice in a Rule 32 proceeding, the presiding judge, or his or her designee, shall appoint counsel for the defendant within 15 days if requested and the defendant is determined to be indigent. Upon the filing of all other notices in non-capital cases, the appointment of counsel is within the discretion of the presiding judge. In non - capital cases appointed counsel for the defendant shall have sixty days from the date of appointment to file a petition raising claims under Rule 32.1. On a showing of good cause, a defendant in a non-capital case may be granted a thirty day extension within which to file the petition. Additional extensions of thirty days shall be granted only upon a showing of extraordinary circumstances.

In a Rule 32 of-right proceeding, counsel shall investigate the defendant's case for any and all colorable claims. If counsel determines there are no colorable claims which can be raised on the defendant's behalf, counsel shall file a notice advising the court of this determination. Counsel's role is then limited to acting as advisory counsel until the trial court's final determination. Upon receipt of the notice, the court shall extend the time for filing a petition by the defendant in propria persona. The extension shall be 45 days from the date the notice is filed. Any extensions beyond the 45 days shall be granted only upon a showing of extraordinary circumstances.

A defendant proceeding without counsel shall have sixty days to file a petition from the date the notice is filed or from the date the request for counsel is denied.

d. Transcript preparation. -- If the trial court proceedings have not been previously transcribed, the defendant may request on a form provided by the clerk of court that certified transcripts be prepared. The court shall expeditiously review the request and order only those transcripts prepared that it deems necessary to resolve the issues to be raised in the petition. The preparation of the transcripts shall be at county expense if the defendant is indigent. The time for filing the petition shall be tolled from the time a request for the transcripts is made until the transcripts are prepared or the request is denied. Certified transcripts shall be prepared and filed within sixty days of the order granting the request.

e. Assignment of judge. -- The proceeding shall be assigned to the sentencing judge where possible. If it appears that the sentencing judge's testimony will be relevant, that judge shall transfer the case to another judge.

f. Stay of execution of death sentence; notification by Supreme Court. -- If the defendant has received a sentence of death and the Supreme Court has fixed the time for execution of the sentence, no stay of execution shall be granted upon the filing of a successive petition except upon separate application for a stay to the Supreme Court, setting forth with particularity those issues not precluded under Rule 32.2. The Clerk of the Supreme Court shall notify the defendant, the Attorney General, and the Director of the State Department of Corrections of the granting of a stay.

HISTORY: Amended Oct. 21, 1980, effective Dec. 1, 1980; amended Oct. 11, 1989, effective Dec. 1, 1989; amended June 2, 1992, effective Sept. 30, 1992; amended Sept. 24, 1992, effective Sept. 30, 1992; amended and effective Feb. 25, 1993; amended July 28, 1993, effective Dec. 1, 1993; amended Oct. 31, 2000, effective Dec. 1, 2000; amended May 31, 2002, effective June 1, 2002; amended by R-05-0009, effective Dec. 1, 2005; amended eff. Jan. 1, 2007 by R-05-0037.

NOTES:
COMMENT

[1973 PROMULGATION]
RULE 32.4(A). For purposes of uniformity, completeness, and efficiency, the rules require the petition to be filed on a standard form. See Rule 32.5(a).

Copies of the petition are to be sent to the attorney general as well as to the county attorney in order to comply with the jurisdictional requirements of Ariz. Rev. Stat. Ann. § 13-1516 (Cum. Supp. 1972). Subject to Rule 32.2, the petition may be filed at any time after entry of judgment and sentence. This is to provide an immediate remedy for issues not part of the trial record and not appropriate for post-trial motions under Rule 24.

RULE 32.4(B). If a petition is filed while an appeal is pending, the appellate court, under Rule 31.4(a), may stay the appeal until the petition is adjudicated. Any appeal from the decision on the petition will then be joined with the appeal from the judgment or sentence. See Rule 31.4(b)(2).

RULE 32.4(C). This rule favors the policy of giving a judge already familiar with the case the opportunity to correct any errors. Nothing in this section is intended to prohibit the sentencing judge from excusing himself if he believes that it may be inappropriate for him to preside over and decide the case, ABA, Standards, supra, at § 1.4(c), nor to limit a party's right to disqualify a judge under Rule 10.1 and 10.2

[1992 AMENDMENT]

COMMENT TO RULE 32.4 (F)
Warrants of execution will not be issued until the first petition for post-conviction relief is resolved. Therefore, Rule 32.4(f) only addresses staying warrants of execution in the case of second or subsequent petitions.

COMMITTEE COMMENT TO 1993 AMENDMENT

The 1993 amendment to Rule 32.4 was designed to adapt the rule to the circumstances in all courts. It deleted language in Rule 32.4(a) referring to the "clerk of the court," leaving only "the court." It also added "the prosecutor" to the list of persons to whom a copy of the notice of post-conviction relief is sent, for cases in which it is not appropriate to send the notice to the attorney general.

COMMENT TO 2000 AMENDMENT

Amendments to subsection (a) are to meet the requirements of Montgomery and State v. Pruett, 185 Ariz. 128, 912 P.2d 1357 (App. 1996). In Pruett, the court held that a pleading defendant is constitutionally entitled to effective assistance of counsel on the first petition for post-conviction relief, the counterpart to a direct appeal. Consequently, the rule is amended to allow the pleading defendant thirty days within which to file a second notice if the defendant seeks to challenge counsel's effectiveness in the Rule 32 of-right proceeding.

Amendments to subsection (c) are to separate capital from non-capital cases. Paragraph (1) brings the rule in line with new A.R.S. § 13-4041 and Rule 6.8 as adopted by the Supreme Court on October 22, 1996, effective November 1, 1996, which requires notification to the Supreme Court if a petition is not filed within 180 days from the filing of the notice for post-conviction relief, and requires monthly status reports thereafter.

Paragraph (2) requires appointment of counsel upon the timely filing of a first notice in a Rule 32 proceeding, when requested, but makes all other appointments of counsel in non-capital cases discretionary. The paragraph adds language to permit counsel to comply with Lammie v. Barker, 185 Ariz. 263, 915 P.2d 662 (1996).

Subsection (d) is amended to substitute "transcripts" for "record", provides for expeditious review of a request for transcripts, allows the court to limit transcripts to those deemed necessary to resolve the issues to be raised, and prescribes a time limit for preparation of transcripts.

JUDICIAL DECISIONS

ANALYSIS

IN GENERAL

Petitioner seeking habeas corpus relief under 28 U.S.C.S. § 2254 was precluded by Ariz. R. Crim. P. 32.2(a)(3) and this rule from obtaining relief in state court on his claims of the violation of his Fourteenth Amendment rights arising out of the state's failure to collect biological evidence from the petitioner in the form of breath, blood or urine samples, despite knowledge of his potential intoxication at the time of the crimes or his arrest. Rogovich v. Schriro, -- F. Supp. 2d --, 2006 U.S. Dist. LEXIS 37041 (D. Ariz. June 6, 2006).

State rules do not bar federal review if they are so unclear that they do not provide a reasonable opportunity to seek relief in state court; subsection (c) incorporates express provisions for extensions based upon good cause, but no criteria for good cause are provided. The rule has not been exercised consistently to bar a capital petition as untimely and is not firmly established. Williams v. Schriro, 423 F. Supp. 2d 994, 2006 U.S. Dist. LEXIS 12424 (D. Ariz. 2006).

CLAIM DEFAULTED

Because a prisoner never presented a claim of ineffective assistance based on appellate counsel's failure to raise an allegation of cumulative error, he was now precluded under Ariz. R. Crim. P. 32.2(a)(3) and 32.4 from presenting the claim in state court and could not establish the claim as cause for procedural default for purposes of habeas relief. McKinney v. Ryan, -- F. Supp. 2d --, 2009 U.S. Dist. LEXIS 73958 (D. Ariz. 2009).

State prisoner was not entitled to habeas corpus relief because his claims that: (1) His guilty plea was not knowing, intelligent, and voluntary; (2) Appellate counsel was ineffective; (3) His constitutional rights were violated by the cumulative deficiency of trial, appellate, and post-conviction relief counsel; and (4) Arizona's death penalty statute was unconstitutional, were technically exhausted but procedurally defaulted for purposes of Ariz. R. Crim. P. 32.1(d)-(h), Ariz. R. Crim. P. 32.2(a)(3) and (b), and Ariz. R. Crim. P. 32.4(a). Djerf v. Schriro, -- F. Supp. 2d --, 2008 U.S. Dist. LEXIS 89565 (D. Ariz. Sept. 29, 2008).

Although several sentencing claims by a death-sentenced Arizona inmate were procedurally defaulted under Ariz. R. Crim. P. 32.2(a)(3) and this rule, the inmate was entitled to consideration of his claim that the trial court violated U.S. Const. amends. VIII and XIV by failing to consider and weigh relevant mitigating evidence under A.R.S. § 13-703 because the Arizona Supreme Court's actual review of the trial court's consideration and weighing of mitigating evidence sufficiently exhausted the claim for purposes of 28 U.S.C.S. § 2254(b)(1). Lopez v. Schriro, -- F. Supp. 2d --, 2005 U.S. Dist. LEXIS 26901 (D. Ariz. 2005).

FILING

Pursuant to 28 U.S.C.S. § 2254, the court dismissed certain aspects of six of the inmate's claims, and nine of the claims, under Ariz. R. Crim. P. 32.2(a)(3) and this rule, because the issues were not raised in state court and were procedurally barred. Murray v. Schriro, -- F. Supp. 2d --, 2005 U.S. Dist. LEXIS 22296 (D. Ariz. Sept. 29, 2005).

The language of subsection (a) of this rule permits a defendant with an appeal pending to file notice of post-conviction relief at any time before 30 days after the mandate in his appeal has been issued by the appellate court. State v. Jones, 182 Ariz. 432, 897 P.2d 734 (Ct. App. 1995).

While subsection (a) establishes the time limits within which a petitioner must file a notice of post-conviction relief, it also provides that a petitioner may pursue, at any time, claims for relief based on Rule 32.1(d), (e), (f) and (g). State v. Pruett, 185 Ariz. 128, 912 P.2d 1357 (Ct. App. 1995).

The Supreme Court amended subsection (a) in 1992 to address potential abuse by defendants caused by the old rule's unlimited filing periods. State v. Jones, 182 Ariz. 432, 897 P.2d 734 (Ct. App. 1995).

NOTICE

This rule requires all post-conviction petitioners to file a notice of post-conviction relief to alert the superior court that it might need to appoint counsel and that notice must contain a request for relief from the judgment of conviction; the post-conviction process cannot go forward until the notice is filed and the guarantee of counsel fulfilled. Isley v. Ariz. Dep't of Corr., 383 F.3d 1054, 2004 U.S. App. LEXIS 19321 (9th Cir. 2004).

PRECLUSION

Where inmate alleged neither cause and prejudice nor that a fundamental miscarriage of justice would occur if his claims were not reviewed on the merits, the preclusive effect could not be avoided. Jones v. Schriro, 450 F. Supp. 2d 1047, 2006 U.S. Dist. LEXIS 63137 (D. Ariz. 2006).

SECOND PETITION

Trial court was not required to, nor did it abuse its discretion by failing to, appoint counsel for defendant in his second post-conviction relief proceeding. State v. McDonald, 192 Ariz. 44, 960 P.2d 644 (Ct. App. 1998).

A second notice of post-conviction relief for a claim of ineffectiveness of previous Rule 32 counsel is timely if filed within 30 days of the order and mandate affirming the trial court's denial of the petitioner's first petition for post-conviction relief. State v. Pruett, 185 Ariz. 128, 912 P.2d 1357 (Ct. App. 1995).

TIME LIMITS

This rule applied to deny petitioner prisoner an extension of time to file a post-conviction claim after Brady material was disclosed; every first request for an extension of time in a capital case had been granted previously in Arizona courts. As a result of the state court's arbitrary application of its rules, there was no state court decision to which a federal habeas court could defer, and thus, the deference for state court determinations did not apply and review of the claim was de novo. Williams v. Ryan, 623 F.3d 1258, 2010 U.S. App. LEXIS 22073 (9th Cir. Oct. 26, 2010).

Magistrate judge correctly found that a 28 U.S.C.S. § 2254 habeas petition filed by an Arizona inmate several years after he was sentenced for manslaughter was untimely. The petition was not filed within one year after the expiration of time for seeking an of-right proceeding under Ariz. R. Crim. P. 32.4, the alleged failure of post-conviction counsel to obtain transcripts was not an impediment caused by the state, and Blakely and Cunningham were not retroactively applicable. Hillman v. Schriro, -- F. Supp. 2d --, 2008 U.S. Dist. LEXIS 97697 (D. Ariz. Dec. 1, 2008).

Prisoner's habeas application under 28 U.S.C.S. § 2254 was dismissed because his habeas claims were procedurally defaulted in that exhaustion of the claims was impossible based on timeliness under Ariz. R. Crim. P. 32.9 and 32.4 and there was no showing of cause and prejudice or a fundamental miscarriage of justice to excuse procedural default. Pickens v. Schriro, -- F. Supp. 2d --, 2009 U.S. Dist. LEXIS 79114 (D. Ariz. Sept. 3, 2009).

Habeas petitioner's claim that she was denied her right to a public trial due to her case being referred to a court commissioner appointed as a judge pro tempore did not fall within the scope of the exceptions enumerated in Ariz. R. Crim. P.32.1(d), (e), (f), (g), or (h). Consequently, she was bound by the time constraints set forth in Rule 32.4(a). Kajander v. Schroeder, -- F. Supp. 2d --, 2009 U.S. Dist. LEXIS 7183 (D. Ariz. Jan. 30, 2009).

Prisoner failed to comply with the requirements of Ariz. R. Crim. P. 32.9, and failed to fairly present claims of prosecutorial misconduct to the Arizona Supreme Court; although the claims were technically exhausted, they were procedurally defaulted because they did not allege facts or law exempting them from preclusion and untimeliness. Wood v. Schriro, -- F. Supp. 2d --, 2006 U.S. Dist. LEXIS 12360 (D. Ariz. Mar. 20, 2006).

State prisoner's claim that the prosecutor engaged in prejudicial misconduct by eliciting bad character evidence that the prisoner had a biker reputation was dismissed as procedurally barred because the prisoner did not fairly present the claim to the state courts; the claim was technically exhausted but procedurally defaulted because the prisoner no longer had an available state remedy. Wood v. Schriro, -- F. Supp. 2d --, 2006 U.S. Dist. LEXIS 12360 (D. Ariz. Mar. 20, 2006).

In a habeas proceeding, a death-sentenced Arizona prisoner was entitled to limited discovery under R. Governing § 2254 Cases U.S. Dist. Cts. 6(a), expansion of the record under R. Governing § 2254 Cases U.S. Dist. Cts. 7, and an evidentiary hearing under R. Governing § 2254 Cases U.S. Dist. Cts. 8 and 28 U.S.C.S. § 2254(e)(2) because he raised a colorable due process claim that the state violated his right to a fair trial under Brady by withholding exculpatory evidence that another potential suspect existed for the offense and because he was diligent in developing his claim in state court. The state court's dismissal of the prisoner's petition as untimely was not an adequate bar to federal review because it is not firmly established under this rule that a capital post-conviction relief petition was subject to dismissal for lack of good cause in seeking a first extension of time to file a petition. Williams v. Schriro, 423 F. Supp. 2d 994, 2006 U.S. Dist. LEXIS 12424 (D. Ariz. 2006).

Dismissal of motion for post-conviction relief was vacated and remanded because once the applicant's sentence no longer existed, no sentencing date was available to be used to calculate the time for initiating a post-conviction proceeding, and the applicant's notice of post-conviction relief, filed just sixteen days after the resentencing, was timely, Ariz. R. Crim. P. 32.4. State v. Viramontes, 211 Ariz. 115, 459 Ariz. Adv. Rep. 9, 118 P.3d 630, 2005 Ariz. App. LEXIS 103 (Ct. App. 2005).

Subsections D and F of § 13-4234, defining time limits for filing a petition for post-conviction relief, conflict with subsection (c) of this rule, and thus violate the separation of powers doctrine. State ex rel. Napolitano v. Brown, 194 Ariz. 340, 982 P.2d 815 (1999).

TOLLING OF LIMITATIONS PERIOD

Defendant failed to demonstrate that equitable tolling of the one-year limitations period of 28 U.S.C.S. § 2244(d) was warranted when he knew at the time he was sentenced on his conviction for attempted child molestation about a letter from one of his stepdaughters, which was used as a basis for his aggravated sentence, and he was made aware of the 90-day period for filing an appropriate state petition for relief under this rule. <u>Burris v. Schriro</u>, -- F. Supp. 2d --, 2006 U.S. Dist. LEXIS 64014 (D. Ariz. Aug. 18, 2006).

Habeas petitioner was granted equitable tolling during the pendency of his state proceedings for post-trial relief, but procedurally defaulted his ineffective assistance claim, and failed to file his federal petition in time, despite the tolling. <u>Flowers v. Gaspar</u>, -- F. Supp. 2d --, 2005 U.S. Dist. LEXIS 25329 (D. Ariz. 2005).

District court improperly dismissed as untimely an inmate's federal habeas petition brought under 28 U.S.C.S. § 2244 on the ground that the petition was not filed within the one-year limitations period set forth in the Antiterrorism and Effective Death Penalty Act of 1996, 28 U.S.C.S. § 2244(d)(1)(A); the inmate's state post-conviction petition was pending within the meaning of § 2244(d) from the date the inmate filed his notice of post-conviction proceeding, as required by this rule, where such notice contained a request for relief from judgment of conviction and began the state post-conviction proceedings. <u>Isley v. Ariz. Dep't of Corr.</u>, 383 F.3d 1054, 2004 U.S. App. LEXIS 19321 (9th Cir. 2004)

Rule 32.5. Contents of petition
The defendant shall include every ground known to him or her for vacating, reducing, correcting or otherwise changing all judgments or sentences imposed upon him or her, and certify that he or she has done so. Facts within the defendant's personal knowledge shall be noted separately from other allegations of fact and shall be under oath. Affidavits, records, or other evidence currently available to the defendant supporting the allegations of the petition shall be attached to it. Legal and record citations and memoranda of points and authorities are required. In Rule 32 of-right and non-capital cases, the petition shall not exceed 25 pages. The response shall not exceed 25 pages, and any reply shall not exceed 10 pages. In capital cases, the petition shall not exceed 40 pages. The response shall not exceed 40 pages, and any reply shall not exceed 20 pages. A petition which fails to comply with this rule shall be returned by the court to the defendant for revision with an order specifying how the petition fails to comply with the rule. A petition that has been revised to comply with the rule shall be returned by the defendant for refiling within 30 days after defendant's receipt of the non-complying petition. If the

petition is not so returned, the court shall dismiss the proceeding with prejudice. The period for response by the state shall begin on the date a returned petition is refiled.

HISTORY: Amended April 11, 1989, effective July 1, 1989; amended June 2, 1992, effective Sept. 30, 1992; amended Sept. 24, 1992, effective Sept. 30, 1992; amended and effective Feb. 25, 1993; amended July 28, 1993, effective Dec. 1, 1993; amended Oct. 31, 2000, effective Dec. 1, 2000; amended Sept. 20, 2006, eff. Jan. 1, 2007 by R-05-0030.

NOTES:

COMMENT TO 2000 AMENDMENT
The amendments prescribe page limitations for petitions for post-conviction relief in all cases. They provide that, where a defendant's non-complying petition has been returned to him and he has not refiled a petition which complies with the rules within 30 days, the court shall dismiss the proceedings with prejudice.

[1973 PROMULGATION]
The petitioner should be afforded appointment of counsel for his or her first petition for post-conviction relief. Upon a subsequent petition for post-conviction relief the court may appoint counsel or decline to appoint counsel. If the court declines to appoint counsel it must state the reason for its decision in writing.

The court shall appoint counsel when petitioner first raises a claim of ineffective assistance of counsel. If the first petition for post-conviction relief includes a claim of ineffective assistance of counsel, then the court is not required to appoint counsel on a second petition claiming ineffective assistance of counsel. Any petition for post-conviction relief filed by a person under sentence of death shall result in the appointment of counsel.

The time within which appointed counsel may file an amended petition is expanded from fifteen (15) days to thirty (30) days. The expansion of time is afforded for the benefit of appointed counsel residing outside of Maricopa and Pima counties. Paperwork associated with the appointment of counsel is frequently delayed and as a matter of course appointed counsel are granted an extension of thirty (30) days in addition to the fifteen (15) days provided by the Rule. It is presumed that expanding the period of time from fifteen (15) to thirty (30) days will reduce the need for additional extensions of time.

RULE 32.5 (A). Rather than prescribing an exhaustive list of contents, section (a) requires the use of a standard form. The form (Form XXV), enables the court to have all relevant information before it as early as possible, facilitates review of the petition's adequacy, and gives additional notice to the petitioner of the requirements of the rule. See ABA, Standards Relating to Post-Conviction Remedies § 3.2 (Approved Draft, 1968); Cf. Post-Conviction Form No. 1, Ariz. Sup. Ct. R. 1 (a).

The rule requires the petitioner to list every ground for relief known to him and to verify under oath that he has done so. This is intended to encourage consolidation of all claims into a single proceeding and to evidence knowing and intelligent relinquishment of claims known but not made, see Rule 32.2. To aid compliance with this requirement, the form contains a check-list of grounds for relief modeled after the form provided by Pennsylvania Rules of Criminal Procedure 1501.

While a memorandum of points and authorities as defined in Ariz. Sup. Ct. R. 5 (b) (9) is not required, arguments which clarify and support the grounds for relief presented are neither precluded nor discouraged.

To afford the petitioner a maximum opportunity to state his claim, incompleteness is grounds for return, not dismissal of the petition.

RULE 32.5 (B). The procedures and standards for appointment of counsel are intended to conform with those in Rule 6. Counsel is appointed at this time in order to permit a full decision on the petition as quickly as possible and to equalize the position of indigent and non-indigent petitioners. No time-consuming preliminary screening is required. Appointed counsel's first duty is to insure that the petitioner has included all his grounds for relief in one petition and to file an amended petition when necessary to do so.

JUDICIAL DECISIONS
ANALYSIS

DUE DILIGENCE

Prisoner was not entitled to depositions to support his 28 U.S.C.S. § 2254 habeas claims of constitutional violations because the request was too vague to show good cause, and the prisoner was not diligent in pursuing the new facts in state court in his post-conviction petition under this rule. Jernigan v. Ryan, -- F. Supp. 2d --, 2009 U.S. Dist. LEXIS 110550 (D. Ariz. Nov. 23, 2009).

Under Arizona law, habeas petitioner had a duty to file affidavits, records, or other evidence available to him to support the allegations raised in his post-conviction relief petition. In failing to include such information, petitioner did not exercise due diligence. Henry v. Ryan, -- F. Supp. 2d --, 2009 U.S. Dist. LEXIS 21510 (D. Ariz. Mar. 17, 2009).

NEW CLAIMS

Trial court properly declined to consider petitioner's claims of ineffective assistance of trial and appellate counsel that were first raised in a post-conviction reply brief because by raising two new claims in the reply brief, petitioner essentially sought to amend the post-conviction petition without leave of the trial court. State v. Lopez, 223 Ariz. 238, 571 Ariz. Adv. Rep. 20, 221 P.3d 1052, 2009 Ariz. App. LEXIS 782 (Ct. App. 2009).

Rule 32.6. Additional pleadings; summary disposition; amendments

a. Prosecutor's response. -- Forty-five days after the filing of the petition, the state shall file with the court and send to the defendant or counsel for the defendant, a response. Affidavits, records or other evidence available to the state contradicting the allegations of the petition shall be attached to it. On a showing of good cause, the state may be granted a thirty day extension to file a response. Additional extensions shall be granted only upon a showing of extraordinary circumstances.

b. Defendant's reply. -- Within fifteen days after receipt of the response, the defendant may file a reply. Extensions shall be granted only upon a showing of extraordinary circumstances.

c. Summary disposition. -- The court shall review the petition within twenty days after the defendant's reply was due. On reviewing the petition, response, reply, files and records, and disregarding defects of form, the court shall identify all claims that are procedurally precluded under this rule. If the court, after identifying all precluded claims, determines that no remaining claim presents a material issue of fact or law which would entitle the defendant to relief under this rule and that no purpose would be served by any further proceedings, the court shall order the petition dismissed. If the court does not dismiss the petition, the court shall set a hearing within thirty days on those claims that present a material issue of fact or law. If a hearing is ordered, the state shall notify the victims, upon the victims' request pursuant to statute or court rule relating to victims' rights, of the time and place of the hearing.

d. Amendment of pleadings. -- After the filing of a post-conviction relief petition, no amendments shall be permitted except by leave of court upon a showing of good cause.

HISTORY: Amended June 2, 1992, effective Sept. 30, 1992; amended Oct. 31, 2000, effective Dec. 1, 2000.

NOTES:

COMMITTEE COMMENT TO 2000 AMENDMENT
The amendments to subsections (a) and (b) clarify that the appropriate party must make a showing of extraordinary circumstances to be granted an extension of time to file pleadings. This does not preclude the court from reviewing the petition on its own initiative.

[1973 PROMULGATION]
RULE 32.6 (A). Section (a) is based upon the second Revised Uniform Post-Conviction Act § 6 (a) (1966), and ABA, Standards Relating to Post-Conviction Remedies §§ 4.2 - 4.4 (Approved Draft, 1968). It requires the prosecutor to respond within 20 days after the petition has been filed and to include those portions of the record and transcript bearing on the issues raised in the petition. Ariz. Sup. Ct. R. 1 (e) and 4 (b) permit only 5 days for a response.

RULES 32.6 (C) AND (D).
Section (c) makes clear that plenary consideration is available for petitions raising factual issues, legal issues or both. It also instructs the court to make a final adjudication of all the petitioner's claims--those lurking in the background as well as those specified. For this reason, section (d) provides a liberal policy toward amendments to the pleadings. If the court finds from the pleadings and record that all of the petitioner's claims are frivolous and that it would not be beneficial to continue the proceedings, it may dismiss the petition. Such decision should be made without regard to defects in form. Both § 6 (b) of the Uniform Act, supra, and §§ 4.2, 4.3 (d) and (e) of the ABA, Standards, supra, provide for a summary disposition at this stage. However, if the court finds any colorable claim, it is required by Townsend v. Sain, 372 U.S. 293 (1963) to make a full factual determination before deciding it on its merits.

JUDICIAL DECISIONS
ANALYSIS

APPLICABILITY
Where defendant filed his notice of post-conviction relief on February 28, 1994, his case was governed by the current version of the rule. State v. Rodriguez, 183 Ariz. 331, 903 P.2d 639 (Ct. App. 1995).

BAR TO FEDERAL HABEAS REVIEW
Because Ariz. R. Crim. P. 32.6(d) allowed amendments even for dismissed petitions, and the state judge did not conduct an analysis on whether good cause for the amendment was shown, it was not an adequate and consistently applied state procedural rule barring the federal court's review of petitioner state death row

inmate's proposed ineffective assistance of trial counsel claims. Scott v. Schriro, 567 F.3d 573, 2009 U.S. App. LEXIS 11932 (9th Cir. 2009).

CLAIM FOR RELIEF

Petitioner set out a colorable claim for relief in arguing that counsel's failure, at the murder trial, to offer a witness' prior testimony to demonstrate a claim of perjury fell below an objective standard of reasonableness as measured by prevailing professional norms. State v. Prince, 211 Ariz. Adv. Rep. 40, 1996 Ariz. App. LEXIS 43 (Ct. App. March 5, 1996).

Defendant who claimed that he was induced to accept plea agreement on advice of trial counsel, based on counsel's allegedly incorrect statements of the possible sentence for armed robbery with a simulated weapon while on probation, presented a colorable claim of prejudice in the plea agreement, and was entitled to an evidentiary hearing on the claim. State v. Bowers, 192 Ariz. 419, 966 P.2d 1023 (Ct. App. 1998).

DISCRETION TO DISMISS

A trial court has discretion to dismiss a petition on the grounds of preclusion without awaiting the state's response. State v. Curtis, 185 Ariz. 112, 912 P.2d 1341 (Ct. App. 1995).

Disapproved to the extent that the question of whether an asserted ground is of sufficient constitutional magnitude to require a knowing and intelligent waiver, depends on the merits of the particular grounds, in Stewart v. Smith, 202 Ariz. 446, 46 P.3d 1067 (Ariz. 2002)).

"GOOD CAUSE."

Good cause exists when appointed counsel does not indicate until the 60-day period has expired that he declines to file a petition. State v. Rodriguez, 183 Ariz. 331, 903 P.2d 639 (Ct. App. 1995).

NEW CLAIM

Trial court properly declined to consider petitioner's claims of ineffective assistance of trial and appellate counsel that were first raised in a post-conviction reply brief because by raising two new claims in the reply brief, petitioner essentially sought to amend the post-conviction petition without the leave of the trial court, as required by this rule. State v. Lopez, 223 Ariz. 238, 571 Ariz. Adv. Rep. 20, 221 P.3d 1052, 2009 Ariz. App. LEXIS 782 (Ct. App. 2009).

Rule 32.7. Informal conference

The court may at any time hold an informal conference to expedite the proceeding. In a capital case, the court shall hold an informal conference within 90 days after the appointment of counsel on the first notice of a petition for post-conviction relief. The defendant need not be present if the defendant is represented by counsel who is present.

HISTORY: Amended June 2, 1992 amended Oct. 31, 2000, effective Dec. 1, 2000, effective Sept. 30, 1992; amended Oct. 31, 2000, effective Dec. 1, 2000; amended by R-08-0042, effective Jan. 1, 2010.

NOTES:
COMMENT

[1973 PROMULGATION]

This provision authorizes a prehearing conference. Such a conference may be useful in reducing the length or, perhaps, entirely disposing of some plenary hearings. The hearing may be used to hear argument on issues of law, narrow the disputed issues of fact, explore issues which may arise at an evidentiary hearing, or otherwise expedite the hearing. (As amended by R-08-0042, effective Jan. 1, 2010.)

Rule 32.8. Evidentiary hearing

a. Evidentiary hearing. -- The defendant shall be entitled to a hearing to determine issues of material fact, with the right to be present and to subpoena witnesses. If facilities are available, the court may, in its discretion, order the hearing to be held at the place where the defendant is confined, giving at least 15 days notice to the officer in charge of the confinement facility. In superior court, the hearing shall be recorded.

b. Evidence. -- The rules of evidence applicable in criminal proceedings shall apply, except that the defendant may be called to testify at the hearing.

c. Burden of proof. -- The defendant shall have the burden of proving the allegations of fact by a preponderance of the evidence. If a constitutional defect is proven, the state shall have the burden of proving that the defect was harmless beyond a reasonable doubt.

d. Decision. -- The court shall rule within 10 days after the hearing ends except in extraordinary circumstances where the volume of the evidence or the complexity of the issues require additional time. If the court finds in favor of the defendant, it shall enter an appropriate order with respect to the conviction, sentence or detention, any further proceedings, including a new trial and conditions of release, and other matters that may be necessary and proper. The court shall make specific findings of fact, and state expressly its conclusions of law relating to each issue presented.

e. Transcript. -- The court may, and shall upon request of a party within the time for filing a petition for review, order that a certified transcript of the evidentiary hearing be prepared. The preparation of the evidentiary hearing transcript shall be at county expense if the defendant is indigent.

HISTORY: Amended June 2, 1992, effective Sept. 30, 1992; amended Apr. 16, 1993, effective June 1, 1993; amended July 28, 1993, effective Dec. 1, 1993; amended Oct. 31, 2000, effective Dec. 1, 2000; amended eff. Jan. 1, 2007 by R-05-0037.

NOTES:

[1973 PROMULGATION]

This rule provides general guidance to the court in conducting an evidentiary hearing. It generally follows ABA, Standards Relating to Post-Conviction Remedies § 4.6 (Approved Draft, 1968).

RULE 32.8 (A) The petitioner's presence is required. The right to subpoena witnesses is included to provide the full fact-finding hearing required by Townsend v. Sain, 372 U.S. 293 (1963). Where for reasons of safety and convenience the court determines that the petitioner or perhaps some of his supporting witnesses should not be transported back to the place of trial, it may order that the hearing be held at the petitioner's place of confinement. A record of the proceedings is required for appellate review and for use as prior recorded testimony upon retrial. See ABA, Standards, supra, at § 4.6 (c); Uniform Act, supra, at § 7; State v. Raybould, 15 Ariz. App. 520, 489 P.2d 1222 (1971) vacated, 108 Ariz. 370, 498 P.2d 458 (1972). The use of prior recorded testimony is governed by Rule 19.3 (c).

RULE 32.8 (B). In keeping with the characterization of the proceedings in Rule 32.3, subsection (b) incorporates the safeguards of the criminal rules of evidence, but accepts the petitioner's right to stand mute. The situation here may be distinguished from the usual criminal proceeding in that the defendant is the moving party and the issues will not normally focus on the question of guilt.

RULE 32.8 (C). This provision contains the generally applicable standards governing burden of proof. See ABA, Standards, supra, at § 4.6 (d) and Rule 32.2 (d).

RULE 32.8 (D). The court may fashion an appropriate dispositive remedy under section (d). See Uniform Act, supra, at § 7. The time limit for rendering a decision is imposed to prevent undue delay. Specific findings of law and fact are required in every case, but may be made either orally on the record or in writing.

COMMITTEE COMMENT TO 2000 AMENDMENT

The 1993 amendment to Rule 32.8(a) substituted "complete" for "verbatim," and added language making a record mandatory only in the superior court. The heading of subsection (a) is changed from "Plenary" to "Evidentiary." Subsection (e) clarifies that a party is entitled to a transcript of any evidentiary hearing held pursuant to this rule and that preparation of the transcript shall be at county expense if the defendant is indigent.

JUDICIAL DECISIONS
ANALYSIS

EVIDENCE
--NEWLY DISCOVERED

When DNA evidence was discovered after defendant's first degree murder and sexual abuse trial, the superior court needed to make additional specific findings of fact and conclusions of law to facilitate the Supreme Court's review of defendant's request for post-conviction relief. State v. Tankersley, 211 Ariz. 323, -- Ariz. Adv. Rep. --, 121 P.3d 829, 2005 Ariz. LEXIS 132 (2005).

IN GENERAL

Defendant presented a colorable claim for ineffective assistance of counsel where trial counsel failed to move to suppress evidentiary fruits of a warrantless search, and thus the case was remanded for an evidentiary hearing on that issue. State v. Fillmore, 187 Ariz. 174, 927 P.2d 1303 (Ct. App. 1996).

There is no broad rule that third-party affidavits alleging that the victim recanted automatically entitle a Rule 32 petitioner to an evidentiary hearing. If a third-party affidavit appears particularly credible or reliable, or if other evidence tends to support the affidavit or the recantation, a trial court should order an evidentiary hearing. State v. Krum, 183 Ariz. 288, 903 P.2d 596 (1995).

Rule 32.9. Review

a. Motion for rehearing; response; reply. -- Any party aggrieved by a final decision of the trial court in these proceedings may, within fifteen days after the ruling of the court, move the court for a rehearing setting forth in detail the grounds wherein it is believed the court erred. No response to a motion for rehearing will be filed unless requested by the court, but a motion for rehearing will not be granted in the absence of such a response. A reply, if any, shall be filed within 10 days after the service of the response. The filing of a motion for rehearing in the trial court is not a prerequisite to the filing of a petition for review pursuant to paragraph (c) of this rule.

b. Disposition when motion granted. -- If the motion for rehearing is granted, the court may either (1) amend its previous ruling without a hearing, or (2) grant a new hearing and then either amend or reaffirm its previous ruling. In either case, if the court amends its previous ruling, it shall set forth its reasons for amending the previous ruling. The state shall notify the victim, upon request, of any action taken by the court.

c. Petition for review. -- Within thirty days after the final decision of the trial court on the petition for post-conviction relief or the motion for rehearing, any party aggrieved may petition the appropriate appellate court for review of the actions of the trial court. A cross-petition for review may be filed within 15 days after service of a petition for review. The petition for review, cross-petition and all responsive pleadings filed pursuant to this rule shall be filed in the appellate court. Within 3 days after filing a petition or cross-petition for review, the petitioner and cross-petitioner, if any, shall file a notice of such filing with the trial court. The notice of filing may include a designation of record adding to the record defined in Rule 32.9(e) any additional certified transcripts of trial court proceedings that were prepared pursuant to Rule 32.4(d) or that were otherwise available to the trial court and the parties and that are material to the issues raised in the petition for review. Motions for extensions of time to file petitions or cross-petitions shall be filed in and ruled upon by the trial court. All other motions shall be filed in the court in which the petition is to be filed.

1. Form and contents. -- The petition or cross-petition for review shall comply with the form requirements of Rule 31.12 of the rules of criminal appellate procedure and contain a caption setting forth the name of the appellate court, the title of the case, a space for the appellate court case number, the trial court case number, and a brief descriptive title. An original and seven copies of the petition and an original and one copy of the appendix, if any, shall be filed if review is being sought in the Supreme Court. An original and four copies of the petition and an original and one copy of the appendix, if any, shall be filed if review is being sought in the

Court of Appeals. An original and one copy shall be filed if review is being sought in the superior court. The parties shall be designated as in the trial court proceedings. The petition or cross-petition shall not exceed 20 pages, exclusive of the appendix, shall not have a cover or be bound, but shall be fastened with a single staple in the upper left corner, and shall contain the following:

 I. Copies of the trial court's rulings entered pursuant to rules 32.6(c), 32.8(d) and 32.9(b).

 II. The issues which were decided by the trial court and which the defendant wishes to present to the appellate court for review.

 III. The facts material to a consideration of the issues presented for review.

 IV. The reasons why the petition should be granted. In Rule 32 of-right and non-capital cases, an appendix is not required, but the petition for review shall contain specific references to the record.

 The filing of a motion for rehearing pursuant to paragraph (a) of this rule does not limit the issues that may be raised in the petition or the cross-petition for review. Failure to raise any issue that could be raised in the petition or the cross-petition for review shall constitute waiver of appellate review of that issue.

2. Service; response; reply. -- The petitioner or cross-petitioner shall serve a copy of the petition or cross-petition on the adverse party. A response may be filed within 30 days from the date upon which the petition or cross-petition is served. The response shall comply with the form requirements of Rule 32.9(c)(1) and shall not exceed 20 pages, exclusive of any appendix. Appendices shall conform to the requirements of Rule 32.9(c)(1). A reply, if any, may be filed within 10 days after the service of a response. The reply shall also comply with the form requirements of Rule 32.9(c)(1). The reply shall be limited to matters addressed in the response and shall not exceed 10 pages. No appendices shall be submitted with a reply.

d. Stay pending review. -- A motion for rehearing or a petition for review filed by the state pursuant to this section shall stay an order granting a new trial until final review is completed. For any other relief granted to a defendant, a stay pending further review is within the discretion of the trial or appellate court. The state shall notify the victim upon request of any action taken.

e. Filing of the record. -- In Rule 32 of-right and non-capital cases, within 45 days after the receipt of the notice of filing of a petition for review, the record, including the trial court file and the certified transcript, shall be transmitted to the appellate court.

In capital cases, the record of the post-conviction proceedings shall not be transmitted to the appellate court unless requested by that court. If requested by the appellate court, the record shall consist of copies of the notice of post-conviction relief, the petition for post-conviction relief, response and reply, all motions and responsive pleadings filed and all minute entries and orders issued in the post-conviction proceedings, plus the certified transcript and any exhibits admitted by the trial court in the post-conviction proceedings.

f. Disposition when petition granted. -- The appellate court may, in its discretion, grant review and may order oral argument upon the petition if deemed necessary and may issue such orders and grant such relief as it deems necessary and proper. The state shall notify the victim, upon request, of any action taken by the appellate court.

g. Reconsideration and review of appellate court decision. -- The provisions governing the filing of motions for reconsideration and petitions for review in criminal appeals set forth in Rules 31.18 and 31.19 shall apply to and govern motions for reconsideration and petitions for review of an appellate court decision entered pursuant to Rule 32.

h. Return of the record. -- In Rule 32 of-right- and non-capital cases, when the matter is determined, the clerk of the appellate court shall return the record to the appropriate trial court for retention according to law. In capital cases, the clerk of the appellate court shall return any exhibits to the appropriate trial court.

HISTORY: Amended May 31, 2000 and Oct. 31, 2000, effective Dec. 1, 2000; amended Oct. 15, 2001, effective Dec. 1, 2001, as corrected Jan. 4, 2002; amended and effective Oct. 12, 2005; amended effective. Jan. 1, 2007 by R-05-0030 and R-05-0037.

NOTES:

COMMITTEE COMMENT TO 1993 AMENDMENT
The 1993 amendments to Rule 32.9(c) and (h) adapted the rule to all courts by deleting the phrase "clerk of the," leaving only "trial court."

COMMENT TO 2000 AMENDMENT
Subsection (a) is amended to provide that no response to a motion for rehearing is to be filed unless requested by the court.

Subsection (c) changes the place of filing a petition for review to the appropriate appellate court and requires the petitioner to file a notice of such filing with the superior court. It allows the trial court to rule on motions for extensions of time for filing, but prescribes that the appellate court will rule on motions for additional pagination. This procedure is deemed advisable to achieve uniformity -- some trial judges grant additional pagination, some do not -- without burdening the appellate court with motions for extension of time better decided by the trial courts, e.g., extension may be necessary due to lack of transcripts from that judge's court.

Paragraph (1) changes the form of caption to the appellate court because the petition for review will be filed in that court. It provides that petitions for review are not to have covers or bindings.

Subparagraph (i) eliminates the need for a synopsis of the trial court's rulings.

Subsection (c) also removes the requirement for appendices in non-capital cases.

Subsection (e) retains the requirement for filing the record in non-capital cases, but provides that the record is not to be transmitted in capital cases unless requested by the appellate court. This differs from non-capital cases because the record in capital cases remains in the Arizona Supreme Court. In non-capital cases, the record is returned to the trial court, as set forth in subparagaph (h).

COMMENT (2007 AMENDMENT)

Rule 5(j)(2) of the Arizona Rules of Civil Procedure was added in 2004 to reduce the clerks' burden of producing and distributing minute entries by requiring counsel to submit with their stipulations and motions proposed forms of orders along with a sufficient number of copies to be conformed and pre-addressed stamped envelopes for each party to the action. This subdivision of the rule, like other provisions in Rule 5, is to be followed by attorneys in criminal cases, unless otherwise provided for by the presiding judge.

JUDICIAL DECISIONS
ANALYSIS

CONSTRUCTION

Policy reason Arizona courts advance for disallowing argument in appendices is that an appendix may not be used to circumvent the page limitations, and this policy would be equally important in petitions for review as it is in direct appeals under this rule; there is no reason why Arizona courts would permit an appendix to be used to circumvent a page limit in a petition for review of a petition-for-post-conviction-relief when the Arizona courts do not permit such a tactic on direct review. Laliberte v. Ryan, -- F. Supp. 2d --, 2009 U.S. Dist. LEXIS 44252 (D. Ariz. May 26, 2009).

State prisoner sentenced to death procedurally defaulted his claim that the trial court violated his Eighth and Fourteenth Amendment rights when it denied his request for neuromatic brain mapping, because the claim was not exhausted on direct appeal either by fair presentation in the prisoner's appellate brief or by virtue of the supreme court's independent sentencing review, nor was it fairly presented in state post-conviction proceedings. Wood v. Schriro, -- F. Supp. 2d --, 2006 U.S. Dist. LEXIS 12360 (D. Ariz. Mar. 20, 2006).

APPEAL GRANTED

Appellate court granted review to consider whether the warrant issued to search defendant's property violated the Fourth Amendment, and if so, whether defense counsel's failure to challenge the legality of the search warrant violated defendant's constitutional right to effective assistance of counsel. State v. Ray, 185 Ariz. 89, 912 P.2d 1318 (Ct. App. 1995).

CLAIMS REJECTED

Although a habeas corpus inmate presented evidence concerning his pre-trial counsel's reputation in the community, he did not show that there were independent witnesses to support an alibi defense, or that he did not participate in the murders; as a result, he did not show that pre-trial counsel's ineffective assistance, if any, resulted in a fundamental miscarriage of justice. The inmate could not excuse his procedural default, and the district court properly found that his ineffective assistance claim was barred. Cook v. Schriro, 516 F.3d 802, 2008 U.S. App. LEXIS 3511 (9th Cir. 2008).

State prisoner's claim that the prosecutor engaged in prejudicial misconduct by eliciting bad character evidence that the prisoner had a biker reputation was dismissed as procedurally barred because the prisoner did not fairly present the claim to the state courts and, if he returned to state court to litigate under Ariz. R. Crim. P. 32.2(a)(3) and 32.4(a) because it did not fall within an exception to preclusion. Wood v. Schriro, -- F. Supp. 2d --, 2006 U.S. Dist. LEXIS 12360 (D. Ariz. Mar. 20, 2006).

Where defendant raised an equal protection claim and also contended the trial court abused its discretion regarding sentencing, but defendant simply referred to memoranda filed below, the petition for review failed to comply with this Rule and the claims were rejected. State v. French, 198 Ariz. 119, 7 P.3d 128, 2000 Ariz. App. LEXIS 95 (Ct. App. 2000). Overruled to the extent that the question of whether a claim is of sufficient constitutional magnitude to require a knowing and intelligent waiver, depends on the merits of the particular grounds rather than upon the particular right alleged to have been violated in Stewart v. Smith, 202 Ariz. 446, 46 P.3d 1067 (Ariz. 2002)).

DEFENDANT'S RIGHTS.

Because review from denial of post-conviction relief is discretionary, a pleading defendant does not have a right to appointed counsel in such proceedings. State v. Smith, 184 Ariz. 456, 910 P.2d 1 (1996).

EXTENSION OF TIME

On remand, a trial court abused its discretion in denying petitioner's motion to extend the time for filing a petition for review of the denial of his motion for post-conviction relief because the motion to extend the time for filing a petition for review had been filed within the time limits of this rule. State v. Miller, -- Ariz. --, -- Ariz. Adv. Rep. --, -- P.3d --, 2006 Ariz. LEXIS 28 (Mar. 15, 2006).

FEDERAL HABEAS CORPUS

Prisoner's federal habeas petition under 28 U.S.C.S. § 2254 was dismissed as untimely. Under 28 U.S.C.S. § 2244(d), he was not entitled to statutory tolling because his petition for state post-conviction relief was not properly filed under this rule, so he did not comply with the requirements of § 2244(d)(2) and he did not meet his burden for equitable tolling. Miller v. McWilliams, -- F. Supp. 2d --, 2010 U.S. Dist. LEXIS 6027 (D. Ariz. Jan. 25, 2010).

Prisoner's habeas application under 28 U.S.C.S. § 2254 was dismissed because his habeas claims were procedurally defaulted in that exhaustion of the claims was impossible based on timeliness under Ariz. R. Crim. P. 32.9 and 32.4 and there was no showing of cause and prejudice or a fundamental miscarriage of justice to excuse procedural default. Pickens v. Schriro, -- F. Supp. 2d --, 2009 U.S. Dist. LEXIS 79114 (D. Ariz. Sept. 3, 2009).

Arizona prisoner's federal habeas petition was denied where the prisoner's claims, which were not presented to the Arizona Court of Appeals, were procedurally defaulted, being time-barred under this rule. Laws v. Harkins, -- F. Supp. 2d --, 2006 U.S. Dist. LEXIS 56018 (D. Ariz. July 24, 2006).

MINUTE ENTRY

Defendant's petition was not untimely, although his counsel failed to file the petition within 30 days of the trial court's minute entry denying post-conviction relief, because minute entry did not contain the trial court's dispositive ruling. State v. Herrera, 183 Ariz. 642, 905 P.2d 1377 (Ct. App. 1995).

Rule 32.10. Review of mental retardation determination [Effective January 1, 2011]

In any capital case, within ten days after the trial court makes a finding on mental retardation, the state or the defendant may file a petition for special action with the court of appeals. The filing of the petition for special action is governed by the rules of procedure for special actions, except that the court of appeals shall exercise jurisdiction and decide the issue raised.

HISTORY: Adopted by R-10-0010, effective January 1, 2011.

Rule 32.11. Extensions of time; notification of victims. [Effective January 1, 2011]

In any capital case, if the victim has filed a notice of appearance as specified in A.R.S. § 13-4234.01, a party seeking an extension of time to file a brief must provide notice of the request to the victim. Notice shall be provided through the prosecutor's office handling the post-conviction relief proceeding, unless the victim specifies a different method in the notice of appearance. The victim may specify in the notice of appearance whether notification should be served directly on the victim or on another person, including the prosecutor, and whether service may be made electronically, by telephone, or by regular mail. If the victim has requested direct notification, the party seeking an extension of time shall serve notice on the victim within 24 hours of filing the extension request. If the prosecutor has the duty to notify the victim on behalf of the defendant, the prosecutor shall serve notice within 24 hours of receipt of the extension request. Service shall be made in the manner specified in the notice of appearance, or if no method is specified, by regular mail. In ruling on any request for an extension of a time limit set in this rule, the court shall consider the rights of the defendant and any victim to prompt and final conclusion of the case.

HISTORY: Added Jan. 30, 2002, effective June 1, 2002; adopted as modified by R-06-012, effective Sept. 18, 2006; and made permanent effective Sept. 5, 2007; renumbered by R-10-0010 from Rule 32.10 of Criminal Procedure, effective January 1, 2011.

NOTES:
EDITOR'S NOTE
R-10-0010, dated September 2, 2010, adopted a new Criminal Rule 32.10 and renumbered the existing Rule 32.10 as Rule 32.11, effective January 1, 2011.

COMMENT
To implement the victim's right to a prompt and final conclusion of the case, see Ariz. Const. Art. 2, § 2.1(A)(10), the victim shall be permitted to file a statement with the court, at the inception of the proceeding, which expresses his or her views with respect to any extensions; or the victim can request, pursuant to A.R.S. § 13-4411, that the prosecutor's office communicate the victim's views to the court concerning any extensions.

Bland v. California DOC, 20 F.3d 1469, 1474 (9th Cir. 1994)
When the state's return fails to dispute the factual allegations contained in the petition and traverse, it is essentially admits those allegations.

Colson v. Smith, C.A. 5 (GA) 1970, 427 F.2d 143, conform to 315 F.Supp. 179, affirmed, 438 F.2d 1075
Where District Court in granting habeas corpus, found that petitioner had made prima facie case, under rebuttal by the state with respect to one of his claims, but the state made no findings on other claims, and where case involved many issues inextricably bound together, case would be remanded for findings of fact and conclusions of law on issues presented but not decided.

Hohn v. US, 262 F.3d 811 (8th Cir. 2001)
Courts interpret pro se petitions for post-conviction post-conviction relief liberally.

Pearson v. Norris, 52 F.3d 740 (8th Cir. 1995)

If direct appeal or another avenue of collateral attack is created by the state, it must conform to due process standards.

Re Currency in the amount of $26,980, 199 Ariz. 291, 297 ¶ 20, 18 P.3d 85, 91 (App. 2000)

When the state does not respond to issue it is thereby a confession of error.

State v. Bell, (App. Div1 1975) 23 Ariz. App. 169, 531 P.2d 545, opinion after remand, 24 Ariz. App.

526, 540 P.2d 145 Preclusion of post-conviction relief on grounds that matter is still raisable on a direct appeal applies only to those matters in which sufficient factual basis exists in record for appellate court to resolve matter.

State v. Bennett, 213 Ariz. 562, 146 P.3d 525, 526 (2006)

Our Supreme Court acknowledged in State v. Spreitz, 202 Ariz. 1, 39 F.3d 525, 526 (2002), that General, claims of ineffective assistance of counsel that were raised or could have been raised in an initial post-conviction proceeding are regarded as waived and precluded if raised in a successive petition. But, that rule does not apply when appellate counsel and counsel in the first rule 32 proceeding are one in the same because appellate counsel is not expected to raise and argue his or her own ineffectiveness.

Bennett, 213 Ariz. 562, 146 P.3d at 67

Bennett is not implicated here because Swoops was represented by different attorneys on appeal and in his first rule 32.

State v. Henderson, 210 Ariz. 516, 19, 115 P.3d 601, 607 (2005)

Fundamental error is going to the foundation for case, error that takes from the defendant a right essential to his defense, and error of such magnitude that the defendant could not possibly have received a fair trial.

State v. Robbins, 166 Ariz. 531, 533, 803P.2d 942,944 (Ariz. App. 1991)

Ineffective assistance of counsel that prejudice is the defendant is a ground for relief under A.R.Cr.P. Rule 32.1 (a) as the conviction or sentence would be one that violates the Constitution of the United States or the state of Ariz.. The petitioner must only shows such violation by a preponderance of the evidence. See A.R.Cr.P. Rule 32.8 (c).

State v. Shrock, 149 Ariz. 433, 441, 719 P.2d 1041 (1986)
State v. Jeffers, 135 Ariz. 404, 427, 661 P.2d 1105,1128, cert. denied, 464 US 865,104 S.Ct. 199, 78 L.Ed.2d 174 (1983)
To present a colorable claim, the issue must appear to be invalid, that is the petitioner's allegations are to be true, would the outcome of the proceedings be different.

State v. Spreitz, 202 Ariz. 1, 2-3, ¶ ¶ 5-9, 39 F.3d 525, 526-27 (2002)
Reviewing case law and holding that ineffective assistance claims must be brought in a petition for post-conviction relief prior to appellate consideration.

Stuart v. Smith, 202 Ariz. 446, 46 P.3d 1067 (2002)
In Smith our Supreme Court examined the distinction between claims that may be precluded under A.R.Cr.P. Rule 32.2 based on the defendant smear failure to raise them previously and claims that require a personal waiver before they may be deemed that waived and, therefore, precluded. As the court pointed out, the comment to rule 32.2 acknowledges that claims of sufficient constitutional magnitude must be knowingly, voluntarily, and intelligently waived before they may be precluded pursuant to rule 32.2 (a) (3). The court stated the question whether and asserted ground, is of sufficient constitutional magnitude to require a knowing, voluntary and intelligent waiver for purpose of rule 32.2 (a) (3), see comment to rule 32.2 (a) (3), does not depend upon the merits of the particular ground. It depends merely upon the particular right alleged to have been violated. 202 Ariz. 446, 10, 46 P.3d 1071.

As the Supreme Court noted in Smith, when rule 32.2 was amended in 1992, the following comment was added: "for most claims of trial error, the state may simply show that the defendant did not raised in her at trial, on appeal, or in a previous collateral proceeding and that would be sufficient to show that the defendant has waived the claim. If defense counsels failure to raise an issue at trial, on appeal or in a previous collateral proceeding is so egregious as to result in prejudice as that

241

term has been constitutionally defined, such failure may be raised by means of the claim of ineffective assistance of counsel." The court explained in Smith howl this analytical framework is applied to claims of ineffective assistance of counsel.

If a petitioner asserts ineffective assistance of counsel and sentencing, and, in a later petition, asserts ineffective assistance of counsel at trial, precluded and is required without examining facts. The grounds of ineffective assistance of counsel cannot be raised repeatedly. There is a strong policy against piecemeal litigation. See State v. Spreitz, 202 Ariz. 1, 39 F.3d 525(2002). In other situations the court must determine the particular right in default by looking at the facts of the claim, not decide its merits, but decided whether, at its core, the claim implicates a significant right that requires a knowing, voluntary and intelligent waiver for precluded in to apply under rule 32.2 (a) (3).

Thus if petitioner asserts ineffective assistance of counsel for the first time in a successive rule 32 petition, the question of precluded in is determined by the nature of the right allegedly affected by counsels ineffective performance. If that right is of sufficient constitutional magnitude to require personal waiver by the defendant and there has been no personal waiver the claim is not precluded. It is not such a magnitude, the claim is precluded.

Waiver of trial error need not be personal to be valid. And although it is true by failing to raise an issue, a defendant forfeits the right to obtain appellate relief unless, the defendant can prove that fundamental error occurred.

US v. Berger, 473 F.3d 1080, 1094-95 (9th Cir. 2007)
State v. Sanchez, 130 Ariz. 295, 299, 635 P.2d 12 (App. 1981)
State v. Perez, 115 Ariz. 3 0, 563 P.2d 285-86 (1977)
State v. Armenta, 112 Ariz. 352, 541 P.2d 1154 (1975)
Bustamante v. Eyman, 456 F.2d 269, 272, 274 (9th Cir. 1972)
For the proposition that the defendant's presence is a right of constitutional magnitude that must be personally waived when trial court answers a deliberating juries question concerning a pivotal factual issue.

<u>US v. Prudden</u>, 424 F.2d 1021 (1970)

Silence can only be equated with fraud where there is a legal or moral duty to respond our where an inquiry left unanswered would be misleading.

Search & Seizure

Arizona v. Hicks, 480 US 321, 328 (1987)

The court held that to establish the incriminating character of an item, the police must show that after an inspection of "what is already exposed to plain view" they are able to determine that it is evidence or contraband.

Austin v. US, 509 US 125 L.Ed.2d 488, 113 S.Ct. (1993)

Eighth Amendment excess fines clause held to apply to drug related forfeitures of property to United States under 21 USCS §§881(a)(4) and 881(a)(7).

Boyer v. County Of Washington, 971 F.2d 100 (8th Cir. 1992)

Under Fourth Amendment warrant can be validly issued only by neutral and detached magistrate.

California v. Ciraolo, 476 US 207, 90 L.Ed.2d 210, 106 S.Ct. 1809 (1986)
Oliver v. US, 466 US 170. 80 L.Ed.2d 214, 104 S.Ct. 1736 (1984)

Warrantless aerial observation of individuals fenced in backyard held not to violate Fourth Amendment.

Canedy v. Boardman, 16 F.3d 183 (7th Cir. 1994)
Schmerber v. California, 384 US 757, 16 L.Ed.2d 908, 86 S.Ct. 1826 (1966)

Right to be free of strip searches and degrading body inspections is basic to concept of privacy, and thus, state's right to interfere with persons bodily integrity by means of strip searches is subject to constitutional limits.

California v. Greenwood, 486 US 35. 100 L.Ed.2d 30, 108 S.Ct. 1625 (1988)

Warrantless search and seizure of garbage bags left for collection on curb outside home upheld.

Florida v. Royer, 460 US 491, 75 L.Ed.2d 229, 103 S.Ct. 1319 (1983)

Excellent case on airport profiles. The defendants consent to the opening of his luggage was tainted by his illegal detention.

Florida v. Wells, 495 US 1, 109 L.Ed.2d 1, 110 S.Ct. 1632 (1990)
US v. Kelly, 913 F.2d 261 (6th Cir. 1990)
Absent exigent circumstances or consent, officer is not to search locked suitcase without a search warrant.

Funaway v. New York, 445 US 573, 63 L.Ed.2d 639, 100 S.Ct. 1371 (1980)
For an arrest to be valid under the Fourth Amendment probable cause must first exist.

Gasho v. US, 39 F.3d 1420 (9th Cir. 1994)
Citizen retains right to refuse consent to warrantless search of bag containing personal effects, even if consent is given to search of vehicle in which bag is located.

Hayes v. Florida, 470 US 811, 84 L.Ed.2d 705, 105 S.Ct. 1643 (1985)
Transporting suspect to police station for fingerprinting without probable cause warrant, or consent held violative of Fourth Amendment.

Jackson v. Gates, 975 F.2d 648 (9th Cir. 1992)
Police officer was fired for refusing to give a urine sample, he sued on a number of grounds and won a $150,000 settlement.

Jackson v. Vannoy, 49 F.3d 175 (5th Cir. 1995)
Passenger has standing to challenge constitutionality of vehicle stop given that stop results in seizure of passenger.

Lavicky v. Burnett, 75/8F.2d 468, 475 (10th Cir. 1985)
Warrantless seizure in search of defendants tromp invalid because of vehicle in movable due to dismantle the engine and on private property.

Maryland v. Garrison, 480 US 79, 84 (1987)
Anderson v. Maryland, 427 US 463, 480 (1976)
Particular at the requirement prevents the seizure of one thing under a warrant describing another.

McDonnell v. Hunter, 809 F.2d 1302 (8th Cir. 1987)
Urinalysis is search and seizure within meaning of Fourth Amendment.

Michigan State Police v. Sitz, 496 US 444, 110 L.Ed.2d 412, 110 S.Ct. 2481 (1990)
Stop of motorist at highway sobriety checkpoints held not to violate Fourth Amendment.

Minnesota v. Dickerson, 508 US 124 L.Ed.2d 334, 113 S.Ct. (1993)
Seizure of a cocaine lump detected in person's pocket during pat down search held violative of Fourth Amendment where determination that lump was contraband was made only after further search.

Minnesota v. Olsen, 495 US 91, 109 L.Ed.2d 85, 110 S.Ct. 1684 (1990)
The arrest of an overnight guest following a warrantless, non-consensual entry violated suspects rights under Fourth Amendment.

Moya v. US, 761 F.2d 322 (7th Cir. 1985)
Brown v. Texas, 443 US 47, 61 L.Ed.2d 357, 99 S.Ct. 2637 (1979)
People are entitled to refuse to provide information to police.

Nix v. Williams, 467 US 431, 81 L.Ed.2d 377, 104 S.Ct. 2501 (1984)
Unlawfully obtained evidence held admissible if untimely or inevitably it would have been discovered by lawful means.

Note: Federal law requires that federal officers executing a search warrant must first knock and announce their authority and purpose before entering.

Note: Police may force a door open only if they have given express notice of both their authority and purpose; not just one or the other (see 18 USC §3109). 24. Reasonable belief that firearms may have been within residence was alone insufficient to excuse violations of statutory knock and announce rule without exigent circumstances.

Reid v. Georgia, 448 US 438, 65 L.Ed.2d 890, 100 S.Ct. 2752 (1980)
Courts must be especially cautious when the evidence that is alleged to establish probable cause is entirely inconsistent with innocent behavior.

Rimie v. City of Hedwig Village, Texas, 765 F.2d 490 (5th Cir. 1985)
Whalen v. Roe, 429 US 589, 51 L.Ed.2d 64, 97 S.Ct. 869 (1977)
The Constitution protects individuals against invasion of their privacy by the government.

Smith v. Ohio, 494 US 541, 108 L.Ed.2d 464. 110 S.Ct. 1288 (1990)
US v. Most, 876 F.2d 191 (D.C. Cir. 1989)
Warrantless search of grocery bag which provided probable cause for arrest, held not justified incident to arrest.

Spear v. Sowders, 33 F.3d 576 (6th Cir. 1994)
Reasonable suspicion of prison officials must support scope of search of prison visitor as well as initiation of search.

Swoboda v. Dubach, 992 F.2d 186 (10th Cir. 1993)
Excessive force during arrest violates a person's Fourth Amendment right against unreasonable searches and seizures.

Terry v. Ohio, 392 US 1, 20 (1968)
Katz v. US, 389 US 347, 357 (1967)
Police must, whenever practicable, obtain advanced judicial approval of searches and seizures through the warrant procedure.

Thompson v. Louisiana, 469 US 17, 83 L.Ed.2d 246, 105 S.Ct. 409 (1984)
Warrantless "murder scene" search of defendants home held unconstitutional.

US v. $124.570 In US Currency, 873 F.2d 1240 (9th Cir. 1989)
Person had the above money seized while clearing thru an airport security check. The case was vacated on the grounds that the individual did not give his consent for a general search of his luggage.

US v. Almonte, 952 F.2d 20 (1st Cir. 1991)
Unless exigent circumstances exist. warrantless searches are impermissible.

US v. Carey, 172 F.3d 1268, 1275-76 (10th CIR. 1989)
Closed computer files containing child pornography deemed out of plain view.

US v. Cohen, 796 F.2d 20 (2nd Cir. 1986)
Search of a pre-trial detainee's cell can be challenged under the Fourth Amendment if undertaken at the direction of the prosecutor and aimed at uncovering evidence for use at the detainee's trial.

US v. Gooch, 6 F.3d 673 (9th Cir. 1993)
1. Fourth Amendment protects expectations of privacy in movable, closed containers. 2. Automobile exception to warrant requirements applies only when vehicle is on open road or is capable of movement and is in place not regularly used for residential purposes, temporary or otherwise.

US v. Good Real Property, 126 US 1126 L.Ed.2d 490, 114 S.Ct. (1993)
Fifth Amendment due process clause held to generally prohibit federal government from seizing real property in civil forfeiture without prior notice and hearing.

US v. Hall, 47 F.3d 1091 (11th Cir. 1995)
Law of trespass forbids intrusions onto land that Fourth Amendment would not proscribe.

US v. Hardy, 52 F.3d 147 (7th Cir. 1995)
US v. ARCH, 7 F.3d 1300 (7th Cir. 1993)
Motel room occupied as temporary residence is entitled to same constitutional protection from warrantless searches as is person's home.

US v. Hodge, 19 F.3d 51 (D.C. Cir. 1994)
US v. Fierro, 38 F.3d 761 (5th Cir. 1994)
Government has burden to prove consent to search by preponderance of the evidence.

US v. Hogan, 23 F.3d 690 (8th Cir. 1994)
US v. Garcia, 23 F.3d 1331 (8th Cir. 1994)
Suspicion is not such "reasonable suspicion" as will justify investigatory stop if it is no more than inchoate and un-particularized suspicion or "hunch".

US v. Johnson, 9 F.3d 506 (6th Cir. 1993)
Exigent circumstances justify warrantless entry into residence only where there is also probable cause to enter residence.

US v. Johnson, 12 F.3d 760 (8th Cir. 1993)
US v. Halliman, 923 F.2d 873 (D.C. Cir. 1991)
Police themselves cannot create exigency such that warrant requirements will be suspended under exigent circumstances exception.

US v. Jones, 994 F.2d 1051 (3rd Cir. 1993)
Probable cause to arrest does not automatically provide probable cause to search arrestee's home.

US v. Kyles, 40 F.3d 519 (2nd Cir. 1994)
Police officers authority to search premises described in warrant is not unbounded.

US v. Layne, 43 F.3d 127 (5th Cir. 1995)
Fourth Amendment prohibits general warrants authorizing officials to rummage through person's possessions looking for any evidence of crime.

US v. Lee, 916 F.2d 814 (2nd Cir. 1990)
Fourth Amendment's protection against unreasonable searches and seizures do not extend to abandoned property.

US v. Mans, 999 F.2d 966 (6th Cir. 1993)
California v. Acevedo, US 114 L.Ed.2d 619, 111 S.Ct. 1982 (1991)
When police have probable cause to believe that vehicle contains contraband, they may search entire vehicle and any containers located within it.

US v. Manuel, 992 F.2d 272 (10th Cir. 1993)
Exercise of right to refuse consent to search cannot alone be basis of reasonable suspicion supporting detention of suspect.

US v. Mendenhall, 446 US 544,554 (1980)
The opinion of Justice Stewart was, "A person has been "seized" within the fourth amendment only if, in view of all the circumstances surrounding the incident, a reasonable person would have believed that he was not free to leave." See also: Terry v. Ohio, 392 US 1, 16-19 (1968); US v. Brigoni-Ponce, 422 US 873, 878 (1975); Reid v. Georgia, 448 US 438 (1980)

US v. Millan, 36 F.3d 886 (9th Cir. 1994)
Because interrogation and search were direct result of illegal traffic stop, all evidence had to be suppressed.

US v. Obase, 15 F.3d 603 (6th Cir. 1994)
Fourth Amendment seizure occurs when police detain an individual under circumstances where reasonable person would feel that he or she is not at liberty to leave.

US v. Padro, 52 F.3d 120 (6th Cir. 1995)
US v. Mendonsa, 989 F.2d 366 (9th Cir. 1993)
Anonymous informant's tip alone, without any statement for basis of her knowledge, could not justify finding of probable cause to search.

US v. Parra, 2 Hid 1058 (10th Cir. 1993)
Peyton v. New York, 445 US 573, 63 LED2d 639, 100 S.Ct. 1371 (1980)
Absent consent or exigent circumstances, police may not enter a citizen's home without a warrant. Mere presence of weapons or destructible evidence does not, by itself, create exigent circumstances.

US v. Parcel of Land, Etc., 507 US 122 L.Ed.2d 469, 113 S.Ct. (1993)
An innocent individual who buys land with alleged drug money is entitled to the "innocent owner" defense.

US v. Pierre, 932 F.2d 377 (5th Cir. 1991)

Although interior of automobile is not subject to same expectations of privacy that exist in one's home, car's interior is protected under Fourth Amendment from unreasonable intrusion by police.

US v. Prieto - Villa, 910 F.2d 601 (9th Cir. 1990)

Even if police have a warrant, fact that a person is in the company of person for whom a warrant has been issued does not constitute probable cause for search of that person.

US v. Robles, 45 F.3d I (1st Cir. 1995)
Collidge v. New Hampshire, 403 US 443, 29 L.Ed.2d 564, 91 S.Ct. 2022 (1968)
Katz v. US, 389 US 347, 357, 19 L.Ed.2d 576, 99 S.Ct. 507 (1967)

Under plain view exception to search warrant requirement. incriminating nature of object must be readily apparent, officers must have had lawful access to object, and it must have been in plain view.

US v. Saadeh, 61 F.3d 510 (7th Cir. 1995)

Government bears burden of proving by preponderance of evidence that consent to search was freely and voluntarily given.

US v. Scopo, 19 F.3d 777 (2nd Cir. 1994)
US v. Hassan El, 5 F.3d 726 (4th Cir. 1993)

Any evidence seized based upon illegal traffic stop is subject to fruit of the poisonous tree doctrine and may be suppressed.

US v. Snow, 919 F.2d 1458 (10th Cir. 1990)

When law enforcement officer grossly exceed scope of search warrant, suppression of all evidence seized under that warrant is required.

US v. Tedford, 875 F.2d 446 (5th Cir. 1989)
Wong Son v. US, 371 US 471, 9 L.Ed.2d 441, 83) S.Ct. 407 (1963)

The "fruit of the poisonous tree doctrine" is not triggered by a rule violation that does not rise to constitutional proportions.

US v. Todd, 963 F.2d 207 (8th Cir. 1992)

Florida v. Bostick, 501 US 115 L.Ed.2d 389, 111 S.Ct. 2382 (1991)

US v. Childs, 944 F.2d 491 (9th Cir. 1991)

As long as the police do not convey a message that compliance with their requests is required they can ask questions, request to search, and request ID (Authors note: you always have the right to shut up and walk away).

US v. Turner, 169 F.3d 87

Incriminating nature of computer files containing child pornography was not immediately apparent, despite presence of sexually suggestive image on the screen and file names such as "young and young with breasts."

US v. Velarde, 25 F.3d 848 (9th Cir. 1994)

US v. Strahan, 984 F.2d 155 (6th Cir. 1993)

Terry v. Ohio, 392 US 1, 20 I Ed2d 889, 88 S.Ct. 1868 (1968)

TERRY allows only for an examination for concealed objects and prohibits searching for anything other than weapons (see Strahan).For an "Investigative Stop" to be valid there must be "reasonable articulable suspicion" (see Terry). To support TERRY stop in airport, police must identify specific facts which distinguish suspect from numerous innocent travelers who erratically dash through airports.

US v. Van Cauwenberghe, 814 F.2d 1329 (9th Cir. 1987)

To prevail on motion for return of seized property, criminal defendant must demonstrate that he is entitled to lawful possession of the seized property, property is not contraband and either seizure was illegal or government's need for property as evidence has ended.

US v. Van Leeuwen, 397 US 249, 25 L.Ed.2d 282, 90 S.Ct. 1029 (1970)

Garmon v. Foust, 741 F.2d 1069 (8th Cir. 1984)

The protection of the Fourth Amendment extends to items in the mail.

US v. Warren, 42 F.3d 647 (D.C. Cir. 1994)
A search by government agents is presumptively unreasonable under Fourth Amendment unless conducted pursuant to warrant issued by judicial officer upon finding of probable cause.

US v. Welliver, 976 F.2d 1148 (8th Cir. 1992)
One claiming Fourth Amendment violation must show that he had a legitimate expectation of privacy and that the expectation was invaded by government action.

US v. Wulferdinger, 782 F.2d 1473 (9th Cir. 1986)
Franks v. Delaware, 438 US 154, 57 L.Ed.2d 667, 98 S.Ct. 2674 (1978)
A "Franks" hearing is used to determine whether the search warrant was invalid because the affidavit provided to the magistrate issuing the warrant was misleading or incorrect.

Wilson v. Arkansas, 514 US 131 L.Ed.2d 976, 115 S.Ct. (1995)
US v. Finch, 998 F.2d 349 (6th Cir. 1993)
Miller v. US, 357 US 301. 2 L.Ed.2d 1332. 78 S.Ct. 1190 (1958)
Common law knock and announce principle held part of reasonableness inquiry under Federal Constitution's Fourth Amendment guarantee against unreasonable searches and seizures.

Selective Prosecution

Bar MK Ranches v. Yeuther, 994 F.2d 735 (10th Cir. 1993)
Administrative agencies are required to follow their own regulations.

Bivens v. Six Unknown Agents, 403 US 388, 29 L.Ed.2d 619, 91 S.Ct. 1999 (1970)
When a government agent acts in an unconstitutional manner it becomes liable for money damages.

Bushanell v. Rossetti, 750 F.2d 298 (4th Cir. 1984)
Government's prosecutorial power may not be used either to exact releases of related civil rights claims or to retaliate for civil prosecution of such claims.

Curry v. Pucinski, 864 F. Supp. 839 (N.D. IL 1994)
A court clerk can be sued when critical documents are missing from an individual's appellate record.

Gaudreault v. Municipality Of Salem, Mass., 923 F.2d 203 (1st Cir. 1990)
O'Neil v. Krezeminski, 839 F.2d 9 (2nd Cir. 1988)
Police officer who is present at scene and fails to take reasonable steps to protect victim of another officer's use of excessive force in violation of Fourth Amendment can be held liable under § 1983 for nonfeasance.

Guam v. Dergurgur, 800 F.2d 1470 (9th Cir. 1986)
Blackledge v. Perry, 417 US 21, 40 LEM 628, 94 S.Ct. 2098 (1974)
It is unconstitutional deprivation of due process for government to penalize person merely because he has exercised protected statutory or constitutional right.

Mahoney v. Kesery, 976 F.2d 1054 (7th Cir. 1992)
Police officer who procures prosecution by lying to prosecutor or the grand jury is subject to prosecution.

Meriwether v. Coughlin, 879 F.2d 1037 (2nd Cir. 1989)
Supervisory liability may be imposed under §1983 when an official has actual or constructive notice of unconstitutional practices and demonstrates "gross negligence" or "deliberate indifference" by failing to act.

North Carolina v. Pearce, 395 US 711, 23 L.Ed.2d 656, 89 S.Ct. 2072 (1969)
Supreme Court coined the phrase "Prosecutorial Vindictiveness."

Sanchez v. US, 49 F.3d 1329 (8th Cir. 1995)
BIVENS actions are governed by same statute of limitations as §1983 actions.

Strength v. Hubert, 854 F.2d 421 (11th Cir. 1988)
Freedom from malicious prosecution is a federal right protected by §1983.

US v. Allen, 954 F.2d 1160 (6th Cir. 1992)
Prosecutor's decision in determining which case to prosecute cannot be based on defendant's race, sex, religion, or exercise of statutory or constitutional right.

US v. Armstrong, 48 F.3d 1508 (9th Cir. 1995)
Colorable basis for selective prosecution entitles defendant to discovery concerning the alleged discrimination.

US v. Hudson, 982 F.2d 160 (5th Cir. 1993)
US v. Cueruelo, 949 F.2d 559 (2nd Cir. 1991)
Outrageous conduct defense is available when conduct of government agents is so outrageous that due process principles bar government from invoking judicial process to obtain conviction.

US v. Sneed, 34 F.3d 1570 (10th Cir. 1994)
"Excessive governmental involvement" occurs when government engineers and directs criminal enterprise from start to finish and defendant contributes nothing more than his presence and enthusiasm.

US v. Solivan, 937 F.2d 1146 (6th Cir. 1991)
US v. Johnson, 968 F.2d 768 (8th Cir. 1992)
"Single Misstep" on part of prosecutor may be so destructive of right to a fair trial that reversal is required.

US v. Woods, 36 F.3d 945 (10th Cir. 1994)
Once defendant meets initial burden on vindictive prosecution claim, burden shifts to government to justify its charging decisions with legitimate, articulable, objective reasons.

Yick Wo v. Hopkins, 118 US 356, 30 L.Ed 220, 96 S.Ct. 1064 (1886)
Case in which the Supreme Court coined the term "Evil eye and an uneven hand."

Sentencing

A.R.Cr.P Rule 26.13 Concurrent or consecutive sentences.
The discretion to impose consecutive sentences rests with the discretion of the trial judge.

Alexander v. Perrill, 916 F.2d 1392 (9th Cir. 1990)
Prison officials who are under duty to investigate claims of computational errors in calculation of prison sentences may be liable for failure to do so when reasonable request is made.

Barden v. Keohane, 921 F.2d 476 (3rd Cir. 1990)
Individual served a state sentence first where the state judge clearly intended that both the state and succeeding federal sentence be served concurrently. The federal BOP refused to even consider his request that the state time served be considered as 'credit' against his federal sentence. The case carried a "serious potential for miscarriage of justice and warranted habeas relief."

Blackledge v. Perry, 417 US 21, 40 L.Ed.2d 628, 94 S.Ct. 2098 (1974)
Vindictiveness on the part of the prosecutor.

Blockburger v. US, 284 US 299, 76 L.Ed.2d 306, 52 S.Ct. 180 (1932)
Consecutive punishments should not be imposed for violations of separate statutes when only one "offense" has been committed.

Boynton v. Anderson, 1 CA-SA 03-0014 , COURT OF APPEALS OF ARIZONA, DIVISION ONE, DEPARTMENT C, 205 Ariz. 45; 66 P.3d 88; 2003 Ariz. App. LEXIS 59; 397 Ariz. Adv. Rep. 41, April 8, 2003, Filed , Released for Publication July 17, 2003. Review denied by Boynton v. Anderson, 2003 Ariz. LEXIS 89 (Ariz., June 30, 2003)
Where crime of luring a minor for sexual exploitation was not listed as punishable as a "dangerous crime against children," appellate court held that the legislature did not intend the crime to be considered a "dangerous crime against children."

Burns v. US, 501 US 115L.Ed.2d 123, 111 S.Ct. (1991)
Before departing upward on its own motion from Sentencing Guidelines' sentencing range the district court must give parties reasonable notice that court is contemplating such action.

Cunningham v. California, 549 US (2007)
Held: the DSL, (determinate sentencing law) by placing sentence - elevating fact-finding within the judge's province, violates the defendants right to trial by jury safeguarded by the sixth and fourteenth amendment's, Page 8 - 22.

In Apprendi v. New Jersey, this court held that under the sixth amendment, any fact (other than a prior conviction) that exposes a defendant to a sentence in excess of the relevant statutory maximum must be found by a jury, not a judge, and established beyond a reasonable doubt, not merely by a preponderance of the evidence. The Booker court held that "the federal guidelines incompatible with the sixth amendment because they were mandatory and impose binding requirements on all sentencing judges." 543 US at 233 This court's decisions make plain, falls within the province of the jury employing a beyond a reasonable doubt standard, not the bailiwick of a judge determining whether preponderance of the evidence lies.

Davis v. Bryan, 889 F.2d 445 (2nd Cir. 1989)
Prisoner has due process interest in having correct sentence imposed by proper authority. 20 Years.

In re James P., 1 CA-JV 06-0074 , COURT OF APPEALS OF ARIZONA, DIVISION ONE, DEPARTMENT D, 214 Ariz. 420; 153 P.3d 1049; 2007 Ariz. App. LEXIS 38; 498 Ariz. Adv. Rep. 23, March 1, 2007, Filed AFFIRMED IN PART, REVERSED IN PART.
A juvenile court erred in concluding that assault was a lesser-included offense of child molestation where assault under Ariz. Rev. Stat. § 13-1203.A.1 contained an element, causing physical injury, which child molestation under Ariz. Rev. Stat. § 13-1410.A did not contain. The evidence was sufficient to convict the juvenile of child molestation.

Jackson v. Schneider, 1 CA-SA 03-0268 , COURT OF APPEALS OF ARIZONA, DIVISION ONE, DEPARTMENT C, 207 Ariz. 325; 86 P.3d 381; 2004 Ariz. App. LEXIS 32; 421 Ariz. Adv. Rep. 5, March 18, 2004, Filed.
Special action petitioner was previously convicted of a misdemeanor. Sentencing court unlawfully imposed lifetime probation. Trial judge wrongfully denied petitioner's request to terminate probation early.

Kellogg v. Shoemaker, 46 F.3d 503 (6th Cir. 1995)
Focus in determining whether new law violates ex post facto clause is time that offense was committed.

Kelly v. US, 29 F.3d 1107 (7th Cir. 1994)
Failure to give defendant notice before trial begins that sentence for drug offense may be enhanced as result of prior conviction, deprives district court of jurisdiction to impose enhanced sentence.

Larson v. Farley, 106 Ariz. 119, 471 P.2d 731 (1970)
A statute should be explained in conjunction with other statutes which relate to the same subject or have the same general purpose.

Mistretta v. US, 488 US 361, 102 L.Ed.2d 714, 109 S.Ct. 647 (1989)
Case where the new "Sentencing Guidelines" were upheld as being constitutional.

Nichols v. US, 511 US 128 L.Ed.2d 745, 114S.Ct. (1994)
The use of an uncounseled misdemeanor conviction, as to which prison term was imposed, could be used to enhance a prison term for a subsequent offense (adverse law).

North Carolina v. Pearce, 395 US 711, 23 L.Ed.2d 656, 89 S.Ct. 2072 (1969)
Vindictiveness on the part of the judge.

Note: Prison labor is voluntary. The Constitution prohibits involuntary servitude except as a punishment for a crime. However, judges; must sentence you accordingly, that is either to a term of labor or a Term of imprisonment. However, the government, courts and the establishment do not recognize such distinctions in the law.

Note: Title 18, USC. 3582 authorizes the Attorney General or if the Director of the Bureau of Prisons to file a motion for reduction of sentence. Also, this same law allows for retroactive guideline amendments that reduce either your sentence or offense level.

Note: Sentencing court's refusal to depart downward is reviewable if it rests on misconstruction of its authority to depart.

Nulph v. Faatz, 27 F.3d 451 (9th Cir. 1994)
Penal law that is applied retrospectively to disadvantage of offender is unconstitutional ex post fact law.

Russell v. Collins, 998 F.2d 1287 (5th Cir. 1993)
It is impermissible to sentence a person to death solely on basis of acts of accomplice; there must be evidence from which jury could determine defendants individual culpability.

Seritt v. State Of Alabama, 731 F.2d 728 (11th Cir. 1984)
US v. HOLLIS, 718 F.2d 277 (8th Cir. 1983)
Eighth Amendment prohibits imposition of a sentence that is grossly disproportionate to severity of the crime.

Simmons v. South Carolina, 512 US 129 L.Ed.2d 133, 114 S.Ct. (1994)
Due process held violated by South Carolina trial court's refusal to allow capital sentencing jury to be informed that defendant was ineligible for parole under state law.

Smith et al. v. Doe et al., 538 US (9th Cir. 2003)
The Ninth Circuit held "the court's conclusion is not altered by the fact that the acts implementing procedural mechanisms required the trial court to inform the defendant of the acts requirements and, as if possible the period of registration required."

Solem v. Helm, 463 US 277, 77 L.Ed.2d 637, 103 S.Ct. 3001 (1983)
Eighth Amendment held to proscribe life sentence without possibility of parole for seventh nonviolent felony.

Solem v. Helm, 463 US 277, 292, 103 S.Ct. 3001, 3011, 77 L.Ed.2d 637 (1983)
Solem set forth a three-part test to determine whether a sentence was disproportionate to the crime and therefore violated the eighth amendment's prohibition against cruel and unusual punishment Id. The test required examination of the following factors: (a) the severity of the penalty as compared to the seriousness of the offense, (b) the jurisdictions penalty as for crimes that a more serious than the offense at issue (the intra jurisdictional analysis), and (c) the sentences other jurisdictions impose for the same crime (the inter jurisdictional analysis).

State v. Barnett, NO.02 CA 65, 2004 WL3090228, at 26, ¶ 153 (Ohio App. Dec. 28, 2004)
Courts from around the country have recognized that a criminal defendant whose appeal was pending at the time Blakely was decided does not waive his Blakely-related arguments simply because he did not make those same arguments at trial.

State v. Bartlett, 164 Ariz. 229, 792 P.2d 692
Defendant was convicted in the Superior Court, Cochise County, No. CR-87-00020, Richard A. Winkler, J., of two counts of sexual conduct with a minor under 15 years of age and sentenced to mandatory minimum consecutive sentences totaling 40 years without possibility of early release. The Court of Appeals affirmed, and the defendant petitioned for further review. The Supreme Court, Corcoran, J., held that defendant's sentences under dangerous crimes against children act of 15 years for first offense and 25 years for second offense were disproportionate to his crimes involving participation in nonviolent, non-

261

incestuous, non-incestuous, heterosexual, and consensual sexual intercourse with two 14-year-old girls and therefore violated Eighth Amendment proscription against cruel and unusual punishment. Remanded for re-sentencing.

State v. Brown, 191 Ariz. 102, 103, 952P.2d 746, 747 (App. 1998)
"We do find fundamental error in trial court's imposition of enhanced sentence. The state alleged pursuant to A.R.S. 13-604.01 that count line was a predicate, to the remaining counts, count to less a predicate to the remaining counts and so on."

State v. Brown, 99 P.3d 15, 2004 WL 2390005 (Ariz.)
The Supreme Court held that application of statutes 13-702 and 13-702.01 was unconstitutional and the aggravating elements must be submitted to a jury before a sentence can be aggravated. This would be a fundamental error if the judge alone found aggravating circumstances to enhance the defendant sentence, a sixth amendment violation, right to have jury decided factual issues. See Blakely v. Washington at (A7)

State v. Conn, 98 P.3d 881 (Ariz. 2004) ¶8.
Arizona law has long recognized the state's ability to give pre-trial notice of factors that could enhance a defendant's sentence.

State v. Cox, 201 Ariz. 464, 468 ¶ 13P.3d 437, 441 (App.2 2002)
Imposition of an illegal sentence constitutes fundamental error. Fundamental error is subject to harmless error review. Will be reversed on appeal despite a lack of objection in trial court.

State v. Davis, Arizona Supreme Court No. CR-01-0423-PR , SUPREME COURT OF ARIZONA, 206 Ariz. 377; 79 P.3d 64; 2003 Ariz. LEXIS 132; 415 Ariz. Adv. Rep. 48, October 30, 2003, Filed , US Supreme Court certiorari denied by Arizona v. Davis, 158 L. Ed. 2d 723, 124 S. Ct. 2097, 2004 US LEXIS 3353 (US, May 3, 2004)
Defendant's 52-year sentence for four counts of sexual misconduct with a minor was grossly disproportionate to his crimes, because the post-pubescent victims were willing participants. They sought out defendant by voluntarily going to his home.

State v. Gonzalez, 216 Ariz. 11, 162 P.3d 650

Gonzalez argues that the statute under which he was sentenced, § 13-604.01(I), does not include attempted sexual conduct with a victim under the age of twelve. Gonzalez also contends that, although § 13-604.01(A) and (B) provide a sentencing range for, inter alia, sexual conduct with a minor twelve years old or under and with a minor under the age of twelve, respectively, those subsections do not apply to attempted sexual conduct, the relevant offense in this case. Gonzalez argues that, because nowhere in § 13-604.01 is the offense of attempted sexual conduct with a victim under the age of twelve addressed, he was illegally sentenced under that statute. Accordingly, because we conclude that the sentence imposed was illegal under § 13-604.01, we grant the petition for review, grant relief, and remand this matter to the trial court for re-sentencing. It may hold a hearing, if necessary, to establish the victim's age. If the court concludes the victim was eleven years old when Gonzalez committed the offense, it shall re-sentence Gonzalez, as he has requested, in accordance with A.R.S. §§ 13-701 and 13-702.

State v. Hana, 126 Ariz. 575, 576, 617 P.2d 527, 528 (1980)

Here as in Brown supra all petitioners' convictions took place at the same time. Section 604 (M) provides: "convictions for two or more offenses committed on the same occasion shall be counted as only one convictions for purposes of this section."

State v. Harrison, 195 Ariz. 1, 4, ¶ 12, 1985 P.2d 486, 489 (1999)

Finding that A.R.S. 13-702 (B) requires court to express reason in support of aggravating factors and failure to substantially comply with this requirement mandates that aggravated sentence be vacated. ¶ 13 In State v. Benati; we chose to follow Aprendi's logic and Ring's clear message that a fact exposing defendant to increase sentence, not the actual sentence imposed, is the litmus test. See Ring. For that recently find a logical disconnect in the reasoning of the many courts that have concluded that the need for a right to a jury determination of sentence enhancers is dependent on the sentence actually imposed. The reason we believe, puts the cart before the horse - something we in Ariz. do not permit. ¶ 14 in this regard we agree with State v. Gross, 201 Ariz. 41, 31 P.3d 815 (App. 2001) when it emphasized that "the relevant inquiry is law that none of form, but of effect - does that required finding expose the defendant to a grader punishment and then authorized by the jury's guilty verdict?" <u>Aprendi</u>: 530 US at 494, 120 S.Ct. at 494, 120 S.Ct. at 2365, 147 L.Ed.2d at 457. If it does, then it is the fundamental equivalent of an element of a grader offense than the one covered by the jury's guilty verdict. Indeed it fits squarely within the usual definition of an "element of the offense." Id. at 494 n.19, 120 S.Ct. (at 2365 n.19, 147 L.Ed.2d at 457 n. 19)

<u>State v. Harrison Jr.</u>, 195 Ariz.1, 985 P.2d 486 (1999) (en Banc)
A.R.S. 13-702 (B) must set forth factual findings and reasons in support of aggravating and mitigating factors in support of such findings and set forth on the record at the time of sentencing. The court's words in <u>State v. Holstun</u>, 139 Ariz. 196, 677 P.2d 1304 (App. 1983) bear repetition: there is a value in requiring every sentencing judge to say why he or she is enhancing or reducing a sentence [from the presumptive term]. Such a practice can bring to light the judges occasional misapprehension of the facts, it ensures that the judge is not relying on matters that are not properly aggravating or mitigating, and tends to a sure that judges will give slot to whether or not each sentence, even a stipulated one, is appropriate. In the case of an aggravated sentence it affirms the defendant's individuality while driving home to him the severity of the consequence of his crime. In the case of a vacated sentence it explains to the community lie a convicted person is receiving a lesser sentence and others who violated the same law... The requirement that reasons for sentencing be articulated helps ensure the process does not become purely mechanical. 139 Ariz. at 197, 677P.2d at 1305.

As the Court of Appeals has said, the victim, the defendant and the public have the right to know why a particular sentence was imposed... Substantial compliance will suffice, but at a minimum this means articulating at sentencing the facts that judge considered to be aggravating or mitigating and explaining how these factors led to the sentence and pilots. Anything less would force the appellate courts as well as the victim, the defendant, and the public to speculate or infer. A harmless error will leg is essentially affirms the judge's decision so long as the record contains facts that may support the result. While such a rule may be appropriate for most situations, we believe it is inappropriate for most situations, we believe it is inappropriate when a trial judge imposes an aggravated or mitigating sentence because A.R.S. 13-702 expressly prohibits searching beyond sentencing transcript for support for the imposed sentence... Substantial compliance means that the factors supporting an aggravated or mitigating sentence must be in the sentencing transcript. The Galliano down would be to conduct a harmless error analysis...

State v. Henderson, 209 Ariz. 300,100 P.3d 911 (App. 2004)
Resendis - Felix. We will find error harmless only if we conclude, beyond a reasonable doubt, but the error did not contribute to or affect the sentence imposed. If a reasonable doubt exists on whether the air has affected the outcome, and the error is not harmless, in the case must be remanded for a new sentencing hearing. See: State v. Sansing, 206 Ariz. 232, 77 P.3d 30 (2003);Resendis - Felix.

State v. Hutton, 87 Ariz 176
Defendant pleaded guilty to one count of first-degree burglary and one count of grand theft. The grand theft charge arose out of defendant's stealing a saddle from a building that he had burglarized. The trial court convicted defendant on the two charges and imposed consecutive sentences. Defendant sought review of the trial court's judgment. On appeal, the court modified the trial court's decision, exercising its power under Ariz. Rev. Stat. § 13-1717(B) to impose concurrent sentences to be served by defendant in the interest of justice. The court otherwise affirmed the trial court's ruling, holding that defendant could be sentenced for both offenses because he actually committed the separate acts of first-degree burglary and grand theft. The court modified the trial court's judgment convicting defendant of first degree burglary and grand theft so that the sentences would run concurrently, and affirmed the trial court's judgment as modified.

State v. Johnson, 23 Ariz. 358, 360, 903 P.2d 1116, 1118 (App. 1995)
Concluding court may convene a second jury to try allegation of prior conviction and nothing in rules or statute prohibits practice.

State v. Munninger, 209 Ariz. 473, 104 P.3d 204
Defendant was convicted by jury of aggravated assault with finding that offense was dangerous, and the Superior Court, Maricopa County, Cause No. CR2002-091835, Alfred M. Fenzel, J., imposed aggravated sentence. Defendant appealed. The Court of Appeals vacated defendant's sentence, but granted State's motion for reconsideration.

Holdings: On reconsideration, the Court of Appeals, Lankford, P.J., held that: 1. Defendant did not waive error under Blakely v. Washington; 2. Single properly found aggravating factor did not satisfy Blakely when sentence also rested on other aggravating factors; 3. Error in failing to submit to jury aggravating factor of extraordinary severity of harm to victim was harmless; 4. Error in failing to submit to jury aggravating factor of viciousness of defendant's actions was not harmless; 5. Relying on aggravating factor of use of dangerous instrument or deadly weapon was improper as double-counting this fact; and 6. Remand was required for trial court to reweigh aggravating and mitigating factors. Vacated and remanded.

State v. Patience, 944 P.2d 381
Defendant pleaded guilty and was convicted in Third District Court, Pat B. Brian, J., of attempted forgery, and defendant appealed sentence. The Court of Appeals, Jackson, J., held that: (1) defendant was entitled to benefit of lesser penalty afforded by amended statute that was in effect prior to sentencing; (2) statements at sentencing hearing of defendant's previous employer concerning prior incidents of embezzlement were properly considered; and (3) doctrine that theft counts may be consolidated into one offense does not apply to forgery cases. Affirmed in part and reversed in part and remanded.

State v. Patton, No. 1 CA-CR 5143, Court of Appeals of Arizona, Division One, Department B, 136 Ariz. 243; 665 P.2d 587; 1983 Ariz. App. LEXIS 443, April 7, 1983 Reversed.
Defendant's conviction for sexual assault upon a trial for child molestation was reversed because sexual assault was not a lesser-included offense. However, double jeopardy did not prevent his re-trial on a proper charge of sexual assault.

State v. Pena, 104 P.3d 873 (Ariz. App. Div. 1 2005)
Defendant argues that we must remand for resentencing because the court improperly found the aggravating circumstances of serious physical injury and emotional harm to the victim. He argues that by statute, an element of the offense cannot be used as an aggravating factor. Whether it is an element of the offense is a question of law that we review de novo.

State v. Poling, 125 Ariz. 90, 11, 606 P.2d 827, 829 (App. 1980)
As the Court of Appeals has said, it would be "better practice for a trial judge to state in the more precise terms of the statute" that he or she has found or considered certain specific circumstances. Not only is this better practice, it is required by present statute.

State v. Ramsey, 136 Ariz.166, 665 P.2d 48, 1983 Ariz. LEXIS 189
We have always assumed and we so hold now, that the state must prove the existence of aggravating circumstances beyond a reasonable doubt.

State v. Ring, 204 Ariz. 534, 6 5P.3d 915 (2003) (Ring 3)
Our Supreme Court essentially rejected its analysis in the capital sentencing context, finding 6th amendment - complaint factor insufficient, in and of itself to permit a trial court to find additional aggravating factors, notwithstanding that an Ariz. capital defendant technically becomes eligible for the death penalty when a single capital aggravating factor is established. In Ring 3 our Supreme Court found that the state had to narrowly construed the US Supreme Court's holding in Ring v. Ariz. 536 US 584, 122 S.Ct. 2428, 153 L.Ed.2d 556 (2002) (Ring 2), ruling instead that Ring 2 requires any jury finding each aggravating factor. We cannot find embraced within the Legislature's intent the concept the state urges here---having both the jury and record finding aggravating factors under different standards. In sum, we can find no principal between the considerations grounding in Ring 3, in which our Supreme Court rejected the same argument the state advanced in the capital context and the application of those same considerations in non-capital context. Absent weighing all aggravators A.R.S. 13-702 prescribes cannot occur if a jury has not found beyond a reasonable doubt each aggravating factor the court considers. ¶ 13 (Harmless error) the state further argues that any error was harmless. Blakely error is subject to a harmless error analysis Resendis - Felix. We will not consider harmless any finding of an aggravating factor is evidence and witness credibility could be laid differently by a jury and it was by a sentencing judge.

State v. Shepler, No. 2 CA-CR 3358, Court of Appeals of Arizona, Division Two, 141 Ariz. 43; 684 P.2d 924; 1984 Ariz. App. LEXIS 422, June 26, 1984

A defendant's consecutive sentences of probation were modified so as to provide that the terms of probation were to run concurrently because the "stacking" of defendant's probationary term was unlawful.

State v. Stewart, 139 Ariz. 50, 676P.2d 1108 (1984)

As long as the convictions are for distinct and separate crimes, consecutive sentences are proper if the trial judge sets out his reasons for consecutive sentences.

State v. Suniga, 145 Ariz. 389

Once defendant began to serve a lawful sentence, he could not be sentenced to an increased term. To do so violated the constitutional proscription against double jeopardy.

State v. Timmons, 103 P.3d 315, 2005 WL 30494 (Ariz. App. Div. 2, 2005)

Division I of Court of Appeals held one Blakely complaint factor increases the maximum prison sentence outweighed by any guilty verdict or plea to the aggravated term from the offense.

State v. Tschilar, 200 Ariz. 427, 432 ¶ 15, 27 P.2d 331, 336 (App. 2001)

The court does considered the emotional harm of the victim as an aggravating factor. Defendant argues that the record is devoid of any evidence of emotional harm. The state does not responded to this contention and thereby confesses error. See: In Re US Currency in amount of $26,980, 199 Ariz. 291, 297 ¶ 20, 18 P.3d 85, 91 (App. 2000)

State v. Tsinnijinnie, 1 CA-CR 02-0958 , COURT OF APPEALS OF ARIZONA, DIVISION ONE, DEPARTMENT D, 206 Ariz. 477; 80 P.3d 284; 2003 Ariz. App. LEXIS 199; 414 Ariz. Adv. Rep. 8, December 11, 2003, Filed , Review denied by State v. Tsinnijinnie, 2004 Ariz. LEXIS 78 (Ariz., June 29, 2004) Affirmed in part, reversed in part, and ...

Trial court's sentencing of defendant to concurrent sentences was reversed; pursuant to applicable statute, the trial court was required to impose consecutive sentences for defendant's convictions for sexual assault and molestation of a child.

State v. Viramontes, 204 Ariz. 360, 64 P.3d 188
Upon further appeal, the Supreme Court, Zlaket, Retired Justice, consolidated the cases and held that: (1) aggravating factors set out in death or life imprisonment sentencing statute were the only factors the trial court could consider in first-degree murder prosecutions in which the state had not sought the death penalty, and thus trial court could not consider factors contained in felony sentencing statute during sentencing, and (2) aggravating factors only needed to be supported by reasonable evidence in non-capital cases. Vacated and remanded.

State v. Vargas-Burgos, 162 Ariz. 325, 783 P.2d 264
Defendant pled no contest in the Superior Court, Pima County, Cause No. CR-24337, Thomas Meehan, J., to charge of unlawful possession of marijuana. State appealed from sentence imposed by trial court. The Court of Appeals, Howard, J., held that: (1) trial court's failure to impose mandatory fine raised question of subject matter jurisdiction which was not waived by State's failure to object below, and (2) sentence not in compliance with mandatory provisions of sentencing statute was illegal and appealable. Sentence vacated and matter remanded.

State v. Vaughn, 147 Ariz. 28, 708 P.2d 453 (1985)
State v. Girdler, 138 Ariz. 482, 675 P.2d 130 (1983) cert. denied, 467 US 1244, 104 S.Ct. 3519, 82 L.Ed.2d 826 (1984)
When a consecutive sentence is imposed by trial judge must state his reasons for the sentence on the record.

State v. Watson, 134 Ariz. 1, 4, 653 P.2d 351, 354 (1982)
We have said that minimal competence at the sentencing stage requires the attorney at least "to challenge the admission of aggravating evidence where reasonably possible and to present available mitigating evidence."

State v. Waggoner, 144 Ariz. 237, 238, 697 P.2d 320, 321 (1985)
Four days before trial, the state filed an allegation under A.R.S. 13-604.01 (now A.R.S. 13-604.02 (2001)) that the defendant committed offense while on parole, which mandated prison term. Defendant argued timeliness of pre-trial motion A.R.Cr.P. 16.1 (b) require, 20 days before trial. Trial court found allegation true and resentenced defendant.

State v. Wagstaff, 164 Ariz. 485, 492, 794, P.2d 11/8, 125 (1990)
Thus redundancy in the statute especially as it applies to attempted child molestation creates constitutional uncertainty. Uncertainty in a criminal statute, the conduct is forbidden, or the punishment imposed.

Tucker v. US, 404 US 443, 30 L.Ed.2d 592, 92 S.Ct. 589 (1972)
Gideon v. Wainwright, 372 US 335, 9 L.Ed.2d 799, 83 S.Ct. 792 (1963)
A prior conviction in which the defendant was denied his Sixth Amendment right to counsel cannot be used in a later proceeding to support a conviction or enhance the punishment.

US v. Alvarez, 51 F.3d 36 (5th Cir. 1995)
District court may impose sentence below statutory minimum only on government's motion and only for purpose of reflecting defendant's substantial assistance.

US v. Anderson, 5 F.3d 795 (5th Cir. 1993)
Departure based on circumstances already adequately considered by Sentencing Guidelines is incorrect application of the Guidelines.

US v. Arrellano - Rios, 799 F.2d 520 (9th Cir. 1986)
Narcotics offenses are not "crimes of violence" within meaning of statute prohibiting use of firearm in connection with those crimes.

US v. Austin, 54 F.3d 394 (7th Cir. 1995)
Double counting is not permitted under Sentencing Guidelines.

US v. Barnes, 948 F.2d 325 (7th Cir. 1991)

Groppi v. Leslie, 404 US 496, 30 L.Ed.2d 632, 92 S.Ct. 582 (1972)

Federal Criminal Procedure Rule 32(a) requires that a defendant be given the right to personally address the court before sentence is passed in an attempt to mitigate punishment.

US v. Becker, 36 F.3d 708 (7th Cir 1994)

Generally, in absence of language to contrary, sentences imposed on more than one offense at same time are presumed to run concurrently.

US v. Bost, 968 F.2d 729 (8th Cir. 1992)

US v. Baker, 961 F.2d 1390 (8th Cir. 1992)

Government bears burden of proof in establishing enhancement under Sentencing Guidelines.

US v. Brady, 26 F.3d 282 (2nd Cir. 1994)

Criminal or penal law is ex post facto if it is retrospective and it disadvantages affected offender.

US v. Brown, 47 F.3d 198 (7th Cir. 1995)

Defendants need not "come clean" on relevant conduct beyond offense of conviction in order to obtain reduction in Sentencing Guidelines offense level for acceptance of responsibility.

US v. Cantu, 12 F.3d 1506 (9th Cir. 1993)

Post-traumatic Stress Disorder, an emotional illness, can be the basis for downward departure on the basis of "significantly reduced mental capacity."

US v. Chatlin, No. 94-10247, UNITED STATES COURT OF APPEALS FOR THE NINTH CIRCUIT, 51 F.3d 869; 1995 US App. LEXIS 6618; 95 Cal. Daily Op. Service 2400; 95 Daily Journal DAR 4162, November 4, 1994, * Submitted* The panel unanimously finds this case suitable for disposition without oral argument. Fed. R. App. P. 34(a); 9th Cir. R. 34-4., April 3, 1995, Filed

Defendant's sentence for sexual abuse of a minor on an Indian reservation was not proper because the lower court relied on aggravated sexual abuse as an additional ground for its departure from the sentencing guidelines.

US v. Condelee, 961 F.2d 1351 (8th Cir. 1992)
Sentencing judge has the authority to depart downward from sentencing guidelines without any government motion in unusual circumstances such as extraordinary restitution.

US v. Cooper, 35 F.3d 1248 (8th Cir. 1994)
Sentencing court should apply Sentencing Guidelines in effect at time of sentencing unless doing so is violative of ex post facto clause.

US v. Curran, 925 F.2d 59 (1st Cir. 1991)
US v. Mueller, 902 F.2d 336 (5th Cir. 1990)
Defendants, including those who plead guilty, have a due process right to be sentenced upon information which is not false or materially incorrect.

US v. Davidson, No. 00-50033 , UNITED STATES COURT OF APPEALS FOR THE NINTH CIRCUIT, 246 F.3d 1240; 2001 US App. LEXIS 7153; 2001 Cal. Daily Op. Service 3100; 2002 Daily Journal DAR 3827, December 7, 2000, Argued and Submitted, Pasadena, California , April 19, 2001, Filed.
Amendment of probation to include sex offender registration vacated where the federal crime to which appellant plead guilty was not punishable, at the time he committed it, as a state law offense requiring registration.

US v. Davis, 906 F.2d 829 (2nd Cir. 1990)
Chapman v. US Dept. Of Health & Human Services, 821 F.2d 523 (10th 1987)
1. Under doctrine of "Dual Sovereignty" federal prosecution does not bar subsequent state prosecution of same person for same acts, and state prosecution does not bar federal one. 2. Exception to doctrine of "Dual Sovereignty" exists which bars successive prosecutions if one prosecuting sovereign can be said to be acting as "tool" of other, of it one prosecution is merely sham and cover for another.

US v. De Albs Pagan, 33 F.3d 125 (1st Cir. 1994)
District court's failure to afford defendant right of allocation or its functional equivalent required vacation of sentence.

US v. DeCosta, 37 F.3d 5 (1st Cir. 1994)
Sentencing court is entitled to depart from Sentencing Guidelines in cases that fall outside "heartland" contemplated by guidelines.

US v. Dean, No. 06-30562, UNITED STATES COURT OF APPEALS FOR THE NINTH CIRCUIT, 238 Fed. Appx. 320; 2007 US App. LEXIS 19416, July 10, 2007, Argued and Submitted, Seattle, Washington, August 10, 2007, Filed, PLEASE REFER TO FEDERAL RULES OF APPELLATE PROCEDURE RULE 32.1 GOVERNING THE CITATION TO UNPUBLISHED OPINIONS.
In sentencing defendant for, inter alia, interstate transportation with intent to engage in criminal sexual activity, district court plainly erred by failing to inform him that it was considering sentence more than twice the top-end of advisory USSG range, as required by Fed. R. Crim. P. 32(h), as failure seriously affected fairness of proceeding.

US v. Demers, 13 F.3d 1381 (9th Cir. 1993)
Sentencing Guidelines commentary regarding role in offense adjustment, by mandating fact based inquiry into relative seriousness of defendant's offense of conviction compared to his actual criminal convicted of possession with intent to distribute, provided his role and culpability in trafficking scheme are sufficiently minor compared to that of other participants.

US v. Dolt, 27 F.3d 235 (6th Cir. 1994)
Prior convictions requirement of Sentencing Guidelines' career offender provision is to be interpreted strictly.

US v. Droge, 961 F.2d 1030 (2nd Cir. 1992)
Bordenkircher v. Hayes, 434 US 357, 54 LEM 604, 98 S.Ct. 663 (1978)
A trial court may not use the sentencing process to punish a defendant, notwithstanding his guilt, for exercising his right to receive a full and fair trial.

Where trial court imposes lengthy sentence out of personal spite and in retaliation for defendant's assertion of his statutory rights, resentencing is required.

US v. Epley, 52 F.3d 571 (6th Cir. 1995)
Court of Appeals may review sentence based on legal error, even if within range of Sentencing Guidelines.

US v. Evans-Martinez, No. 05-10280, UNITED STATES COURT OF APPEALS FOR THE NINTH CIRCUIT, 530 F.3d 1164; 2008 US App. LEXIS 13972, April 7, 2006, Argued and Submitted, San Francisco, California, July 2, 2008, Filed.
Defendant's sentence was vacated and the matter was remanded for resentencing because the court failed to provide notice of its intent to depart from the sentencing range suggested by the sentencing guidelines as required by Fed. R. Crim. P. 32(h) after he pled guilty to sexual abuse of a minor, sexual exploitation of minors and witness tampering.

US v. Fendley, No. 90-50085, UNITED STATES COURT OF APPEALS FOR THE NINTH CIRCUIT, 1991 US App. LEXIS 4846, January 10, 1991, Submitted, ** Pasadena, California** The panel unanimously finds this case suitable for submission on the record and briefs and without oral argument pursuant to Fed. R. App. P. 34(a), Ninth Circuit Rule 34-4., March 20, 1991, Filed , THIS DISPOSITION IS NOT APPROPRIATE FOR PUBLICATION AND MAY NOT BE CITED TO OR BY THE COURTS OF THIS CIRCUIT EXCEPT AS PROVIDED BY THE 9TH CIR. R. 36-3. , Reported as Table Case 928 F.2d 1137, 1991 US App. LEXIS 9707.
District court's denial of an acceptance of responsibility departure in sentencing was reversed and remanded where it was unclear from the record whether a defendant's denial of a separate crime was equivalent to a denial of the offense conduct.

US v. Fones, 51 F.3d 663 (7th Cir. 1995)
Application of new guideline which would result in imposition of more severe sentence would constitute violation of ex post facto clause.

US v. Fortier, 911 F.2d 100 (8th Cir. 1990)
Confrontation clause also applies at sentencing.

US v. Fox, 941 F.2d 480 (7th Cir. 1991)
Defendant whose crimes occurred before the November 1st, 1987 effective date of Sentencing Guidelines, was not subject to Sentencing Guidelines.

US v. Furman, 31 F.3d 1034 (10th Cir. 1994)
In imposing sentence, sentencing court may consider various factors including need to avoid unwarranted sentencing disparity among codefendants involved in same criminal activity.

US v. Gessa, 57 F.3d 493 (6th Cir. 1995)
US v. Logan, 54 F.3d 452 (8th Cir. 1995)
US v. Goins, 51 F.3d 400 (4th Cir. 1995)
Violation of criminal rule concerning plea hearings cannot be considered harmless if defendant had no knowledge of mandatory minimum sentence at time of plea.

US v. Gonzales, 12 F.3d 298 (1st Cir. 1993)
US v. Chincy, 1 F.3d 1501 (6th Cir. 1993)
Sentencing court must apply guideline in effect at time of sentencing.

US v. Greene, 41 F.3d 383 (8th Cir. 1994)
US v. Sanders, 41 F.3d 480 (9th Cir. 1994)
Government bears burden of proving of fact of prior conviction for purposes of sentence enhancement under Sentencing Guidelines.

US v. Hankton, 432 F.3d 779 (7th Cir. 2005)
State v. Jordan, 126 Ariz. 283, 286, 614P.2d 825, 828 (1980)
A defendant has due process right to be sentenced on basis of accurate information.

US v. Harrison - Philpot, 971 F.2d 234 (9th Cir. 1992)
US v. ROSA, 946 F.2d 505 (7th Cir. 1991)
Government has the burden of presenting sufficient evidence to allow the district court to properly determine the amount of drugs: burden is not on the defendant.

US v. Hays, 899 F.2d 515 (6th Cir. 1990)

Three part test used in reviewing sentencing court's decision to depart from guidelines requires determination of whether case was sufficiently unusual to warrant departure, whether circumstances relied on to support departure actually existed, and whether weight given to particular aggravating or mitigating was reasonable.

US v. Hayes, 49 F.3d 178 (6th Cir. 1995)

Defendant may appeal his sentence even when sentence imposed falls within range advocated by defendant, as long as defendant can identify specific legal error.

US v. Herndon, 982 F.2d 1411 (10th Cir. 1992)

When judge sentences are wrong, sentencing guideline range constitutes fundamental error affecting substantial rights.

US v. Hicks, 948 F.2d 877 (4th Cir. 1991)

False statement made by defendant to probation officer during pre-sentence interview about amount of attorney fees defendant had paid was material so as to justify two level upward adjustment in base offense level (Authors note: although it is not required by law that counsel be present you should never talk to a parole of probation officer unless counsel is present).

US v. Hill, 53 F.3d 1151 (10th Cir. 1995)

Government must prove sentence enhancement by preponderance of evidence.

US v. Howard, 894 F.2d 1085 (9th Cir. 1990)

The government bears the burden of proof if it is attempting to adjust the legal level upward, but the defendant bears the burden of proof if he is attempting to lower the offense level.

US v. Hoyungowa, 930 F.2d 744 (9th Cir. 1991)
US v. Beaulieu, 900 172d 1531 (10th Cir. 1990)

Remand was required where sentencing court failed to explain level of its upward departure sentence.

US v. Hulshof, 23 F.3d 1470 (8th Cir. 1994)
Government bears burden of proving disputed facts at sentencing by preponderance of evidence.

US v. Jackson, 32 F.3d 1101 (7th Cir. 1994)
Defendants must receive advance notice of all proposed enhancements or adjustments in pre-sentence report, the prosecutor's recommendation, or from sentencing judge well in advance of sentencing.

US v. Jenkins, 58 F.3d 611 (11th Cir. 1995)
When a criminal statute is ambiguous in its application to certain conduct, rule of lenity requires it to be construed narrowly.

US v. Jones, 841 F.2d 1022 (10th Cir. 1988)
US v. Naas, 755 F.2d 1133 (5th Cir. 1985)
Ambiguity in definition of conduct to be punished must be settled against turning single transaction into multiple offenses.

US v. Juvenile Male, 819 F.2d 468 (4th Cir. 1987)
Critical date for determining the law to be applied in ex post facto analysis is date when the crime was committed, not when defendant was sentenced.

US v. Kammerdiener, 945 F.2d 300 (9th Cir. 1991)
Under the sentencing guidelines, for conviction may not be included in a defendant's criminal history calculation.

US v. Kaufman, 951 F.2d 793 (7th Cir. 1992)
Judgment which lacks finality cannot authorize imprisonment of defendant.

US v. Keller, 58 F.3d 884 (2d Cir. 1995)
Generally a sentence in court must use the version of the guidelines in effect at the time of defendants sentencing not that extant at the time the offense was committed. Yet when the guidelines are amended provision calls for a more severe penalty in the original on, the guidelines in effect at the time the offense was

committed covering the imposition of sentence. The reason for this is to avoid violation of the ex post facto clause of the Constitution.

US v. Khang, 904 F.2d 1219 (8th Cir. 1990) 110.
The Sentencing Guidelines must be strictly construed. Guideline Sentencing is adversarial proceeding; burden of proof falls on party asserting the sentencing adjustment.

US v. Kienenberger, 13 F.3d 1354 (9th Cir. 1994)
Ex post facto clause prohibits any statute, which makes more burdensome punishment for crime, after its commission.

US v. Kirk, 894 F.2d 1162 (10th Cir. 1990)
Government bears burden of proof for sentence increases under sentencing guidelines while defendant bears burden of proof for 220 year sentence decreases: evidence which does not preponderate or is in equipoise fails to meet required burden of proof.

US v. Lande, 40 F.3d 329 (10th Cir. 1994)
At sentencing hearing, burden rests on government to establish by a preponderance of the evidence the type and quantity of methamphetamine involved in the offense.

US v. Leung, 40 F.3d 577 (2nd Cir. 1994)
Defendant's race or nationality may play no adverse role in administration of justice, including at sentencing.

US v. Maggi, 44 F.3d 478 (7th Cir. 1995)
Sentence based on incorrect Sentencing Guidelines range constitutes error affecting substantial rights and thus can constitute plain error, even though error is of less than four levels.

US v. McNeese, 901 F.2d 585 (7th Cir. 1990)

US v. Jones, 908 F.2d 365 (8th Cir. 1990)

Under BIFULCO rule of lenity, criminal penalties must be narrowly construed; any ambiguity in criminal statute, including sentencing, must be resolved in favor of lenity.

US v. Meyers, 32 F.3d 411 (9th Cir. 1994)

Harmless error rule does not apply to law of contractual plea agreements.

US v. Monaco, 852 F.2d 1143 (9th Cir. 1988)

Failure to individualize sentence compels reversal or resentencing.

US v. Montmayor, 703 F.2d 109 (5th Cir. 1983)

Under "concurrent sentence doctrine," existence of one valid conviction may make unnecessary review of other convictions when concurrent sentences have been given.

US v. Nottingham, 898 F.2d 390 (3rd Cir. 1990)

Despite mandatory language of guidelines requiring consecutive terms for crimes committed on parole, district court had discretion to impose concurrent or consecutive sentences.

US v. Osmani, 20 F.3d 266 (7th Cir. 1994)

Mere fact that defendant goes to trial does not automatically disqualify him from reduction pursuant to United States Sentencing Guidelines for acceptance of responsibility.

US v. Paris, 812 F.2d 417 (9th Cir. 1987)

When there is substantial disparity in sentences imposed on defendants engaged in the same criminal activity and defendant's constitutional right to stand trial is implicated, proper reasons for the disparity must be readily discernible from the record.

US v. Pinnick, 47 F.3d 434 (D.C. Cir. 1995)
US v. Williams, 46 F.3d 57 (10th Cir. 1995)
Anderson v. US, 405 F.2d 492, 493 (10th Cir. 1995 per curiam cert. denied 394 US 965)
A criminal sentence must be definite and certain.

US v. Pito, 433 F.3d 53 (1st Cir. 2006)
Regardless of length of a sentence based on an error of law is per se unreasonable.

US v. Ponce, 51 F.3d 820 (9th Cir. 1995)
While hearsay statements may be considered at sentencing, due process requires that such statements be corroborated by extrinsic evidence.

US v. Reed, 49 F.3d 895 (2nd Cir. 1995)
When sentencing court resolves disputed issue of fact, it is required to state its findings with sufficient clarity to permit appellate review.

US v. Reese, 33 F.3d 166 (2nd Cir. 1994)
Guidelines to be used when imposing sentence are those in effect on date of sentencing, unless ex post facto concerns are implicated.

US v. Restrepo, 986 F.2d 1462 (2nd Cir. 1993)
US v. Chasmer, 952 F.2d 50 (3rd Cir. 1991)
US v. Khoury, 901 F.2d 975 (11th Cir. 1990)
Where conflict existed between oral pronouncement of sentence and judgment, oral controlled.

US v. Restrepo, 999 F.2d 640 (2nd Cir. 1993)
Defendant's status as an alien may serve as a basis for downward departure under the Sentencing, Guidelines.

US v. Robinson, 20 F.3d 270 (7th Cir. 1994)
Sentence based on incorrect guideline range constitutes error affecting substantial rights and can thus constitute plain error.

US v. Romero, 57 F.3d 565 (7th Cir. 1995)

Court may not enhance defendant's sentence for obstruction of justice merely for reason that defendant testified at trial and lost.

US v. Sarault, 975 F.2d 17 (1st Cir. 1992)

US v. Califano, 978 F.2d 65 (2nd Cir. 1992)

When sentencing court determines that departure is warranted, it enjoys substantial leeway in determining extent of departure, and its decision in this regard will be reviewed for reasonableness.

US v. Shoupe, 35 F.3d 835 (3rd Cir. 1994) Sentencing court may depart downward on defendant's offense level if defendant's career offender status over represents his criminal history and likelihood of recidivism.

US v. Simpson, 8 F.3d 546 (7th Cir. 1993)

US v. Villagrana, 5 F.3d 1048 (7th Cir. 1993)

Due process requires that defendant be sentenced on basis of accurate information.

US v. Smith, 893 F.2d 1573 (9th Cir. 1990)

Defendants sentence may not be enhanced based on his failure to cooperate by implicating others.

US v. Stites, 56 F.3d 1020 (9th Cir. 1995)

US v. Alpert, 28 F.3d 1104 (11th Cir. 1994)

Disappearing from jurisdiction and not disclosing one's whereabouts to government does not warrant enhanced punishment for obstruction of justice.

US v. Stoneking, 34 F.3d 651 (8th Cir. 1994)

Sentencing Guidelines permit, but do not mandate, retroactive application of amended provision for calculating drug quantity to previously sentenced individual.

US v. Streich, 987 F.2d 104 (2nd Cir. 1993)

US v. Cantero, 995 F.2d 1407 (7th Cir. 1993)

Government bears brunt of establishing by preponderance of evidence that facts justify an upward adjustment of defendant's offense level under the Sentencing Guidelines.

US v. Thomas, 961 F.2d 1110 (3rd Cir. 1992)

It was error to make upward departure to compensate for governments decision not to charge defendant with more serious crime.

US v. Tillman, 8 F.3d 17 (11th Cir. 1994)

Government carries burden of persuasion with respect to inclusion of negotiated but undelivered amounts of drugs in sentencing calculations.

US v. Tolliver, 61 F.3d 1189 (5th Cir. 1995)

Where three charges of possession of firearm in relation to drug offense were predicated on single conspiracy count, consecutive sentences could not be imposed.

US v. Torres, 53 F.3d 1129 (10th Cir. 1995)

When sentencing drug conspiracy defendants, government bears burden of proving, by preponderance of evidence, quantities of drugs attributable to each defendant.

US v. Washington, 44 F.3d 1271 (5th Cir. 1995)

If defendant is not afforded opportunity to speak on his own behalf before sentence is imposed, resentencing is required.

US v. Webb, 30 F.3d 687 (6th Cir. 1994)

Defendant could not be sentenced to additional term of supervised release following his imprisonment upon revocation of his initial term of supervised release.

US v. Webster, 995 F.2d 209 (9th Cir. 1993)

Remand was required to determine whether defendant was entitled to downward adjustment under Sentencing Guidelines on grounds that he was minor participant in the offense, where district court made no factual findings regarding defendant's role and culpability with regard to relevant conduct, including collateral conduct beyond charged offense.

US v. Wilson, 503 US 1117 L.Ed.2d 593, 112 S.Ct (1992)

Federal sentencing credit under Title 18 (3585[b]) for certain pre-sentence time served held required to be computed by the Attorney General after convicted federal defendant began to serve sentence.

Wasman v. States, 468 US 559, 82 LEM 424, 104 S.Ct. 3217 (1984)

After re-trial and conviction following a successful appeal, sentencing authority could justify an increased sentence based on conduct subsequent to original sentencing.

Weaver v. Graham, 450 US 24, 67 L.Ed.2d 17, 101 S.Ct. 960 (1981)
US v. Arzate - Nunez, 18 F.3d 730 (9th Cir. 1994)

The Ex Post Facto clause prohibits the enactment of laws that either impose punishments for acts not punishable at the time they were committed or increase punishment over that previously prescribed.

Wilson v. US, 962 F.2d 996 (11th Cir. 1992)

Defendant has constitutional right to effective assistance or counsel at sentencing.

Sexual Abuse

State v. Bartlett, (1992) 171 Ariz. 302, 830 P.2d 823, cert. denied, 113 S.Ct. 511, 506 US 992, 121 L.Ed.2d 445

Sentence of 40 years without possibility of early release was grossly disproportionate to offense of sexual conduct with minors, two girls just under 15 years of age, in light of girls testimony that sex was consensual, absence of violation or any threats of violence by defendant, defendants lack of prior record of any crime, let alone crime involving children, and reality that sexual conduct among post pubescent teenagers was not uncommon.

State v. Patton, (App. 1983) 136 Ariz. 243, 665 P.2d 587

Since the sexual abuse statute, 13-1401 prohibits any direct or indirect fondling manipulating of any part of the genitals, anus, or female breasts of a person under the age of 15, and the child molesting statute, 13-1410 prohibits any person from causing a child under the age of 15 to fondle, play with, or touch the private parts, which include the gentle and excretory organ but not the female breasts, fondling the breasts of a female under the age of 15 may amount to sexual abuse under 13-1404, but it is not child molesting, and sexual abuse is not a lesser included offense of child molesting.

S.O.T.P.

<u>US v. Antelope</u>, 395 F.3d 1128 (9th CIR. 2005)
As long as a defendant retains his right to appeal use in court of information obtained in psycho-sexual counseling constitutes a 5th Amendment right violation as it causes a person to incriminate oneself.

Note: It is always best to get an order from the court regarding use immunity of defendant's statements if a defendant retains his right to appeal and will be ordered by the court to participate in sex offender treatment program.

Speedy Trial

Barker v. Wingo, 407 US 514, 33 L.Ed.2d 101, 92 S.Ct. 2183 (1972)
Four part test by the Supreme Court on speedy trial.

Cowart v. Hargett, 16 F.3d 642 (5th Cir. 1994)
Rights to speedy trial applies to states.

Dogget v. US, 505 US, 120 L.Ed.2d 520, 112 S.Ct. (1992)
US v. Doggett, 906 F.2d 573 (11th Cir. 1990)
Defendant need not show actual prejudice in order to prevail on constitution speedy trail claim, where first 3 Barker (407 US 514) factors all weigh heavily against government. (Editor's Note: The lower court case went to the US Supreme Court where it was upheld).

Hakeem v. Beyer, 990 F.2d 750 (3rd Cir. 1993)
1. At its core, Sixth Amendment guarantees of speedy trial shield individual from deprivation of personal liberty. 2. Delay of 14 1/2 months between defendant's arrest and trial was sufficient to trigger further inquiry into Barker speedy trial factors.

Michel v. Louisiana, 350 U.S. 91
Three Negroes were sentenced to death in Louisiana courts for aggravated rape. They challenged the composition of the grand jury which indicted them, charging that there was a systematic exclusion of Negroes from the panel. The state courts rejected this attack because it was not made before the expiration of the third judicial day following the end of the grand jury's term, as required by a Louisiana statute. In case No. 32 it appears that an attorney was appointed in open court on the day on which the grand jury's term ended, but that he did not consider himself appointed until he received official notice of his appointment; however, the state courts found that the appointment was made in open court. In case No. 36 it appears that one of the defendants (Poret) fled the state of Louisiana and was not returned to the state until it was too late for him to raise objections to the composition of the grand jury, and that during all of this time he was without counsel. Counsel for the other defendant (Labat) was appointed more than two

months before the termination of the grand jury's term, but failed to make a timely challenge. The issue before the United States Supreme Court as to all the defendants was whether the Louisiana statute as applied violated the due process clause of the Fourteenth Amendment. The conviction of Labat should be vacated because he was jointly indicted with Poret by the same grand jury whose composition is challenged on constitutional grounds. Cf. Ashcraft v. Tennessee, 322 U.S. 143.

Redd v. Sowders, 809 F.2d 1266 (6th Cir. 1987)
Held: a ten month delay was oppressive and constituted prejudice.

Ringstaff v. Howard, 861 F.2d 644 (11th Cir. 1988)
A delay of 23 months between arrest and trial was presumptively prejudicial when the state caused most of the delay.

Snyder v. Donato, 211 Ariz. 117
Accordingly, we accept jurisdiction and grant relief from the order designating this as a complex case. A "complex case" is a case so complicated, by virtue of its nature or because of the evidence required that the ordinary limits for the time to trial are insufficient and must be extended so as to afford the party more time to prepare in order to fairly and fully present its case. Because this is not a "complex case," we grant relief from the court's order. Our holding, however, does not preclude the court from granting a continuance on the basis of another rule if it properly finds that the circumstances justify it.

US v. Aviles - Alvarez, 868 F.2d 1108 (9th Cir. 1989)
Defense counsel who wishes to protect client's right to trial within 70 days should request that all pre-trial motions be completed, or that government be compelled to comply with discovery order, before statutory time for trial on issue of guilt has run its course.

US v. Bond, 956 F.2d 628 (6th Cir. 1992)
Seventy day period for commencing trial under the Speedy Trial Act following vacation of defendant's guilty plea began running from date district court vacated the guilty plea.

US v. Butz, 982 F.2d 1378 (9th Cir. 1993)
If several defendants are joined, 70 day limit in Speedy Trial Act is measured form the date on which last codefendant is arraigned.

US v. Crawford, 982 F.2d 199 (6th Cir. 1993)
Speedy Trial Act requires that trial of criminal defendant commence within 70 days from date of arrest, filing of indictment or information, or first appearance before court, which ever date last occurs; if government falls to bring defendant to trial within 70 day period, government must dismiss indictment or information on motion of defendant.

US v. Hayes, 40 F.3d 362 (11th Cir. 1994) 13.
For speedy trial purposes, government has duty to make diligent. good faith effort to bring indicted defendant to trial promptly. For purposes of speedy trial claim, prejudice to defendant may be presumed in cases involving lengthy delay.

US v. Lindsey, 47 F.3d 440 (D.C. Cir. 1995)
Any delay of one year or more in bringing a defendant to trial triggers scrutiny under the Sixth Amendment speedy trial provision.

US v. Neal, 27 F.3d 1035 (5th Cir. 1994)
US v. Duranseau, 26 F.3d 804 (8th Cir. 1994)
When Speedy Trial Act violation occurs, dismissal is mandatory on motion of the defendant.

US v. Sandoval, 990 F.2d 481 (9th Cir. 1993)
"Accused" i.e., someone who has been either arrested or indicted, is prohibited from pre-trial delay not by the Fifth Amendment due process clause but by the more stringent requirements of the Sixth Amendment speedy trial right. Accused does not waive Sixth Amendment speedy trial right by failing to assert it.

US v. Theron, 782 F.2d 1510 (10th Cir. 1986)
Due process required that incarcerated defendant be released on bond or tried within 30 days: defendant had been incarcerated 4 months, had taken no steps to delay trial, and government was ready for trial (delays were due to codefendant).

US v. White, 985 F.2d 271 (6th Cir. 1993)
Speedy trail test under the Sixth Amendment requires courts to balance length of delay, reason for delay, whether and how defendant asserted speedy trial right, and amount of prejudice suffered by defendant.

State / Federal Law

Abdul - Hakeem v. Koehler, 910 F.2d 66 (2nd Cir. 1990)
A §1983 action is proper remedy for state prisoner who is making constitutional challenge to conditions of his prison life, but not to fact or length of his custody. i.e., when he is challenging conditions of his confinement (such an action requires exhaustion of state remedies).

Abramson v. Gonzalez, 949 F.2d 1567 (11th Cir. 1992)
If statement may not be censored by the federal government it is also protected from censorship by the states.

Bell v. Stigers, 937 F.2d 1340 (8th Cir. 1991)
Claim under §1983 must allege that conduct of defendant acting under color of state law deprived plaintiff of right, privilege, or immunity secured by constitution or laws of United States.

Blake v. Papadakos, 953 F.2d 68 (3rd Cir. 1992)
Federal courts have no jurisdiction to review state official's compliance with state law.

Burk v. Beene, 948 F.2d 489 (8th Cir. 1991)
State may waive its sovereign immunity and consent to suit in federal court.

James v. Kentucky, 466 US 341, 80 L.Ed.2d 346. 104 S.Ct. 1830 (1984)
The judge refused to give requested instructions, the Supreme Court reversed and held that state statutes did not take precedent over constitutional law and that the judge had to give the requested instruction/admonition.

K - S Pharmacies v. American Home Products, 962 F.2d 728 (7th Cir. 1992)
Federal court may interpret state law (Authors note: in other words federal law takes precedent over state law).

Kellas v. Lane, 923 F.2d 492 (7th Cir. 1990)
While §1983 confers no substantive federal rights, it is designed to remedy deprivations of federal rights by state actor.

Mackenzie v. City Of Rockledge, 920 F.2d 1554 (11th Cir. 1991)
Unequal application of state law may violate equal protection clause.

Mannhalt v. Reed, 847 F.2d 576 (9th Cir. 1988)
To prevail on claim for habeas corpus, state prisoner must show that his detention violates the Constitution. a federal statute. or a treaty.

Noble v. White, 996 F.2d 797 (5th Cir. 1993)
Federal courts may, under limited circumstances, exercise jurisdiction over state law claims.

Note: State prisoners now serving a federal consecutive sentence may receive 'credit on their federal sentence for the entire time spent in a state institution. Simply put, a state prisoner who first serves a state sentence followed by a consecutive federal sentence can have them credited in such a way that the federal sentence will be run concurrent with the state sentence. See Barden v. Keohane, 921 F.2d 476.

O'Bar v. Pinion, 953 F.2d 74 (4th Cir. 1991)
If a term of imprisonment can be shortened or modified by rights conveyed under state law, those rights cannot be denied without due process.

Orozco v. US I.N.S., 911 F.2d 539 (1Ith Cir. 1990)
Filing of "detainer" is informal process advising prison officials that prisoner is wanted on other pending charges and requesting notification prior to prisoner's release.

Pearson v. Norris, 52 F.3d 740 (8th Cir. 1995)
If direct appeal or another avenue of collateral attack is created by state, it must conform to due process standards.

Qyzel v. Marks, 6 F.3d 116 (3rd Cir. 1993)
The Fourteenth Amendment directs that all persons similarly situated be treated alike.

US v. Alaska Public Utilities Comm., 23 F.3d 257 (9th Cir. 1994)
Supremacy clause establishes federal law as the supreme law of the land.

US v. Cephas, 937 F.2d 816 (2nd Cir. 1991)
Government cannot launch detainer against defendant and then throw out the clock every time it dismisses charges, only to start clock anew by bringing new set of charges.

US v. Marvro, 436 US 340. 56 L.Ed.2d 329. 98 S.Ct. 1934 (1978)
US v. Reed, 910 F.2d 621 (9th Cir. 1990)
Prosecutions jurisdiction's failure to bring prisoner to trial within 180 days after prisoner requests speedy trial under Interstate Agreement on Detainers Act required dismissal of indictment.

US v. Union Gas Co., 792 F.2d 372 (3rd Cir. 1986)
States immunity may be avoided in only two ways. Congress may abrogate it by providing through statute for suits against state. or states can waive their sovereign immunity and consent to be sued.

Williamson v. Jones, 936 F.2d 1000 (1991)
State court's interpretation of state law is binding upon federal court in habeas corpus proceeding.

State Procedural Bar

Coleman v. Thompson, 501 US 722, 750 (1991)

The requirement of an independent and adequate state procedural rule is a strict one: federal courts on habeas corpus review of state prisoner claim... will presumed that there is no independent and adequate state ground for a state court decision when... the adequacy and independence of any possible state law ground is not clear from the face of the opinion. Id at 734-735.

Davis v. Wechseler, 263 US 22, 23 (1923)

The assertion of federal rights, when plainly and reasonably made, is not to be defeated under the name of local practice.

Gretzler v. Stewart, (1996)
State v. Neal, 692 P.2d 272, 280 (Ariz. 1984)
State v. Durgin, 517 P.2d 1246, 1249 (Ariz. 1974)

At the time of Gretzler's trial, evidence of intoxication whether induced by alcohol or drugs, was admissible to show lack of specific intent to commit to crime charged.

Lambright v. Stewart, 191 F.3d 1181, 1185 (9th Cir. 1999)

All sentencing errors are treated as implicitly raised, removing the bar of procedural default.

Michael v. Louisiana, 350 US 91, 93-94 (1955)

In a criminal case, the test for whether a state procedural rule constitutes an inseparable barrier to the assertion of a federal right is whether the defendant has had a reasonable opportunity to have the issue as to the claimed right heard and determined by the state court.

Michel v. Louisiana, 350 US 91, 93-94 (1955)
English, 146 F.3d at 1260-64

State statute that is unreasonably restrictive on exercise of the federally protected constitutional right to counsel and therefore is inadequate to bar federal review.

Staub v. City of Blakely, 355 US 313,325 (1958)

The court has held that if a state procedural rule frustrates the exercise of a federal right, that rule is inadequate to preclude federal courts from reviewing the merits of the federal claims. Holding that denial of petitioner's constitutional claims for failure to attack specific sections of the challenged ordinance was inadequate state law grounds. The inadequate state grounds doctrine is rooted in a concern that a state's rigid hearings to technical requirements of dubious validity may result in fundamental unfairness or federal rights are at stake.

Wager v. Pro, 603 F.2d 1005, 195 US App. D.C. 423 (1979)

"Intent", as is used in international torts, has been defined as the desire to bring about a result that will invade the interests of another. W. Prosser, Law of Torts s 8, and 31 (1971). In contrast gross negligence implies an "extreme departure from the ordinary standard of care. Id at 184.

Wainwright v. Sykes, 433 US 72, 81 (1977)

When a state court litigant raises a federal claim in a manner that does not comply with a state procedural rule, the state court may dismiss that claim as defaulted. So long as the dismissed relies on a state law ground that is independent of the federal question and adequate to support the judgment, it will be insulated from federal review.

Structural Error

Arizona v. Fulminante, 499 US 279, 308-09 (1991)
Trial error which occurred during the presentation of case to the jury, and which may therefore be quantitatively assessed in the context of other evidence presented in order to determine whether its admission was harmless beyond a reasonable doubt. Id. at 307-08. In contrast structural defects affect the framework within the trial proceeds and involve the basic protections, without which a criminal trial cannot reliably serve its function as a vehicle for determination of guilt or innocence, and no criminal punishment may be regarded as fundamentally fair. Id. at 307-09.

Hoffman v. Arave, 236 F.3d 523, 5 40-41 (9th Cir. 2001) Although defendant was denied right to counsel during pre-sentence interview a critical stage of proceedings, error is subject to harmless error review.

Neder v. US, 527 US 1, 8-9) 1999)
Rose v. Clark, 478 US 570, 5 77-78 (1986)
When structural error occurs, we automatically reversed the judgment. Id. at 552, ¶ 45, 65 P3d at 933. No consideration is given to factual setting and whether the error may or may not be harmless. Structural error requires reversal.

Powell v. Galaza, 282 F.3d 1089, 1096 (9th Cir. 2002)
Rose v. Clark, 478 US 570, 5 77-78 (1986)
Improper to apply harmless error analysis or structural errors rendered trial fundamentally unfair, vacated on other grounds by 123 S.Ct. 362 (2002)

State v. Garcia-Contreras, 191 Ariz. 144, 953 P.2d 536
Defendant was convicted by jury upon re-trial in the Superior Court, Maricopa County, No. CR 91-02873, Stephen A. Gerst, J., of child molestation charges. Defendant appealed. Following remand, the Court of Appeals affirmed convictions. Granting petition for review, the Supreme Court, Zlaket, C.J., held that: (1) defendant's choice not to be present at jury selection, after trial court denied request for continuance to allow defendant's civilian clothing to arrive, was not voluntary and did not constitute waiver of right to be present; (2) denial of

continuance was abuse of discretion; and (3) error in denying continuance was structural error that was not subject to harmless error review. Convictions reversed; case remanded for new trial

State v. Henderson, 133 Ariz. 259, 650 P.2d 1241 (Ariz. App. 1982)
As our Supreme Court explained in State v. Ring, 204 Ariz. 534, 65 P.3d 915 (2003) (Ring 3) structural errors deprive defendants of basic protections, without which a criminal trial cannot reliably serve its function as a vehicle for determination of guilt or innocence... And no criminal punishment may be regarded as fundamentally fair. Id. at 552, ¶ 45, 65 P.3d at 933.

US v. Annigoni, 96 F.3d 1132, 1143 (9th Cir. 1996) (en Banc) There is not a rigid dichotomy between trial errors and structural error. The court's opinion in Fulminante does not mean that any violation of the same constitutional right is a structural defect regardless of whether the error is significant or trivial. To determine if a particular error is structural, courts must look not only at the right violated but also at the particular nature, context and significance of the violation.

Summary Judgment

Allen v. Wright, 468 US 737, 82 L.Ed.2d 556, 104 S.Ct. 3315 (1984)
"Standing" is granted if "The person seeking redress has suffered, or is threatened with, some 'distinct and palpable injury' the 'personal stake requirement is satisfied ... and, if there is some casual connection between the asserted injury and the conduct being challenged."

City Management Corp. Vs. US Chemical Co. Inc., 43 F.3d 244 (6th Cir. 1994)
Role of judge at summary judgment stage is not to weight evidence, but to determine whether there is genuine issue of material fact.

Duke v. Cleland, 5 F.3d 1399 (11th Cir. 1993)
Haines v. Kerner, 404 US 519, 30 L.Ed.2d 652, 92 S.Ct.594 (1972)
Complaint should not be dismissed unless it appears beyond doubt that plaintiff can prove no set of facts in support of his claim which would entitle him to relief.

Fallen v. US, 378 US 139, 12 L.Ed.2d 760, 84 S.Ct. 1689 (1964)
Hibernia Nat. Bank v. Adm. Cen. Soc. Anonima., 776 F.2d 1277 (5th Cir 1985)
Because the plaintiff did all that could be reasonable expected the motion to dismiss was denied.

Gallo v. Prudential Residential Services, 22 F.3d 1219 (2nd Cir. 1994)
Latrieste Restaurant and Cabaret Inc. v. Village of Port Chester, 40 F.3d 587 (2nd Cir. 1994)
Adickes v. Kress & Co., 398 US 144, 26 L.Ed.2d 142, 90 S.Ct. 1598 (1970)
On motion for summary judgment, court is required to resolve all ambiguities and draw all factual inferences in favor of party against whom summary judgment is sought. On summary judgment, all facts and inferences therefrom are to be construed in favor of party opposing motion.

Hamm v. Groose, 15 F.3d 110 (8th Cir. 1994)
Cramer v. Skinner, 931 F.2d 1020 (5th Cir. 1991)
Cooper v. Pate, 378 US 546, 12 L.Ed.2d 1030, 84 S.Ct. 1733 (1964)
Court must accept allegations in pleadings as true.

Ingram v. Becher, 3 F.3d 1050 (7th Cir. 1993)
Trial court ordinarily should permit litigant, especially pro se litigant, opportunity to amend complaint before dismissing complaint for failure to state a claim.

Johnson v. US Dept. Of Treasury, 939 F.2d 820 (9th Cir. 1991)
Dismissal is harsh penalty, and should be imposed only in extreme circumstances.

Justice v. US, 6 F.3d 1474 (11th Cir. 1993)
Dismissal with prejudice is a sanction of last resort proper only where there is a clear record of delay or willful contempt.

Keywell Corp. v. Weinstein, 33 F.3d 159 (2nd Cir. 1994)
Party seeking summary judgments bear burden of demonstrating absence of any genuine factual dispute.

Nikwei v. Ross School of Aviation, Inc., 822 F.2d 939 (10th Cir. 1987)
Montalbano v. Easco Hand Tools Inc., 766 F.2d 737 (2nd Cir. 1985)
Ordinarily, insufficient service of process will be squashed and the action preserved, where there is a reasonable prospect that plaintiff ultimately will be able to serve defendant properly, Rule 4(c)(2)(C)(ii) SERVICE BY MAIL. Where defendant attempts to hide, thereby making service by mail nearly impossible, service is perfected and court has jurisdiction.

Sudeikis v. Chicago Transit Authority, 774 F.2d 766 (7th Cir. 1985)
Moses Cone Hosp. v. Mercury Const., 460 US 1, 74 L.Ed.2d 765, 103 S.Ct. 927 (1983)
Fact that a state lawsuit on an issue is pending is not generally a bar to federal suit on same issue.

Thompson v. I.N.S., 375 US 374, 11 L.Ed.2d 404, 74 S.Ct. 397 (1967)
Harris Truck Lines v. Cherry Meat Packers, 371 US 215, 9 L.Ed.2d 261, 83 S.Ct. 383 (1962)
These cases have the criteria for "Excusable Neglect" and "Unique Circumstances."

Tolentino v. Friedman, 46 F.3d 645 (7th Cir. 1995) Summary judgment is not granted unless there are not triable issues.

US v. Chamberlin, 139 F.Supp. 2d 637)
Minors and their parents sued photographer who took nude pictures of minors for violation of Protection of Children Against Sexual Exploitation Act, infliction of emotional distress, invasion of privacy, and negligent supervision. On photographer's motion for summary judgment, the District Court, Caputo, J., held that: (1) some photographs did not contain exhibition of minors' genitals as required to establish violation of Act; (2) other photographs which did exhibit genitals were not lascivious; (3) affidavits describing photographs not in record did not establish lasciviousness; and (4) there was no affirmative reason to retain jurisdiction over state-law claims. Summary judgment granted in part, and claims dismissed in part.

US v. Koreh, 59 F.3d 431 (3rd Cir. 1995)
At summary judgment stage, court must give benefit of all inferences to nonmoving party.

Time Periods

ARCrP Rule 1.3 Five days is added to all time periods at issue, due to the fact that services may be made by mail.

ARCrP Rule 31.2. Notice of appeal; automatic appeal; joint appeals.
a. Filing the notice of appeal. -- Unless a defendant has been sentenced to death, an appeal or cross-appeal shall be taken by filing a written notice of appeal with the clerk of the trial court, within the time allowed by Rule 31.

b. Automatic appeal when defendant is sentenced to death. -- When a defendant has been sentenced to death, the clerk, pursuant to Rule 26.15, shall file a notice of appeal on his or her behalf at the time of entry of judgment and sentence. Such notice shall be sufficient as a notice of appeal by the defendant with respect to all judgments entered and sentences imposed in the case. Within 10 days after the filing of the notice of appeal in any capital case, the clerk of the superior court shall notify all authorized transcribers assigned to transcribe any portion of the proceedings that they are required to transmit their portions of the certified transcript to the clerk of the Supreme Court.

c. Joint appeals. -- If 2 or more persons are entitled to appeal from a judgment or order of the superior court, and their interests are such as to make a joinder practicable, they may file a joint notice of appeal, or may join in the appeal after filing separate timely notices of appeal, and proceed as in the case of a single appellant.

d. Content of the notice of appeal. -- Except as provided in Rule 31.2(b), the notice of appeal shall identify the order, judgment and sentence appealed from and shall be signed by the appellant or his or her attorney, if any, or by the prosecutor if the appeal or cross-appeal is taken by the state. If the appeal or cross-appeal is taken by the state, in whole or in part, based upon violation of a substantial right of the victim, the attorney for the state shall so state in the notice of appeal or opening brief or memorandum and shall certify that the victim has requested the appeal or cross-appeal, in whole or in part, on that basis.

e. Additional information. -- The appellant should attach to the notice of appeal:

1) The name and address of the defendant;

2) The name and address of the attorney for the defendant, if any;

3) The name and address (if known) of any co-defendant at trial; and,

4) Whether the defendant was represented by appointed counsel at the determination of guilt or at sentencing.

f. Service of the notice of appeal.

1) When defendant appeals. -- When a defendant appeals, within 8 days of the filing of the notice of appeal, the clerk of the trial court shall send a copy of the notice of appeal to the prosecutor of the county in which the defendant was tried, to the attorney general, to each co-defendant at trial who is not a joint-appellant and defendant's counsel of record, if any, to the appropriate certified court reporter or reporters, or to the court's designated transcript coordinator, if the record was made by electronic or other means, and to the clerk of the proper Appellate Court.

2) When the state appeals. -- When the state appeals or cross-appeals, within 8 days of the filing of the notice of appeal, the clerk of the trial court shall send a copy of the notice of appeal to each defendant and defendant's counsel of record, if any, to the appropriate certified court reporter or reporters, or to the court's designated transcript coordinator, if the record was made by electronic or other means, and to the clerk or the proper Appellate Court.

3) Notice of right to counsel. -- The clerk shall include with any notice of appeal sent to a defendant, and shall send to a defendant filing notice of appeal pro se, a notice advising the defendant of his or her rights to counsel under Rule 6.

4) Notice to the appellate court of pending post-trial motions. -- The clerk shall include with the copy of the notice of appeal sent to the appellate court, a copy of any motion filed by any party under Rule 24 which has not yet been decided by the trial court.

5) Manner of service. -- The notice of appeal shall be sent to the defendant at his or her address of record or at his or her place of incarceration and to his or her counsel of record.

g. Entry by the clerk. -- The clerk shall make an entry in the docket when a notice of appeal is filed and shall note whether the defendant had appointed counsel at the determination of guilt or at sentencing. The clerk shall also enter in the docket the names and addresses of the parties to whom copies of the notice of appeal are mailed together with the date of mailing.

HISTORY: Amended Nov. 12, 1991, effective Dec. 31, 1991; amended July 28, 1993, effective Dec. 1, 1993; amended Mar. 18, 1994, effective Apr. 1, 1994; amended eff. Jan. 1, 2007 by R-05-0037.

NOTES:

COMMENT TO 1991 AMENDMENT
The 1991 amendment to Rule 31.2(d) was among those adopted in order to implement the Victims' Bill of Rights, which was incorporated into the Arizona Constitution in 1990 as Art. II, § 2.1. For a related statutory provision, see A.R.S. § 13-4032(4), adopted by Laws 1991, Ch. 229 § 1 et seq. (the "Victims' Rights Implementation Act").

[1973 PROMULGATION]
This rule is intended to provide a simple means for taking appeals and to insure that all persons directly affected by the taking of an appeal are promptly notified. It is drawn from Federal Rules of Appellate Procedure 3.

RULES 31.2 (A) AND (C)
As under the 1956 Arizona Rules of Criminal Procedure, Rule 350, the notice of appeal is filed with the clerk of the trial court. Section (c) is taken directly from Federal Rules of Appellate Procedure 3 (b). Together with Rule 31.4 (b), permitting consolidation of appeals, it is intended to encourage the taking of joint appeals in order to reduce the case load of the appellate court and the workload of clerks and court reporters.

RULE 31.2 (B). Section (b), providing for automatic appeal, is similar to Cal. Penal Code § 1239 (b) (West 1970), Ill. Ann. Stat. § 38:121-12 (a) (Smith-Hurd 1964), and Ala. Code § 15:382 (2) (1958). RULES 31.2 (D) & (E) Except for automatic appeals, only the signature of the appellant or his counsel and a statement of the judgment, sentence or order being appealed from is required for a proper notice of appeal. See 1956 Arizona Rules of Criminal Procedure, Rule 350. The other information is to aid service by the clerk and to expedite transcription of the record and appointment of counsel. See Rules 31.5 and 31.8 (b) and (d). The term "determination of guilt" is defined in Rule 26.1 (c).

RULE 31.2 (F) The burden of advising other interested persons that an appeal has been filed is shifted from the parties to the clerk of the trial court. Cf. 1956 Arizona Rules of Criminal Procedure, Rules 351 and 352 and Federal Rules of Appellate Procedure 3 (d).

A copy of the notice of appeal and attachment is sent to the court reporter or reporters who reported pretrial hearings, the trial or plea hearing, sentencing and any other superior court proceedings in the case, in order to alert them, at the earliest possible moment, of the need to prepare a transcript and to inform them whether or not the appeal is being taken by a person declared indigent under Rule 6. See Rule 31.2 (e) (4). Rules 31.8 (d) and (e) govern payment of the court reporter by non-indigent parties and Rule 31.5 (a)(2) allows a person who did not proceed as an indigent prior to conviction to so proceed on appeal if he now qualifies.

Paragraph (4) is to provide notice to the appellate court of any post-trial motions then pending so that the court can exercise its power, under Rule 31.4, to stay the appeal. Rules 24.2 (c) and 32.4 (b) provide for notice to the appellate court of any post-trial motions or petitions filed while an appeal is pending. Service on counsel is required in addition to service on the defendant.

Service may be accomplished by ordinary mail and is complete upon mailing. See 1956 Arizona Rules of Civil Procedure 5 (c).

RULE 31.2 (G) The notation that the defendant has proceeded below as an indigent will automatically serve as authorization for him to proceed as an indigent on appeal unless the trial court orders otherwise. See Rule 31.5.

JUDICIAL DECISIONS
ANALYSIS

DIRECT APPEAL
Under Ariz. R. Crim. P. 26.15 and 31.2(b), direct appeal to the Supreme Court of Arizona is mandatory when the trial court imposes a sentence of death. State v. Rutledge, 205 Ariz. 7, 397 Ariz. Adv. Rep. 21, 66 P.3d 50, 2003 Ariz. LEXIS 33 (2003).

FAILURE TO APPEAL
Since the state failed to appeal in accordance with the provisions of this rule, the question raised by the state was not properly before the appellate court. State v. LeMaster, 137 Ariz. 159, 669 P.2d 592 (Ct. App. 1983).

FILING
The state's filing of a notice of appeal under the wrong cause number does not deprive the court of appeals of jurisdiction. State v. Rasch, 188 Ariz. 309, 935 P.2d 887 (Ct. App. 1996).

ARCrP Rule 31.3. Time for taking appeal
The notice of appeal shall be filed with the clerk of the trial court within 20 days after the entry of judgment and sentence, except that: A notice of cross-appeal may be filed within 20 days after service of the appellant's notice of appeal; and A notice of delayed appeal shall be filed within 20 days after service of an order granting a delayed appeal under rule 32.1(f).

NOTES:

[1973 PROMULGATION]
This rule reduces the time in which an appeal may be taken from 60 to 20 days after entry of judgment and sentence and the time for filing a cross-appeal from 30

to 20 days after the filing of the notice of appeal. See Arizona Rules of Criminal Procedure, Rules 348, 349. The entry of judgment and sentence is taken as a single benchmark for determination of the timeliness of an appeal, with 2 exceptions. For cross-appeals, the filing of the notice of appeal is the point from which the 20-day period will run. Cross-appeals are not required in every case. For delayed appeals, the service of the order is the benchmark. The order itself is not used to trigger the appellate process because it lacks the additional information accompanying the notice of appeal. See Rule 32.1 (f).

JUDICIAL DECISIONS
ANALYSIS

CONSTRUCTION
Rule 1.3 applies to this rule just as it does to Rules 10.2 and 32.9, both of which also prescribe time running from an event. State v. Rabun, 162 Ariz. 261, 782 P.2d 737 (1989).

FAILURE TO APPEAL
Petitioner's conviction became final for habeas purposes after the 20 day period during which petitioner could have, but did not, file a notice of appeal to the Arizona Court of Appeals. Matthews v. Schiriro, -- F. Supp. 2d --, 2005 U.S. Dist. LEXIS 22317 (D. Ariz. Sept. 22, 2005). Although defendant did not separately appeal the denial of modification of sentence, failure to appeal the denial of modification did not deprive court of jurisdiction to consider his appeal of the original sentence, which raised the same issues. State v. Renner, 177 Ariz. 395, 868 P.2d 978 (Ct. App. 1993).

RIGHT TO APPEAL
The state was precluded by principles of finality from attacking the validity of a dismissal order; the state is given the right to appeal from an order dismissing an indictment, information or complaint or count of an indictment, information or complaint, but where it failed to do so, the order of dismissal became final after the expiration of 20 days from the date of its entry. State v. Kangas, 146 Ariz. 155, 704 P.2d 285 (Ct. App. 1985).

UNTIMELINESS

Trial court did not err in failing to consider mitigation evidence under A.R.S. §§ 13-701, 13-702 and in considering the prisoner's drug use as an aggravating factor; the prisoner was precluded from relief under Ariz. R. Crim. P. 32.2(a)(3) because he failed to fairly present the claims to the post-conviction review court, and a return to state court would be futile because the time for the prisoner to file a direct appeal under this rule had elapsed. Deberry v. Schriro, -- F. Supp. 2d --, 2009 U.S. Dist. LEXIS 99081 (D. Ariz. Oct. 22, 2009).

Where appellant's notice of appeal was filed 50 days after the denial of a motion for rehearing, the appeal was not timely filed. State v. Littleton, 146 Ariz. 531, 707 P.2d 329 (Ct. App. 1985).

A.R.Cr.P. Rule 31.4. Motion to stay appeal; notice of reinstatement of appeal; consolidation of appeals.

a. Motion to stay appeal; notice of reinstatement of appeal.
    1) The appellate court, on motion of a party or on its own initiative, may stay an appeal while a motion under Rule 24 or a petition under Rule 32 is pending. If a stay is ordered, the clerk of the appellate court shall notify all parties, the clerk of the trial court, and, if the certified transcript has not yet been filed, the appropriate authorized transcribers.

    2) Within 20 days after the trial court's decision on the motion or petition, the appellant shall file with the clerk of the appellate court, and send to all persons notified of the stay, either a notice of reinstatement of the appeal or a motion to dismiss the appeal under Rule 31.15 (a) (2).

b. Consolidation of appeals
    1) Appeals which raise a common question of law or fact may be consolidated at any time by order of the appellate court upon its own initiative after opportunity has been given to the parties to raise objections or upon motion of a party or upon stipulation by the parties.
    2) An appeal from a final decision on a Rule 24 motion or Rule 32 petition filed prior to a notice of appeal or filed while an appeal is pending and

decided while the appeal is stayed, shall be consolidated with an appeal from the judgment or sentence, unless good cause is shown why such consolidation should not occur.

HISTORY: Amended by R-06-0037, effective Jan. 1, 2007.

NOTES:

[1973 PROMULGATION]
This rule is intended to prevent unnecessary duplication and to further define the relationship between appeals and collateral post-conviction procedures. See Rules 31.2 (f) (4), 24.2 and 32.2.

RULE 31.4 (A). Under Rule 31.3 a notice of appeal must be filed within 20 days of entry of judgment and sentence, and under Rule 31.11 the appeal is perfected at the time the first major filing is due in the appellate court. Under Rules 24.2 and 24.3 (a), a defendant may move the trial court to vacate a judgment or unlawful sentence before an appeal is perfected. Under Rule 32.1 a party may file a petition for post-conviction relief at any time subject to Rule 32.2, which precludes the filing of a petition based on any issue still raisable on appeal or in a Rule 24 post-trial motion. In effect, during the pendency of an appeal, a Rule 32 petition is available only after perfection of the appeal and only to raise issues not still raisable on appeal, such as those for which there is no record. Thus, it is possible that proceedings may be pending in both the trial and appellate courts.

Section (a) is intended to empower the appellate court to stay the appeal whenever this jurisdictional overlap threatens to waste the efforts of the courts or the parties. There is no mandatory stay provision. The decision is left with the sound discretion of the appellate court, to balance the delay in prosecution of the appeal against possible gains in judicial efficiency, including elimination of the appeal if the motion or petition is granted or consolidation of an appeal from the decision on the motion or petition with the appeal already pending.

RULE 31.4 (B). Rule 31.4 (b) encompasses two situations. Paragraph (1) governs when separate appeals are taken from the same or similar cases such as when co-defendants file separate appeals. Consolidation is discretionary. The parties have an opportunity to raise objections to consolidation whether it is suggested by a party or by the court. See Rules 35.1 and 35.3.

Paragraph (2) governs the situation covered in Rule 31.4 (a) and is made virtually mandatory since the parties to the appeal from the Rule 24 motion or Rule 32 petition and to the appeal from judgment and sentence will nearly always be identical.

Such appeals should be consolidated automatically unless it can be shown that such consolidation would substantially prejudice one of the parties.

JUDICIAL DECISIONS

CONSOLIDATION
A defendant should seek to consolidate post-conviction proceedings with a direct appeal. State v. Valdez, 160 Ariz. 9, 770 P.2d 313 (1989).

ARCrP Rule 31.5. Appeals by indigents
a. Determination of indigency.
   1) A defendant who had appointed counsel at the determination of guilt or at sentencing may proceed on appeal as an indigent without further authorization, unless, after a notice of appeal is filed, the trial court finds that the defendant is now able to employ counsel and pay for a certified copy of the record on appeal and the certified transcript.

   2) A defendant who did not proceed as an indigent in the trial court may so proceed on appeal by filing in the trial court a request to proceed as an indigent, together with the sworn questionnaire required by Rule 6.4(b). The clerk shall immediately deliver a copy of the request and questionnaire to the prosecutor by hand. The court shall require the defendant to appear for an inquiry into his or her ability to pay. It shall grant or deny the request within 3 days of filing, using the standard set forth in Rule 31.5(a)(1).

b. Contribution by the defendant. -- The trial court may order an indigent defendant to contribute to the costs of appeal and services of counsel in the manner prescribed by Rule 6.7 (d).

c. Petition to appellate court. -- If the trial court finds that the defendant is not entitled to proceed as an indigent, the defendant may file a petition to so proceed, together with a copy of the sworn questionnaire required by Rule 31.5 (a) (2), in the appellate court. The appellate court, or a single member thereof, shall decide the matter within 3 days after the petition is filed.

d. Notice to clerk of the appellate court and to the certified court reporter or to the court's designated transcript coordinator. -- A copy of any order or decision made under this rule shall be sent to the parties, the clerk of the appellate court and to the appropriate certified court reporter or reporters, or to the court's designated transcript coordinator, if the record was made by electronic or other means.

HISTORY: Amended May 7, 1975, effective Aug. 1, 1975; amended July 28, 1993, effective Dec. 1, 1993; amended eff. Jan. 1, 2007 by R-05-0037.

NOTES:

[1975 AMENDMENT]
RULE 31.5 (A). Paragraph (1) provides that a person who had appointed counsel at trial, at a Rule 17 plea hearing, or at sentencing, may automatically proceed as an indigent on appeal unless the court finds that his financial condition has changed. The standard used combines the Rule 6.4 (a) standard drawn from Ariz. Rev. Stat. Ann. § 11-584 (1) and Ariz. Rev. Stat. Ann. § 13-1714 (1956).

A defendant who proceeded as an indigent below but does not wish to do so on appeal should notify the trial court promptly.

Paragraph (2) sets forth the procedure for a defendant who has not had counsel appointed under Rule 6. The questionnaire notification of the prosecutor and opportunity for a hearing is to comply with verification requirement in Ariz. Rev.

Stat. Ann. § 13-1714 (1956). Cf. Arizona Rules of Criminal Procedure 361 (B); see Rule 6.4 (b). Immediate in hand delivery and determination within 3 days is required to avoid unduly delaying the proceedings. See Rule 6.4 (b).

Rule 6.6 insures that appellate counsel will be appointed when previously appointed counsel is precluded by law or legal ethics from continuing to represent the defendant or when the public defender is unable to prosecute a timely appeal because of lack of resources. Appointed appellate counsel for indigents is constitutionally required on an appeal of right by Douglas v. California, 372 U.S. 353 (1963). See Rule 6.1. The provision of free transcripts and records of prior proceedings is constitutionally required for indigents under Griffin v. Illinois, 351 U.S. 12 (1956). See Draper v. Washington, 372 U.S. 487 (1963); Britt v. North Carolina, 404 U.S. 226 (1971).

RULE 31.5 (B). Section (b) gives the court the discretion to order the defendant to make partial payment under the guidelines and procedures set forth in Rule 6.7 (d). See comment to Rule 6.7 (d)

RULE 31.5 (C) This section provides a prompt review procedure for those denied counsel.

RULE 31.5 (D). The notice required in this rule is to implement the early docketing provided in Rule 31.7 and to permit the court reporter to begin transcribing the record as soon as possible. See Rule 31.2 (g) and comments thereto.

ARCrP Rule 31.7. Docketing in the appellate court; designation of the parties.
a. Docketing the appeal. -- Within 10 days after filing the notice of appeal, the clerk of the appellate court shall docket the appeal.
b. Designation of the parties. -- An appeal shall be docketed under the title given to the action in the trial court with the appellant identified as such, but if such title does not contain the name of the appellant, his or her name, identified as appellant, shall be added to the title.

HISTORY: Amended July 28, 1993, effective Dec. 1, 1993; amended eff. Jan. 1, 2007 by R-05-0037.

NOTES:

[1973 PROMULGATION]
RULE 31.7. The early docketing provided by this rule is to encourage appellate court supervision of the preparation of appeals by the parties, the clerk of the trial court and the court reporter. See ABA, Standards Relating to Criminal Appeals § 3.1 (Approved Draft, 1970).

RULE 31.7 (B). This rule is equivalent to the 1956 Ariz. Rules of Criminal Procedure, Rule 347 and is taken from the Federal Rules of Appellate Procedure 12 (a).

ARCrP Rule 31.8. The record on appeal; transcript; duty of the authorized transcriber

a. Composition of the record on appeal; additions; deletions.
   1) Composition. -- The record on appeal to the appellate court shall be a certified transcript, all documents, papers, books and photographs introduced into evidence, and all pleadings and documents in the file -- (other than subpoenas and proceedings not specifically designated), and if authorized by the appellate court, an electronic recording of the proceeding.
   2) Additions and deletions.
      i. By the Appellant. -- Within 5 days after the filing of the notice of appeal the appellant may file with the clerk of the trial court a designation to include in the record the subpoenas and proceedings appellant deems necessary, and to delete from the record all the documents, papers, books and photographs he or she deems unnecessary.
      ii. By the Appellee. -- Within 12 days after the filing of the notice of appeal the appellee may file with the clerk of the trial court a designation to include in the record those subpoenas and proceedings

appellee deems necessary, and any document, paper, book or photograph deleted by the appellant.

iii. By the Appellate court. -- An exhibit other than those listed in section (a) (1) including the excised portion, if any, of a pre-sentence, diagnostic or mental health report may be added to the record on appeal only by order of the appellate court. Such an order may be made at any time.

b. Certified transcript: composition, additions and exclusions.

1) For the purpose of these rules, an "authorized transcriber" is a certified court reporter or a transcriber under contract with an Arizona court.

2) Composition. -- Except in cases where the death penalty has been imposed, a certified transcript of the following proceedings shall be provided:

i. Any voluntariness hearing or hearing to suppress the use of evidence.

ii. The trial, except that the record of voir dire of the jury and the opening and closing arguments of counsel shall not be included unless specifically designated by a party.

iii. Entry of judgment and sentence.

iv. Probation violation proceeding.

v. Aggravation-mitigation hearing.

3) Composition where the death penalty has been imposed. -- The certified transcript shall consist of all recorded proceedings, including grand jury proceedings.

4) Additions and deletions. -- Within 5 days after the filing of the notice of appeal, the appellant may request the certified court reporter or the court's designated transcript coordinator, if the record was made by electronic or other means, to add to the certified transcript any proceeding not automatically included, and to exclude from the certified transcript any portion of the proceedings the appellant deems unnecessary for the proper hearing of his or her appeal.

Within 12 days after the filing of the notice of appeal, the appellee may request the certified court reporter or the court's designated transcript coordinator, if the record was made by electronic or other means, to add to the certified transcript any portion deleted by the appellant or not automatically included under paragraph (1).

c) Notice to other parties. -- Any designation or request made under sections (a) or (b) shall be sent to all other parties at the time it is filed or submitted.

d) Duty of the authorized transcriber; payment for certified transcript; number of copies.

1) The authorized transcriber shall prepare the certified transcript promptly upon receipt of a notice of appeal by the state or a notice of appeal indicating that the appellant proceeded as an indigent at the determination of guilt or at sentencing.

2) Within 5 days after the filing of the notice of appeal or within 5 days after denial or a request to proceed as an indigent, an appellant who is not proceeding as an indigent shall make arrangements with the authorized transcriber to pay for the certified transcript. Thereupon the authorized transcriber shall promptly prepare the certified transcript. The authorized transcriber shall notify the appellate court if the appellant fails to make satisfactory arrangements within the prescribed time.

3) The authorized transcriber shall promptly make any additions and deletions requested by the parties.

i. For non-electronically filed transcripts. -- The authorized transcriber shall prepare an original and two copies of the certified transcript unless further copies are ordered. The authorized transcriber shall file the original certified transcript with the clerk of the appellate court within the time for the clerk to file the record pursuant to Rule 31.9(a). When the state is the appellee the authorized transcriber shall send one copy of the certified transcript to the Office of the Attorney General. When the state is the appellant, the authorized transcriber shall send one copy of the certified transcript to the agency that prosecuted the case in Superior Court. The authorized transcriber shall submit the copy for the defendant to the clerk of the Superior Court, who will retain the copy for release to the defendant's appellate counsel or to the defendant if he or she is proceeding pro se, unless there is a local rule or administrative order providing otherwise, in which case the authorized transcriber shall distribute the defendant's copy as provided by such rule or order. Notice of service of the certified transcript shall be lodged with the appellate court reflecting when and upon whom service was made.

ii. For electronically filed transcripts. -- In courts that accept electronic filings, the authorized transcriber shall file the original certified electronic transcript with the clerk of the appellate court within the time for the clerk to file the record pursuant to Rule 31.9(a). When the state is the appellee, the authorized transcriber shall send an electronic copy of the certified transcript to the Office of the Attorney General and the appropriate county attorney's office, if any. When the state is the appellant, the authorized transcriber shall send an electronic copy of the certified electronic transcript to the agency that prosecuted the case in Superior Court. The authorized transcriber shall submit the electronic transcript for the defendant to the clerk of the Superior Court, who will provide the electronic transcript to the defendant's appellate counsel or to the defendant if he or she is proceeding pro se. If a paper transcript is required or requested in lieu of an electronic transcript, the authorized transcriber shall submit the paper copy for the defendant to the clerk of the Superior Court, who will retain the copy for release to the defendant's appellate counsel or to the defendant if he or she is proceeding pro se, unless there is a local rule or administrative order providing otherwise, in which case the authorized transcriber shall distribute the defendant's copy as provided by such rule or order. Notice of service of the certified transcript shall be lodged with the appellate court reflecting when and upon whom service was made.

iii. Retention of transcript copies. -- Copies of transcripts retained under this rule shall be retained for 90 days.

e) Responsibility for payment. -- Non-indigent parties shall pay for all portions of the record on appeal and certified transcript which they have designated or requested. In addition, non-indigent appellants shall pay for those portions of the record on appeal and certified transcript required under Sections (a)(1), (b)(1), and (b)(2) and not deleted.

f) Statement of the evidence for proceedings when no report was made or when the transcript is unavailable. -- If no report of the evidence or proceedings at trial was made or if the transcript is unavailable, the clerk of the trial court shall immediately serve notice of the unavailability upon the parties and upon the clerk of the Appellate Court. Within 10 days of receipt of such notice the appellant may prepare a statement of the evidence or proceedings from the best available means, including the appellant's recollection, which shall be filed with the trial court and sent to the appellee. Within 10 days after service of the appellant's statement, the appellee may prepare objections and propose amendments thereto and submit them to the trial court for approval. If the appellant does not prepare such a statement within the specified time, the appellee may prepare his or her own statement and submit it to the trial court for approval within 20 days of service of the notice of unavailability.

g) The statement, as approved, shall be included in the record on appeal.

h) Agreed statement as the record on appeal. – In lieu of the record on appeal as defined above, the parties may prepare and sign a statement of the case showing how the issues presented by the appeal arose and were decided in the trial court, setting forth only so many of the facts averred and proved or thought to be proved as are essential to a decision of the issues presented. Notice that a statement is being prepared shall be served promptly on the appropriate authorized transcriber and on the clerk of the trial court.

i) The agreed statement shall be submitted for the trial court's approval within 20 days of the filing of the notice of appeal. The court may make such additions as it considers necessary fully to present the appeal.

j) Correction or modification of the record. -- If any controversy arises as to whether the record discloses what actually occurred in the trial court, the difference shall be submitted to and settled by the trial court. If anything material to either party is omitted from the record or is misstated therein, the parties by stipulation, the trial court, either before or after the record is transmitted to the appellate court, or the appellate court on motion or on its own initiative, may direct that the omission or misstatement be corrected, and if necessary that a supplemental record be certified and transmitted. All other questions as to the form and content of the record shall be presented to the appellate court.

HISTORY: Amended May 7, 1975, effective Aug. 1, 1975; amended Feb. 23, 1981, effective Mar. 1, 1981; amended July 26, 1982, effective Sept. 1, 1982; amended Oct. 29, 1991, effective Dec. 1, 1991; amended July 28, 1993, effective Dec. 1, 1993; amended Mar. 18, 1994, effective Apr. 1, 1994; amended June 10, 1997, effective January 1, 1998; amended Oct. 6, 1998, effective Dec. 1, 1998; amended eff. Jan. 1, 2007 by R-05-0037.

NOTES:

COMMITTEE COMMENT TO THE 1997 AMENDMENTS
Superior courts in the respective counties may adopt local rules ensuring that each defendant appearing pro se timely receives a copy of the transcript for appeal. See Rule XIV, Uniform Rules of Practice of the Superior Court. The Superior Court Clerks should also maintain an accurate record of when a defendant's copy of a transcript has been lodged with the office of the clerk and when and to whom such copy has been released.

[1975 AMENDMENT]
Only those papers and portions of the proceedings normally needed on appeal are automatically included in the record and transcript.

RULES 31.8 (A) & (C) The record on appeal will consist of copies of the maTTers in the file, not the original documents. This will allow the permanent file to remain in the trial court for reference in case of later Rule 32 petitions, or concurrent Rule 24 motions. Under Rule 28.1, the clerk of the appellate court is authorized to destroy the copies used for the appeal when they are no longer needed by the appellate court.

Paragraph (1) replaces Arizona Rules of Criminal Procedure 360 (A) and includes all the items listed in that rule except exhibits other than documents, papers, books and photographs. In addition, a copy of the complaint, if any, and the order holding the defendant to answer, if any, should be included.

The term documents, papers, books and photographs introduced into evidence includes those items introduced at trial and those introduced during sentencing proceedings including the excised presentence report and any diagnostic or mental health reports. See Rules 26.4, 26.5, 26.6 and 26.7 (c). The appellate court may send for an exhibit not included in the record on appeal at any time.

Each party is given the opportunity to add those portions of the record not included automatically. The appellant may request the omission of any portion of the record or any exhibit he does not need and does not want to pay for, but the appellee may request its reinsertion at his own expense. Stringent time limits are imposed on such requests in order to permit the clerk and court reporter to complete their duties within the prescribed time.

The appellant must file and serve his request within 5 days after filing the notice of appeal and the appellee has 7 days more -- i.e., about 5 days after he receives his copy of any request of the appellant -- to file and serve his request.

RULE 31.8 (D) Paragraph (1) requires the reporter to begin transcribing as soon as possible after receiving a notice of appeal by the state or by an appellant who proceeded as an indigent below. Payment in those cases is assured and there is no reason to wait. See Rules 34.5 (d) and 34.2 (g).

Private parties who are able to pay must make arrangements to do so promptly in order to permit timely filing of the record. The number of copies filed conforms to the present practice in the 9th Circuit.

RULE 31.8 (F). This rule is based on the 1956 Arizona Rules of Criminal Procedure, Rule 363. The clerk of the trial court is in a better position than the appellant to know at the earliest possible moment, that a transcript is unavailable; hence, he has the duty of notifying the parties. Cf. the Federal Rules of Appellate

Procedure 10 (d). If the clerk should find that the transcript is unavailable within a few days of the filing of the notice of appeal, the time limits prescribed in this section should still allow the appeal to proceed within the general time limits of Rule 31. If the unavailability of the transcript should only become apparent later, this would be grounds for extending the time for transmission of the record under Rule 31.9 (c). Cf. Arizona Rules of Criminal Procedure 75 (k).

RULE 31.8 (G). Rule 31.8 (g) is based upon Federal Rules of Appellate Procedure 10 (d). It provides a money-saving alternative for the parties and a way of relieving the burden on the clerk and other court personnel. Cf. Arizona Rules of Civil Procedure 75 (f).

RULE 31.8 (H). This section is taken from Federal Rules of Appellate Procedure 10 (e) and is intended to prevent major delays and confusion when mistakes or omissions occur. Cf. Arizona Rules of Civil Procedure 75 (h).

JUDICIAL DECISIONS
ANALYSIS

MISTAKE OR OMISSION
Where a jury of 12 members returned verdicts convicting defendant of certain criminal offenses, where the jurors were individually polled, where the court reporter's transcript only contained the polling of 11 of the 12 jurors and omiTTed any mention of juror number six, and when defendant appealed his conviction on the basis that he was denied his right to a 12-person jury, the state could and should have asked the appellate court to employ Ariz. R. Crim. P. 31.8(h) to clarify what actually occurred during the polling process; that procedure would have beTTer served the goals of timely administering justice and searching for the truth and would have quickly revealed that the omission of the polling of juror number six from the trial transcript was merely attributable to court reporter error. State v. Diaz, 223 Ariz. 358, 575 Ariz. Adv. Rep. 41, 224 P.3d 174, 2010 Ariz. LEXIS 10 (2010).

RECORD INADEQUATE

Where the trial judge's pronouncement of sentence was fully set forth, but much of that proceeding, most notably defendant's statement on his own behalf and a statement by defense counsel, were not transcribed, record of sentencing hearing was clearly inadequate to enable proper review of defendant's death sentence. A new hearing was required. State v. Schackart, 175 Ariz. 494, 858 P.2d 639 (1993), cert. denied, 511 U.S. 1046, 114 S. Ct. 1578, 128 L. Ed. 2d 220 (1994).

TRIAL EXHIBITS

In defendants' consolidated appeals from convictions on alcohol-related driving charges, the court included in its review the exhibits, primarily scientific articles, that were admitted at trial because, contrary to the state's assertion, such were part of the record on appeal pursuant to Ariz. R. Crim. P. 31.8(a)(1). State v. Esser, 205 Ariz. 320, 403 Ariz. Adv. Rep. 12, 70 P.3d 449, 2003 Ariz. App. LEXIS 108 (Ct. App. 2003).

ARCrP Rule 31.9. Transmission of the record

a. Time for transmission. -- Within 45 days after the filing of the notice of appeal, the clerk of the superior court shall transmit to the appellate court a copy of the pleadings, documents, and minute entries, and the original paper and photographic exhibits of a manageable size filed with the clerk of the superior court.

b. Duty to certify and transmit the record. -- After certifying that it is true, correct, and complete as ordered, the clerk of the trial court and the authorized transcriber shall transmit to the clerk of the appellate court the portions of the record on appeal for which each is responsible. Each shall number the items comprising that portion of the record on appeal and shall transmit with that portion a list of the items so numbered.

c. Extension and reduction of time for transmission of the record. -- The appellate court, on a showing of good cause, may grant one extension of the time for transmitting the record on appeal which shall not exceed 20 days or it may require the record to be transmitted at any time within the prescribed period. A copy of any order issued under this section shall be sent to the parties, the clerk of the trial court, and to the requesting authorized transcriber.

d. Transmission of other exhibits. -- The court, or any party upon motion made to the appellate court, may request the transmission of exhibits not automatically transmitted under Rule 31.9(a) when such are necessary to the determination of the appeal.

HISTORY: Amended May 7, 1975, effective Aug. 1, 1975; amended July 28, 1993, effective Dec. 1, 1993; amend. June 10, 1997, effective January 1, 1998; amended Jan. 30, 2002, effective June 1, 2002; amended eff. Jan. 1, 2007 by R-05-0037.

NOTES:

[1975 AMENDMENT]
This rule is drawn from the 1956 Arizona Rules of Criminal Procedure, Rules 360 (B) and 361 (A), and Federal Rules of Appellate Procedure.

RULES 31.9 (A) & (C). Rule 31.9 (a) allows 25 days more than the former rule for filing the record. The 1956 Arizona Rules of Criminal Procedure, Rule 361 (A). Rule 31.9 (c) permits one extension of up to 20 days on a showing of good cause. Such extension can be granted only by the appellate court. The notice requirement is to insure that all persons concerned will be aware of any change in the date on which the record or any portion thereof is due.

RULE 31.9 (B). Section (b) requires each person responsible for preparing a portion of the transcript to transmit that portion to the appellate court himself. The rule allows transmittal of the clerk's portion of the record and of the transcript as soon as each is ready. The rule does not prevent the clerk and reporter from assembling and transmitting the record and transcript in a single package.

Rule 31.9 (b) retains the certification requirement of the 1956 Arizona Rules of Criminal Procedure, Rule 360 (B) and 361 (A), but omits the requirement that the clerk affix his seal. Added is a requirement, taken from Federal Rules of Appellate Procedure 11 (b), that the clerk and reporter number the items in the record and transcript and attach a list of the items so numbered.

ARCrP Rule 31.11. Perfection of the appeal No new matter, other than a petition for post-conviction relief not precluded under Rule 32.2, may be filed in the trial court by any party to an appeal later than 15 days after the record on appeal has been filed.

NOTES:

[1973 PROMULGATION]

Perfection of an appeal is delayed to give the parties an adequate opportunity to file corrective motions in the trial court. This section delays the perfection of the appeal until the due date for the first filing which directly affects the course of the appeal and which can only be decided by the appellate court -- the request to file briefs. See Rule 31.12. This gives parties who appeal about the same time to file corrective motions as they had under the former rules -- about 60 days -- and equalizes the time for filing motions under Rule 24.2 for those who do and those who do not appeal. Formerly, an appeal was perfected upon the filing of the notice of appeal and payment of the docketing fee. See Arizona Rules of Civil Procedure 73 (d); and the 1956 Arizona Rules of Criminal Procedure, Rule 348.

Perfection, under this section, merely designates to what court new matters relating to the appeal must be addressed. It does not remove the trial court's jurisdiction to decide motions filed before the cut-off date, or petitions for post-conviction relief based upon issues which are not raisable on appeal and were not raised in a post-trial motion. See Rules 24.2; 24.3; 32.1; 32.2. Thus, a Rule 24 motion which was filed before perfection may be decided by the trial court after perfection whether or not the appeal has been stayed under Rule 31.4 (a). The phrase "15 days after the record of appeal has been filed" refers to 15 days after the date on which the parties are notified under Rule 31.10.

JUDICIAL DECISIONS

NEW MATTER

The revocation of probation is not a new matter within the meaning of that term in this rule. State v. Albe, 148 Ariz. 87, 713 P.2d 288 (Ct. App. 1984).

ARCrP Rule 31.12. Form of motions

All papers relating to motions may be produced by any process that results in a clear black image on white paper, including typing, printing, or photocopying. The paper must be white, opaque, and unglazed, and only one side of the paper may be used. Motion papers shall be on paper 8 1/2 by 11 inches and shall contain a caption setting forth the name of the court, the title of the case, the case number, and a brief descriptive title. Text shall be double-spaced; headings, quotations and footnotes may be indented and single-spaced. Either a proportionately spaced typeface of 14 points or more, or a monospaced typeface of no more than 10 1/2 characters per inch, shall be used for text, quotations, and footnotes. A proportionately spaced typeface has characters with different widths (e.g., an acceptable proportionately spaced typeface is Times New Roman, 14 point). A monospaced typeface has characters with the same advanced width (e.g., an acceptable monospaced typeface is Courier New, 12 point). All margins must be at least 1 inch. Page numbers shall be placed in the bottom margin, but no text or footnotes may appear there. Text shall be in roman, non-script text, although italics, underline, or bold may be used for emphasis. Case names and signals shall be underlined or in italics. Headings shall be underlined, in italics, or in bold. All parties must file the original and four copies of all motions filed in the Court of Appeals and the original and seven copies of all motions filed in the Supreme Court.

HISTORY: Adopted June 10, 1997, effective January 1, 1998; amended Jan. 24, 2001, effective June 1, 2001; amended effective Oct. 12, 2005.

Rule 31.13. Appellate briefs [Effective until January 1, 2011]

a. Time for filing; manner of filing. -- In all cases other than capital cases, the appellant's opening brief shall be filed within 40 days after the mailing of the notice as provided for by Rule 31.10. The appellee's brief shall be filed within 40 days after service of the appellant's brief. The appellant may file a reply brief within 20 days after service of the appellee's brief, or the appellant may file a notice to the effect that no reply brief will be filed, at which time the appeal will be deemed to be "at issue." Otherwise, the appeal will be deemed to be "at issue" upon the filing of the reply brief or 20 days after service of the appellee's brief, whichever first occurs. The time for filing briefs in capital cases shall be governed by subdivision (f) of this rule. Briefs and appendices may be filed by mail, which shall include every type of delivery service except same day hand delivery. Briefs and appendices shall be deemed timely filed if, within the time allowed for filing, they are either (i) received by the Clerk of the Court, or (ii) they are addressed to the Clerk of the Court and picked up by or delivered either to a third party commercial carrier for delivery within three calendar days or to the United States Postal Service. Except in the case of same day hand delivery, filing by third-party commercial carrier or by mail must be accompanied by the party's or attorneys separate signed certification indicting the date of delivery to or pick up by either the carrier or the United States Postal Service.

b. Form and length.

1) Form. -- A brief shall comply with Rule 31.12, except that the brief's covers and the components of the brief excluded from the word count computation are exempt from the 14 point or 10 1/2 characters per inch typeface requirement. Briefs shall be in pamphlet form and shall have covers. The front cover shall contain (1) the name of the court, (2) the number of the case, (3) the title of the case, (4) the title of the brief (e.g., opening brief), and (5) the name and address and state bar number of counsel representing the party on which behalf the brief is filed. The covers of briefs shall be colored as follows: the appellant's opening brief, blue; the appellee's answering brief, red; any reply brief, gray; the brief of an intervenor or amicus curiae, green.

2) Length. -- Except by permission of the court, (i) a principal brief in a non-capital case prepared in a proportionately spaced typeface may not exceed 14,000 words, and a reply brief may not exceed 7,000 words, and neither may have an average of more than 280 words per page, including footnotes and quotations; and (ii) a principal brief in a non-capital case prepared in a monospaced typeface may not exceed 40 pages, and a reply brief may not exceed 20 pages. The above word and page limits do not include the table of contents, table of citations, certificate of service, certificate of compliance,

and any addendum containing statutes, rules, regulations, etc. The brief must be accompanied by a certificate of compliance that states the brief's line spacing and states either (i) the brief uses a proportionately spaced typeface, together with the typeface, point size, and word count, or (ii) the brief uses a monospaced typeface, together with the number of characters per inch. A party preparing this certificate may rely on word count of the processing system used to prepare the brief. The length of briefs in capital cases is governed by subsection (f) of this rule.

3) Briefs not clearly legible shall be stricken by the court.

c. Contents

1) Appellant. -- The appellant's brief shall include:

i. A table of contents with page references.

ii. A table of citations, which shall alphabetically arrange and index the cases, statutes, and other authorities cited, with references to the pages of the brief on which they are cited.

iii. A statement of the case, indicating briefly the basis of the appellate court's jurisdiction, the nature of the case, the course of the proceedings and the disposition in the court below.

iv. A statement of facts relevant to the issues presented for review, with appropriate references to the record. The statement shall not contain evidentiary matter unless material to a proper consideration of the issues presented, in which instance a reference shall be made to the record or page of the transcript where such evidence appears. The statement of facts may be combined with the statement of the case.

v. A statement of the issues presented for review. The statement of an issue presented for review will be deemed to include every subsidiary issue fairly comprised therein.

vi. An argument which shall contain the contentions of the appellant with respect to the issues presented, and the reasons therefor, with citations to the authorities, statutes and parts of the record relied on. The argument may include a summary. With respect to each contention raised on appeal, the proper standard of review on appeal shall be identified, with citations to relevant authority, at the outset of the discussion of that contention. Citation of authorities shall be to the volume and page number of the official reports and also when possible to the unofficial reporters.

vii. A short conclusion stating the precise relief sought.

viii. An appendix if desired.

1) Appellee. -- The appellee's brief shall be of like character and arrangement as that of the appellant except that no statement of the case is required unless the appellee finds the statement presented by the appellant to be insufficient or incorrect.

2) Reply brief. -- The reply brief shall be confined to a response to questions of law or fact raised by the appellee's brief.

3) Appendix.

i. The appellate brief for either party may include an appendix of pertinent statutes, treaties, regulations, rules, and instructions.

ii. In addition, the appendix to an appellate brief may include extended quotations from cases and authorities where such quotations are required for proper presentation of the issues.

d. Extension of time. -- Upon a showing of exceptional circumstances, the appellate court may extend the time for filing a brief.

e. Non-compliance. -- The appellate court may strike a brief which does not substantially conform to the requirements of this rule.

f. Capital cases.

1) Time for filing. -- In capital cases, the appellant's opening brief shall be filed within 70 days after the mailing of the notice as provided for by Rule 31.10. The appellee's brief shall be filed within 40 days after service of the appellant's brief. Appellant's reply brief shall be filed within 20 days after service of appellee's brief.

2) Length. -- Except by permission of the court, (i) a principal brief in a capital case prepared in a proportionately spaced typeface may not exceed 28,000 words and a reply brief may not exceed 14,000 words, and neither may have an average of more than 280 words per page, including footnotes

and quotations; and (ii) a principal brief in a capital case prepared in a monospaced typeface may not exceed 80 pages, and a reply brief may not exceed 40 pages. All other requirements for the form of the briefs shall be as specified in subsection (b) of this rule.

HISTORY: Amended May 7, 1975, effective Aug. 1, 1975; amended Oct. 24, 1991, effective Nov. 15, 1991; amended Feb. 18, 1992, effective Sept. 1, 1992; amended June 10, 1998, effective January 1, 1998; amended Oct. 6, 1998, effective Dec. 1, 1998; amended Jan. 24, 2001; effective June 1, 2001.

NOTES:

COMMITTEE COMMENT TO THE 1997 AMENDMENTS
This rule has been amended to conform to corresponding rules of the Arizona Rules of Civil Appellate Procedure. See the comments to ARCAP 15 concerning formatting of briefs. In addition, this rule has been amended to make the structure of any brief identical to the structure of briefs in civil appeals under ARCAP 13. The time for filing briefs has been extended and motions for additional time to file briefs will be rarely granted.

[1975 AMENDMENT]
This rule is drawn from Ariz. Sup. Ct. R. 5 and Federal Rules of Appellate Procedure 28 and 32. The appellate memorandum will be the standard appellate pleading. Briefs are permitted only on motion under Rule 31.12.

RULE 31.13 (A) The appellant's memorandum is due within 20 days after the filing of the record or 10 days after denial of a request to file briefs; the appellee's memorandum is due about 20 days later. This compares to 30-day periods for briefs under this rule and under Ariz. Sup. Ct. R. 5 (f). No reply memoranda are permitted. Reply briefs are due 20 days after service of the appellee's brief, as under current Ariz. Sup. Ct. R. 5 (f) (3). Service shall be in accordance with Rule 31.21. The filing of the record refers to the date of notice specified in Rule 31.10.

RULE 31.13 (B) The requirements in paragraph (1) which govern both memoranda and briefs are taken directly from Ariz. Sup. Ct. R. 5 (a) except that all appellate pleadings are to be on letter size paper rather than the 7" x 10" paper required by Ariz. Sup. Ct. R. 5 (a). These rules standardize the paper size for all documents in criminal cases. See Rule 35.1.

Appellate memoranda under paragraph (2) may be 15 pages long. Briefs may be about the same length as previous practice -- ca. 9,600 words. Appellate memoranda need only have stiff backing, but briefs, because of their greater bulk must have covers and be bound in pamphlet form.

RULE 31.13 (C) Part (1) of this section is based on Federal Rules of Appellate Procedure 28 (a). A statement of the issues is included within the table of contents rather than as a separate requirement. In briefs the issues presented should substantially conform to those listed in the statement of issues under Rule 31.12. There is no reason for the contents of the brief to differ substantially from that of the memorandum. The only difference herein is the provision in paragraph (4) (ii) permitting the appendix to an appellate memorandum to contain extended quotations where they are absolutely necessary.

The restrictions on the reply brief in paragraph (3) are taken from Ariz. Sup. Ct. R. 5 (e).

RULE 31.13 (E) This rule changes Ariz. Sup. Ct. R. 5 (a) (3) in that the power to reject a memorandum or brief is given to the appellate court rather than to the clerk.

JUDICIAL DECISIONS
ANALYSIS

CONSTITUTIONALITY
There was no deprivation of defendant's constitutional rights resulting from the page limitation applied to his opening brief. State v. Atwood, 171 Ariz. 576, 832 P.2d 593 (1992), cert. denied, 506 U.S. 1084, 113 S. Ct. 1058, 122 L. Ed. 2d 364 (1993); overruled on other grounds by State v. Nordstrom, 200 Ariz. 229, 25 P.3d 717 (2001).

Where defendant was permitted to file a brief more than twice the size normally accepted, to file a 34-page reply brief, and to engage, through his counsel, in oral argument before the court, and as all arguable issues were raised and analyzed in the brief submitted, the court-mandated editing of defendant's appellate brief did not violate his constitutional rights. State v. Amaya-Ruiz, 166 Ariz. 152, 800 P.2d 1260 (1990), cert. denied, 500 U.S. 929, 111 S. Ct. 2044, 114 L. Ed. 2d 129 (1991).

IN GENERAL

The type of issues an appellant can raise in an appeal and the number of issues an appellant can raise are not limited by a rule per se; as a long-standing practice, however, this court, like other appellate courts, will not tolerate a party's presentation of claims that have no arguable merit. State v. Carriger, 143 Ariz. 142, 692 P.2d 991 (1984), cert. denied, 471 U.S. 1111, 105 S. Ct. 2347, 85 L. Ed. 2d 864 (1985).

PURPOSE

The appellate process is designed to give prompt, full appellate review to those who have grounds to believe they have not had a fair trial; important policy considerations require that all claims be raised in the appeal. State v. Carriger, 143 Ariz. 142, 692 P.2d 991 (1984), cert. denied, 471 U.S. 1111, 105 S. Ct. 2347, 85 L. Ed. 2d 864 (1985).

FAILURE TO RAISE ISSUE

Defendant failed to comply with this rule; therefore, the appellate court considered only defendant's argument that the indictment was allegedly duplicitous. State v. Ramsey, 211 Ariz. 529, 466 Ariz. Adv. Rep. 3, 124 P.3d 756, 2005 Ariz. App. LEXIS 159 (Ct. App. 2005). Where a defendant did not develop an argument that his sentencing violated A.R.S. § 13-116, the argument was not preserved for review. State v. Burdick, 211 Ariz. 583, 467 Ariz. Adv. Rep. 3, 125 P.3d 1039, 2005 Ariz. App. LEXIS 166 (Ct. App. 2005).

Defendant contended, on appeal, that there was a lack of foundation for the admission of sentencing documents to prove defendant's two prior felony convictions; appellate court rejected this argument as summarily waived because defendant did not provide sufficient argument on appeal. State v. Cons, 208 Ariz. 409, 430 Ariz. Adv. Rep. 63, 94 P.3d 609, 2004 Ariz. App. LEXIS 107 (Ct. App. 2004).

Where defendant appealed generally from the revocation of his probation and sentence but did not set forth any issues, absent fundamental error, he waived any claims on appeal. State v. Holguin, 177 Ariz. 589, 870 P.2d 407 (Ct. App. 1993).

If an error is not fundamental, an appellant's failure to raise an issue on appeal constitutes a waiver of that issue. Because such a waiver constitutes abandonment of the claim, an appellant may not raise a claim of error for the first time in his reply brief. State v. Lee, 160 Ariz. 489, 774 P.2d 228 (Ct. App. 1989).

Since defendant's brief listed his concerns without providing argument with respect to counsel's failure to object to the hearsay and to counsel's identification of evidence, these claims were therefore abandoned and waived. State v. Nirschel, 155 Ariz. 206, 745 P.2d 953 (1987).

Issue of whether suppression was an appropriate remedy was not addressed in the state's opening brief, and was not raised until the state filed its reply brief; it was thus waived. State v. Doolittle, 155 Ariz. 352, 746 P.2d 924 (Ct. App. 1987).

LEGIBILITY
There is no requirement that pleadings be typed this rule requires that briefs be clear and legible. Knight v. Superior Court ex rel. County of Maricopa, 161 Ariz. 551, 779 P.2d 1290 (Ct. App. 1989).

PAGE LIMIT
Policy reason Arizona courts advance for disallowing argument in appendices is that an appendix may not be used to circumvent the page limitations, and this policy would be equally important in petitions for review as it is in direct appeals under this rule; there is no reason why Arizona courts would permit an appendix to be used to circumvent a page limit in a petition for review of a petition-for-post-conviction-relief when the Arizona courts do not permit such a tactic on direct

review. Laliberte v. Ryan, -- F. Supp. 2d --, 2009 U.S. Dist. LEXIS 44252 (D. Ariz. May 26, 2009).

Attachment of arguments as an "appendix" to appellant's opening brief is improper under this rule, as argument must be in the body of the brief. State v. Walden, 183 Ariz. 595, 905 P.2d 974 (1995), cert. denied, 517 U.S. 1146, 116 S. Ct. 1444, 134 L. Ed. 2d 564 (1996).

Supreme Court's rejection of defendant's oversize (175 page) brief and order that he file a brief within the 80-page limit did not deny him due process when he wasted many pages on precluded issues and raised many issues repeatedly rejected in recent decisions. State v. Bolton, 182 Ariz. 290, 896 P.2d 830 (1995).

Barring an advance showing of the most extraordinary circumstances, the appellate court is committed to enforcing the page limitations set by the rules. State v. West, 176 Ariz. 432, 862 P.2d 192 (1993), cert. denied, 511 U.S. 1063, 114 S. Ct. 1635, 128 L. Ed. 2d 358 (1994), overruled on other grounds, State v. Rodriguez, 192 Ariz. 58, 961 P.2d 1006 (1998).

ARCrP Rule 31.13. Appellate briefs [Effective January 1, 2011]
a. Time for filing; manner of filing. -- In all cases other than capital cases, the appellant's opening brief shall be filed within 40 days after the mailing of the notice as provided for by Rule 31.10. The appellee's brief shall be filed within 40 days after service of the appellant's brief. The appellant may file a reply brief within 20 days after service of the appellee's brief, or the appellant may file a notice to the effect that no reply brief will be filed, at which time the appeal will be deemed to be "at issue." Otherwise, the appeal will be deemed to be "at issue" upon the filing of the reply brief or 20 days after service of the appellee's brief, whichever first occurs. The time for filing briefs in capital cases shall be governed by subdivision (f) of this rule. Briefs and appendices may be filed by mail, which shall include every type of delivery service except same day hand delivery. Briefs and appendices shall be deemed timely filed if, within the time allowed for filing, they are either (i) received by the Clerk of the Court, or (ii) they are addressed to the Clerk of the Court and picked up by or delivered either to a third party commercial carrier for delivery within three calendar days or to the United States

Postal Service. Except in the case of same day hand delivery, filing by third-party commercial carrier or by mail must be accompanied by the party's or attorney's separate signed certification indicting the date of delivery to or pick up by either the carrier or the United States Postal Service.

b. Form and length.

1) Form. -- A brief shall comply with Rule 31.12, except that the brief's covers and the components of the brief excluded from the word count computation are exempt from the 14 point or 10 1/2 characters per inch typeface requirement. Briefs shall be in pamphlet form and shall have covers. The front cover shall contain (1) the name of the court, (2) the number of the case, (3) the title of the case, (4) the title of the brief (e.g., opening brief), and (5) the name and address and state bar number of counsel representing the party on which behalf the brief is filed. The covers of briefs shall be colored as follows: the appellant's opening brief, blue; the appellee's answering brief, red; any reply brief, gray; the brief of an intervenor or amicus curiae, green.

2) Length. -- Except by permission of the court, (i) a principal brief in a non-capital case prepared in a proportionately spaced typeface may not exceed 14,000 words, and a reply brief may not exceed 7,000 words, and neither may have an average of more than 280 words per page, including footnotes and quotations; and (ii) a principal brief in a non-capital case prepared in a monospaced typeface may not exceed 40 pages, and a reply brief may not exceed 20 pages. The above word and page limits do not include the table of contents, table of citations, certificate of service, certificate of compliance, and any addendum containing statutes, rules, regulations, etc. The brief must be accompanied by a certificate of compliance that states the brief's line spacing and states either (i) the brief uses a proportionately spaced typeface, together with the typeface, point size, and word count, or (ii) the brief uses a monospaced typeface, together with the number of characters per inch. A party preparing this certificate may rely on word count of the processing system used to prepare the brief. The length of briefs in capital cases is governed by subsection (f) of this rule. 8. Briefs not clearly legible shall be stricken by the court.

c. Contents.

    1)Appellant. -- The appellant's brief shall include:

        i. A table of contents with page references.

        ii. A table of citations, which shall alphabetically arrange and index the cases, statutes, and other authorities cited, with references to the pages of the brief on which they are cited.

        ii. A statement of the case, indicating briefly the basis of the appellate court's jurisdiction, the nature of the case, the course of the proceedings and the disposition in the court below.

        iv. A statement of facts relevant to the issues presented for review, with appropriate references to the record. The statement shall not contain evidentiary matter unless material to a proper consideration of the issues presented, in which instance a reference shall be made to the record or page of the transcript where such evidence appears. The statement of facts may be combined with the statement of the case.

        v. A statement of the issues presented for review. The statement of an issue presented for review will be deemed to include every subsidiary issue fairly comprised therein.

        vi. An argument which shall contain the contentions of the appellant with respect to the issues presented, and the reasons therefor, with citations to the authorities, statutes and parts of the record relied on. The argument may include a summary. With respect to each contention raised on appeal, the proper standard of review on appeal shall be identified, with citations to relevant authority, at the outset of the discussion of that contention. Citation of authorities shall be to the volume and page number of the official reports and also when possible to the unofficial reporters.

        vii. A short conclusion stating the precise relief sought.

        viii. An appendix if desired.

4) Appellee. -- The appellee's brief shall be of like character and arrangement as that of the appellant except that no statement of the case is required unless the appellee finds the statement presented by the appellant to be insufficient or incorrect.

5) Reply brief. -- The reply brief shall be confined to a response to questions of law or fact raised by the appellee's brief.

6) Appendix

i. The appellate brief for either party may include an appendix of pertinent statutes, treaties, regulations, rules, and instructions.

ii. In addition, the appendix to an appellate brief may include extended quotations from cases and authorities where such quotations are required for proper presentation of the issues.

d. Extension of time. -- Upon a showing of exceptional circumstances, the appellate court may extend the time for filing a brief.

e. Non-compliance. -- The appellate court may strike a brief which does not substantially conform to the requirements of this rule.

f. Capital cases

1) Time for filing. -- In capital cases, the appellant's opening brief shall be filed within 90 days after the court issues a notice that the record is complete. The appellee's brief shall be filed within 60 days after service of the appellant's brief. Appellant's reply brief shall be filed within 30 days after service of appellee's brief.

2) Length. -- Except by permission of the court, (i) a principal brief in a capital case prepared in a proportionately spaced typeface may not exceed 28,000 words and a reply brief may not exceed 14,000 words, and neither may have an average of more than 280 words per page, including footnotes and quotations; and (ii) a principal brief in a capital case prepared in a monospaced typeface may not exceed 80 pages, and a reply brief may not exceed 40 pages. All other requirements for the form of the briefs shall be as specified in subsection (b) of this rule.

HISTORY: Amended May 7, 1975, effective Aug. 1, 1975; amended Oct. 24, 1991, effective Nov. 15, 1991; amended Feb. 18, 1992, effective Sept. 1, 1992;

amended June 10, 1998, effective January 1, 1998; amended Oct. 6, 1998, effective Dec. 1, 1998; amended Jan. 24, 2001; effective June 1, 2001; amended by R-09-0032, effective January 1, 2011.

NOTES:

ARCrP Rule 31.14. Request for oral argument; precedence of criminal appeals.

a. Request of oral argument. -- An appeal may be scheduled for oral argument if, on or before the earlier of the ten (10) days after the date the reply brief is due or filed, a party files with the Court of Appeals a separate instrument requesting oral argument. If any party believes that extended argument should be permitted, the reasons therefor should be filed as part of the request for oral argument, or in a separate instrument, no later than 10 days after the request for oral argument is filed. The clerk of the appellate court shall notify the parties of the specific time and place at which oral argument will be heard at least 20 days prior to the date fixed for oral argument. The notice shall inform the parties as to the appellate court's allocation of time to each side at oral argument. An appeal may be considered and decided without oral argument if the appellate court determines that (1) the appeal is frivolous; (2) the dispositive issue or set of issues presented has been recently authoritatively decided; or (3) the facts and legal arguments are adequately presented in the briefs and record and the decisional process would not be significantly aided by oral argument. When such a determination is made that a case is to be submitted without oral argument, the clerk of the appellate court shall give the parties prompt written notice of such determination, and any party shall have 10 days from the date of such notice from the clerk in which to file a statement setting forth the reasons why, in the opinion of that party, oral argument should be heard.

b. Precedence of criminal appeals. -- Appeals in criminal cases shall have precedence over all other appeals except those from juvenile actions or where otherwise provided by law. Appeals under Rule 31.2 (b) shall have precedence over all other appeals.

HISTORY: Amended Mar. 31, 1992, effective June 1, 1992; amend. June 10, 1997, effective January 1, 1998; amend. effective Jan. 1, 2007 by R-05-0036.

NOTES:

COMMENT TO 1992 AMENDMENT

The 1992 amendment was deemed necessary to correct an existing inequity, whereby oral argument was mandatory in civil cases but discretionary in criminal cases. The revision was intended to make oral argument more readily available to criminal litigants while reducing unnecessary oral argument in civil cases.

[1975 AMENDMENT]

RULE 31.14 (A) Whether or not it has received or denied a request for oral argument, the court may request it on its own initiative. The phrase "at any time" is meant to include the period after a motion for rehearing has been granted by the appellate court or after a petition for review has been granted by the Supreme Court.

This section allows the appellate court to decide whether oral argument will be heard. In so doing it differs from previous practice. Ariz. Sup. Ct. R. 6 made oral argument automatic upon a party's request. Requests shall be filed and served in accordance with Rule 31.21.

RULE 31.14 (B) This section is taken form Ariz. Sup. Ct. R. 16 (b) and Ariz. R. Juv. Ct. P. 24 (c) (giving juvenile actions precedence over everything except extraordinary writs and special actions).

ARCrP Rule 31.17. Disposition and ancillary orders; warrants of execution.
a. Ancillary orders. -- The appellate court may issue such orders in aid of the proceedings as it deems necessary.

b. Disposition, in general. -- The appellate court may reverse, affirm, or modify the action of the lower court and issue any necessary and appropriate orders.

c. Fixing the date of execution after a death sentence is affirmed.

1. Initial execution warrant. After a conviction and sentence of death are affirmed and the first post-conviction relief proceeding pursuant to Rule 32.4(a) has concluded by the denial of a petition for review filed pursuant to Rule 32.9(c) or, if no petition for review has been filed, upon the filing of a notice by the state that the time for filing such petition has expired, the Supreme Court shall fix a twenty-four hour time period for execution of the sentence and shall issue a warrant of execution.

2. Subsequent execution warrant. In the event the warrant is stayed by any court beyond the time period fixed for the execution of sentence, the Supreme Court shall issue subsequent warrants of execution upon motion by the state.

3. Date and time of execution. The time period for execution shall be fixed for thirty-five days after the Supreme Court's order denying review, order acting on a notice of non-filing, or order granting a motion for warrant of execution, unless good cause renders it impracticable to fix it at thirty-five days, but in such case no more than sixty days. The warrant of execution shall state the date for commencement of the execution time period. The warrant shall further state that it is valid for twenty-four hours beginning at an hour to be designated by the director of the state department of corrections. The warrant shall include an order to the director to provide written notice of the designated hour to the Supreme Court and parties at least twenty calendar days prior to the execution date. The warrant shall authorize the director to carry out the execution at any time during the duration of the warrant.

4.Return on warrant. The superintendent of the state prison shall make a return on the warrant to the Supreme Court showing the manner and time of execution.

d. Modification of judgment upon finding of insufficient evidence at trial. -- When the appellate court finds that the evidence introduced at trial is not legally sufficient to establish the defendant's guilt of the offense of which he was convicted, but is legally sufficient to establish his guilt of a necessarily included

336

offense, it may modify the judgment to one of conviction for the lesser offense and remand the case to the trial court for resentencing.

e. Brief form of opinion. -- The appellate court may issue a brief form of opinion where the facts and issues of law are clear and the interests of justice will be served.

HISTORY: Amended July 28, 1993, effective Dec. 1, 1993; amend. June 30, 1997, effective December 1, 1997; amended June 25, 1998.

NOTES:

[1973 PROMULGATION]
This rule is intended to replace Ariz. Sup. Ct. R. 22 and the 1956 Arizona Rules of Criminal Procedure, Rule 364.

RULE 31.17 (A) This section reflects the appellant court's inherent power to issue orders during the course of appeal regarding release pending appeal, appointment of counsel, referral to the trial court for an evidentiary hearing, and any other appropriate matter.

RULE 31.17 (B) Section (b) is meant to encompass the powers granted by Ariz. Rev. Stat. Ann. §§ 13-1716 and 13-1717 (1956) and includes affirming, reversing or modifying the judgment, correcting or reducing sentence and affirming, modifying, or vacating any order made by the lower court, including but not limited to those concerning new trials, arrest of judgment, or dismissal of the indictment or information. The appellate court may, in addition, remand a case for a new trial, and take any other action that appears just and proper under the circumstances. Cf. Ariz. R. Juv. Ct. P. 27.

RULE 31.17 (C) The provision alters the language of Ariz. Sup. Ct. R. 22 (d) so as to provide for the automatic appeal from a sentence of death. See comment to Rule 31.2 (b).

RULE 31.17 (D) This rule is based on N.Y. Crim. Pro. L. § 470.15 (2) (a) (McKinney 1971) and follows an already established Arizona procedure. See Ariz. Rev. Stat. Ann. § 13-1716 (1956) (power to modify judgment); State v. Hunter, 102 Ariz. 472, 433 P.2d 22 (1967); State v. Rowland, 12 Ariz. App. 437, 471 P.2d 322 (1970). When the appellate court concludes that modification is appropriate under this rule, it is to remand the case to the trial court for resentencing.

RULE 31.17 (E) Summary opinions are opinions in the form previously used by the supreme court for per curiam denials of writs of habeas corpus, e.g., Pina v. State, 100 Ariz. 47, 410 P.2d 658 (1966); Leonard v. State, 101 Ariz. 42, 415 P.2d 570 (1966). They are limited to those cases in which the issues presented have been clearly decided in past opinions. A similar but broader rule has been adopted by the United States Court of Appeals for the District of Columbia Circuit. See D.C. Cir. R. 13 (c). Ariz. Const. art. 6, § 2 (Cum. Supp. 1972) and Ariz. Rev. Stat. Ann. 12-120.17(A) (Cum. Supp. 1972) require that appellate decisions "be in writing and [have] the grounds stated," but do not demand a full exposition of the facts of the case or of the reasoning supporting the decision.

ARCrP Rule 31.19. Petition for review
a. Time for filing; cross-petition. -- Within 30 days after the filing of a decision or within 15 days after the clerk has mailed notice of the determination of a motion for reconsideration, any party may file with the clerk of the Court of Appeals a petition for review by the Supreme Court. A cross-petition for review may be filed with the clerk of the Supreme Court within 15 days after service of a petition for review.

b. Priority of motion for reconsideration. -- In the event of the timely filing of a petition for review prior to the disposition of a motion for reconsideration, further proceedings relating to the petition or cross-petition for review shall be stayed until the clerk of the Court of Appeals has mailed notice of the court's ruling on the motion for reconsideration.

If a motion for reconsideration is granted, proceedings relating to the petition or cross-petition for review shall be further stayed until the clerk of the Court of Appeals has mailed notice of the court's ruling on any motion for reconsideration

338

of the decision upon reconsideration, or until the time for filing a motion for reconsideration of such decision upon reconsideration has expired. In the event a petition or cross-petition has become moot by reason of the granting of a motion for reconsideration, the petitioner or cross-petitioner shall give immediate written notice of such mootness to the clerk of the Court of Appeals prior to the transmittal of the partial record to the clerk of the Supreme Court as provided in Rule 31.19(d).

c. Form, length and contents. -- The petition and cross-petition for review shall be bound or fastened and shall comply with Rule 31.12. An original and seven copies of the petition or cross-petition and an original and two copies of any separately bound or fastened appendices shall be filed. The parties shall be designated as in the Court of Appeals. Except by permission of the court (1) a petition for review prepared in a proportionately spaced typeface may not exceed 3500 words and may not have an average of more than 280 words per page, including footnotes and quotations; (2) a petition for review prepared in a monospaced typeface may not exceed 10 pages and may not have an average of more than 350 words per page including footnotes and quotations; and (3) a handwritten petition for review may not exceed 12 pages. The petition shall be accompanied by a certificate of compliance that states either (1) that the petition for review uses a proportionately spaced typeface of 14 points or more, is double spaced using a roman font and contains [blank] words, or (2) that the petition for review uses a monospaced typeface of no more than 10.5 characters per inch and does not exceed 10 pages or (3) that the petition for review was handwritten and does not exceed 12 pages. A party preparing this certificate may rely on the word count of the processing system used to prepare the petition for review.

A copy of the Court of Appeals' decision shall be attached to the petition. Where the Court of Appeals' decision is simply an order declining to accept jurisdiction of a special action, a copy of the Superior Court's decision from which the petition for special action was taken shall also be attached to the petition. The petition shall contain concise statements of the following:

> 1) The issues which were decided by the Court of Appeals and that the petitioner wishes to present to the Supreme Court for review. The petitioner

shall also list, separately and without argument, those additional issues which were presented to, but not decided by, the Court of Appeals and which may need to be decided if review is granted.

2) The facts material to a consideration of the issues presented to the Supreme Court for review with appropriate references to the record on appeal. No evidentiary matter shall be included unless material to a proper consideration of the issues presented, in which instance a reference shall be made to the record or page of the transcript where such evidence appears.

3) The reasons the petition should be granted, which may include, among others, the fact that no Arizona decision controls the point of law in question, that a decision of the Supreme Court should be overruled or qualified, that conflicting decisions have been rendered by the Court of Appeals, or that important issues of law have been incorrectly decided. If there are documents in the record on appeal that are necessary for a determination of the issues raised by the petition or cross-petition, the petitioner and cross-petitioner shall file, simultaneously with a copy of the petition and cross-petition, an appendix consisting only of such documents. If the appendices exceed 15 pages in length, such appendices shall be bound or fastened together separately from the petition and the copy of the Appeals Court's decision or the cross-petition.

Any petition for review presented for filing that does not substantially comply with this rule may, in the discretion of the clerk of the appellate court, be returned to the petitioner by the clerk with written instructions to the petitioner to file a proper petition within 30 days from the date on which the written instructions are mailed to the petitioner.

d. Transmittal of partial record upon filing of a petition for review. -- Upon the filing of a petition for review, the clerk of the Court of Appeals shall transmit to the clerk of the Supreme Court the original and all copies of the petition, the original and all copies of the briefs filed in the Court of Appeals, and one copy of the decision of the Court of Appeals.

e. Service and response. -- The petitioner and cross-petitioner shall serve a copy of the petition and cross-petition and any appendices on all parties who have appeared in the Court of Appeals. Any party wishing to oppose the petition or cross-petition may file with the clerk of the Supreme Court a response within 30 days from the date upon which the petition or cross-petition for review is served. The response and any appendices shall comply with form, length, and number of copy requirements of Rule 31.19(c). If there are documents in the record on appeal that are necessary for a determination of the issues raised by the petition or cross-petition, the respondent shall file, simultaneously with a copy of the response, an appendix consisting only of such documents which were not included in the appendix filed with the petition or cross-petition. If the appendices exceed 15 pages in length such appendices shall be bound or fastened together separately from the response. Failure to file a response shall not be considered an admission that the petition should be granted.

If a response is filed, the response shall list, separately and without argument, those additional issues, if any, were presented to, but not decided by, the Court of Appeals, that were not listed by the petitioner, and that may need to be decided if review is granted. No reply shall be filed by petitioner unless the Court has so directed by specific order, in which event a reply may be filed within the time set by the Court.

f. Order granting review. -- If the Supreme Court grants review, its order shall specify the issue or issues which are to be reviewed. The Supreme Court may order that the parties file additional briefs or that oral argument be heard, or both. If the order granting review does not provide for supplementation of briefs or for oral argument, either party may, within 15 days after the clerk mails notice of the Court's order, request the Court to do so by motion, specifying reasons for supplementation or for oral argument, or both.

g. Transmittal of remaining record. -- Upon notification by the clerk of the Supreme Court that a petition or cross-petition for review has been granted, the clerk of the Court of Appeals shall transmit the remaining record on appeal to the clerk of the Supreme Court.

h. Denial of petition. -- When all petitions and cross-petitions for review have been denied, the clerk of the Supreme Court shall so notify the clerk of the Court of

Appeals and the parties, and return the briefs and the petition or cross-petition for review to the clerk of the Court of Appeals.

i. Dispositions

1) If an appeal is resolved by agreement of the parties after a petition for review by the Supreme Court is filed, the Supreme Court may order that the decision of the Court of Appeals be vacated, or that any opinion of the Court of Appeals be re-designated as a Memorandum Decision.

2) When a review has been granted, the Supreme Court may remand the appeal to the Court of Appeals for reconsideration in light of authority identified in the Supreme Court's order.

3) If issues were raised in, but not decided by, the Court of Appeals and review has been granted, the Supreme Court may consider and decide such issues, may remand the appeal to the Court of Appeals for decision of such issues, or may make such other disposition with respect to such issues as it deems appropriate.

j. Motions to extend time. -- The court of appeals shall have authority to grant or deny motions to extend time to file motions for reconsideration of its decisions or opinions or to extend the time to file a petition for review. These motions shall be filed in the court of appeals.

k. Amicus curiae. -- The Supreme Court may permit participation by amicus curiae as provided for in Rule 31.25 of these rules.

HISTORY: Amended May 24, 1983, effective Sept. 1, 1983; amended Sept. 15, 1987, effective Nov. 15, 1987; amended May 24, 1989, effective Aug. 1, 1989; amended Mar. 28, 1990, effective July 1, 1990; amended Sept. 25, 1990, nunc pro tunc effective Aug. 1,1989; amended Mar. 1, 1994, effective Apr. 1, 1994; amended Apr. 26, 1994, effective June 1, 1994; amended June 10, 1997, effective January 1, 1998; amended Oct. 6, 1998, effective Dec. 1, 1998; amended effective Oct. 12, 2005; amended by R-07-0014 and R-07-0025 Sept. 16, 2008, effective Jan. 1, 2009.

NOTES:

COMMITTEE COMMENT TO THE 1997 AMENDMENTS
The page limit for a petition for review has been changed from 20 pages to 12 pages. The format of a petition for review has been changed to avoid any need to provide a synopsis of the decision below. The appendices no longer have to include every record item referred to in the petition or response. While only record items necessary for a determination of the issues identified in the petition need to be included in the appendix, any factual statement still must refer to a record item so the opposing party and the court can easily locate that portion of the record and ensure that the factual statement is accurate. Any documents filed after the petition are now to be filed with the Supreme Court, not the Court of Appeals, thus speeding up the process of considering the petition. Finally, only an original and two copies of any separate appendices must be filed, as opposed to an original and six copies under the prior rule.

NOTE TO 1989 AMENDMENTS
Notwithstanding any statements to the contrary in the Supreme Court's Supplemental Opinion in State v. Ikirt, 160 Ariz. 113, 770 P.2d 1159 (January 17, 1989), the separate listing, in the petition or a cross-petition for review, or the response thereto, of issues presented to, but not decided by, the Court of Appeals, as required by Rules 23(c) and (e), as amended, shall be sufficient to preserve such issues for review and disposition by the Supreme Court, if necessary.

[1983 AMENDMENT]
[(c)4.] The 1983 amendments to Rule 31.19 contemplate that review will not be sought as a matter of course. Review procedure is intended for those cases in which there is a tenable claim involving substantial issues of law or procedure, or in which serious injustice is claimed to have occurred.

No attempt should be made to include the entire record in the appendix. Where it is necessary for the court to review large portions of the record, a motion should be filed requesting transmittal of the entire record rather than including the entire record as part of the appendix. However, it is contemplated that most issues such as sufficiency of the evidence or lack of competent counsel could ordinarily be supported by summary or by reference to limited portions of the record included in the appendix rather than by the whole record.

[(h)] Note that a response to a petition for review or cross-petition for review should not be filed in the Supreme Court until the time for filing a motion for reconsideration has expired and the Court of Appeals has disposed of any pending motion for reconsideration. Note also that Rule 31.19(b) extends the time for the filing of such responses.

[1973 PROMULGATION]

This provision alters Ariz. Sup. Ct. R. 47 (b) by reducing the period in which to file a petition from 15 to 5 days, and by eliminating the necessity of filing additional copies of the pleadings. Provisions for filing and service are contained in Rule 31.21. The 1983 amendments to Rule 31.19 contemplate that review will not be sought as a matter of course. Review procedure is intended for those cases in which there is tenable claim involving substantial issues of law or procedure, or in which serious injustice is claimed to have occurred.

No attempt should be made to include the entire record in the appendix. Where it is necessary for the court to review large portions of the record, a motion should be filed requesting transmittal of the entire record rather than including the entire record as part of the appendix. However, it is contemplated that most issues such a sufficiency of the evidence or lack of competent counsel could ordinarily be supported by summary or by reference to limited portions of the record included in the appendix rather than by the whole record.

NOTE TO 1989 AMENDMENTS

Notwithstanding any statements to the contrary in the Supreme Court's Supplemental Opinion in State v. Ikirt, 160 Ariz. 113, 770 P.2d 1159 (January 17, 1989), the separate listing, in the petition or a cross-petition for review, or the response thereto, of issues presented to, but not decided by, the Court of Appeals, as required by Rules 23(c) and (e), as amended, shall be sufficient to preserve such issues for review and disposition by the Supreme Court, if necessary.

COMMITTEE COMMENT TO THE 1997 AMENDMENTS

The page limit for a petition for review has been changed from 20 pages to 12 pages. The format of a petition for review has been changed to avoid any need to provide a synopsis of the decision below. The appendices no longer have to include every record item referred to in the petition or response. While only record items necessary for a determination of the issues identified in the petition need to be included in the appendix, any factual statement still must refer to a record item so the opposing party and the court can easily locate that portion of the record and ensure that the factual statement is accurate. Any documents filed after the petition are now to be filed with the Supreme Court, not the Court of Appeals, thus speeding up the process of considering the petition. Finally, only an original and two copies of any separate appendices must be filed, as opposed to an original and six copies under the prior rule.

JUDICIAL DECISIONS
ANALYSIS

IN GENERAL

The Supreme Court is not required to accept petitions for review in any case. State v. Sandon, 161 Ariz. 157, 777 P.2d 220 (1989).

CONSTRUCTION

Other than an appeal pursuant to this section, there is nothing in either the Rules of Criminal Procedure or the Superior Court Rules of Appellate Procedure -- Criminal which authorizes the court of appeals to review a final judgment of the superior court. State v. Aguilar, 170 Ariz. 292, 823 P.2d 1300 (Ct. App. 1991).

EXHAUSTION OF APPEALS

In cases other than those carrying a life sentence or the death penalty, a decision by the court of appeals and its search for error exhausts a defendant's right of appeal in this jurisdiction; thus, when the court of appeals' decision has been rendered, the attorney should advise the defendant about his legal rights, but the attorney has no obligation to seek further relief through the appellate process. State v. Shattuck, 140 Ariz. 582, 684 P.2d 154 (1984).

ILLUSTRATIVE CASES

In light of the importance of the issue and the uncertainty of the law on the point, the Supreme Court granted review of rape defendant's claim regarding admission of police expert's testimony about the odds of a random match between defendant's DNA and DNA extracted from semen stains at the scene of the crime. State v. Johnson, 186 Ariz. 329, 922 P.2d 294 (1996).

JURISDICTION

To permit a petitioner to file a petition for review in the court of appeals from a case that originated in city court would impermissibly enlarge Rule 32 jurisdiction. State v. Aguilar, 170 Ariz. 292, 823 P.2d 1300 (Ct. App. 1991).

NO GROUNDS FOR APPEAL

If defendant's counsel has conscientiously searched the record for error and has found no meritorious grounds for appeal in the first instance, then counsel should not bring the case to the Supreme Court by petitioning for review. State v. Shattuck, 140 Ariz. 582, 684 P.2d 154 (1984).

PETITION

A rule 31.19 petition for review is the pleading the parties file to engage Supreme Court review of a court of appeals decision. This rule specifically only encompasses review by the supreme court from a court of appeals decision; it does not cover review of a lower court decision by the court of appeals. State v. Aguilar, 170 Ariz. 292, 823 P.2d 1300 (Ct. App. 1991).

PROCEDURE

District court found that the U.S. Court of Appeals for the Ninth Circuit's decision in Insyxiengmay v. Morgan, which held that a prisoner's claims were sufficiently presented to the Washington Supreme Court, although not argued in the prisoner's petition for review, because the original petition was attached and contained the federal grounds for each claim, did not apply to claims which an Arizona inmate made in his petition for post-conviction relief because it was based on Washington law, and the Arizona Rules of Criminal Procedure were different. Detrich v. Schriro, -- F. Supp. 2d --, 2005 U.S. Dist. LEXIS 30292 (D. Ariz. November 29, 2005).

Although a defendant has the right to an appeal in a criminal case, the appeal must be properly initiated by presenting a record on appeal which contains the material to which objection is made and by raising and arguing the issue relied upon in the appeal. State v. Ikirt, 160 Ariz. 113, 770 P.2d 1159, cert. denied, 493 U.S. 872, 110 S. Ct. 202, 107 L. Ed. 2d 156 (1989).

RIGHT OF APPEAL

Once the defendant has been given the appeal to which he has a right, state remedies have been exhausted. State v. Sandon, 161 Ariz. 157, 777 P.2d 220 (1989).

ARCrP Rule 31.22. Supplemental citation of legal authority

When pertinent and significant authorities come to the attention of a party after the party's brief has been filed, or after oral argument but before decision, a party may supplement the citation of legal authority previously presented in that party's appeal brief or briefs by filing with the appellate court a list of supplemental citations of legal authority. If filed less than 5 days before oral argument, a list shall not be assured of consideration by the court at oral argument unless good cause is shown for a later filing; provided, however, that no supplemental citation of legal authority shall be rejected for filing on the grounds that it was filed less than 5 days before oral argument. The list of supplemental citations shall clearly identify by page number which portion or portions of the party's appeal brief is intended to be supplemented thereby, and the relevant page or pages of the supplemental authority, and shall further state concisely and without argument the legal proposition for which each supplemental authority is cited. This list shall be typewritten in pica type and double spaced on 8.5 by 11 inch white, opaque, unglazed paper. The list shall contain a caption setting forth the name of the Court, the title of the case, the case number and a brief descriptive title.

HISTORY: Added Jan. 14, 1991, effective Jan. 14, 1991.

ARCrP Rule 31.23. Issuance of mandates by appellate courts and mandates from United States Supreme Court.

a. Mandates by appellate courts.

1) If there has been no motion for reconsideration and no petition for review filed, the clerk of the Court of Appeals shall issue the mandate at the expiration of the time for the filing of such motion or petition.

2) If a motion for reconsideration has been filed, the mandate shall not issue until the motion has been disposed of and until the expiration of the time provided by Rule 31.19 for the filing of a petition for review.

3) If a petition for review is filed, the clerk of the Court of Appeals shall not issue a mandate until 15 days after the receipt by the clerk of the Court of Appeals of an order of the Supreme Court denying the petition for review.

4) When the Supreme Court has filed any decision which requires the issuance of a mandate, the clerk of the Supreme Court shall not issue the mandate until 15 days after the filing of the decision, or if a motion for reconsideration has been filed, 15 days after the motion is disposed of.

5) Any exhibits or other objects transmitted as originals by the clerk of the superior court to the appellate court pursuant to Rule 31.8 shall be returned with the mandate to the clerk of the appropriate court or agency. The papers, exhibits, minute entries or other objects which were transmitted as certified copies to the appellate court may be returned with the mandate to the clerk of the appropriate court or agency, or destroyed after issuance of the mandate pursuant to rule or administrative order of the appellate court.

b. Stay of mandate pending application for certiorari.

1) Automatic stay in capital cases affirming death sentence. -- The clerk of the Supreme Court shall issue the mandate in capital cases when the time for filing a petition for writ of certiorari in the United States Supreme Court from the decision affirming the defendant's conviction and sentence on direct appeal has expired, or, in a case in which a petition for writ of certiorari has actually been filed, when the clerk of the Supreme Court is notified by the United States Supreme Court that the petition has been

denied. The filing of a petition for rehearing of the denial of a petition for writ of certiorari shall not delay the issuance of the mandate.

2) In all other cases.

i. A stay of the issuance of the mandate of either the Court of Appeals or the Arizona Supreme Court pending application to the United State Supreme Court for a writ of Certiorari may be granted upon request.

ii. An application for a stay of the issuance of a mandate of the Arizona Supreme Court may be filed with the clerk of the Arizona Supreme Court within 15 days after the filing of the court's opinion, memorandum decision or order denying a motion for reconsideration.

iii. An application for a stay of the issuance of a mandate of the Court of Appeals may be filed with the clerk of the Court of Appeals within 15 days after an order of the Supreme Court denying a petition for review, or in any other situation requiring the Court of Appeals to issue a mandate.

iv. The stay shall not exceed 90 days unless the period is extended for cause shown. If, during the period of the stay, there is filed with the clerk of the appropriate court a notice that the party who has obtained the stay has filed a petition for a writ of certiorari, the stay shall continue until the clerk is notified by the United States Supreme Court that the writ has been denied or, in a case in which the writ has been granted, that a mandate has been issued by the United States Supreme Court.

c. Mandates from United States Supreme Court. -- Upon receipt of a mandate by the clerk of the appellate court from the Supreme Court of the United States in any action brought to the appellate court on appeal and taken from the appellate court by appeal or writ of error or certiorari to the Supreme Court of the United States, the clerk shall forthwith issue under the clerk's hand and the seal of the appellate court a remittitur to the superior court of the county in which the original judgment was rendered, commanding such court to take such action in the premises as is proper under the mandate.

HISTORY: Added Feb. 24, 1994, effective June 1, 1994.

ARCrP Rule 31.25. Amicus curiae.

a. Filing and form of brief; participation in oral argument. -- A brief of an amicus curiae may be filed only if accompanied by written consent of all parties or by leave of court granted upon motion. The brief shall be lodged with the motion, if any. The motion for leave shall identify the interest of the applicant, state that the applicant has read the relevant brief, petition or motion and shall state the reasons accepting applicant's amicus curiae brief would be desirable. A party desiring to respond to the amicus brief shall file the response within 20 days of service of a brief filed with consent, or within 20 days of the Court's order granting a motion for leave to file an amicus brief. Rules 31.13, Arizona Rules of Criminal Procedure, shall govern the form of an amicus brief, except that it shall not exceed 12,000 words in length if done in proportionately spaced typeface, or 35 pages if done in monospaced typeface, unless otherwise permitted by the court. An amicus curiae may participate in the oral argument only by leave of the appellate court.

b. Time and length limits applicable to amicus briefs in the Supreme Court. -- Parties desiring to file an amicus curiae brief shall file such briefs as provided by this rule, except that an amicus curiae brief relating to a special action petition shall be filed as expeditiously as possible after the special action petition is filed, as provided for in Rule 7(g), Rules of Procedure for Special Actions.

> 1) Briefs filed prior to a decision by the Court to grant review. -- Unless otherwise ordered by the Court, an amicus brief in support of a petition for review or a response to a petition for review accompanied by written consent of all parties, or a motion for leave to file the brief shall be filed no later than 21 days after the filing of the response to the petition for review. Such briefs shall comply with the form and length requirements of Rule 31.19(c) exclusive of any appendix.
>
> 2) Briefs filed after the Court has granted review. -- After the Court has granted review, and unless otherwise ordered, an amicus brief accompanied by written consent of all parties, or a motion for leave to file an amicus brief, shall be filed no later than 10 days after the date ordered by the Court at the time review was granted for filing supplemental briefing by the parties in the particular case. Such briefs shall comply with rule 31.13 and shall not exceed the page limitation imposed for the parties' supplemental briefs.

3) Responses to amicus curiae briefs. -- A party wishing to respond to an amicus brief shall file the response within 20 days of service of a brief filed with consent, or within 20 days of the Court's order granting a motion for leave to file an amicus brief. The response shall comply with the page and formatting requirements imposed on the particular amicus brief to which it relates.

4) Late-filed briefs and responses. -- Leave for filing a late amicus or response brief shall be granted only for good cause shown.

HISTORY: Added Oct. 6, 1998, effective Dec. 1, 1998; amended by R-07-0014 and R-07-0025 Sept. 16, 2008, effective Jan. 1, 2009.

NOTES:

COMMENT TO THE 1998 AMENDMENTS

Although the 1998 amendments to Rule 31.25 permit amicus briefs to be filed without leave of court with consent of all parties, amicus curiae should keep in mind the purpose of an amicus brief. As the name implies, an amicus curiae brief should assist the Court, not advocate a particular litigant's case. Ideally, it should not duplicate the briefs of the parties, nor merely extend the length of a litigant's brief. Rather, it should provide a broader, more abstract presentation of law that is not narrowly tied to the facts of the case. It should provide background and context for the Court's decision. Amicus briefs should normally be allowed when a party is not represented competently or is not represented at all, when the amicus has an interest in some other case that may be affected by the decision in the present case, or when the amicus can provide information, perspective, or argument that can help the Court beyond the help that the lawyers for the parties have provided.

Additionally, an amicus brief should clearly identify the group or organization sponsoring the brief and the interest of the sponsoring entity in the outcome of the appeal. Counsel for a party should not be permitted to write the amicus brief in whole or in part.

ARCrP Rule 31.27. Extensions of time; notification of victim

In any capital case, if the victim has filed a notice of appearance as specified in A.R.S. § 13-4042, a party seeking an extension of time to file a brief must provide notice of the request to the victim. Notice shall be provided through the prosecutor's office handling the appellate proceeding, unless the victim specifies a different method in the notice of appearance. The victim may specify in the notice of appearance whether notification should be served directly on the victim or on another person, including the prosecutor, and whether service may be made electronically, by telephone, or by regular mail. If the victim has requested direct notification, the party seeking an extension of time shall serve notice on the victim within 24 hours of filing the extension request. If the prosecutor has the duty to notify the victim on behalf of the defendant, the prosecutor shall serve notice within 24 hours of receipt of the extension request. Service shall be made in the manner specified in the notice of appearance, or if no method is specified, by regular mail. In ruling on any request for an extension of a time limit set in this rule, the court shall consider the rights of the defendant and any victim to prompt and final conclusion of the case.

HISTORY: Added Jan. 30, 2002, effective June 1, 2002; adopted as modified by R-06-0012, effective Sept. 11, 2006.

NOTES:

COMMENT

To implement the victim's right to a prompt and final conclusion of the case, see Ariz. Const. Art. 2, § 2.1(A)(10), the victim shall be permitted to file a statement with the court, at the inception of the proceeding, which expresses his or her views with respect to any extensions; or the victim can request, pursuant to A.R.S. § 13-4411, that the prosecutor's office communicate the victim's views to the court concerning any extensions.

ARCrP Rule 32.6(b), (c)

Defense is given 15 days to file response. The court has 20 days after defendant's reply [is] due to determine whether an evidentiary hearing is required.

ARC Rule 8.2. Time limits

a. General. -- Subject to the provisions of Rule 8.4, every person against whom an indictment, information or complaint is filed shall be tried by the court having jurisdiction of the offense within the following time periods:

> 1) Defendants in custody. -- 150 days from arraignment if the person is held in custody, except as provided in subsection (a), paragraph (3) of this section.
>
> 2) Defendants released from custody. -- 180 days from arraignment if the person is released under Rule 7, except as provided in subsection (a), paragraph (3) of this section.
>
> 3) Complex cases. -- 270 days from arraignment if the person is charged with any of the following:
>
>> i. First degree murder, except as provided in paragraph (a)(4) of this rule;
>>
>> ii. Offenses that will require the court to consider evidence obtained as the result of an order permitting the interception of wire, electronic or oral communication;
>>
>> iii. Any complex cases as determined by a written factual finding by the court.
>
> 4) Capital Cases. -- Eighteen months from arraignment, if the state files a notice of intent to seek the death penalty.

b. Waiver of appearance at arraignment. -- If a person has waived an appearance at arraignment pursuant to Rule 14.2, the date of the arraignment held without the defendant's presence shall be considered the arraignment date for purposes of subsection (a), paragraphs (1), (2), (3), and (4) of this rule.

c. New trial. -- A trial ordered after a mistrial or upon a motion for a new trial shall commence within 60 days of the entry of the order of the court. A trial ordered upon the reversal of a judgment by an appellate court shall commence within 90 days of the service of the mandate of the Appellate Court.

d. Extension of time limits. -- These time limits may be extended pursuant to Rule 8.5. 5. Trial dates. -- In all superior court cases except those in which Rule 8 has been suspended pursuant to Rule 8.1(e), the court shall, either at the time of arraignment in superior court or at a pretrial conference, set a trial date for time certain.

ARS 12-541 Statute Of Limitations For Civil Suits

Malicious prosecution; false imprisonment; libel or slander; seduction or breach of promise of marriage; breach of employment contract; wrongful termination; liability created by statute; one year limitation

1. There shall be commenced and prosecuted within one year after the cause of action accrues, and not afterward, the following actions:

2. For malicious prosecution, or for false imprisonment, or for injuries done to the character or reputation of another by libel or slander.

3. For damages for seduction or breach of promise of marriage.

4. For breach of an oral or written employment contract including contract actions based on employee handbooks or policy manuals that do not specify a time period in which to bring an action.

5. For damages for wrongful termination.

6. Upon a liability created by statute, other than a penalty or forfeiture.

Snyder v. Donato, 211 Ariz. 117

Accordingly, we accept jurisdiction and grant relief from the order designating this as a complex case. A "complex case" is a case so complicated, by virtue of its nature or because of the evidence required that the ordinary limits for the time to trial are insufficient and must be extended so as to afford the party more time to prepare in order to fairly and fully present its case. Because this is not a "complex case," we grant relief from the court's order. Our holding, however, does not preclude the court from granting a continuance on the basis of another rule if it properly finds that the circumstances justify it.

Transcripts

<u>Hardy v. US</u>, 375 U.S. 277, 84 S.Ct. 424, 11 L.Ed.2d 331 (1964)

<u>Douglas v. California</u>, 372 U.S. 353, 361 (1963)

<u>Griffin v. Illinois</u>, 351 U.S. 12, 34, 35 (1956)

On direct appeal, if you're determined to be indigent, you would be entitled to transcripts of the entire trial proceedings. (Note: The free transcripts that you are entitled to will be given to your attorney when counsel is appointed. This case law does not entitle you to your own personal copy, but once he is done with his part, the entire file must be turned over to defendant upon request which includes any and all transcripts.)

<u>Ex Parte Perales</u>, 215 S.W.3d 418

The Court of Criminal Appeals, Johnson, J., held that the record supported habeas court's determination that no evidence supported conviction. Relief granted.

<u>State v. Tomlinson</u>, 121 Ariz. 313

Presumption was that defendant needed transcript of first trial for effective defense. State failed to carry burden of establishing contrary because it did not prove that defendant had alternative available that was equivalent to trial transcript.

Uncontested Affidavit

<u>Melorich Builders v. Superior Ct. San Bernardino Co. (Serabia)</u>, 207 Cal. Rptr. 47 (Cal. App.4 Dist. 1984)
Uncontested affidavit taken as true in opposition to summary judgment.

<u>Morris v. NCR</u>, 44 SW2d 433
An affidavit if not contested in a timely manner is considered undisputed facts as a matter of law.

<u>Seltzer v. Seltzer</u>, 80 Cal. Rptr.
Uncontested affidavit taken as true in support of summary judgment.

<u>State v. Jackson</u>, 170 Ariz 89, 821 P.2d 1374, 1991 Ariz. App. LEXIS 394, 103 Ariz. Adv. Rep.6
<u>State v. Linsey</u>, 149 Ariz. 472, 720 P.2d 73 (1986)
Disposition: Affirmed HN 4 expert testimony. One expert can testify concerning the behavioral characteristics of victim of child abuse, and expert cannot testify about the accuracy, reliability or trustfulness of the victim in the case before the jury, or quantity of the percentage of victims who are truthful.

<u>U.S. v. Henderson</u>, 409 F.3d 1293 (11th Cir. 2005)
Essential difference between expert and lay witnesses is expert's ability to answer hypothetical questions.

<u>U.S. v. Pruden</u>, 424 F.2d 1021 (1970)
Silence can only be equated with fraud where there is a legal or moral duty to respond or where an inquiry left unanswered would be intentionally misleading.

Verdict

Blacks Law Dictionary: Compromise verdict. A verdict is reached when jurors, to avoid a deadlock, concede some issues so that other issues will be resolved as they went.

Defective verdict. A verdict on which a judgment cannot be based because of irregularities or legal inadequacies.

Legally inconsistent verdict. A verdict in which the same elements are found to exist and not to exist, as when a defendant is acquitted of one offense and convicted for another, even though the offenses arise from the same set of facts and an element of the second offense requires proof that the first offense has been committed. Arizona vigorously supports inconsistent verdicts because they keep people in prison.

Partial verdict. A verdict by which the jury finds a criminal defendant not guilty of some charges and guilty of others.

Repugnant verdict. A verdict that contradicts itself in that the defendant is convicted and acquitted of different crime having identical elements.

Witnesses

ARS 13-1407 Defenses (1998 version)

Evidence of reputation or prior acts to demonstrate the unchastity of the victim and a sexual assault prosecution is inadmissible, except if the defendant can show that the victim has made unsubstantiated charges of rape in the past. See: State v. Superior Court, 154 Ariz. 624, 744 P. 2d 725 (Ct. App. 1987)

Cummings v. Malone, 995 F.2d 817 (8th Cir. 1993)

Ability to introduce specific prior crime is not a license to flaunt its details; cross-examiners are limited to eliciting the name, date and disposition of felony committed.

Francis v. Clark Equipment Co., 993 F.2d 545 (6th Cir. 1993)

Refusal to permit cross-examination of witness concerning matters testified to on direct examination constitutes prejudicial error.

G.L.J. Note page 1605, 1606 (1994)

Many children have trouble distinguishing fact from fiction and are willing to lie if they are rewarded for telling such stories.

Harris v. White, 745 F.2d 523 (8th Cir. 1984)

The Sixth Amendment establishes the right of a defendant to require the presence of a witness at trial and implies a reciprocal right for the government.

Hubbard v. US, 514 US 131 L.Ed.2d 779, 115 S.Ct. (1995)

Federal court held to be neither department nor agency within meaning of 18 USCS §1001, proscribing false statements made in matter within jurisdiction of federal department or agency.

Kopf v. Skyum, 993 F.2d 374 (4th Cir. 1993)

Person may qualify to render expert testimony in any one of five ways listed in rules governing admissibility of expert testimony; knowledge, skill, experience, training or education.

Mesareosh v. US, 352 US 1, 1 L.Ed.2d 1, 77 S.Ct. 1 (1956)
Truthfulness of testimony... "The dignity of the United States Government will not permit the conviction of any person on tainted testimony.

Murray v. Carrier, 477 U.S. 478, 106 S.Ct. 2639
Respondent was convicted by a jury in a Virginia state court of rape and abduction. The trial judge denied respondent's counsel's pretrial motion to discover the victim's statements to police describing her assailants, their vehicle, and the location of the alleged rape. Without consulting respondent, counsel filed a petition for appeal that failed to include any claim that the trial judge erred in not permitting counsel to examine the victim's statements, notwithstanding a Virginia Supreme Court Rule providing that only errors assigned in the petition for appeal will be noticed and that no error not so assigned will be admitted as a ground for reversal. The Supreme Court, Justice O'Connor, held that petition for habeas review of procedurally defaulted discovery claim was subject to dismissal for failure to establish cause for default. Reversed and remanded.

Starkins v. Bateman, 150 Ariz. 537, 724 P.2d 1206 (Ct. App. 1986)
Witnesses have a right to testify about their opinions concerning the mental condition of a party.

State v. Castro, No. 1 CA-CR 12318, Court of Appeals of Arizona, Division One, Department D, 163 Ariz. 465; 788 P.2d 1216; 1989 Ariz. App. LEXIS 321; 48 Ariz. Adv. Rep. 34, November 24, 1989 , Reconsideration Denied January 24, 1990. Review Denied April 17, 1990. Reversed and Remanded.
The trial court violated defendant's right to confrontation when it precluded defendant from cross-examining victim regarding medical emergency resulting from her self-induced abortion or miscarriage, which prompted her to accuse defendant of rape.

State v. Hopkins, 1 CA-CR 91-1576, COURT OF APPEALS OF ARIZONA, DIVISION ONE, DEPARTMENT E, 177 Ariz. 161; 866 P.2d 143; 1993 Ariz. App. LEXIS 194; 147 Ariz. Adv. Rep. 59, September 9, 1993, Filed , Petition for Review DENIED on February 1, 1994 by Arizona Supreme Court No. CR-93-0525-PR. REVERSED AND REMANDED.

Defendant could obtain reversal of his conviction for sexual abuse of minor and child molestation; trial court's admittance of evidence of emotional propensity to molest based on acts as remote in time as 10 years required reliable medical testimony.

State v. Hummer, 184 Ariz. 603, 911 P.2d 609 (Ct. App. 1995)
Expert testimony is appropriate when the trier of fact cannot understand the evidence or determine a fact in issue without specialized knowledge.

State v. Hummert, 188 Ariz. 119
This case is unlike Bible and Johnson because it involves a qualitative, not quantitative, description of the significance of a match. The experts in this case testified that they had never seen two samples from unrelated donors that matched over three probes, that the possibility of a random match was "rare," and that DNA can "uniquely identify" a person. These conclusions [***32] were based upon their own scientific experience. Neither expert relied upon a controversial scientific principle. I agree with the court, therefore, that Frye is not applicable. The experts' opinions concerning the "uniqueness of DNA" and their personal experience are admissible under Rule 702, Ariz. R. Evid. The data supporting their opinions are admissible under Rule 703, Ariz. R. Evid. We are judges, not scientists. It is enough for us to be able to identify the legitimacy of a principle and its proponents so as to exclude junk science. Qualitative descriptions of the significance of a match are admissible.

State v. Martin, No. 1 CA-CR 5542, Court of Appeals of Arizona, Division One, Department B, 135 Ariz. 556; 663 P.2d 240; 1982 Ariz. App. LEXIS 685, September 23, 1982 , Review Granted December 7, 1982. Reversed and remanded. Judgment reversed, 663 P.2d 236 Defendant's child molestation conviction was reversed because the trial court improperly admitted prior consistent statements of the 11-year-old victim that were made after defendant married her mother, when she had a motive to falsify her story.

State v. Moran, No. 6753-PR, Supreme Court of Arizona, 151 Ariz. 378; 728 P.2d 248; 1986 Ariz. LEXIS 300, November 19, 1986. REVERSED AND REMANDED.

It was improper to allow testimony by experts vouching for the credibility of a victim of sexual abuse, and when there was no evidence of the crime other than the victim's statement, the error was prejudicial to defendant.

State v. Ortega, 2008 WL 4571814 (Ariz. App. Div. 2)

Defendant was convicted in the Superior Court, Pima County, No. CR20071579, Nichols, J., of sexual conduct with minor, molestation of child, and threatening and intimidating. Defendant appealed. The Court of Appeals, Vásquez, J., held that: (1) Whether victim was less than 15 years of age was element of sexual conduct with minor; (2) Separate convictions for sexual conduct with minor and child molestation arising from same act violated prohibition against double jeopardy; and (3) Prosecutor was permitted to use transcript of witness' interview with police about alleged threats defendant made against witness to refresh witness' recollection. Conviction and sentence for molestation of child vacated; otherwise affirmed.

State v. Rivera, No. 5953-PR, Supreme Court of Arizona, 139 Ariz. 409; 678 P.2d 1373; 1984 Ariz. LEXIS 196, February 16, 1984 , Reconsideration Denied April 3, 1984. Reversed and remanded Child molestation conviction was reversed. Child's statement to her mother regarding molestation was not excited utterance exception to hearsay where there was no evidence of stress or excitement, and thus, it should not have been admitted at trial.

State v. Roberts, No. 4898, Supreme Court of Arizona, 126 Ariz. 92; 612 P.2d 1055; 1980 Ariz. LEXIS 224, May 19, 1980 , Rehearing Denied June 24, 1980. Reversed and remanded.

Defendant was improperly convicted of child molestation when a trial court denied his motion to invoke the rule on exclusion of witnesses because exclusion was mandatory upon request and prejudicial if not granted.

State v. Salzman, No. 2 CA-CR 2944, Court of Appeals of Arizona, Division Two, 139 Ariz. 521; 679 P.2d 544; 1984 Ariz. App. LEXIS 371, January 12, 1984 , Review Denied April 10, 1984.

The wife's claim of marital privilege did not prevent the state from forcing her to testify against her husband because the privilege did not pertain in a case in which a child's abuse was at issue.

State v. Thompson, 169 Ariz. 471, 820 P.2d 335

Defendant was convicted in the Superior Court, La Paz County, Cause No. CR-86-140, Michael Irwin, J., of sexual conduct with minor, and defendant appealed. The Court of Appeals, 167 Ariz. 230, 805 P.2d 1051, reversed and remanded. The Supreme Court granted review and remanded. The Court of Appeals, McGregor, J., held that: (1) hearsay statements of victim were not admissible under excited utterance exception; (2) videotaped interview of victim was not admissible as statement made for purpose of medical diagnosis or treatment; and (3) erroneous admission of hearsay statements was not harmless. Reversed and remanded.

State v. Tucker, 165 Ariz 340

Dr. Harrison's testimony went beyond what our supreme court has said is permissible. Essentially, he was allowed to testify as to the believability of the victim in violation of Lindsey and Moran. When Dr. Harrison related each of his credibility factors to the specific facts of this case, he was really testifying that the victim was truthful and not lying. His testimony was "nothing more than advice to [the] jurors on how to decide the case." Moran, 151 Ariz. at 383, 728 P.2d at 253. After reviewing the evidence, we cannot say that the errors which occurred in the trial were harmless. It was the victim's word against the defendant's. The physical evidence was inconclusive. We cannot say that, beyond a reasonable doubt, the errors did not affect the verdict. [***31] See Lindsey, 149 Ariz. at 477, 720 P.2d at 78; State v. Allen, 157 Ariz. 165, 755 P.2d 1153 (1988). For the reasons stated herein, the convictions are reversed and the case is remanded for new trial.

State v. Uriarte, 1 CA-CR 97-0351, COURT OF APPEALS OF ARIZONA, DIVISION ONE, DEPARTMENT B, 194 Ariz. 275; 981 P.2d 575; 1998 Ariz. App. LEXIS 149; 276 Ariz. Adv. Rep. 20, August 27, 1998, Filed , Petition for Review Denied on March 23, 1999 by Arizona Supreme Court CR-98-0454-PR. AFFIRMED IN PART; REVERSED AND REMANDED.
Victim of child molestation had a right to her mother's presence at trial even though the mother was to testify and the trial court had ordered that all prospective witnesses be excluded.

State v. Williams, No. 2984, Supreme Court of Arizona, 111 Ariz. 511; 533 P.2d 1146; 1975 Ariz. LEXIS 271, April 10, 1975. Reversed.
Testimony concerning defendant's alleged rape of his sister was inadmissible for impeachment purposes during defendant's trial because the evidence was collateral and irrelevant to the charged offense.

Trammel v. US, 445 US 40, 63 L.Ed.2d 186, 100 S.Ct. 906 (1980)
A spouse can testify against the other party if the marriage is irretrievably broken.

US v. Acker, 52 F.3d 509 (4th Cir. 1995)
Adverse spousal privilege is vested in witness's spouse, who may neither be compelled to testify, nor foreclosed from testifying.

US v. Alonso, 48 F.3d 1536 (9th Cir. 1995)
Expert witness may not state his opinion about defendant's guilt.

US v. Butler, 56 F.3d 941 (8th Cir. 1995) Although leading questions are generally prohibited during direct examination except as necessary to develop witness's testimony, exception to this rule exists when witness is child.

US v. Cooks, 52 F.3d 101 (5th Cir. 1995)
Giglia v. US, 405 US 150, 31 L.Ed.2d 104, 92 S.Ct. 763 (1972)
Napue v. Illinois, 360 US 264, 2 LEM 1217, 79 S.Ct. 1173 (1959)
Where the government fails to disclose evidence of any understanding or agreement as to future prosecution of a key government witness, due process may require reversal of the conviction ... also ... the government has a duty to disclose

such understandings for they directly affect the credibility of the witness. This duty of disclosure is even more important where the witness provides the key testimony against the accused. Importance of and need to safeguard right to cross-examination is enhanced when witness is crucial to prosecution.

US v. DeSalvo, 26 F.3d 1216 (2nd Cir. 1994)
Witness is entitled to claim Fifth Amendment privilege against self-incrimination if testimony might reveal perjury in a prior proceeding.

US v. Fierro, 38 F.3d 761 (5th Cir. 1994)
Prosecution may not comment directly or indirectly on defendant's failure to testify.

US v. Foster, 986 F.2d 541 (D.C. Cir. 1993)
In criminal trial, informer's privilege must give way when information sought is relevant and helpful to defense of accused.

US v. Gecas, 50 F.3d 1549 (11th Cir. 1995)
1. Fifth Amendment privilege against self-incrimination supports two goals: (1) constraining government from overzealous prosecution of individuals and (2) securing individual liberties.
2. Fifth Amendment privilege against self-incrimination is personal right; it is matter of individual dignity.

US v. Jones, 766 F.2d 412 (9th Cir. 1985)
Davis v. Alaska, 415 US 308. 39 LEM 347, 94 S.Ct. 1105 (1974)
Pointer v. Texas, 380 US 400, 13 LEM 923, 85 S.Ct. 1065 (1965)
Violation of the confrontation clause requires reversal unless they are harmless beyond a reasonable doubt.

US v. Kaba, 999 F.2d 47 (2nd Cir. 1993)
US v. Kelly, 953 F.2d 562 (9th Cir. 1992)
Voluntary statement" is one that is the product of rational intellect and free will. Voluntariness of confession must be established by preponderance of the evidence. Post - arrest statement may not be admitted if because of mental illness, drugs, or

intoxication, statement was not product of rational intellect and free will. Coerced or otherwise involuntary statement may never be used for any purpose.

US v. Kelly, 35 F.3d 929 (4th Cir. 1994)
1. Due process requires government to disclose material evidence affecting credibility of government witnesses. 2. Conviction must be reversed if there is any reasonable likelihood that false testimony could have affected judgment of jury, even if testimony relates only to credibility of government witness and other evidence also has called into question credibility of witness.

US v. Kilgroe, 959 F.2d 802 (9th Cir. 1992)
Witness who has been subpoenaed remains free to refuse to answer questions that would incriminate him.

US v. Kunzman, 54 F.3d 1522 (10th Cir. 1995) Experience alone can qualify witness to give expert testimony.

US v. Kreiser, 15 F.3d 635 (7th Cir. 1994)
Lee v. Illinois, 476 US 530, 90 L.Ed.2d 514, 106 S.Ct. 2056 (1986)
Bruton v. US, 391 US 123, 20 L.Ed.2d 476, 88 S.Ct. 1620 (1968)
When two defendants are tried jointly, pretrial confession of one cannot be admitted against another unless confessing defendant takes stand.

US v. Nanni, 59 F.3d 1425 (2nd Cir. 1995)
State statute granting use immunity protects witness from use of his testimony by federal, as well as state authorities.

US v. Necoechea, 986 F.2d 1273 (9th Cir. 1993)
US v. Agurs, 427 US 97, 49 L.Ed.2d 342, 96 S.Ct. 2392 (1976)
White v. Ragen, 324 US 760, 89 L.Ed 1348, 65 S.Ct. 978 (1953)
When the prosecution is or should be aware that it is presenting perjured testimony, a strict standard of materiality will be applied, and/or conviction will be set aside if there is any reasonable likelihood that the false testimony could have affected the judgment of the jury. Conviction obtained by knowing use of perjured

testimony must be set aside if there is any reasonable likelihood that the false testimony could have affected the outcome of the trial.

US v. Newton, 44 F.3d 913 (11th Cir. 1995)
It is improper for prosecution to place prestige of the government behind a witness by making explicit personal assurances of witness' veracity.

US v. Porter, 986 F.2d 1014 (6th Cir. 1993)
Adverse spousal testimony privilege" protects one spouse from being compelled to testify against the other.

US v. Quintanilla, 2 F.3d 1469 (7th Cir. 1993)
Authority to immunize witness is explicitly executive branch responsibility; in enacting use immunity statute, Congress expressly left this decision exclusively to Justice Department.

US v. Sanchez - Galvez, 33 F.3d 829 (7th Cir. 1994)
US v. Sepulveda. 15 F.3d 1161 (1st Cir. 1993)
Government may not imply that non - testifying defendant's silence is evidence of guilt.

US v. Taylor, 17 F.3d 333 (11th Cir. 1994)
US v. Baptista - Rodriguez, 17 F.3d 1354 (11th Cir. 1994)
Importance of full cross-examination into possible bias increases where witness is the star government witness or participated in crimes for which the defendant is being prosecuted.

US v. Waterman, 732 F.2d 1527 (8th Cir. 1984)
Government cannot, consistent with due process, offer favorable treatment to prosecution witness contingent upon success of prosecution. Since testimony was critical to support of defendant's conviction it was vacated.

US v. Weitzenhoff, 35 F.3d 1275 (9th Cir. 1993)

US v. Dunnigan, 507 US 122 L.Ed.2d 445, 113 S.Ct. 1111 (1993)

A sentencing increase based on false testimony does not unconstitutionally burden a defendant's right to testify. "A Defendant's right to testify does not include a right to commit perjury" 113 S.Ct. at 1117.

US v. Young, 952 F.2d 1252 (10th Cir. 1991)

US v. Perkins, 926 F.2d 1271 (1st Cir. 1991)

Defendants are entitled to adequate leeway to impeach witness' credibility and motivation during criminal trial. Confrontation clause guarantees right to effective cross-examination when attempting to show bias.

Webb v. Lewis, 1994 US App LEXIS 34997

As the use of the videotape alone was such a substantial violation of Webb's Confrontation Clause rights, we need not on this appeal evaluate the further violations alleged by the admission of hearsay reported by Connie Martin and by Leslie Morton. If, however, these statements are to be used again they must be reevaluated in the light of this opinion and of Idaho v. Wright. Their earlier admission under a statute now found by Arizona to be unconstitutional is now irrelevant. Accordingly, the judgment of the district court is reversed. The district court is ordered to issue the writ sixty days from the issuance of the mandate, unless within that time the state of Arizona indicates to the district court its intention to retry Webb. In that event, the district court shall order Webb released to the proper authorities [**21] for the purposes of retrial.

Chapter 12 Addresses

US JUDICIAL & RELATED DEPARTMENTS

Alcohol, Tob. & Fire, 1200 Pennsylvania Ave., Washington, D.C. 20004	202-566-7235
Civil Rights, Tenth St. & Constitution Ave. NW, Washington, D.C. 20530	202-633-2151
Court of Claims, 717 Madison Pl. N.W., Washington, D.C. 20005	202-633-7257
Customs Service, 1301 Constitution Ave. NW, Washington, D.C. 20002	202-566-5286
Drug Enforcement Admin., 700 Army Navy Dr., Arlington, VA 20537	202-307-1000
Federal Aviation Admin., 800 Independence Ave. SW, Wash., D.C. 20003	202-426-3883
Federal Bureau of Invest., Ninth St. & Penn. Ave. NW, Wash., D.C. 20535	202-324-3444
F.O.I.A., 2201 C. St. N.W., Washington, D.C. 20520	202-632-8484
House of Representatives, Capitol Building, Washington, D.C. 20001	202-224-3121
Internal Revenue Service, 11 Constitution Ave. NW, Wash., D.C. 20002	202-566-4743
Justice Department, Tenth St & Constitution Ave. NW, Wash., D.C. 20530	202-633-2000
Library of Congress, 10 First St. S.E., Washington, D.C. 20024	202-287-5000
Marshals Service, One Tysons Comer Center McLean, Virginia 22102	703-285-1131
Postal Service, 475 L'Enfant Plaza North S.W., Washington D.C. 20024	202-245-4034
Secret Service, 1800 G Street N.W., Washington D.C. 20006	202-535-5708
The Senate, Capitol Building, Washington D.C. 20001	202-224-3121
Tax Court, 400 Second Street N.W., Washington D.C. 20004	202-376-2754
White House, 1600 Pennsylvania Ave. N.W., Washington D.C. 20006	202-456-1414

Supreme Court of the U.S., 1 First St. N.E., Washington D.C. 20543	202-479-3000
UNITED STATES COURTS OF APPEALS	
District of Columbia, U.S. Courthouse, 3rd & Constitution Ave. N.W.,Washington D.C. 20001	202-535-3308
First Circuit. 1606 John W. McCormack Post Office and Courthouse, Boston, Massachusetts 02109	617-223-9057
Second Circuit, U.S. Courthouse, Foley Square, N.Y., N.Y. 10007	212-791-0103
Third Circuit, 21400 U.S. Courthouse, Philadelphia, PA 19106	215-597-2995
Fourth Circuit, Tenth & Main Streets, Richmond, Virginia 23219	804-771-2213
Fifth Circuit, 100 U.S. Courthouse, 600 Camp St., New Orleans, LA 70130	504-589-6514
Sixth Circuit, 502 U.S. Post Office & Courthouse Building, Fifth & Walnut Streets, Cincinnati, Ohio 45202	513-684-2953
Seventh Circuit, 219 South Dearborn St., Chicago, Illinois 60604	312-435-5850
Eighth Circuit. 511 US Court & Custom House, St. Louis, Missouri 63101	314-539-3609
Ninth Circuit, P.O. Box 547, San Francisco, California 94101	415-556-7340
Tenth Circuit, 1929 Stout Street, Denver, Colorado 80294	303-844-3157
Eleventh Circuit, 56 Forsyth St. N.W., Atlanta, Georgia 30303	404-331-6187
U.S. Court of Appeals for the Federal Circuit, 717 Madison Place N.W., Washington D.C. 20439	202-633-6550
Temporary Emergency Court of Appeals, 1130 U.S. Courthouse, 3rd & Constitution Ave. N.W., Washington D.C. 20001	202-535-3390
U.S. Claims Court, 717 Madison Pl. N.W., Washington D.C. 20005	202-633-7257
U.S. Court of International Trade, One Federal Plaza, N.Y., N.Y. 10007	212-264-2814
U.S. Court of Military Appeals, 450 E. Street N.W., Wash. D.C. 20442	202-272-1448
U.S. Tax Court, 400 Second St. N.W., Washington D.C. 20217	202-376-2754

UNITED STATES DISTRICT COURTS	
Alabama, Northern, 1729 5th Avenue North, Birmingham 35203	205-731-1025
Alabama, Northern, 101 Holmes Ave. N.E., Huntsville 35801	205-534-6495
Alabama, Northern, 12th & Noble Streets, Anniston 36201	205-237-5631
Alabama, Northern, P.O. Box 1289, Decatur 35601	205-353-2817
Alabama, Northern, P.O. Box 2597, Tuscaloosa 35403	205-752-0426
Alabama, Middle, P.O. Box 711, Montgomery 36101	205-832-7308
Alabama, Southern, P.O. Box 2625, Mobile 36652	205-690-2371
Alaska, 222 West 7th Avenue #4, Anchorage 99513	907-271-5568
Alaska, 101 12th Ave., Box 1, Fairbanks 99701	907-452-3163
Alaska, Box 349, Juneau 99802	907-586-7458
Alaska, 415 Main St., Rm. 400, Ketchikan 99901	907-225-3195
Alaska, Box 130, Nome 99762	907-443-5216
Arizona, 230 North 1st Avenue, Phoenix 85025	602-261-3341
Arizona, 55 E. Broadway, Tucson 85701	602-629-6575
Arizona, 320 N. Central Ave.. Suite 200. Phoenix 85004	602-261-3561
Arkansas, Eastern, P.O. Box 869. Little Rock 72203	501-378-5353
Arkansas, Eastern, 312 Federal Building 2. Jonesboro 72401	501-972-4610
Arkansas, Eastern, P. 0. Box 8307, Pine Bluff 71611	501-536-1190
Arkansas, Western, P.O. Box 1523, Fort Smith 72902	501-783-6833
Arkansas, Western, P.O. Box 1566. El Dorado 71730	501-862-1202
Arkansas, Western, Rm. 523, Fed. Bldg. Fayetteville 72701	501-521-6980
Arkansas, Western, P.O. Drawer 1, Hot Springs 71901	501-623-6411
Arkansas, Western, P.O. Box 2746, Texarkana 75501	501-773-3381
California, Northern, P.O. Box 36060. San Francisco 94102	415-556-3031
California, Northern, 280 South First Street, San Jose 95113	408-291-7783
California, Northern, 214 Post Office Bldg., Oakland 94612	415-273-7212
California, Northern, 1450 Guerneville Rd., Bldg. G. Santa Rosa 95403	707-525-8520
California, Eastern, 650 Capitol Mail, Sacramento 95814	916-551-2615
California, Eastern, 1130 "0" Street. Fresno 93721	209-487-5083
California, Eastern P.O. Box 5276, Modesto 95352	209-521-5160
California, Central, 312 N. Spring Street, Los Angeles 90012	213-894-3535
California, Central, 34 Civic Center Plaza, Santa Ana 92701	714-836-2993
California, Central, 699 N. Arrowhead Ave., San Bernardino 92401	714-383-5600
California, Southern, 940 Front Street, San Diego 92189	619-557-5600
Colorado, 1929 Stout Street, Denver 80294	303-844-3433
Connecticut, 141 Church Street, New Haven 06510	203-773-2140

Connecticut, 915 Lafayette Blvd., Bridgeport 06604	203-579-5861
Connecticut, 450 Main Street, Hartford 06103	203-240-3200
Delaware, Lockbox 18, 844 King Street, Wilmington	302-573-6170
District Of Columbia, 3rd & Constitutional Ave. Washington DC 20001	202-535-3594
Florida, Northern, 110 East Park Ave., Tallahassee 32301	904-681-7165
Florida, Northern, P.O. Box 990, Pensacola 32502	904-435-8440
Florida, Middle, P.O. Box 53558, Jacksonville 32201	904-791-2854
Florida, Middle, 80 N. Hughey Ave., Orlando 32801	407-648-6366
Florida, Middle, 105 U.S. Courthouse, Tampa 33602	813-228-2105
Florida, Middle, First & Lee Street, Ft. Myers 33901	813-332-3655
Florida, Southern, 301 N. Miami Ave., Miami 33128	305-536-4131
Florida, Southern, 299 E. Broward Blvd., Ft. Lauderdale 33301	305-527-7075
Florida, Southern, 701 Clematis St., West Palm Beach 33701	407-655-8710
Georgia, Northern, 75 Spring Street S.W., Atlanta 30335	404-331-6496
Georgia, Northern, 201 Federal Building, Gainesville 30501	404-534-5954
Georgia, Northern, P.O. Box 939, Newman 30264	404-253-8847
Georgia, Northern, P.O. Box 1186, Rome 30161	404-291-5629
Georgia, Middle, P.O. Box 1906, Albany 31702	912-430-8431
Georgia, Middle, P.O. Box 124, Columbus 31902	404-649-7816
Georgia, Middle, P.O. Box 68, Valdosta 31601	912-226-3651
Georgia, Southern, P.O. Box 1130, Augusta 30903	404-722-2074
Georgia, Southern, P.O. Box 1636, Brunswick 31521	912-265-1758
Hawaii, P.O. Box 50129, Honolulu 96850	808-541-1300
Guam, Pacific News Building, 238 O'Hara Street, Agana, Guam 96910	
Idaho, 550 West Fort Street, Box 040, Boise 83724	208-334-1361
Illinois, Northern, 219 South Dearborn Street, Chicago 60604	312-435-5670
Illinois, Northern, 211 South Court Street, Rockford 61101	815-987-4355
Illinois, Central, P.O. Box 315, Springfield 62705	217-492-4020
Illinois, Central, P.O. Box 786, Danville 61832	217-431-4805
Illinois, Central, 100 N.E. Monroe, Peoria 61602	309-671-7117
Illinois, Central, Rm. 40, P.O. Bldg., Rock Island 61201	309-793-5778
Illinois, Southern, 750 Missouri Ave., E. St. Louis 62202	618-492-9371
Illinois, Southern, 501 Belle Street, Alton 62002	618-463-6402
Illinois, Southern, 301 W. Main Street, Benton 62812	618-435-2109
Indiana, Northern, 204 S. Main Street, South Bend 46601	219-236-8260
Indiana, Northern, 1300 S. Harrison St., Fort Wayne 46801	219-424-7360
Indiana, Northern, 507 State Street, Hammond 46320	219-937-5235

Indiana, Northern, P.O. Box 1498, Lafayette 47902	317-742-0512
Indiana, Northern, 610 Connecticut St., Gary 46402	219-881-3335
Indiana, Southern, 46 East Ohio Street, Indianapolis 46204	317-226-6670
Indiana, Southern, 101 N.W. 7th Street, Evansville 47708	812-465-6426
Indiana, Southern, 210 Federal Bldg., New Albany 47150	FTS 358-5238
Indiana, Southern, 210 Federal Bldg., Terre Haute 47808	FTS 335-8346
Iowa, Northern, 101 First St. S.E., Cedar Rapids 52401	319-399-2566
Iowa, Northern, 320 Sixth Street, Sioux City 51101	712-233-3203
Iowa, Southern, E. Ist & Walnut Streets, Des Moines 50309	515-284-6348
Iowa, Southern, P.O. Box 307, Counsel Bluffs 51502	712-325-5517
Iowa, Southern, P.O. Box 256, Davenport 52805	319-322-3223
Kansas, 401 Market Street, Wichita 67202	316-269-6491
Kansas, 812 North 7th Street, Kansas City 66101	913-236-3719
Kansas, 444 S.E. Quincy Street, Topeka 66683	913-295-2610
Kentucky, Eastern, P.O. Box 741, Lexington 40586	606-233-2503
Kentucky, Eastern, 1405 Greenup Avenue, Ashland 41101	606-329-2465
Kentucky, Eastern, P.O. Box 1073, Covington 41012	606-292-3167
Kentucky, Eastern, P.O. Box 1040, Frankfort 40602	502-223-5225
Kentucky, Eastern, P.O. Box 689, London 40741	606-864-5137
Kentucky, Eastern, 102 Main Street, Pikeville 41501	606-437-6160
Kentucky, Western, 601 West Broadway, Louisville 40202	502-582-5156
Kentucky, Western, 242 East Main Street, Bowling Green 42101	502-781-1110
Kentucky, Western, P.O. Box 538, Owensboro 42302	502-683-0221
Kentucky, Western, 5th & Broadway, Paducah 42001	502-443-1347
Louisiana, Eastern, U.S. Courthouse, 500 Camp Street 70130	504-589-2946
Louisiana, Middle, P.O. Box 2630, Baton Rouge 70821	504-389-0321
Louisiana, Western, 500 Fannin Street, Room 106, Shreveport 71101	318-226-5273
Louisiana, Western, P.O. Box 1269, Alexandria 71309	318-473-7415
Louisiana, Western, 705 Jefferson Street, Lafayette 70501	318-232-2106
Louisiana, Western, P.O. Box 393, Lake Charles 70601	318-376-7246
Louisiana, Western, 306 Federal Building, Opelousas 70570	318-948-8594
Maine, P.O. Box 7505 DTS, Portland 04111	107-780-3357
Maine, P.O. Box 1007, Bangor 04401	FTS 833-7357
Maryland, 101 W. Lombard Street, Baltimore 21201	301-962-2600
Maryland, 451 Hungerford Drive, Rockville 02085	301-443-7010
Massachusetts, John W. McCormack Post Office Rm 707, Boston 02109	617-223-9152
Massachusetts, 1550 Main Street, Springfield 01103	413-785-0214

Massachusetts. 10 Mechanic Street, Worcester 01608	617-793-0518
Michigan, Eastern, 231 W. Lafayette Blvd.. Rm 133, Detroit 48226	313-226-7200
Michigan, Eastern, 200 E. Liberty Street. Ann Arbor 48107	313-668-2380
Michigan, Eastern, 1000 Washington Avenue. Bay City 48706	517-892-6571
Michigan, Eastern, 600 Church Street, Flint 48502	313-766-5021
Michigan. Western, 110 Michigan Street N.W., Grand Rapids 49503	616-456-2381
Michigan, Western, 410 West Michigan Avenue Kalamazoo 49005	616-349-2922
Michigan, Western, P.O. Box 698, Marquette 49855	906-226-2021
Minnesota, 316 N. Robert Street, St. Paul 55101	612-290-3212
Minnesota, 515 W. First Street, Duluth 55802	218-720-5250
Minnesota, 110 South 4th Street, Minneapolis 55401	218-348-1821
Minnesota, 118 South Mill Street, Fercus Falls 56537	218-739-4671
Mississippi, Northern, P.O. Box 727, Oxford 38655	601-234-1971
Mississippi, Northern, P.O. Box 704, Aberdeen 39730	601-369-4952
Mississippi, Northern, P. 0. Box 190, Clarksdale 38614	601-624-6208
Mississippi, Northern, P. 0. Box 190, Greenville 38701	601-335-1651
Mississippi, Southern, 245 E. Capitol Street, Suite 416. Jackson 39201	601-960-4439
Mississippi, Southern. P.O. Box 369, Biloxi 39533	601-431-8623
Mississippi, Southern, P.O. Box 511, Hattiesburg 39401	601-583-2433
Mississippi, Southern, P.O. Box 1186. Meridian 39301	601-693-2883
Missouri, Eastern, 1114 Market Street, St. Louis 63101	314-425-6056
Missouri, Western, 811 Grand Avenue, Kansas City 64106	816-426-2811
Missouri, Western. 131 West High Street, Jefferson City 65102	314 636 6124
Missouri, Western, 302 Joplin Street, Joplin 64801	417-623-6536
Missouri, Western, 222 John Q. Hammons Parkway, Springfield 65806	417-665-7719
Missouri, Western, 201 S. 8th Street, St. Joseph 64501	816-279-2428
Montana, 316 N. 26th Street, Billings 59101	406-657-6366
Montana, Federal Building, Butte 59701	FTS 585-2329
Montana, P.O. Box 2186, Great Falls 59403	406-453-3378
Montana, P.O. Box 8537, Missoula 59807	405-329-3598
Nebraska, P.O. Box 129 DTS, Omaha 68101	402-221-4761
Nebraska, 1100 Centennial Mail North, Lincoln 68508	402-437-5225
Nevada, 300 Las Vegas Blvd. South, Las Vegas 89101	702-388-6351
Nevada, 300 Booth Street, Reno 89509	702-784-5515

New Hampshire, P.O. Box 1498, Concord 03301	603-225-1423
New Jersey, P.O. Box 419, Newark 07102	210-645-3730
New Jersey, P.O. Box 2797, Camden 08101	606-757-5021
New Jersey, P.O. Box 515, Trenton 08603	609-989-2068
New Mexico, P.O. Box 689, Albuquerque 87103	505-766-2851
New Mexico, 200 E. Griggs Avenue, Las Cruces 88001	505-523-8220
New Mexico, P.O. Box 2384, Santa Fe 87501	505-988-6481
New York, Northern, P.O. Box 1037, Albany 12201	518-472-5651
New York, Northern, 15 Henry Street, Binghamton 13901	607-773-2893
New York, Northern, 100 South Clinton Street, Syracuse 13260	315-423-5549
New York, Northern, 10 Board Street, Utica 13501	315-793-8151
New York, Southern, U.S. Courthouse, Foley Square, New York 10007	212-791-0108
New York, Southern, 176 Church Street, Poughkeepsie 12602	912-452-4200
New York, Southern, 101 East Post Road, White Plains 10601	914-683-9755
New York, Eastern, 225 Cadman Plaza East, Brooklyn 11201	718-330-2105
New York, Eastern, 300 Rabro Drive, Hauppauge 11787	516-582-1100
New York, Eastern, Uniondale Ave. & Turnpike, Uniondale 11553	516-485-6500
New York, Western, 68 Court Street, Buffalo 14202	716-846-4211
New York, Western, 100 State Street, Rochester 14614	716-263-6263
North Carolina, Eastern, P.O. Box 25670, Raleigh 27611	919-856-4370
North Carolina, Eastern, P.O. Box 43, Fayetteville 28302	919-483-9509
North Carolina, Eastern, P.O. Box 1336, New Bern 28560	919-638-8534
North Carolina, Eastern, P.O. Box 338, Wilmington 28401	919-343-4663
North Carolina, Middle, P.O. Box V 1, Greensboro 27402	919-333-5347
North Carolina, Western, 100 Otis Street, Asheville 28801	704-259-0648
North Carolina, Western, 401 W. Trade Street, Charlotte 48202	704-371-6200
North Carolina, Western, P.O. Box 466, Statesville 28677	704-873-7112
North Dakota, P.O. Box 1193, Bismarck 58502	701-250-4295
North Dakota, P.O. Box 870, Fargo 58107	701-239-5377
Northern Mariana Islands, P.O. Box 687, Saipan CM 96950	
Ohio, Northern, 201 Superior Avenue, N.E., Cleveland 44114	216-522-4359
Ohio, Northern, Two S. Main Street, Akron 44308	216-375-5705
Ohio, Northern, 1716 Spielbusch Avenue, Toledo 43624	419-259-6411
Ohio, Northern, 9 West Front Street, Youngstown 44503	216-746-3351
Ohio, Southern, 85 Marconi Boulevard, Columbus 43215	614-469-6945
Ohio, Southern, 5th & Walnut Streets, Cincinnati 45202	513-684-2777
Ohio, Southern, P.O. Box 970, Dayton 45402	513-225-2896

Oklahoma, Northern, 333 W. 4th Street, Tulsa 74103	918-581-7796
Oklahoma, Northern 200 N.W. 4th Street, Oklahoma City 73102	405-231-4792
Oklahoma, Eastern, P.O. Box 607, Muskogee 74401	918-687-2471
Oklahoma, Western, 200 N.W. 4th Street, Oklahoma City 73102	405-231-4792
Oregon, 620 S.W. Main Street, Portland 97205	503-326-2202
Oregon, 211 East 7th Street, Eugene 97401	503-687-6423
Pennsylvania, Eastern, 601 Market Street, Philadelphia 19106	401-528-5100
Pennsylvania, Middle, P.O. Box 1148, Scranton 18501	215-597-7950
Pennsylvania, Middle, P.O. Box 983, Harrisburg 17108	717-347-5623
Pennsylvania, Middle, 197 S. Main Street, Wilkes - Barre 18701	717-782-4445
Pennsylvania, Middle, P.O. Box 608, Williamsport 17701	717-823-8034
Pennsylvania, Western, P.O. Box 1805, Pittsburgh 15230	717-323-6380
Pennsylvania, Western, P.O. Box 1820, Erie 16507	412-644-3528
Puerto Rico, P.O. Box 3671, San Juan 00904	814-453-4829
Rhode Island, 119 Federal Building & U.S. Courthouse, Providence 02903	809-729-6701
South Carolina, P.O. Box 867, Columbia 29202	803-765-5816
South Carolina, P.O. Box 835, Charleston 29402	803-724-4225
South Carolina, P.O. Box 2317, Florence 29503	803-662-1223
South Carolina, P.O. Box 10768, Greenville 29603	803-233-2781
South Dakota, 400 S. Phillips Avenue, Sioux Falls 57102	605-3358-5566
South Dakota, 515 Ninth Street, Rapid City, 57701	605-342-3066
South Dakota, 405 U.S. Courthouse, Pierre 57501	605-224-5849
Tennessee, Eastern, P.O. Box 2348, Knoxville 37901	615-673-4227
Tennessee, Eastern, P.O. Box 591, Chattanooga 37401	615-752-5200
Tennessee, Eastern, 101 Summer Street, West, Greeneville 37743	605-639-3105
Tennessee, Middle, 801 Broadway, Nashville 37203	615-736-5728
Tennessee, Western. 167 North Main Street. Memphis 38103	901-521-3317
Tennessee, Western, 109 S. Highland Avenue, Jackson 38301	901-427-6586
Texas, Northern, 1100 Commerce Street, Dallas 75242	214-767-0787
Texas, Northern, P.O. Box 1218, Abilene 79604	615-677-6311
Texas, Northern, P.O. Box F 13240, Amarillo 79189	806-376-2352
Texas. Northern, 202 U.S. Courthouse, Fort Worth 76102	817-334-3132
Texas, Northern, 1205 Texas Avenue, Lubbock 79401	806-743-7624
Texas, Northern, 33 E. Twohig Street, San Angelo 76903	915-655-4506
Texas, Northern, P.O. Box 1234, Wichita Falls 76307	817-767-1902
Texas, Southern, P.O. Box 61010, Houston 77208	713-221-9505
Texas, Southern, P.O. Box 2299, Brownsville 78520	512-548-2500

Texas, Southern, 521 Starr Street, Corpus Christi 78401	512-888-3142
Texas, Southern, P.O. Box 2300, Galveston 77553	409-766-3530
Texas, Southern, P.O. Box 597, Laredo 78042	512-723-3542
Texas, Southern, P.O. Box 5059, McAllen 78501	512-631-2205
Texas, Southern, P.O. Box 1541, Victoria 77902	512-575-3512
Texas, Eastern, 211 We. Ferguson Street, Tyler 75702	214-592-8195
Texas, Eastern, 300 Willow Street, Beaumont 77701	409-839-2645
Texas, Eastern, P.O. Box 1499, Marshall 75672	214-935-2912
Texas. Eastern, 101 E. Pecan Street, Sherman 75090	214-892-2921
Texas, Eastern, P.O. Box 2667, Texarkana 75501	214-794-8561
Utah, 350 South Main Street, Salt Lake City 84101	801-524-5160
Vermont, P.O. Box 945, Burlington 05402	802-951-6301
Vermont, P.O. Box 607, Rutland 05701	802-773-0245
Virgin Islands, P.O. Box 720, Charlotte Amalie, St. Thomas 00801	809-774-0640
Virgin Islands, P.O. Box 3439, Christiansted, St. Croix 00820	809-773-1130
Virginia, Eastern, 200 S. Washington Street, Alexandria 22320	703-557-5127
Virginia, Eastern, P.O. Box 494, Newport News 23607	804-244-0539
Virginia, Eastern, 600 Granby Street, Norfolk 23510	804-441-6677
Virginia, Eastern, P.O. Box 2 AD, Richmond 23205	804-782-2611
Virginia, Western, P.O. Box 1234, Roanoke 24006	703-982-6224
Virginia, Western, P.O. Box 398, Abingdon 24210	703-628-5116
Virginia, Western, P.O. Box 490, Big Stone Gap 24219	703-523-3557
Virginia, Western, 255 W. Main Street, Room 305, Charlottesville 22901	804-296-9284
Virginia, Western, P.O Box 52, Danville 24540	703-793-7147
Virginia. Western, P.O. Box 1207, Harrisonburg 22801	703-434-3181
Virginia, Western, P.O. Box 744, Lynchburg 24505	804-847-5722
Washington, Eastern. P.O. Box 1493, Spokane 99210	509-353-2150
Washington, Western, 1010 Fifth Avenue, Seattle 98104	206-442-5598
Washington, Western, P.O. Box 1935, Tacoma 98401	206-442-5598
West Virginia, Northern, P.O. Box 1518, Elkins 26241	304-636-1445
West Virginia, Northern, P.O. Box 2857, Clarksburg 26302	304-622-8513
West Virginia, Northern, P.O. Box 471, Wheeling 26003	304-232-0011
West Virginia, Southern, P.O. Box 2546, Charleston 25329	304-342-5154
West Virginia, Southern, Box 4128, Bluefield 27702	304-327-9798
West Virginia, Southern, P.O. Box 1570, Huntington 25716	304-529-5588
West Virginia, Southern, P.O. Box 1526. Parkersburg 26102	304-420-6490
West Virginia, Southern, 1002 Federal Bldg., Beckley 25801	304-253-7481

Wisconsin, Eastern, 517 East Wisconsin Avenue, Milwaukee 53202	414-291-3372
Wisconsin, Western, P.O. Box 432. Madison 53701	608-264-5156
Wisconsin, Western. 500 S. Barstow Street, Eau Claire 54701	715-839-2980
Wyoming, P.O. Box 727, Cheyenne 82001	307-772-2145
PUBLIC DEFENDERS AND LEGAL ASSISTANCE	
Alaska, 800 A Street, Room 205, Anchorage 99501	907-271-2277
Arizona, 97 East Congress, Suite 130, Tucson 85701	602-629-6521
Arizona, 320 N. Central Avenue, Suite 200, Phoenix 85004	602-261-3561
California, Northern, 450 Golden Gate Avenue, San Francisco 94102	415-556-7712
California, Northern, 280 South First Street, San Jose 95113	408-291-7753
California, Eastern, 1125 Firehouse Alley, Sacramento 95814	916-551-1067
California, Eastern, 1313 P Street, Suite 104, Fresno 93721	209-487-5561
California, Central, 312 N. Spring Street, Los Angeles 90012	213-894-2854
California. Central, 751 W. Santa Ana Blvd., Santa Ana 92701	714-836-2252
California, Southern, "Federal Defenders of San Diego, Inc.", 225 Broadway, Suite 500, San Diego 92101	619-234-8467
Colorado, 110 16th Street #800, Denver 80202	303-620-4888
Connecticut, 450 Main Street, Room 710, Hartford 06103	203-240-3357
Connecticut, 234 Church Street, Suite 1001, New Haven 06510	202-773-2148
Florida, Northern, 227 N. Bronough Street, Tallahassee 32301	904-681-7439
Florida, Northern, 17 S. Palafox Street, Suite 394, Pensacola 32501	904-432-1418
Florida, Middle, 80 N. Hughey Avenue, Orlando 32801	407-648-6338
Florida, Middle, P.O. Box 4998, Jacksonville 32201	904-791-3039
Florida, Middle, 500 Zack Street, Room 204, Tampa 33602	813-228-2715
Florida, Southern, 301 N. Miami Avenue, Miami 33128	305-536-6900
Florida, Southern, 299 E. Broward Blvd., Fort Lauderdale 33301	305-527-7293
Florida, Southern, 224 Datura Street, Suite 601, West Palm Beach 33401	407-833-6288
Georgia, Northern, "Federal Defender Program, Inc., Suite 3310, 101 Marietta Tower, Atlanta 30303	404-688-7530
Georgia [All!] "Georgia State University College of Law," University Plaza, Atlanta 30303	404-651-2898
Hawaii, P.O. Box 50269, Honolulu 96850	808-541-2521
Illinois, Northern, 219 South Dearborn Street, Chicago 60604	312-435-5580
Illinois, Central, 1114 Market Street, St. Louis, Missouri 63101	314-539-6186
Illinois, Southern, 1114 Market Street, St. Louis, Missouri 63101	314-539-6186

Kansas, 401 N. Market Street, Wichita 67202	316-269-6455
Kansas, 812 North 7th Street, Kansas City 66101	913-236-3712
Kansas, 444 S.E. Quincy Street, Topeka 66683	913-295-2595
Louisiana, Eastern, 500 Camp Street, New Orleans 70130	504-589-2468
Louisiana, Eastern/Middle/Western: Eastern, 348 Baronne, Suite 420, New Orleans 70112	504-522-0578
Maryland, Suite 612, 2 Hopkins Plaza, Baltimore 21201	301-962-3962
Massachusetts, 195 State Street, Boston 02109	617-565-8335
Michigan, Eastern, "Legal Aid & Defender Assoc. of Detroit, 2255 Penobscot Building, 645 Griswold Street, Detroit 48226	313-961-4150
Minnesota, 110 S. 4th Street, Minneapolis 55401	612-348-1755
Mississippi, Northern/Southern, P.O. Box 510, Jackson 39205	601-353-1750
Missouri, Eastern, 1114 Market Street, St. Louis 63101	314-539-6186
Missouri, Western, 911 Walnut, 12th Floor, Kansas City 64106	816-426-5851
Missouri, Western, 1949 East Sunshine, Suite 3104, Springfield 65804	417-881-4090
Nevada, 330 South 3rd Street, Suite 1050, Las Vegas 89101	702-388-5677
Nevada, 300 Booth Street, Reno 89509	702-784-5626
New Jersey, 976 Broad Street, Newark 07101	201-645-6347
New Jersey, 330 Market Street, Camden 08102	609-757-5341
New Jersey, 402 E. State Street, Room 110, Trenton 08615	609-989-2160
New Mexico, 118 New Mexico, P.O. Box 306, Albuquerque 87103	505-766-3293
New Mexico, South Downtown Mall, Las Cruces 88001	505-523-8366
New York, Southern, "The Legal Aid Society" 15 Park Row, New York 10038	212-577-3313
New York, Southern, "Federal Defender Services Unit" 52 Duane Street, New York 10007	212-285-2838
New York, Southern, 158 Grand St., Rm. 7 1st Floor, White Plains 10601	914-428-7214
New York, Eastern, "Legal Aid Society" 50 Court Street, Room 1103, Brooklyn 11201	718-330-1200
North Carolina, 128 East Hargett St., Raleigh 27611	919-856-4236
Ohio, Northern, 75 Public Square, Suite 410, Cleveland 44113	216-522-4856
Oklahoma, Northern/Eastern/Western: 215 Dean McGee Ave., Suite 524, Oklahoma City 73102	405-231-5725
Oklahoma, 222 S. Houston, Suite C, Tulsa 74127	918-581-7656
Oregon, 615 W. Broadway, Suite 200, Portland 97205	503-326-2123
Oregon, 44 W. Broadway, Suite 406, Eugene 97401	503-687-6937

Pennsylvania, Eastern, "Defender Assoc. of Philadelphia" Cast Iron Bldg., Suite 500S, 718 Arch Street, Philadelphia 19106	215-925-9220
Pennsylvania, Middle, 100 Chestnut Street, Suite 306, Harrisburg 17101	717-782-2237
Pennsylvania, Middle, 401 Adams Avenue, Scranton 18510	717-343-6285
Pennsylvania, Western, 960 Penn Avenue, Pittsburgh 15222	412-644-6565
Pennsylvania, Western, P.O. Box 1776, Erie 16507	814-455-8089
Puerto Rico, P.O. Box 3832, San Juan 00904	809-729-6775
South Carolina, 1835 Assembly Street, Room 146, Columbia 29201	803-765-5147
South Carolina, P.O. Box 11311, Columbia 29211	803-765-0650
Tennessee, Eastern, 1225 17th Avenue South, Nashville 37212	615-327-8791
Tennessee, Middle, 808 Broadway, Nashville 37203	615-736-5047
Tennessee, Middle, 1225 17th Avenue South, Nashville 37212	615-327-8791
Tennessee, Western, 167 North Main Street, Memphis 38103	901-521-3895
Tennessee, Western, 1225 17th Avenue South, Nashville 37212	615-327-8791
Texas, (All Texas) "University of Texas School of Law" 727 East 26th Street, Austin 78705	512-471-5151
Texas, Western, 727 E. Durango Boulevard, San Antonio 78206	512-229-6700
Texas, Western, 700 E. San Antonio, El Paso 79901	915-534-6525
Texas, Southern, P.O. Box 61508, Houston 77208	713-220-2194
Texas, Southern, P.O. Box 2163, Brownsville 78522	512-548-2573
Texas, Southern, P.O. Box 1562, Laredo 78042	512-726-2218
Texas, Southern, 1701 W. Highway 83, Suite 905, McAllen 78501	512-630-2995
Virgin Islands, P.O. Box 3450, Christiansted, St. Croix 00820	809-773-3585
Virgin Islands, P.O. Box 720, Charlotte Amalie, St. Thomas 00801	809-774-4449
Washington, Western, 1111 Third Avenue, Suite 380, Seattle 98101	206-442-1100
West Virginia, Southern, 500 Quarrier Street, Charleston 25301	304-343-9551
U. S. PAROLE COMISSION & BUREAU OF PRISONS	
United States Sentencing Commission 1331 Pennsylvania Ave NW, Suite 1400, Washington DC 20004	202-662-8800
Parole Commission, 5550 Friendship Blvd, Chevy Chase, MD 20815	310-792-5990
N Central Region, 10920 Ambassador Cr., Kansas City, MO 64153	816-891-1395
NE Region, Scott Plaza 11, Philadelphia, PA 19113	215-596-1868

S. Central Region, Griffin Square Bldg., Dallas, TX 75202	214-767-0024
SE Region, 1718 Peachtree St. N.W., Suite 250, Atl., GA 30309	404-221-3515
W Region, Crocker Financial Center Bldg., Burlingame, CA 04010	415-347-4737
Bureau Of Prisons, 320 First St NW, Washington, DC 20001	202-514-2000
Southeast Region, 523 McDonough Blvd. SE, Atlanta, GA 30315	404-624-5202
FCI, P.O. Box 888, Ashland, Kentucky 41101	606-928-6414
USP, Box PMB, Atlanta, Georgia 30315	404-622-6241
FCI, Old N. Carolina Highway 75, Butner, North Carolina 27509	919-575-4541
FPC, P.O. Box 600, Eglin Air Force Base, Eglin, Florida 32542	904-882-8522
FCI, 1310 West Cherry St, Jessup, Georgia 31545	912-427-0870
FCI, Lexington, Kentucky 40411	606-255-6812
FCI, 100 FCI Rd, Marianna, Florida 32446	904-526-2313
FPC, Maxwell Air Force Base, Montgomery, Alabama 36112	205-834-3681
FCI, 1101 John Denie Road, Memphis, Tennessee 38134	901-372-2269
MCC, 15802 S.W. 137th Avenue, Miami, Florida 33177	305-253-4400
FPC, Symour Johnson Air Force Base, Goldsboro, NC 27531	919-734-8913
FCI, 902 Renfroe Road, Talladega, Alabama 35160	205-362-0410
FCI, Tallahassee, Florida 32301	904-878-2173
FPC, PO Box 40150, Tyndall. Panama City, Florida 32403	904-283-3838
Northeast Region, 2nd & Chestnut Street, Philadelphia, PA 10106	215-596-1868
FCI, Alderson, West Virginia 24910	304-445-2901
FPC, (Allenwood) Montgomery, PA 17752	717-547-1641
FCI, PO Box 5000, Bradford, PA 16701	814-362-8900
FCI, Danbury, Connecticut 06811	203-743-6471
FCI, Fairton, New Jersey	609-825-3110
FPC, Homestead Air Force Base, Homestead, Florida 33039	305-257-7838
USP, Lewisburg, Pennsylvania 17837	717-523-1251
FCI, PO Box 1000, Loretto, Pennsylvania 15940	814-472-4140
FCI, Morgantown, West Virginia 26505	304-296-4416
MCC, 150 Park Row, New York, New York 10007	212-791-9130
FCI, PO Box 600, Otisville, New York 10963	914-386-5855
FCI, Petersburg, Virginia 23804	804-733-7881
FCI, PO Box 300, Ray Brook, New York12977	518-891-5400
North Central Region, 10920 Ambassador Dr., Kansas City, MO 64153	816-891-7007
MCC, 71 W. Van Buren Street, Chicago, Illinois 50505	312-322-7500

FPC, P.O. Box 1000, Duluth, Minnesota 55814	218-722-8634
USP, P.O. Box 1000, Levenworth, Kansas 66048	913-682-8700
USP, Marion, Illinois 62959	618-964-1441
FCI, Milan, Michigan 48160	313-439-1511
FCI, P.O. Box 1000, Oxford, Wisconsin 53952	608-584-5511
Federal Medical Center (FMC), PO Box 4600, Rochester MN 55903	507-287-0674
FCI, Sandstone, Minnesota 55072	612-245-2262
Med Ctr for Fed Pri (MCFP), PO Box 4000, Springfield, MO 65808	417-862-7041
USP, P.O. Box 33, Terre Haute, Indiana 47808	812-238-1531
FPC, PO Box 680, Yankton, SD 57078	605-665-3262
South Central Region, 1607 Main, Suite 700, Dallas, Texas 75201	214-767-0024
FCI, P.O. Box 730, Bastrop, Texas 78602	512-321-3903
FPC, 1900 Simler Ave, Big Springs, Texas 79721	915-263-8304
FPC, 1100 Ursuline, Bryan, Texas 77803	409-823-1879
FPC, PO Box 16300, El Paso, Texas 79902	915-564-6155
FCI, El Reno, PO Box 1500, Oklahoma 73036	405-262-4875
FCI, Fort Worth, Texas 76119	817-535-2111
FDC, P.O. Box 5050, Oakdale, Louisiana 71463	318-335-4070
FCI, (La Tuna) Anthony, New Mexico - Texas 88021	915-886-3422
FCI, Seagoville, Texas 75159	214-287-2911
FCI, PO Box 7000, Texarkana, Texas 75501	212-838-4587
Western Region, Belmont Shores, 1301 Shoreway Dr, Belmont CA 94002	415-347-4737
FPC, P.O. Box 500, Boron, California 93516	619-762-5161
MCC, PO Box 189, Los Angeles 90053	213-485-0439
FCI, (Englewood) 9595 W. Quincy, Littleton, Colorado 90123	303-985-1566
USP, Lompoc, 3901 Klein Blvd, Lompoc, California 93436	805-736-2771
FCI, Box 1680 Black Canyon Stage 1, Phoenix, Arizona 85029	602-256-0924
FCI, (Pleasanton) 5701 8th Street, Dublin, California 94568	415-829-3522
FCI, RR#2, PO Box 820, Safford, Arizona 85546	602-428-6600
MCC, 808 Union St, San Diago, California 92101	619-232-4311
FCI, PO Box 5001, Sheridan, Oregon 97378	503-843-4442
FCI, Terminal Island, California 90731	213-831-8961
MCC, 8901 S. Wilnot Road, Tucson, Arizona 85706	602-741-3100
Bureau of Prisons Training Centers:	

Fed Law Enforcement Training Ctr, Bldg 21, Glynco GA 31524	912-267-2711
Food Management Training Center, C/O FCI, Ft Worth TX 76119	817-535-2111
Management and Specialty Training Center, 601 Chambers Rd, Ste 300, Aruora CO 80011	303-361-0557
Office of Inspections, Dept. of Justice, Washington, D.C. Office to contact if you have a complaint on staff	202-724-3286
Inmate Locater Number (Used for locating inmates)	202-307-3126

Arizona CLU Contact: Legal Department
Address: P.O. Box 17148 Phoenix, AZ 85011-0148
Phone: (602) 650-1967
Fax: (602) 650-1376
E-mail: office@azclu.org
Website: www.azclu.org
Services: Prison conditions (limited to state prisons); limited direct referrals; general community education.

Middle Ground
Contact: Donna Leone Hamm
Address: 139 East Encanto Dr. Tempe, AZ 85281
Phone: (480) 966-8116
Fax: (801) 409-8536
E-mail: middleground@qwest.net
Website: www.middlegroundprisonreform.org
Services: Provide education/training programs; counseling; legislative advocacy for prison reform; litigation on policies and procedures affecting visitors; public speaking on criminal and social justice issues; referrals to social service agencies. Advocacy and public education is performed on state and national levels; direct services are provided statewide in Arizona. Publish periodic newsletter; membership is $3/year for prisoners, $20/year non-prisoners.

Southern Arizona AIDS Foundation
Contact: Danny Blake
Address: 375 S. Euclid Ave. Tucson, AZ 85719
Phone: (520) 628-7223
Fax: (520) 628-7222
E-mail: info@saaf.org
Website: www.saaf.org
Services: Work with prisoners in the Arizona State system - Wilmot Prison in Tucson. The project has provided limited services to prisoners with AIDS.

Dept. of Corrections Central Office
1601 W. Jefferson Phoenix, AZ 85007

Arizona Department of Public Safety
2102 W, Encanto Phoenix, AZ 85005

Apache County Superior Court
P.O. Box 667 St. Johns, AZ 85963

Navajo County Superior Court Navajo Co. Courthouse
P.O. Box 668 Holbrook, AZ 86025

Association of Trial Lawyers
1001 N. Central Ave. Phoenix, AZ 85004

ASPC-Phoenix
2500 E. Van Buren Phoenix, AZ 85008

Arizona Department of Transportation
206 S. 17th Ave. Phoenix, AZ 85007

Cochise County Superior Court
P.O. Drawer CT Bisbee, AZ 85603

PimaCounty Superior Court New Court Bldg.

110 W. Congress Tucson, AZ 85701

Coalition for Prison Family Unity, Inc.
P.O. Box 30416 Tucson, AZ 85751

ASPC-Douglas
P.O. - Brawer 3807 Douglas, AZ 85608

Governor's Office of Women's Services
1700 W. Washington Room 420 Phoenix , AZ 85007

Gila County Superior Court
1400 East Ash Globe, AZ 85501

Pinal County Superior
Court Pinal Co. Courthouse Florence, AZ 85232

Coalition for Prisoners Rights
P.O. Box 1911 Santa Fe, NM 87504

ASPC-Florence
P.O. Box 629 Florence, AZ 85232

Maricopa County Attorney's Office
101 W. Jefferson St. Phoenix, AZ 85003

Coconino County Superior Court
Coconino Co. Courthouse Flagstaff, AZ 85603

Santa Cruz County Superior Court
Santa Cruz County Courthouse Nogales, AZ 85621

Families Against Mandatory Minimum's
1001 Pennsylvania Ave. NW
Suite 200 Washington, D.C. 20000

ASPC-Eyman
P.O. Box 3500
4374 E. Butte Avenue Florence, AZ 85232-5003
Maricopa County Sheriff's Dept.
102 W. Madison Phoenix, AZ 85003

Graham County Superior Court Graham Co.
Courthouse Safford, AZ 85546

Yavapi County Superior Court
Yavapi Co. Courthouse Prescott, AZ 86303

Middle Ground C/O Donna Leone-Hamm
139 East Encanto Drive Tempe, AZ 85281

ASPC-Fort Grant
P.O. Box 4399
St. Hwy. 266 - Spur Fort Grant, AZ 85644

Maricopa County Public Defender
132 S. 3rd Ave. 2nd floor
Phoenix AZ 85003

La Paz County Superior Court
P.O. Box 729 Parker, AZ 85344

American Civil Liberties Union
P.O. Box 17148 Phoenix, AZ 85011

AZ Daily Star P.O. Box 26807 Tucson, AZ 85726

ASPC-Perryville
P.O. Box 3000 Goodyear, AZ 853381

Maricopa County Records Office
111 S. 3rd Avenue Phoenix, AZ 85003

Maricopa County Superior Court
Central Court Build.
201 W. Jefferson St. Phoenix, AZ 85003

NAACP
2160 N. 6th Ave. Tucson, AZ 85034

Arizona Republic
P.O. Box 1950 Phoenix, AZ 85001

ASPC-Safford
Rt. 1, P.O. Box 2222 Safford, AZ 85546

Pima County Attorney
32 N. Stone Ave. Tucson, AZ 85701

EAST Court Build.
101 W. Jefferson St. Phoenix, AZ7 85003

NAACP
1818 S. 16th St. Phoenix, AZ 85034

Mesa Tribune
P.O. Box 1547 Mesa, AZ 85211

ASPC-Tucson
10000 S. Wilmont Tucson, AZ 85777

Pima County Public Defender's Office
33 N. Stone Ave. 21st floor Tucson, AZ 85701

Old Courthouse
125 W. Washington Phoenix, AZ 85003

NAACP
Legal Defense & Educational Fund
99 Hudson St. 16th Floor New York, NY 10013

Prison Legal News
P.O. Box 1684 Lake Worth, FL 33460

ASPC-Winslow
2100 S. Highway 87 Winslow, AZ 86047

Veteran Services Commission
3224 N. Central Ave. Suite 420 Phoenix, AZ

Southeast Courthouse
222 E. Javelina Dr. Phoenix, AZ 85210

Phoenix Chamber of Commerce
201 N. Central Ave. 27th Floor

Phoenix New Times
P.O. Box 2510 Phoenix, AZ 85002

ASPC-Yuma
23115 S. Avenue B. Summerton, AZ 85356

Tucson Chamber Of Commerce
P.O. Box 991 Tucson, AZ 85702

Mojave Co. Superior Ct.
Mojave Co. Courthouse Kingman, AZ 86401

Arizona Supreme Court
1501 W. Washington Phoenix, AZ. 85007

Prison Law Reporter
Hoge Bldg. 15th Floor Seattle, WA 98104

Family Assist. Office
1601 W. Jefferson St. Phoenix, AZ 85007

Chapter 13 Glossary

COMMONLY USED LEGAL WORDS

Absurdity So unreasonable as to be ridiculous

Acrimonious Bitterness or harshness of manner or speech

Adduce To give as a reason for proof

Alleviating Relieve

Ameliorated To make better

Annuity Annul to void

Articulate Able to speak clearly

Axiom A universal truth

Behooves To be incumbent upon, to need.

Capricious Sudden change

Cavalier Casual, arrogant

Chattel A movable item of personal property

Coalesce To unite in a single body

Cognizable That which can be known or perceived

Collateral Attack An attempt to challenge a judgment in another legal forum.

Collateral Estoppel The matter has been decided.

Coterminous Boundary. Having a common boundry.

Credulity Tending to believe, credulous

De - minimis Concerning trifles

Dilatory Causing delay

Draconian Very severe or harsh.

Emphasized To give emphasis to, stress

Empirical Based on experiment or experience

Endeavor Honest attempt

Erudition Learning acquired by studying and reading

Eschew To advocate

Espouse To shun, avoid

Estoppel A bar that stops a plea

Exigent Calling for immediate action or attention

Ex parte From one side

Explicit Clearly stated or shown

Frivolous Of little value

Gratuitous Uncalled for Idiosyncratic One's own view, peculiarity

Inexorable That which cannot be altered or checked

Inimical Hostile, in opposition to

Invidious Such as to incite ill will

Invoked To call on, to resort to

Linked Anything that connects

Malaise A vague feeling of discomfort

Matrix Womb, from within

Meritorious Deserving regard

Microcosm Regarded as world in miniature

Modicum Small amount

Myopic Short sightedness

Mystified To puzzle or perplex

Negate To make ineffective

Nihilistic General rejection of customary beliefs

Objectivity Independent of the mind

Onerous Oppressive

Penumbras A surrounding region where something exists to a lesser degree.

Pernicious Causing great injury

Polemical Attack on the opinion of others

Precedential Decision to be followed by a lower court

Prejudice A preconceived, usually unfavorable idea

Progeny Offspring

Promulgate To make known officially

Quixotic Romantically idealistic

Rebounded Come back, react

Res Judicata The case has already been adjudicated and cannot be re-litigated

Ridiculous Absurd

Rudimentary Slight beginning

Scintilla The least trace

Sham Something false or fake

Smacked A small amount, trace

Standing One who has a right to be a party to the litigation

Static At rest, inactive

Stigma Mark of disgrace

Stigmatize To mark with a stigma

Subterfuge Plan to evade, something different

Succor To help in time of need

Syllogistic A formal argument consisting of a major and a minor premise and a conclusion which must logically be true

Tangential Touching upon

Unambiguous Clear, precise

Unpersuasive Not having the power to persuade

Usufruct The legal right of using and enjoying the fruits or profits of something belonging to another

Vehement Strong feelings

Vehicle A means of communication, thought

Venire From within a jury will be selected

Vindicate To clear from criticism or blame

Vitiate To spoil, corrupt, pervert

Vociferous Noisy, clamorous

Voyeur One that has excessive interest in sex

Zealously Fervent, enthusiastic

LEGAL LATIN

Ab initio From the beginning

Ad damnum To the damage refers to the damages of the plaintiff

Ad hoc For this for a particular purpose

Ad infinitum To go on indefinitely

Ad interim In the meantime

Ad nauseam To the point of disgust

A fortiori By the stronger reason all the more

Amicus curiae Friend of the court

A priori From what is before

Arguendo For arguments sake

Bona vacantia Property with no apparent legal owner.

Coram nobis Before ourselves to seek review in the same court

Corpus delicti The body of the crime/victim

Cui bono Who will profit by this action.

Defacto Something that is "in fact"

Dehors Out of, without, foreign to the record

De jure By right by law

De nova Again, over, anew

Duces tecum You will bring with you

Eo nomine Under that name

Et al And others (et alii)

Ex abundanti cautela Out of an abundance of caution

Ex facie From the face, apparently

Ex officio From or by virtue of the office

Ex parte From or in the interest of one side only

Ex post facto After the fact

i.e. That is (id est)

In camera In a room usually something that is heard in private

In forma pauperis Not able to pay the fees. Not liable for the cost.

In limine At the beginning.

In pari delicto In equal fault equal in guilt

In personam Against the person against a specific person

In re In the matter of usually when there are no opposing parties

In Rem Against the thing against a thing rather than its owner

Infra Refers to a later section of text.

Inter alia Amongst others among other things

Ipse dixit He said it himself a bare assertion

lpso facto By the fact itself Mandamus We command

Mens rea Criminal intent

Nolo prosequi Record entry indicating that party will not proceed any further

Nolo contendere I will not contest it

Non compos mentis Not of sound mind insane

Nunc pro tunc Acts allowed to be done after the time they should be done

Onus prbandi The burden of proof.

Ore tenus By word of mouth

Pendente lite Pending or during suit

Per curiam By the court by the whole court rather than one judge

Prima facie On the first appearance

Pro forma As a matter of form

Pro se To represent oneself.

Pro hac vice Solely in this instance.

Quid pro quo One thing in return for another

Res judicata A matter already decided not to be decided again

Seriatim In the same sequence

Sine qua non A condition or thing that is essential or indispensable

Stare decisis To stand by decided matters prior case law

Sua sponte Of it's own accord

Sub judice The case at hand

Subpoena Writ commanding a person to appear in court to give testimony

Subpoena duces tecum A writ commanding a person to bring specific papers to court

Supra Referring to an earlier section of text.

Ultra vires Beyond the powers

Vel non Or not

TYPES OF RELIEF

1) ANNOYANCE: A discomfort, a nuisance, vexation.

2) ANXIETY: Worry or uneasiness about what may happen

3) COMPENSATORY: The damages recoverable in satisfaction of, or in recompense for loss or injury sustained, including all damages except nominal damages, punitive, or exemplary damages.

4) DECLARATORY: A judgment which declares conclusively the rights and duties, Or the status, of the parties.

5) EXEMPLARY DAMAGES: Damages given as an enhancement of compensatory damages because of the wanton, reckless, malicious. or oppressive character of the acts complained of, and by way of punishment of the defendant and a deterrent to

6) HARASSMENT: To worry or torment.

7) INJUNCTIVE: A court order prohibiting or ordering a given action.

8) MENTAL ANGUISH: Mental suffering as distinguished from physical pain

9) MONETARY: Of money.

10) NOMINAL DAMAGES: An award to which the plaintiff is entitled, although he gives no evidence of any particular amount of loss, because the law infers damage from the breach of an agreement or the invasion of a right.

11) PUNITIVE: Damages which are allowed as an enhancement of compensatory damages because of the wanton, reckless, malicious, or oppressive character which the plaintiff complains. See <u>Smith v. Wade</u>, 461 US 30, 75 L.Ed.2d 63 2, 103 SCt 1625 (1983).

Chapter 14 How the Madness Began

I have often asked myself, "How did the madness begin?" There's no doubt that this is crazy, so madness is a term that fits very well. As I write more on the subject in this chapter the madness will be revealed in all of its nuances, so there will be little room for doubt. You could say that the current situation regarding sex offenses is one of the most rapidly increasing forms of crime in this country. Is it the backlash of pent-up anger and hatred toward men as a result of the repression of women for centuries? You wouldn't be wrong, but you wouldn't be entirely right either. You could say that the current situation is the result of anger and frustration from the inequality between the sexes in our society. You wouldn't be wrong, but you wouldn't be entirely right either. You could say it's the result of the meltdown of the nuclear family and the rise of the latchkey child, that is the real reason these things are happening. This too is correct, but it isn't entirely right either. The point that I'm trying to make here is that these statements while being correct cannot explain every aspect of a very complicated issue. Back in 1980 there was a significant increase in the number of reported cases of child maltreatment. Maltreatment can be anything from physical abuse to sexual abuse.

It was during the '80s that the McMartin preschool trial hit the scene, where the owners of a preschool were falsely accused of molesting the children in their care. This case shattered the myth that children are incapable of lying. As a result of this trial and the revelation that the methods employed by psychologists and social workers in gathering testimonial evidence to be used at trial had failed in detecting the truth, a re-evaluation of child investigative interviews was conducted. In 1998 psychologists Deborah A. Poole and Michael E. Lamb wrote a book entitled Investigative Interviews of Children and it is from this book that I will present some of their views that should help to explain this phenomenon.

Although recognition of child abuse has increased dramatically since 1960, there is little evidence that children are at greater risk today than they were during earlier historical periods. Economic and physical hardship have always been associated with declines in the quality of care offered to children. According to Kessen (1965), however attitudes toward children have changed dramatically since the 17th-century for three major reasons: improved medical care, the Industrial Revolution, and Darwin's theory of evolution.

Before the 17th-century, there were few standards for rearing children and little public interest in the early years of life. During the 17th-century, however, records became sufficiently detailed to arouse widespread concern about child welfare. As Kessen (1965) explained in his book, "The Child", physicians avoided the child so long because they seemed hopelessly resistant to medical intervention. It was only yesterday in human history that the majority of children could be expected to live beyond their fifth year. Before 1750, for example the odds were 3 to 1 against a child in London reaching five years of age. In addition to death by disease, children faced a huge risk of abandonment and little hope of surviving the "foundling" homes that were set up to handle the "dropping" of babies. According to Kessen only 45 out of 10,272 infants survived in a Dublin foundling home during the late 18th century. Not knowing how to improve the survival rate of young children, society expressed little interest in this period of life. Though harsh, conditions during this time represented the continuation of a long history of child maltreatment that included practices such as infanticide and ritual mutilation (Zigler and Hall, 1991)

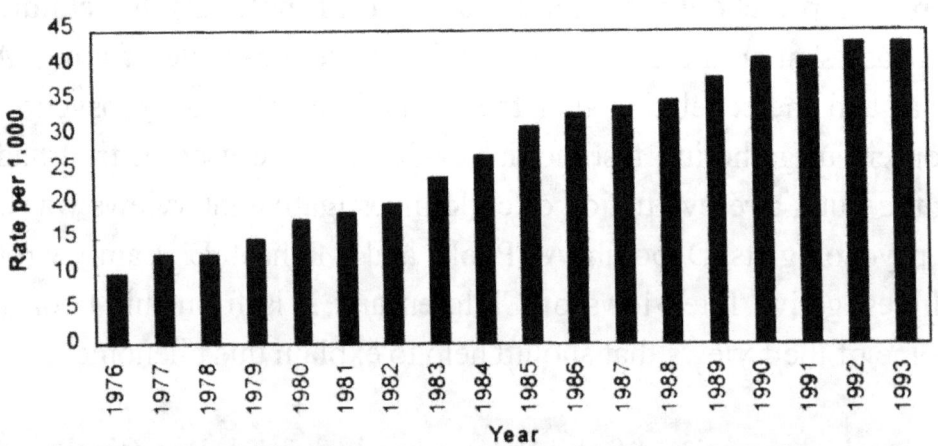

Figure 1.1. Child maltreatment reporting trends: 1976–1993. Adapted from data presented in *Child Maltreatment 1993: Reports From the States to the National Center on Child Abuse and Neglect* (U.S. Department of Health and Human Services, 1995).

The National Center on Child Abuse and Neglect (NCCAN) compiles data on child abuse and neglect referrals and their disposition following investigation. In the 1993 summary, reproduced in figure 1.1, shows a steady increase in referrals between 1976 and 1992, with the 1992 and 1993 figures at 43 reports per 1000 U.S. children under the age of 18 (US Department of Health and Human Services, 1995). Stated differently, 2.9 million reports of maltreatment in 1993 prompted approximately 1.6 million investigations, most of which were conducted without adequate resources to respond effectively. For example, although the number of reports grew tremendously between 1985 and 1991, 35 states held funding steady or reduced support for child protective services during this period (Pence and Wilson, 1994).

Efforts to advocate on behalf of children were complicated not only by the increased number of referrals but also by the changing nature of these reports. Four trends during the 1980s and early 1990s influenced the focus and content of interviewing protocols: a disproportionate increase in allegations of sexual abuse, increased publicity about reports of severe or bizarre abuse, referrals from a wide range of professional and nonprofessional sources, and an increased number of very young alleged victims.

In 1993, 49 percent of all reports or for neglect, 24 percent for physical abuse, 14 percent for sexual abuse, and 22 percent for other types of maltreatment, including emotional maltreatment, medical neglect, abandonment, and congenital drug addiction. (Figures do not add to 100 percent because the same child can experience more than one type of abuse; US Department of Health and Human Services, NCCAN, 1995).

To what extent did the increased number of reports reflect an increased risk to children as opposed to increased awareness of abuse? Because social expectations play a large role in the identification of maltreatment, there probably is no definitive answer to this question. On the one hand, the past two decades were characterized by increases in the number of single parent households, a risk factor for sexual abuse. On the other hand, changing awareness of abuse and mandated reporting also may have fueled the increase in reporting rates. For example, Ceci and Bruck (1995) argued that younger and older adults seemed

397

equally likely to have been sexually abused as children, suggesting that there have been no dramatic changes in prevalence. In addition, although many more cases are reported, the number of cases that are classified as "substantiated" has remained steady or dropped slightly (Besharov, 1990; Ceci and Bruck, 1995). **Nonetheless, the number of arrests for sexual offenses has increased markedly, from approximately 159,200 in 1976 to more than 247,000 in 1991 (US Department of Justice, 1978, 1992).**

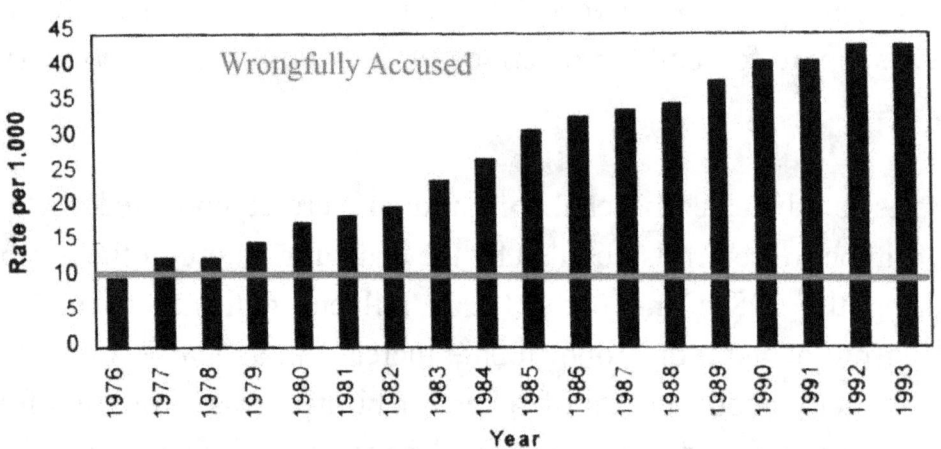

Figure 1.1. Child maltreatment reporting trends: 1976–1993. Adapted from data presented in *Child Maltreatment 1993: Reports From the States to the National Center on Child Abuse and Neglect* (U.S. Department of Health and Human Services. 1995).

Assuming that Besharov, (1990), Ceci and Bruck, (1995) are correct and the number of actual reports of child maltreatment has remained the same or slightly decreased since 1965, then all of the reported incidents of child maltreatment above the black line represent the number of reports that created wrongful accusations per year. A substantial increase which is corroborated by the U.S. Dept. of Justice report above. What this means is that 5,853 innocent people are convicted for child maltreatment every year. **Keep in mind this number doesn't account for the number of wrongful arrests that occurred before and during 1976 and we know in fact there were many, so the real truth is that the number of wrongfully arrested is far worse than is actually depicted here, and what is depicted is pretty damn bad! What you are witnessing is war against the citizens of America by its own government! You can't call it anything else! Numbers don't lie!**

What is science? Science is a way for us to teach how some thing gets to be known. In as much as anything can be known, because nothing is known absolutely. It's how to handle doubt and uncertainty. Science teaches us what the rules of evidence are. We mess with that at our own peril.

(Richard Feynman)

The increased awareness of sexual abuse has paralleled increased publicity about the most violent and unusual forms of child maltreatment. Many professional publications in the 1980s and early 1990s focused on the tragedy of child fatalities, noting that one-half of all fatalities occurred in families that were already known to social service agencies or other helping professionals (Korbin, 1994). Thousands of stranger abductions were reported annually (Finkelhor, Hotaling, and Sedlak, 1990), prompting public service announcements that encourage parents and children to use "code words" to prevent kidnapping. See Best, 1989, for a critical look at the politics of social problem statistics.) Children in the inner cities were exposed to violence with alarming frequency. For example, interviews with parents determined that 51 percent of fifth graders in New Orleans and 32 percent of 6 to 10-year-olds in Washington, D.C., had been victims of violence (see Osofsky, 1995, for a review). These portraits of an increasingly violent world altered adult's perceptions of what was possible or even likely. Media publicity contributed to this perception through coverage of highly publicized trials involving references to ritualistic features such as baby killing, animal sacrifice, religious candles, and other objects of ritual worship (see Ceci and Bruck, 1995, for case studies). In addition, professional workshops on ritualistic/satanic abuse increased dramatically (Nathan and Snedeker, 1995).

According to NCCAN's annual compilation, educators are by far the most frequent source of referrals to child protective services, accounting for 16% of all reports. There followed, in order of prominence, by legal/justice (12%), social service (12%) and medical (11%) professionals, with friends and neighbors (10%), other relatives (10%), parents (7%), child care providers (2%) and even victims and perpetrators (2%) providing the remaining reports (11% are anonymous or unknown, and 7% are listed as "other").

Unfortunately many adults converse with alleged victims before investigative interviews take place, and each conversation provides an opportunity for adults to influence a child's report. On one hand, adults may encourage children to deny abuse, either by making explicit threats or by expressing disapproval or doubt. On the other hand, adult's suspicions of abuse can affect how suggestively they questioned children and, alternately, the quality of information on which decisions must be based. As McGough explained (1996), legal and social service professionals often faced the "honky-tonk the effect"-an inability to piece together what really had happened to children whose accounts had been contaminated and this problem was exacerbated when referrals came from various sources.

As awareness of sexual abuse increased, the problems associated with prosecuting these crimes prompted procedural changes to accommodate children's involvement in the legal system. The process began in 1982, when the American Bar Association's national legal resource center for child advocacy and protection published a list of proposed legal reforms that included altering courtroom environments to minimize children's distress, interagency cooperation to reduce the number of interviews, and changes in the rules of evidence governing the presentation of information at trial (see McGough, 1994, for a review). Changes in the rules of evidence were most controversial because they involved minimizing competency in valuations for child witnesses and permitting the use of children's hearsay statements. As McGough indicated, "the creation of special rules of evidence that apply only to child victims of sexual abuse represented an astonishing detour from the traditional path of the law." (P. 16).

There are number of reasons why researchers have focused on interviews with young children. First, legal reforms have removed barriers that previously impeded the prosecution of cases involving very young children. Indeed, Gray (1993) reported that in one sample sexual abuse cases involving preschool children were disproportionately likely to progress to trial. Second, researchers have been fascinated by evidence that preschoolers can be amazingly accurate undersigned conditions but that they are more likely than older children or adults to succumb to suggestions (Ceci and Bruck, 1993). Finally, the fear that adults might misunderstand young children's comments or overreact to their sexualized behavior has fueled concerned that referrals involving young children are more likely to be invalid. The interviewing protocols that evolved during this period reflected the need to accommodate younger children, suggesting the use of developmentally appropriate language to ensure that young children understand interviewer's questions and avoidance of representational aids such as dolls because some young children do not use props accurately to report events. Unfortunately research and guidelines for meeting the special needs of other groups, such as adolescents, have lagged behind.

It is difficult to estimate how many false allegations are made, because rarely is their certainty about what really happened. In the case of sexual abuse, and external evidence in the form of a confession, consistent medical findings, or other evidence (e.g., pornographic pictures of the child) is very seldom available (e.g., Eliot and Briere, 1994; Lamb et al., 1997). Despite the methodological barriers to estimating false allegations rights, it frequently has been claimed that only approximately 5-8% of sexual abuse allegations are false. This estimate has appeared in numerous articles (e.g., Sink, 1988), was underscored by the American Professional Society on the Abuse of Children (APSAC, 1993), and has been cited by experts in court (Ceci and Bruck, 1995). Several authors, however (e.g., Ceci and Bruck, 1995; Robin, 1991; Wakefield and Underwager, 1991), have argued that this rate is misleadingly low because it includes only delivered attempts to deceive rather than cases in which honest errors were made (e.g., premature judgments about a gentle rash or misinterpretations of children's comments). When the latter are included, estimates jump from 6% to 23% for one comprehensive study (Jones and McGraw, 1987), with rates of approximately 35% or higher when allegations arising in the context of divorce or custody proceedings are included (e.g. Benedik and Schertky, cited in Jones and Seig, 1998; Faller, 1991;Thonnes and Tjaden, 1990).

Everson and Boat in 1989 as to child protective service workers in North Carolina to identify cases in which a child or adolescent made an allegation that the worker believed was false. Common reasonings for identifying an allegation as false were improbable, inconsistent or recanted reports. In 59 percent of these cases, respondents concluded that the child or adolescent had deliberately fabricated in order to obtain secondary gains, such as changes in living arrangements, or to retaliate against a parent.

Over the years, research on the causes of child maltreatment has focused less on parental psychopathology and more on the broader social factors, such as societal attitudes and structures (Cicchetti and Carlson, 1991). This focus on social contexts also is useful for analyzing why concerns developed about investigative interviewing. Six factors are especially relevant: (a) the economic climate of the '80s, (b) a revival of conservative politics in the media, (c) a therapeutic focus on childhood victimization, (d) the increased exposure of children to sexual material at a time when police about the indicators of abuse were changing, (e) changing conceptions of sexual abuse, and (f) in attention to the differences between therapy and investigation when helping professionals were trained.

Many authors have noted how moral panics and resulting controversies often developed during periods of rapid social change. For example, Robin (1991) wrote an insightful essay on how American individualism favors solutions to social problems that focus on individual deviance rather than changes in the basic organization of society. Furthermore, he noted how changes in sexuality, sexual identity, and family roles threats to the traditional family have allowed child abuse to become "a convenient focus for public anxiety about changing social conditions related to the family" (p. 9). Similarly, Tavri (1992) argued that some women who became entangled in the "survivor" movement in the absence of prior concerns about their childhood identified with the sexual-victim culture because it provided "a lightning rod for the inchoate feelings of victimization they have as a result of their status in society at large. It provides a clear focus than such vague enemies as "the system", sexism, deadening work, welfare, or boredom" (p. 321). These and other system-level critiques do not deny the reality of abuse or minimize its consequences. Rather, they attempt to understand the moral panic in recent decades that has fostered increased concerns about false allegations.

During the past decades, the challenges when confronted fueled a market for pop psychology, self-help books written by professionals, and therapy by licensed professionals. In many of these forms, women's depression and anxiety were explained as consequences of individual personalities, decisions, or life experiences rather than as predictable responses to social and economic circumstances.

The tendency to attribute women's problems to their individual experiences is reflected in the intense controversy over repressed memories of childhood sexual abuse. Some of the women who flooded into therapy during the past decade for depression, anxiety, and relationship problems were told that their difficulties resemble those of women who had been sexually abused. Clinicians sometimes used special techniques to help their clients recall abusive experiences-including hypnosis, dream interpretation, and guided imagery-under the assumption that the presumed abuse must be remembered before therapy could be successful. In one study, 25% of the doctor-level therapists surveyed reported that (a) they sometimes concluded after only one session the clients who did not report abuse had in fact been abused as children, (b) abused clients needed to acknowledge our remembered their abuse for therapy to be effective, and (c) they used to or more therapeutic techniques specifically to help clients remembered childhood sexual abuse (Poole, Lindsay, Memon, Bull, 1995) by their own estimates, these American and British therapists often were successful in retrieving memories of abuse. Extrapolation into the population of therapists from which the sample had been drawn suggested that during the two-year period examined by the survey, hundreds of thousands of women were exposed to therapists who held such beliefs (see also Polusny and Follette, 1996).

On a specific calculation of our data, it may be stated that at least 85% of the younger male population could be convicted as sex offenders if law enforcement officials were as efficient as most people expect them to be. The stray boy who is caught and brought before the court may not be different from most of his fellows, but the public, not knowing of the near universality of adolescent sexual activity, heaps the penalty for the whole group upon the shoulders of the one boy who happens to be apprehended. This situation presents a considerable dilemma for law enforcement officials and for students of the social organization as a whole. (Kinsey, 1948 p. 224)

References

Besharov, D. J, (1990), *Recognizing child abuse*. New York: Free Press.

Ceci, S. J, & Bruck, M. (1993), *Suggestibility of the child witness: A historical review and synthesis*. Psychological Bulletin, 113, 403-439.

Ceci, S. J, & Bruck, M. (1995), *Jeopardy in the courtroom: A scientific analysis of children's testimony*. Washington D.C.: American psychological association.

Faller, K. (1991), *Possible explanations for child sexual abuse allegations in divorce*. American Journal of Orthopsychiatry, 61,86-91.

Finkelhor, D., Hotaling, G. T., & Sedlak, A. (1990). *Missing, objected, runaway, and throwaway children in America*; First report. Washington D.C.: Juvenile Justice Clearinghouse.

Gray, E. (1993). *Unequal justice: The prosecution of child sexual abuse*. New York: Mac Millan.

Jones, D., & McGraw, J. M. (1987). *Reliable and fictitious accounts of sexual abuse in children*. Journal of Interpersonal Violence,2, 27-45.

Jones, D. P. H., & Seig, A. (1988). Child sexual abuse allegations in custody or visitation cases: A report of 20 cases. In E. B. Nicholson (Ed.), *Sexual abuse allegations in custody and visitation cases: a resource book for judges and court personnel*. Washington, D.C.: American Bar Association National Legal Resource Center for Child Advocacy and Protection.

Kessen, W. (1965). *The child*. New York: Wiley.

Kinsey, A. C., Pomeroy, W. B. , & Martin, C. E. (1948). *Sexual behavior in the human male*. Philadelphia: Saunders.

Korbin, J. E. (1994). *Perpetrators of fatal child maltreatment*. The APSAC Advisor, 7(4), 45-46.

Lamb, M. E., Sternberg, K. J., Esplin, P. W., Hershkowitz, I., & Orbach, Y. (1997). *Assessing the credibility of children's allegations of sexual abuse: Insights from recent research*. Learning and Individual Differences, 9, 175-194.

Lamb, M. E., Sternberg, K. J., Esplin, P. W., Hershkowitz, I., Orbach, Y., & Hovav, M. (1997). *Criterion based content analysis: a field validation study*. Child Abuse & Neglect, 21, 255-264.

McGough, L. S. (1996). *Commentary: Achieving real reform -- the case for American interviewing protocols*. Monographs of the Society for Research in Child Development, 61 (4-5, Serial No. To 48), 188-203.

McGough, L. S., & Warren, A. R. (1994). *The all-important investigative interview*. Juvenile and Family Court Journal, 45, 13-29.

Nathan, D., & Snedeker, M. (1995). *Satan's silence: Ritual abuse and the making of a modern American witch hunt*. New York: Basic Books.

Osofsky, J. D. (1995. *The effect of exposure to violence on young children*. American Psychologist, 50, 782-788.

Pence, D., & Wilson, C. (1994). *Team investigation of child sexual abuse*. Thousand Oaks, CA: Sage.

Polusny, M. A. , & Follette, V M. (1996). *Remembering childhood sexual abuse: A national survey of psychologists clinical practices, police, and personal experiences*. Professional Psychology: Research and Practice, 27, 41-52.

Poole, D. A., Lindsay, D. S.,Memon, A., & Bull, R. (1995). *Psychotherapy and the recovery of memories of childhood sexual abuse: U.S. and British practitioners opinions, practices, and experiences*. Journal of Consulting and Clinical Psychology, 63, 426-437.

Robin, M. (1991). *The social construction of child abuse and "false allegations." In M. Robin (Ed.), Assessing child maltreatment reports: the problem of false allegations (pp. 1-34).* Binghamton, New York: Haworth Press.

Sink, F. (1988). *Studies of true and false allegations: a critical review.* in E. B. Nicholson (Ed.), *Sexual abuse allegations in custody and visitation cases: A resource book for judges and court personnel (pp. 37-47).* Washington, D.C.: American Bar Association.

Tavris, C. (1992). *The measure of woman.* New York: Touchstone.

Theonnes, M., & Tjaden, P. G. (1990). *The extent, nature and validity of sexual abuse allegations in custody/visitation disputes.* Child Abuse & Neglect, 14, 151-163.

Wakefield, H. & Underwager, R. (1991). *Sexual abuse allegations in divorce in custody disputes.* Behavioral Sciences and the Law, 9,451-468.

Zigler, E., & Hall, N. W. (1991). *Physical child abuse in America: past, present, and future.* In D. Cicchetti & V Carlson (Eds.), Child maltreatment (pp. 38-75). New York: Cambridge University Press.

Have You Been To Jail For Justice

Was it Cesar Chavez or Rosa Parks that day?
Some say Dr. King or Ghandi Set them on their way
No matter who your mentors are it's pretty plain to see
That if you've been to jail for justice
You're in good company

Have you been to jail for justice?
I want to shake your hand
'Cause sitting in and laying down
Are ways to take a stand

Have you sung a song for freedom
Or marched that picket line?
Have you been to jail for justice?
Then you're a friend of mine

You law abiding citizens
Come listen to this song
Laws are made by people
And people can be wrong
Once unions were against the law
But slavery was fine
Women were denied the vote
While children worked the mine
The more you study history
The less you can deny it
A rotten law stays on the books
'til folks with guts defy it!

Have you been to jail for justice?
I want to shake your hand
'Cause sitting in and laying down
Are ways to take a stand

Have you sung a song for freedom
Or marched that picket line?
Have you been to jail for justice?
Then you're a friend of mine

Something To Think About

Bill Hicks used to finish his shows with this. Life is like a ride at an amusement park. When you go on it you think that it's real because that's how powerful our minds are. And the ride goes up and down and round and round. It has thrills and chills, it's very brightly colored and it's very loud and it's very fun - for a while. Some have been on the ride for a long time and they begin to question, "Is this real or is it just a ride?" And other people have remembered and they come back to us and say, "Hey, don't worry, because it's just a ride." **And we kill those people!**

"Shut him up I've got a lot invested in this ride. Shut him up!", "Look at my furrows of worry!", "Look at my big bank account!", "My family just has to be real." But it's just a ride! We try to kill those guys that tell us that. Have you ever noticed that? And let the demons run amok. **But it doesn't matter, because it's just a ride and we can change it anytime we want! It's all in our choice. No effort, no work, no job, no savings, no money. It's just a choice right now! Between fear - and love. (Zeitgeist, The Movie)**

About The Author

My career began in the United States Coast Guard. My first unit was Coast Guard Station Saginaw River. There I was responsible for search and rescue in Saginaw Bay and Lake Huron, where I performed numerous rescues. Earned Coast Guard Good Conduct Award, Meritorious Unit Commendation with Operational Designator and Meritorious Unit Commendation I was also responsible for standing a radio watch, listening for distress calls on the VHF-FM marine radio. I was transferred to Coast Guard Cutter Bristol Bay WTGB 102 where I worked as a Fireman and Oiler. I advanced to the rank of Machinery Technician Third Class at Yorktown, Virginia and spent my last two years of enlisted service at Search and Rescue Station Panama City Florida. Honorably Discharged after 4 years active duty service.

I obtained my FAA Airframe and Powerplant mechanics license in 1988 and began working as a mechanic for the Midway Commuter, which was a wholly owned subsidiary of Midway Airlines. From there I worked for Midway Aircraft Engineering in Miami, Florida working as a mechanic on DC-9 and B-737 aircraft. I advanced to the Position of Senior Aircraft Maintenance Planner where I was responsible for scheduling both routine overnight maintenance and heavy maintenance for one third of Midway's fleet. After Midway went out of business I moved to California and began working as a mechanic on B-747 aircraft which was something that I had always wanted to do. Later I began working in Phoenix, Arizona at Sky Harbor Airport and various repair stations throughout the region.

I obtained a Bachelor of Science Degree in Legal Study's from Kaplan University in 2011 while on the President's List. In 2013, I studied Computer Numeric Control at Glendale Community College and earned a position on the Dean's List and a Certificate of Completion in that program. I was released in 2017 after fighting my case for 14 years and obtained my Certificate of Absolute Discharge from the Arizona Department of Corrections in 2018. My only remaining requirement is to register for life and abide by all local SO laws as well.

It's true. In life one wears many hats.